T0062665

Get the eBook FREE!
(PDF, ePub, Kindle, and liveBook all included)

We believe that once you buy a book from us, you should be able to read it in any format we have available. To get electronic versions of this book at no additional cost to you, purchase and then register this book at the Manning website.

Go to https://www.manning.com/freebook and follow the instructions to complete your pBook registration.

That's it!
Thanks from Manning!

Getting Started with Natural Language Processing

Getting Started with Natural Language Processing

EKATERINA KOCHMAR

MANNING

SHELTER ISLAND

For online information and ordering of this and other Manning books, please visit
www.manning.com. The publisher offers discounts on this book when ordered in quantity.
For more information, please contact

Special Sales Department
Manning Publications Co.
20 Baldwin Road
PO Box 761
Shelter Island, NY 11964
Email: orders@manning.com

Manning Publications Co.
20 Baldwin Road
PO Box 761
Shelter Island, NY 11964

Development editor:	Dustin Archibald
Technical development editor:	Michael Lund
Review editor:	Adriana Sabo
Production editor:	Kathleen Rossland
Copy editor:	Carrie Andrews
Proofreader:	Jason Everett
Technical proofreader:	Al Krinker
Typesetter:	Dennis Dalinnik
Cover designer:	Marija Tudor

ISBN: 9781617296765
Printed and bound by CPI Group (UK) Ltd, Croydon, CR0 4YY

To my family, who always supported me and believed in me.

brief contents

contents

1 Introduction   1

2 Your first NLP example   31

preface

Thank you for choosing *Getting Started with Natural Language Processing*. I am very excited that you decided to learn about natural language processing (NLP) with the help of this book, and I hope that you'll enjoy getting started with NLP following this material and the examples.

Natural language processing addresses various types of tasks related to language and processing of information expressed in human language. The field and techniques have been around for quite a long time, and they are well integrated into our everyday lives; in fact, you are probably benefiting from NLP on a daily basis without realizing it. Therefore, I can't really overemphasize the importance and the impact that this technology has on our lives. The first chapter of this book will give you an overview of the wide scope of NLP applications that you might be using regularly—from internet search engines to spam filters to predictive keyboards (and many more!), and the rest the book will help you to implement many of these applications from scratch yourself.

In recent years, the field has been gaining more and more interest and attention. There are several reasons for this: on the one hand, thanks to the internet, we now have access to increasingly larger amounts of data. On the other hand, thanks to the recent developments in computer hardware and software, we have more powerful technology to process this data. The recent advances in machine learning and deep learning have also contributed to the increasing importance of NLP. These days, large tech companies are realizing the potential of using NLP, and businesses in legal tech, finance, insurance, health care, and many other sectors are investing in it. The reason for that is clear—language is the primary means of communication in all spheres of life, so being able to efficiently process the information expressed in the form of human language is always an advantage. This makes a book on NLP very timely. My goal with this book is to introduce you to a wide variety of topics related to natural language and its processing, and to show how and why these things matter in practical applications—be that your own small project or a company-level project that could benefit from extracting and using information from texts.

I have been working in NLP for over a decade now, and before switching to NLP, I primarily focused on linguistics and theoretical studies of language. Looking back, what motivated and excited me the most about turning to the more technical field of NLP were the incredible new opportunities opened up to me by technology and the ease of working with data and getting the information you need from texts, whether in the context of academic studies about the language itself or in the context of practical applications in any other domain. This book aims to produce the same effect. It is highly practice oriented, and each language-related concept, each technique, and each task is explained with the help of real-life examples.

acknowledgments

Writing a book is a long process that takes a lot of time and effort. I truly enjoyed working on this book, and I sincerely hope that you will enjoy reading it, too. Nevertheless, it would be impossible to enjoy this process, or even to finish the book, were it not for the tremendous support, inspiration, and encouragement provided to me by my family, my partner Ted, and my dear friends Eugene, Alex, and Natalia. Thank you for believing in me!

I am also extremely grateful to the Manning team and all the people at Manning who took time to review my book with such care and who gave me valuable feedback along the way. I'd like to acknowledge my development editor, Dustin Archibald, who was always there for me with his patience and support, especially when I needed those the most. I am also grateful to Michael Lund, my technical development editor, and Al Krinker, my technical proofreader, for carefully checking the content and the code for this book and providing me with valuable feedback. I would also like to extend my gratitude to Kathleen Rossland, my production editor; Carrie Andrews, my copyeditor; and Susan Honeywell and Azra Dedic, members of the graphics editing team, whose valuable help at the final stages of editing of this book improved it tremendously. Thanks as well to the rest of the Manning team who worked on the production and promotion of this book.

I would also like to thank all the reviewers who took the time out of their busy schedules to read my manuscript at various stages of its development. Thanks to their invaluable feedback and advice, this book kept improving from earlier stages until it went into production. I would like to acknowledge Alessandro Buggin, Cage Slagel,

Christian Bridge-Harrington, Christian Thoudahl, Douglas Sparling, Elmer C. Peramo, Erik Hansson, Francisco Rivas, Ian D. Miller, James Richard Woodruff, Jason Hales, Jérôme Baton, Jonathan Wood, Joseph Perenia, Kelly Hair, Lewis Van Winkle, Luis Fernando Fontoura de Oliveira, Monica Guimaraes, Najeeb Arif, Patrick Regan, Rees Morrison, Robert Diana, Samantha Berk, Sumit K. Singh, Tanya Wilke, Walter Alexander Mata López, and Werner Nindl.

about this book

The primary goal that I have for this book is to help you appreciate how truly exciting the field of NLP is, how limitless the possibilities of working in this area are, and how low the barrier to entry is now. My goal is to help you get started in this field easily and to show what a wide range of different applications you can implement yourself within a matter of days even if you have never worked in this field before. This book can be used both as a comprehensive cover-to-cover guide through a range of practical applications and as a reference book if you are interested in only some of the practical tasks. By the time you finish reading this book, you will have acquired

- Knowledge about the essential NLP tasks and the ability to recognize any particular task when you encounter it in a real-life scenario. We will cover such popular tasks as sentiment analysis, text classification, information search, and many more.
- A whole arsenal of NLP algorithms and techniques, including stemming, lemmatization, part-of-speech tagging, and many more. You will learn how to apply a range of practical approaches to text, such as vectorization, feature extraction, supervised and unsupervised machine learning, among others.
- An ability to structure an NLP project and an understanding of which steps need to be involved in a practical project.
- Comprehensive knowledge of the key NLP, as well as machine-learning, terminology.
- Comprehensive knowledge of the available resources and tools for NLP.

Who should read this book

I have written this book to be accessible to software developers and beginners in data science and machine learning. If you have done some programming in Python before and are familiar with high school math and algebra (e.g., matrices, vectors, and basic operations involving them), you should be good to go! Most importantly, the book does not assume any prior knowledge of linguistics or NLP, as it will help you learn what you need along the way.

How this book is organized: A road map

The first two chapters of this book introduce you to the field of natural language processing and the variety of NLP applications available. They also show you how to build your own small application with a minimal amount of specialized knowledge and skills in NLP. If you are interested in having a quick start in the field, I would recommend reading these two chapters. Each subsequent chapter looks more closely into a specific NLP application, so if you are interested in any such specific application, you can just focus on a particular chapter. For a comprehensive overview of the field, techniques, and applications, I would suggest reading the book cover to cover:

- *Chapter 1*—Introduces the field of NLP with its various tasks and applications. It also briefly overviews the history of the field and shows how NLP applications are used in our everyday lives.
- *Chapter 2*—Explains how you can build your own practical NLP application (spam filtering) from scratch, walking you through all the essential steps in the application pipeline. While doing so, it introduces a number of fundamental NLP techniques, including tokenization and text normalization, and shows how to use them in practice via a popular NLP toolkit called NLTK.
- *Chapter 3*—Focuses on the task of information retrieval. It introduces several key NLP techniques, such as stemming and stopword removal, and shows how you can implement your own information-retrieval algorithm. It also explains how such an algorithm can be evaluated.
- *Chapter 4*—Looks into information extraction and introduces further fundamental techniques, such as part-of-speech tagging, lemmatization, and dependency parsing. Moreover, it shows how to build an information-extraction application using another popular NLP toolkit called spaCy.
- *Chapter 5*—Shows how to implement your own author (or user) profiling algorithm, providing you with further examples and practice in NLTK and spaCy. Moreover, it presents the task as a text classification problem and shows how to implement a machine-learning classifier using a popular machine learning library called scikit-learn.
- *Chapter 6*—Follows up on the topic of author (user) profiling started in chapter 5. It investigates closely the task of linguistic feature engineering, which is an essential step in any NLP project. It shows how to perform linguistic feature

engineering using NLTK and spaCy, and how to evaluate the results of a text classification algorithm.

- *Chapter 7*—Starts the topic of sentiment analysis, which is a very popular NLP task. It applies a lexicon-based approach to the task. The sentiment analyzer is built using a linguistic pipeline with spaCy.
- *Chapter 8*—Follows up on sentiment analysis, but unlike chapter 7, it takes a data-driven approach to this task. Several machine-learning techniques are applied using scikit-learn, and further linguistic concepts are introduced with the use of spaCy and NLTK language resources.
- *Chapter 9*—Overviews the task of topic classification. In contrast to the previous text classification tasks, it is a multiclass classification problem, so the chapter discusses the intricacies of this task and shows how to implement a topic classifier with scikit-learn. In addition, it also takes an unsupervised machine-learning perspective and shows how to approach this task as a clustering problem.
- *Chapter 10*—Introduces the task of topic modeling with latent Dirichlet allocation (LDA). In addition, it introduces a popular toolkit called gensim, which is particularly suitable for working with topic modeling algorithms. Motivation for the LDA approach, implementation details, and techniques for the results evaluation are discussed.
- *Chapter 11*—Concludes this book with another key NLP task called named-entity recognition (NER). While introducing this task, this chapter also introduces a powerful family of sequence labeling approaches widely used for NLP tasks and shows how NER integrates into further, downstream NLP applications.

About the code

This book contains many examples of source code both in numbered listings and in line with normal text. In both cases, source code is formatted in a `fixed-width font like this` to separate it from ordinary text. Sometimes code is also **in bold** to highlight code that has changed from previous steps in the chapter, such as when a new feature adds to an existing line of code.

In many cases, the original source code has been reformatted; we've added line breaks and reworked indentation to accommodate the available page space in the book. In rare cases, even this was not enough, and listings include line-continuation markers (➡). Additionally, comments in the source code have often been removed from the listings when the code is described in the text. Code annotations accompany many of the listings, highlighting important concepts.

You can get executable snippets of code from the liveBook (online) version of this book at http://livebook.manning.com/book/getting-started-with-natural-language-processing and from the book's GitHub page at https://github.com/ekochmar/Essential-NLP. The appendix provides you with installation instructions. Please note that if you use a different version of the tools than specified in the instructions, you may get slightly different results to those discussed in the book: such differences are to be expected as the tools are constantly updated; however, the main points made will still hold.

liveBook discussion forum

Purchase of *Getting Started with Natural Language Processing* includes free access to live-Book, Manning's online reading platform. Using liveBook's exclusive discussion features, you can attach comments to the book globally or to specific sections or paragraphs. It's a snap to make notes for yourself, ask and answer technical questions, and receive help from the author and other users. To access the forum, go to https://livebook.manning .com/book/getting-started-with-natural-language-processing/discussion. You can also learn more about Manning's forums and the rules of conduct at https://livebook .manning.com/discussion.

Manning's commitment to our readers is to provide a venue where a meaningful dialogue between individual readers and between readers and the author can take place. It is not a commitment to any specific amount of participation on the part of the author, whose contribution to the forum remains voluntary (and unpaid). We suggest you try asking the author some challenging questions lest their interest stray! The forum and the archives of previous discussions will be accessible from the publisher's website as long as the book is in print.

Other online resources

I hope that this book will give you a start in the exciting field of NLP and will motivate you to learn more about NLP techniques and applications. Even though the book covers a range of different applications, being a single resource, it cannot possibly cover all topics. At the same time, you might also find yourself wanting to know more about some of the topics overviewed in the book and dig deeper. Here are other online resources that will help you on this journey:

- One of the popular NLP toolkits that this book uses a lot is NLTK. If you want to learn more about particular techniques and implementation details, you can always check the documentation at www.nltk.org/. NLTK also comes with a useful book, available at www.nltk.org/book/, which provides further examples with the toolkit.
- Another popular NLP toolkit that you will be using a lot in the course of working with this book's material is spaCy (https://spacy.io). SpaCy aims to provide you with industrial-strength NLP functionalities, its models are constantly updated using state-of-the-art techniques and approaches, and the toolkit is used in a wide variety of educational and industrial projects (see an overview at https://spacy.io/universe). Therefore, I recommend keeping an eye on the updates and checking the documentation and tutorials available on spaCy's website to learn more about its rich functionality.

- The third NLP library that you will be using is gensim (https://radimrehurek .com/gensim/), which is particularly suitable for topic modeling and semantics-oriented tasks. Just like the previous two toolkits, it comes with extensive documentation and a variety of examples and tutorials. I recommend looking into those if you'd like to learn more about this toolkit.

- Finally, if you want to learn more about the theoretical side of things and the developments on various NLP tasks, I'd recommend an excellent comprehensive textbook called *Speech and Language Processing* by Dan Jurafsky and James H. Martin. The book is in its third edition, and a substantial part of it is available at https://web.stanford.edu/~jurafsky/slp3/.

Finally, no book is ever perfect, but if you find this book helpful, I would love to get your feedback. You can share it with me via LinkedIn: www.linkedin.com/in/ekaterina-kochmar-0a655b14/. Updates and corrections will be made available on the book's GitHub page at https://github.com/ekochmar/Essential-NLP.

about the author

 **EKATERINA KOCHMAR** is a lecturer (assistant professor) at the Department of Computer Science of the University of Bath, where she is part of the AI research group. Her research lies at the intersection of artificial intelligence, natural language processing, and intelligent tutoring systems. She holds a PhD in natural language processing, an MPhil in advanced computer science from the University of Cambridge, and an MA in computational linguistics from the University of Tuebingen. She is also a cofounder and the chief scientific officer of Korbit AI, focusing on building an AI-powered dialogue-based tutoring system capable of providing learners with high-quality, interactive, and personalized education. Ekaterina has extensive experience in teaching both within and outside of academia.

about the cover illustration

The figure on the cover of *Getting Started with Natural Language Processing* is *Femme de l'Isle de Santorin* (*Woman of the Island of Santorini*) taken from a collection by Jacques Grasset de Saint-Sauveur, published in 1788. Each illustration is finely drawn and colored by hand.

In those days, it was easy to identify where people lived and what their trade or station in life was just by their dress. Manning celebrates the inventiveness and initiative of the computer business with book covers based on the rich diversity of regional culture centuries ago, brought back to life by pictures from collections such as this one.

Introduction 1

This chapter covers

- Introducing natural language processing
- Exploring why you should know NLP
- Detailing classic NLP tasks and applications in practice
- Explaining ways machines represent words and understand their meaning

Natural language processing (or NLP) is a field that addresses various ways in which computers can deal with natural—that is, human—language. Regardless of your occupation or background, there is a good chance you have heard about NLP before, especially in recent years with the media covering the impressive capabilities of intelligent machines that can understand and produce natural language. This is what has brought NLP into the spotlight, and what might have attracted you to this book. You might be a programmer who wants to learn new skills, a machine learning or data science practitioner who realizes there is a lot of potential in processing natural language, or you might be generally interested in how language works and how to process it automatically. Either way, welcome to NLP! This book aims to help you get started with it.

What if you don't know or understand what NLP means and does? Is this book for you? Absolutely! You might have not realized it, but you are already familiar with this application area and the tasks it addresses—in fact, anyone who speaks, reads, or writes in a human language is. We use language every time we think, plan, and dream. Almost any task that you perform on a daily basis involves some use of language. Language ability is one of the core aspects of human intelligence, so it's no wonder that the recent advances in artificial intelligence and the new, more capable intelligent technology involve advances in NLP to a considerable degree. After all, we cannot really say that a machine is truly intelligent if it cannot master human language.

Okay, that sounds exciting, but how useful is it with your everyday projects? If your work includes dealing with any type of textual information, including documents of any kind (e.g., legal, financial), websites, emails, and so on, you will definitely benefit from learning how to extract the key information from such documents and how to process it. Textual data is ubiquitous, and there is a huge potential in being able to reliably extract information from large amounts of text, as well as in being able to learn from it. As the saying goes, data is the new oil! (A quote famously popularized by the *Economist* http://mng.bz/ZA9O.)

This book will cover the core topics in NLP, and I hope it will be of great help in your everyday work and projects, regardless of your background and primary field of interest. What is even more important than the arguments of NLP's utility and potential is that NLP is interesting, intellectually stimulating, and fun! And remember that as a natural language speaker, you are already an expert in many of the tasks that NLP addresses, so it is an area in which you can get started easily. This book is written with the lowest entry barrier to learning possible: you don't need to have any prior knowledge about how language works. The book will walk you through the core concepts and techniques, starting from the very beginning. All you need is some basic programming skills in Python and basic understanding of mathematical notation. What you will learn by the end of this book is a whole set of NLP skills and techniques. Let's begin!

1.1   *A brief history of NLP*

This is not a history book, nor is it a purely theoretical overview of NLP. It is a practice-oriented book that provides you with the details that you need when you need them. So, I will not overwhelm you with details or long history of events that led to the foundation and development of the field of natural language processing. There are a couple of key facts worth mentioning, though.

> **NOTE**   For a more detailed overview of the history of the field, check out *Speech and Language Processing* by Dan Jurafsky and James H. Martin at (https://web .stanford.edu/~jurafsky/slp3/).

The beginning of the field is often attributed to the early 1950s, in particular to the Georgetown–IBM experiment that attempted implementing a fully automated machine-translation system between Russian and English. The researchers believed they could solve this task within a couple of years. Do you think they succeeded in solving it? Hint: if you have ever tried translating text from one language to another with the use of automated tools, such as Google Translate, you know what the state of the art today is. Machine-translation tools today work reasonably well, but they are still not perfect, and it took the field several decades to get here.

The early approaches to the tasks in NLP were based on *rules and templates* that were hardcoded into the systems: for example, linguists and language experts would come up with patterns and rules of how a word or phrase in one language should be translated into another word or phrase in another language, or with templates to extract information from texts. Rule-based and template-based approaches have one clear advantage to them—they are based on reliable expert knowledge that is put into them. And, in some cases, they do work well. A notable example is the early chatbot ELIZA (http://mng.bz/R4w0), which relies on the use of templates, yet, in terms of the quality of the output and ELIZA's ability to keep up with superficially sensible conversation, even today it may outperform many of its more "sophisticated" competitors.

However, human language is diverse, ambiguous, and creative, and rule-based and template-based approaches can never take all the possibilities and exceptions of language into account—it would never generalize well (you will see many examples of that in this book). This is what made it impossible in the 1950s to quickly solve the task of machine translation. A real improvement to many of the NLP tasks came along in the 1980s with the introduction of *statistical approaches*, based on the observations made on the language data itself and statistics derived from the data, and *machine-learning algorithms*.

The key difference between rule-based approaches and statistical approaches is that the rule-based approaches rely on a set of very precise but rigid and ultimately inflexible rules, whereas the statistical approaches don't make assumptions—they try to learn what's right and what's wrong from the data, and they can be flexible about their predictions. This is another major component to (and a requirement for) the success of the NLP applications: rule-based systems are costly to build and rely on gathering expertise from humans, but statistical approaches can only work well provided they have access to large amounts of high-quality data. For some tasks, such data is easier to come by: for example, a renewed interest and major breakthroughs in machine translation in the 1980s were due to the availability of the parallel data translated between pairs of languages that could be used by a statistical algorithm to learn from. At the same time, not all tasks were as "lucky."

The 1990s brought about one other major improvement—the World Wide Web was created and made available to the general public, and this made it possible to get access to and accumulate large amounts of data for the algorithms to learn from. The web also introduced completely new tasks and domains to work on: for example, before the creation of social media, social media analytics as a task didn't exist.

Finally, as the algorithms kept developing and the amount of available data kept increasing, there came a need for a new paradigm of approaches that could learn from bigger data in a more efficient way. And in the 2010s, the advances in computer hardware finally made it possible to adopt a new family of more powerful and more sophisticated machine-learning approaches that became known as *deep learning*.

This doesn't mean, however, that as the field kept accommodating new approaches, it was dropping the previous ones. In fact, all three types of approaches are well in use, and the task at hand is what determines which approach to choose. Figure 1.1 shows the development of all the approaches on a shared timeline.

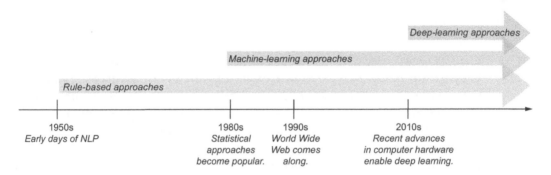

Figure 1.1   NLP timeline showing three different types of approaches

Over the years, NLP got linked to several different fields, and consequently you might come across different aliases, including statistical natural language processing; language and speech processing; computational linguistics; and so on. The distinctions between these are very subtle. What matters more than namesakes is the fact that NLP adopts techniques from a number of related fields:

- *Computer science*—Contributes with the algorithms, as well as software and hardware
- *Artificial intelligence*—Sets up the environment for the intelligent machines
- *Machine learning*—Helps with the intelligent ways of learning from real data
- *Statistics*—Helps coming up with the theoretical models and probabilistic interpretation
- *Logic*—Helps ensure the world described with the NLP models makes sense
- *Electrical engineering*—Traditionally deals with the processing of human speech
- *Computational linguistics*—Provides expert knowledge about how human language works
- *Several other disciplines, such as (computational) psycholinguistics, cognitive science, and neuroscience*—Account for human factors, as well as brain processes in language understanding and production

With so many "contributors" and such impressive advances of recent years, this is definitely an exciting time to start working in the NLP area!

1.2 Typical tasks

Before you start reading the next section, here is a task for you: name three to five applications that you use on a daily basis and that rely on NLP techniques. Again, you might be surprised to find that you are already actively using NLP through everyday applications. Let's look at some examples.

1.2.1 Information search

Let's start with a very typical scenario: you are searching for all work documents related to a particular event or product—for example, everything that mentions management meetings. Or perhaps you decided to get some from the web to solve the task just mentioned (figure 1.2).

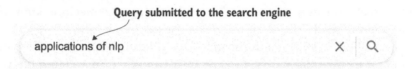

Figure 1.2 **You may search for the answer to the task formulated earlier in this chapter on the web.**

Alternatively, you may be looking for an answer to a particular question like "What temperature does water boil?" and, in fact, Google will be able to give you a precise answer, as shown in figure 1.3.

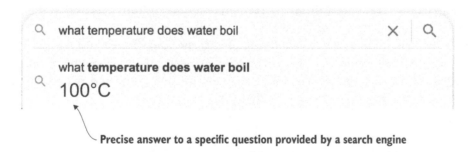

Figure 1.3 **If you look for factual information, search engines (Google in this case) may be able to provide you with precise answers.**

These are all examples of what is in essence the very same task—*information search*, or technically speaking, *information retrieval*. You will see shortly how all the varieties of the task are related. It boils down to the following steps:

1 You submit your "query," the question that you need an answer to or more information on.

2   The computer or search engine (Google being an example here) returns either the answer (like 100°C) or a set of results that are related to your query and provide you with the information requested.

3   If you search for the applications of NLP online, the search engine will provide you with an ordered list of websites that discuss such applications, and if you search for documents on a specific subject on your computer, it will list them in the order of relevance.

This last bit about relevance is essential here—the list of the websites from the search engine usually starts with the most relevant websites that you should visit, even if it may contain dozens of results pages. In practice, though, how often do you click through pages after the first one in the search results? The documents found on your filesystem typically would be ordered by their relevance, too, so you'll be able to find what you're looking for in a matter of seconds. How does the machine know in what order to present the results?

If you think about it, information search is an amazing application: First of all, if you were to find the relevant information on your computer, in a shared filesystem at work, or on the internet, and had to manually look through all available documents, it would be like looking for a needle in a haystack. Secondly, even if you knew which documents and web pages are generally relevant, finding the most relevant one(s) among them would still be a hugely overwhelming task. These days, luckily, we don't have to bother with tasks like that. It is hard to even imagine how much time is saved by the machines performing it for us.

However, have you ever wondered how the machines do that? Imagine that you had to do this task yourself—search in a collection of documents—without the help of the machine. You have a thousand printed notes and minutes related to the meetings at work, and you only need those that discuss the management meetings. How will you find *all* such documents? How will you identify the *most relevant* of these?

The first question might seem easy—you need all the documents that contain words like *meeting* and *management*, and you are not interested in any other documents, so this is simple filtering, as figure 1.4 shows:

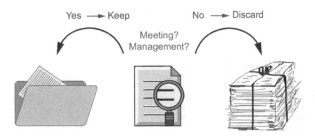

Figure 1.4   Simple filtering of documents into "keep" and "discard" piles based on occurrence of words

Now, it is true that the machines are getting increasingly better at understanding and generating human language. However, it's not true that they truly "understand" language, at least not in the same way we humans do. In particular, whereas if you were to look through the documents and search for occurrences of *meeting* and *management*, you would simply read through the documents and spot these words, because you have a particular representation of the word in mind and you know how it is spelled and how it sounds. The machines don't actually have such representations. How do they understand what the words are, and how can they spot a word, then?

One thing that machines are good at is dealing with numbers, so the obvious candidate for word and language representation in the "mechanical mind" is numerical representation. This means that humans need to "translate" the words from the representations that are common for us into the numerical language of the machines in order for the machines to "understand" words. The particular representation that you will often come across in natural language processing is a *vector*. Vector representations are ubiquitous—characters, words, and whole documents can be represented using them, and you'll see plenty of such examples in this book.

Here, we are going to represent our query and documents as vectors. A term vector should be familiar to you from high school math, and if you have been programming before, you can also relate vector representation to the notion of an *array*—the two are very similar, and in fact, the computer is going to use an array to store the vector representation of the document. Let's build our first numerical representation of a query and a document.

Query = "management meeting" contains only two words, and in a vector each of them will get its own dimension. Similarly, in an array, each one will get its own cell (figure 1.5).

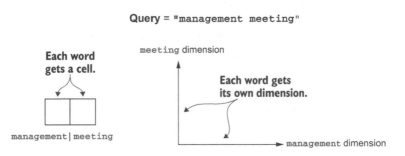

Figure 1.5   In an array, each word is represented by a separate cell. In a vector, each word gets its own dimension.

The cell of the array that is assigned to management will be responsible for keeping all the information related to management, and the cell that is assigned to meeting will similarly be related to meeting. The vector representation will do exactly the same but with the dimensions—there is one that is assigned to management and one that is for meeting. What information should these dimensions keep?

Well, the query contains only two terms, and they both contribute to the information need equally. This is expressed in the number of occurrences of each word in the query. Therefore, we should fill in the cells of the array with these counts. As for the vector, each count in the corresponding dimension will be interpreted as a coordinate, so our query will be represented as shown in figure 1.6.

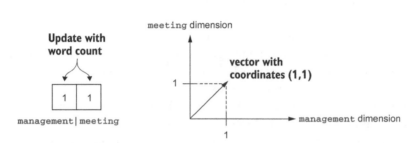

Figure 1.6 The array is updated with the word counts; the vector is built using these counts as coordinates.

Now, the vector is simply a graphical representation of the array. On the computer's end, the coordinates that define the vector are stored as an array.

We use a similar idea to "translate" the word occurrences in documents into the arrays and vector representations: simply count the occurrences. So, for some document `Doc1` containing five occurrences of the word `meeting` and three of the word `management`, and for document `Doc2` with one occurrence of `meeting` and four of `management`, the arrays and vectors will be as shown in figure 1.7.

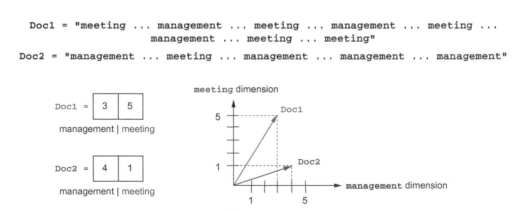

Figure 1.7 Arrays and vectors representing `Doc1` and `Doc2`

Perhaps now you see how to build such vectors using very simple Python code. To this end, let's create a Jupyter Notebook and start adding the code from listing 1.1 to it. The code starts with a very simple representation of a document based on the word occurrences in document Doc1 from figure 1.7 and builds a vector for it. It first creates an array vector with two cells, because in this example we know how many keywords there are. Next, the text is read in, treating each bit of the string between the whitespaces as a word. As soon as the word management is detected in text, its count is incremented in cell 0 (this is because Python starts all indexing from 0). As soon as meeting is detected in text, its count is incremented in cell 1. Finally, the code prints the vector out. Note that you can apply the same code to any other example—for example, you can build a vector for Doc2 as an input using the correspondent counts for words.

> **NOTE** In this book, by default, we will be using Jupyter Notebooks, as they provide practitioners with a flexible environment in which the code can be easily added, run, and updated, and the outputs can be easily observed. Alternatively, you can use any Python integrated development environment (IDE), such as PyCharm, for the code examples from this book. See https://jupyter .org for the installation instructions. In addition, see the appendix for installation instructions and the book's repository (https://github.com/ekochmar/ Getting-Started-with-NLP) for both installation instructions and all code examples.

Listing 1.1 Simple code to build a vector from text

```
doc1 = "meeting ... management ... meeting ... management ... meeting "
doc1 += "... management ... meeting ... meeting"          ◁——— Represents a document
                                                                based on keywords only
vector = [0, 0]        ◁——| Initializes
                          | array vector

for word in doc1.split(" "):          ◁——| The text is read in, and
    if word=="management":               | words are detected.
        vector[0] = vector[0] + 1
    if word=="meeting":          ◁——— Count for "management"
        vector[1] = vector[1] + 1       is incremented in cell 0.
                                   ◁
print (vector)    ◁——| This line should         Count for "meeting" is
                     | print [3, 5] for you.     incremented in cell 1.
```

The code here uses a very simple representation of a document focusing on the keywords only: you can assume that there are more words instead of dots, and you'll see more realistic examples later in this book. In addition, this code assumes that each bit of the string between the whitespaces is a word. In practice, properly detecting words in texts is not as simple as this. We'll talk about that later in the book, and we'll be using a special tool, a *tokenizer*, for this task. Yet splitting by whitespaces is a brute-force strategy good enough for our purposes in this example.

Now, of course, in a real application we want a number of things to be more scalable than this:

- We want the code to accommodate for all sorts of queries and not limit it to a predefined set of words (like management or meeting) or a predefined size (like array of size 2).
- We want it to properly detect words in text.
- We want it to automatically identify the dimensions along which the counts should be incremented rather than hardcoding it as we did in the code from listing 1.1.

And we'll do all that (and more!) in chapter 3. But for now, if you grasped the idea of representing documents as vectors, well done—you are on the right track! This is quite a fundamental idea that we will build upon in the course of this book, bit by bit.

I hope now you see the key difference between what we mean by "understanding" the language as humans do and "understanding" the language in a machinelike way. Obviously, counting words doesn't bring about proper understanding of words or the knowledge of what they mean. But for a number of applications, this type of representation is quite good for what they are. Now comes the second key bit of the application. We have represented the query and each document in a numerical form so that a machine can understand it, but can it tell which one is more relevant to the query? Which should we start with if we want to find the most relevant information about the management meetings?

We used vector representations to visualize the query and documents in the geometrical space. This space is a visual representation of the space in which we encoded our documents. To return the document most relevant to our query, we need to find the one that has *most similar content* to the query. That is where the geometrical space representation comes in handy—each object in this space is defined by its coordinates, and the most similar objects are located close to each other. Figure 1.8 shows where our query and documents lie in the shared geometrical space.

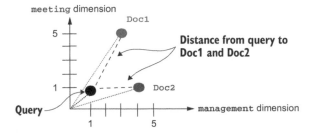

Figure 1.8   The query (denoted with the circle at [1, 1]) and the documents Doc1 [3, 5] and Doc2 [4, 1], represented in the shared space

The circles on the graph show where documents Doc1 and Doc2 and the query are located. Can we measure the distance between each pair in precise terms? Well, the distance is simply the difference between the coordinates for each of the objects along the correspondent dimensions:

- 1 and 3 along the `management` dimension for the query and `Doc1`
- 1 and 5 along the `meeting` dimension for the query and `Doc1`
- 1 and 4 along the `management` dimension for the query and `Doc2`, and so on

The measurement of distance in geometrical space originates with the good ole Pythagorean theorem that you should be familiar with from your high school mathematics course. Here's a refresher: in a right triangle, the square of the hypotenuse (the side opposite to the right angle) length equals the sum of the squares of the other two sides' lengths. That is, to measure the distance between two points in the geometrical space, we can draw a right triangle such that the distance between the two points will equal the length of the hypotenuse and calculate this distance using Pythagorean theorem. Why does this work? Because the length of each side is simply the difference in the coordinates, and we know the coordinates! This is what figure 1.9 demonstrates.

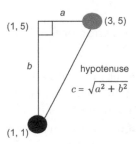

Figure 1.9 In a right triangle, the length of the hypotenuse can be estimated by determining the lengths of the other two sides.

This calculation is called *Euclidean distance*, and the geometrical interpretation is generally referred to as *Euclidean space*. Using this formula, we get

```
ED(query, Doc1) = square_root((3-1)² + (5-1)²) ≈ 4.47 and
ED(query, Doc2) = square_root((4-1)² + (1-1)²) = 3
```

> **Euclidean distance**
> The Euclidean distance between two points in space is measured as the length of the line between these points. In NLP, it can be used to measure the *similarity* between two texts (i.e., the distance between two vectors representing these texts).

Now, in our example, we work with two dimensions only, as there are only two words in the query. Can you use the same calculations on more dimensions? Yes, you can. You simply need to take the square root of the sum of the squared lengths in each dimension.

Listing 1.2 shows how you can perform the calculations that we have just discussed with a simple Python code. Both query and document are hardcoded in this example. Then the `for-loop` adds up squares of the difference in the coordinates in the query and the document along each dimension, using `math` functionality. Finally, the square root of the result is returned.

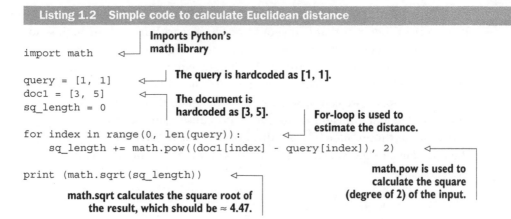

Listing 1.2   Simple code to calculate Euclidean distance

```
import math          ←┘  Imports Python's
                         math library

query = [1, 1]       ←┘  The query is hardcoded as [1, 1].
doc1 = [3, 5]        ←
sq_length = 0            The document is
                         hardcoded as [3, 5].          For-loop is used to
                                                       estimate the distance.
for index in range(0, len(query)):   ←
    sq_length += math.pow((doc1[index] - query[index]), 2)   ←

print (math.sqrt(sq_length))   ←                       math.pow is used to
                                                       calculate the square
        math.sqrt calculates the square root of        (degree of 2) of the input.
        the result, which should be ≈ 4.47.
```

NOTE   Check out Python's math library at https://docs.python.org/3/library/math.html for more information and a refresher.

Our Euclidean distance estimation tells us that `Doc2` is closer in space to the query than `Doc1`, so it is more similar, right? Well, there's one more point that we are missing at the moment. Note that if we typed in `management` and `meeting` multiple times in our query, the content and information need would not change, but the vector itself would. In particular, the length of the vector will be different, but the angle between the first version of the vector and the second one won't change, as you can see in figure 1.10.

New query = "management meeting management meeting"

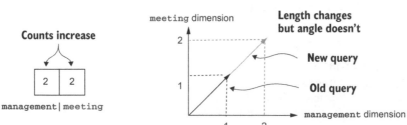

Figure 1.10   Vector length is affected by multiple occurrences of the same words, but angle is not.

Vectors representing documents can get longer without any conceptually interesting reasons. For example, longer documents will have longer vectors: each word in a longer document has a higher chance of occurrence and will most likely have higher counts. Therefore, it is much more informative to measure the angle between the *length-normalized* vectors (i.e., vectors made comparable in terms of their lengths) rather than the absolute distance, which can be dependent on the length of the documents.

As you can see in figure 1.10, the angle between the vectors is a much more stable measure than the length; otherwise the versions of the same query with multiple repetitions of the same words will actually have nonzero distance between them, which does not make sense from the information content point of view. The measure that helps estimate the angle between vectors is called *cosine similarity*, and it has a nice property of being higher when the two vectors are closer to each other with a smaller angle (i.e., more similar) and lower when they are more distant with a larger angle (i.e., less similar). The cosine of a 0° angle equals 1, meaning maximum closeness and similarity between the two vectors. Figure 1.11 shows an example.

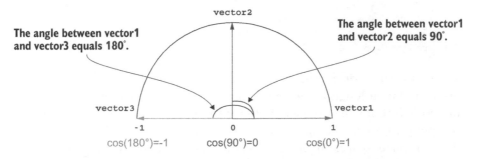

Figure 1.11 The cosine of 0° angle equals 1; `vector1` and `vector2` are at 90° to each other and have a cosine of 0; `vector1` and `vector3` at 180° have a cosine of −1.

> ## Cosine similarity
> *Cosine similarity* estimates the similarity between two nonzero vectors in space (or two texts represented by such vectors) on the basis of the angle between these vectors—for example, the cosine of 0° equals 1, which denotes the maximum similarity, and the cosine of 180° equals −1, which is the lowest value. Unlike Euclidean distance, this measure is not affected by vector length.

`Vector1` in figure 1.11 has an angle of 0° with itself as well as with any overlapping vectors, so the cosine of this angle equals 1, showing maximum similarity. For instance, the query from our previous examples is maximally similar to itself. `Vector1` and `vector2` are at 90° to each other, and the cosine of the angle between them equals 0. This is a very low value showing that the two vectors are not similar: as you can see in figure 1.11, it means that the two vectors are perpendicular to each other—they don't share any content along the two dimensions. `Vector1` has word occurrences along the *x*-axis, but not along *y*-axis, while `vector2` has word occurrences along the *y*-axis but not along *x*-axis. The two vectors represent content that is complementary to each other. To put this in context, imagine that `vector1` represents one query consisting of a single word, `management`, and `vector2` represents another query consisting of a single word, `meeting`.

Vector1 and vector3 are at 180° to each other and have a cosine of –1. In tasks based on simple word counting, the cosine will never be negative because the vectors that take the word occurrences as their coordinates will not produce negative coordinates, so `vector3` cannot represent a query or a document. When we build vectors based on word occurrence counts, the cosine similarity will range between 0 for the least similar (perpendicular, or orthogonal) vectors and 1 for the most similar, in extreme cases overlapping, vectors.

The estimation of the cosine of an angle relies on another Euclidean space estimation: *dot product* between vectors. Dot product is simply the sum of the coordinate products of the two vectors taken along each dimension. For example:

```
dot_product(query, Doc1) = 1*3 + 1*5 = 8
dot_product(query, Doc2) = 1*4 + 1*1 = 5
dot_product(Doc1, Doc2) = 3*4 + 5*1 = 17
```

The cosine similarity is estimated as a dot product between two vectors divided by the product of their lengths. The length of a vector is calculated in exactly the same way as we did before for the distance, but instead of the difference in coordinates between two points, we take the difference between the vector coordinates and the origin of the coordinate space, which is always $(0,0)$. So, the lengths of our vectors are

```
length(query) = square_root((1-0)² + (1-0)²) ≈ 1.41
length(Doc1) = square_root((3-0)² + (5-0)²) ≈ 5.83
length(Doc2) = square_root((4-0)² + (1-0)²) ≈ 4.12
```

And the cosine similarities are

```
cos(query,Doc1) = dot_prod(q,Doc1)/len(q)*len(Doc1) = 8/(1.41*5.83) ≈ 0.97
cos(query,Doc2) = dot_prod(q,Doc2)/len(q)*len(Doc2) = 5/(1.41*4.12) ≈ 0.86
```

To summarize, in the general form we calculate cosine similarity between vectors `vec1` and `vec2` as

```
cosine(vec1,vec2) = dot_product(vec1,vec2)/(length(vec1)*length(vec2))
```

This is directly derived from the Euclidean definition of the dot product, which says that

```
dot_product(vec1,vec2) = length(vec1)*length(vec2)*cosine(vec1,vec2)
```

Listing 1.3 shows how you can perform all these calculations using Python. The code starts similarly to the code from listing 1.2. Function `length` applies all length calculations to the passed argument, whereas length itself can be calculated using Euclidean distance. Next, function `dot_product` calculates dot product between arguments `vector1` and `vector2`. Since you can only measure the distance between vectors of the same dimensionality, the function makes sure this is the case and returns an error otherwise. Finally, specific arguments `query` and `doc1` are passed to the functions, and the cosine similarity is estimated and printed out. In this code, `doc1` is the same as used in other examples in this chapter; however, you can apply the code to any other input document.

Listing 1.3   Cosine similarity calculation

```
import math

query = [1, 1]
doc1 = [3, 5]

def length(vector):
    sq_length = 0
    for index in range(0, len(vector)):
        sq_length += math.pow(vector[index], 2)
    return math.sqrt(sq_length)

def dot_product(vector1, vector2):
    if len(vector1)==len(vector2):
        dot_prod = 0
        for index in range(0, len(vector1)):
            dot_prod += vector1[index]*vector2[index]
        return dot_prod
    else:
        return "Unmatching dimensionality"

cosine=dot_product(query, doc1)/(length(query)*length(doc1))
print (cosine)
```

Length is calculated using Euclidean distance; coordinates (0, 0) are omitted for simplicity.

Function length applies all length calculations to the passed argument.

The code up to here is almost exactly the same as the code in listing 1.2.

Function dot_product calculates dot product between passed arguments.

An error is returned if vectors are not of the same dimensionality.

A numerical value of ≈ 0.97 is printed.

Specific arguments query and doc1 are passed to the functions.

Bits of this code should now be familiar to you. The key difference between the code in listing 1.2 and the code in listing 1.3 is that instead of repeating the length estimation code for both query and document, we pack it up in a function that is introduced in the code using the keyword `def`. The function `length` performs all the calculations as in listing 1.2, but it does not care what vector it should be applied to. The particular vector—query or document—is passed in later as an argument to the function. This allows us to make the code much more concise and avoid repeating stuff.

So, in fact, when the length of the documents is disregarded, Doc1 is much more similar to the query than Doc2. Why is that? This is because rather than being closer only in distance, Doc1 is *more similar* to the query—the content in the query is equally balanced between the two terms, and so is the content in Doc1. In contrast, there is a higher chance that Doc2 is more about "management" in general than about "management meetings," as it mentions *meeting* only once.

Obviously, this is a very simplistic example. In reality, we might like to take into account more than just two terms in the query, other terms in the document and their relevance, the comparative importance of each term from the query, and so on. We'll be looking into these matters in chapter 3, but if you've grasped the general idea from this simple example, you are on the right track!

> ### Exercise 1.1
> Calculate cosine similarity between each pair of vectors: A = [4,3], B = [5,5], and C = [1,10]. Which ones are closest (most similar) to each other?
>
> First, try solving this exercise. Then you can compare your answer to the solution at the end of the chapter. Represent the vectors visually in a geometrical space to check your intuition about distance.

1.2.2   Advanced information search: Asking the machine precise questions

As you've seen in the earlier examples, it is not just the documents that you can find by your query—you can also find direct answers to your questions. For example, if you type into your search engine "What temperature is it now?" you may get an answer similar to that shown in figure 1.12.

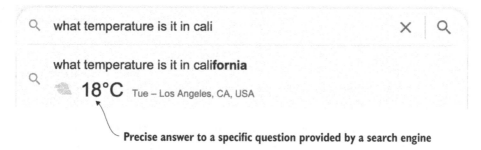

Figure 1.12   If you type into your search engine a question asking about the temperature, you will get an answer straightaway.

Alternatively, you can test your knowledge on any subject by asking the search engine precise factual questions like "When was the Eiffel Tower built?" or "What temperature does water boil at?" (you saw this last question in figure 1.3). In fact, you'll get back both the precise answer and the most relevant web page that explains the stuff, as shown in figure 1.13.

Okay, some of the "magic" behind what's going on should be clear to you now. If the search engine knows that your information need concerns water's boiling point, it can use information-retrieval techniques similar to the ones we've just talked about to

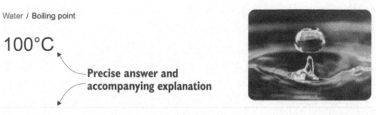

Water / Boiling point

100°C

Precise answer and
accompanying explanation

A liquid at high pressure has a higher boiling point than when that liquid is at atmospheric
pressure. For example, water boils at 100 °C (212 °F) at sea level, but at 93.4 °C (200.1 °F)
at 1,905 metres (6,250 ft) altitude. For a given pressure, different liquids will boil at different
temperatures.

https://en.wikipedia.org › wiki › Boiling_point   ⋮
Boiling point - Wikipedia

**Figure 1.13   The search for factual information on Google returns both the
precise answer to the question and the accompanying explanation.**

search for the most relevant pages. But what about the precise answer? These days you
can ask a machine a question and get a precise answer, and this looks much more like
machines getting real language understanding and intelligence!

Hold on. Didn't we say before that machines don't really "understand" language,
at least not in the sense humans do? In fact, what you see here is another application
of NLP concerned with *information extraction* and *question answering*, and it helps
machines get closer to understanding language. The trick is to

- Identify in the natural language question the particular bit(s) the question is
  about (e.g., the water boiling point).
- Apply the search on the web to find the most relevant pages that answer that
  question.
- Extract the bit(s) from these pages that answer(s) the question.

Figure 1.14 shows this process.

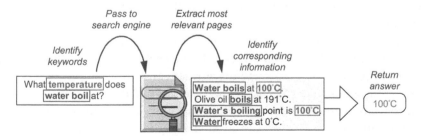

**Figure 1.14   Information extraction pipeline for the query "What temperature does
water boil at?"**

To solve this task, the machine indeed needs to know a bit more about language than just the number of words, and here is where it gets really interesting. You can see from the example here that to answer the question the machine needs to

- Know which words in the question really matter. For example, words like *temperature*, *water*, and *boil* matter, but *what*, *do*, and *at* don't. The group {temperature, water, boil} are called *content words*, and the group {what, do, at} are called *function words* or *stopwords*. The filtering is done by stopwords removal, which you'll learn more about in chapter 3.

- Know about the relations between words and the roles each one plays. For example, it is really the temperature that this question asks about, but the temperature is related to water, and the water is doing the action of boiling. The particular tools that will help you figure all this out are called *part-of-speech taggers* (they identify that words like *water* do the action, and the other words like *boil* denote the action itself) and *parsers* (they help identify how the words are connected to each other). You will learn more about this in chapter 4.

- Know that *boiling* means the same thing as *boil*. The tools that help you figure this out are called *stemmers* and *lemmatizers*, and we'll be using them in this book quite a lot, starting in chapter 3.

As you can see, the machine applies a whole bunch of NLP steps to analyze both the question and the answer, and identify that it is 100°C, and not 0°C or 191°C, that is the correct answer.

1.2.3   *Conversational agents and intelligent virtual assistants*

When reading about asking questions and getting answers from a machine, you might be thinking that it's not as frequently done in a browser these days. Perhaps a more usual way to get answers to questions like "Who sings this song?" or "How warm is it today?" now is to ask an intelligent virtual assistant. These are integrated in most smartphones, so depending on the one you're using, you may be communicating with Siri, Google Assistant, or Cortana. There are also independent devices like Amazon Echo that hosts the Amazon Alexa virtual assistant, which can also be accessed online. There are a whole variety of things that you can ask your virtual assistant, as figure 1.15 demonstrates.

Some of these queries are very similar to those questions that you can type in your browser to get a precise factual answer, so as in the earlier examples, this involves NLP analysis and application of information retrieval and information-extraction techniques. Other queries, like "Show me my tweets" or "Ring my brother at work," require information retrieval for matching the query to the brother's work phone number and some actions on the part of the machine (e.g., actual calling). Yet, there are two crucial bits that are involved in applications like intelligent virtual assistants: the input is no longer typed in, so the assistant needs to understand speech, and apart from particular actions like calling, the assistant is usually required to generate speech, which means translating the speech signal internally in a text form, processing the

Figure 1.15 A set of questions that you can ask your intelligent virtual assistant (Siri in this case; although you can ask similar questions of Alexa, Google Assistant, or Cortana)

query using NLP, generating the answer in a natural language, and producing output speech signal. This book is on text processing and NLP, so we will be looking into the bits relevant to these steps; however, the speech-processing part is beyond the scope of this book, as it usually lies in the domain of electrical engineering. Figure 1.16 shows the full processing pipeline of a virtual assistant.

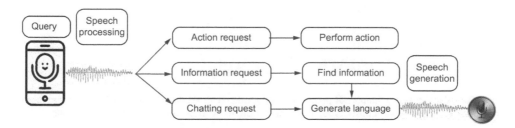

Figure 1.16 Processing pipeline of an intelligent virtual assistant

Leaving the speech-processing and generation steps aside, there is one more step related to NLP that we haven't discussed yet—*language generation*. This may include formulaic phrases like "Here is what I found," some of which might accompany actions like "Ringing your brother at work" and might not be very challenging to generate. However, in many situations and, especially if a virtual assistant engages in some natural conversation with the user like "How are you today, Siri?" it needs to generate a natural-sounding response, preferably on the topic of the conversation. This is also what *conversational agents*, or *chatbots*, do. So how is this step accomplished?

1.2.4   *Text prediction and language generation*

If you use a smartphone, you probably have used the predictive keyboard at least once. This is a good realistic example of text prediction in action. If you use a predictive keyboard, it can suggest the next word or a whole phrase for you, based on what you've typed in so far. You might also notice that the most appropriate word or phrase is usually placed in the middle for your convenience, and the application learns your individual lingo, so it tries to write as you personally do. In addition, modern technology (e.g., Google's Smart Reply) allows the machines to respond to emails for you, with usually quite short answers like `Either day works for me` or `Monday works for me`. Despite the relative simplicity and shortness of the responses, note how very relevant they usually are! Figure 1.17 provides some examples.

Figure 1.17   On the left: examples of predictive keyboards on smartphones, suggesting the most likely next words or phrases given the context typed in so far. On the right: Google's Smart Reply for emails.

Before we look under the hood of this application, here's a short quiz for you. Suppose I provide you with the beginning of a word, for example "langu___," and ask you "What is the next character?" Alternatively, suppose you can see some words beginning a phrase, for instance "natural language _____." Can you guess the next word?

I bet your intuition tells you that the first one is almost certainly "language." The second one might be trickier. You are reading a book on natural language processing, so "processing" might be your most reliable guess. Still, some of you might think of "natural language understanding" or "natural language generation." These are all valid candidates, but intuitively you know which ones are more likely. How does this prediction work?

Since you use language all the time, you know what events (e.g., sequences of characters or words) occur in language and which ones don't, and how often they occur relative to each other. This is our human intuitive understanding of probability. In fact, we are so primed to see the expected sequences of characters and words that we easily miss typos and get the main idea from a text even when only the first and the last letter of the word are correct and all other letters are shuffled—for exmaple, you might miss some spleling miskates in this sentence (got it?).

> **NOTE**   Even though the letters in the words *example, spelling,* and *mistakes* are shuffled, you probably had no trouble understanding what the sentence is saying. Moreover, if you were reading this text quickly, you might have missed these misspellings altogether. See more examples and explanation for this phenomenon at www.mrc-cbu.cam.ac.uk/people/matt.davis/cmabridge/.

Our expectations are strong and are governed by our observations of what usually happens in language. We make such estimations effortlessly, but machines can also learn about what's most common in language if they are given such an opportunity. The estimation of what is common and how common it is, is called *probability estimation*. In practice, you would estimate the probabilities as follows: if we've seen 100 contexts where the phrase "natural language _____" was used, and 90 of those were "natural language processing," 6 were "natural language understanding," and 4 were "natural language generation," then you'd say that

```
Probability("Processing" given "Natural Language" as context) = 90/100 = 90%
Probability("Understanding" given "Natural Language" as context) = 6/100 = 6%
Probability("Generation" given "Natural Language" as context) = 4/100 = 4%
```

That is, based on what you've seen so far (and you make sure that you've seen enough and the data that you observed was not abnormal), you can expect 90% of the time to see "natural language processing." Note that together the estimations add up to 100%. Note also that we can directly compare these probabilities and say that "processing" is more likely given that the beginning of the phrase is "natural language."

This idea of estimating what is most likely to follow can apply to characters and words. We have been trying to predict the next word or next character based on some previous context. In NLP terms, such context used in prediction is referred to as *n*-grams, where *n* represents the number of symbols (i.e., number of characters or words) that are considered as context. For example, *l, a,* and *n* in "language" represent character *unigrams,* while *natural, language,* and *processing* in "natural language processing" are word unigrams. Then *la*, *an*, and so on are character *bigrams*, and "natural language" and "language processing" are word bigrams. Trying to predict pairs of characters or words (i.e., bigrams) based on one previous character or word is called *bigram modeling*, predicting triplets of characters or words based on two previous ones is called *trigram modeling*, and so on. Figure 1.18 summarizes these examples.

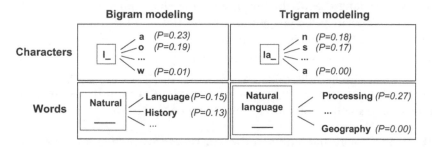

Figure 1.18   Examples of bigram and trigram character and word modeling with probabilities (*P*)

N-gram

An *n-gram* is a continuous sequence of *n* symbols (e.g., characters, words), where *n* denotes the length of the sequence; that is, *n* = 1 is a unigram; *n* = 2 is a bigram, and so on. *N*-grams are widely used in many NLP tasks, such as in text prediction based on previous context.

Why is considering context important, and what is the best *n* to take into account? Let's look at our quiz again. If you were given no context to predict, the task of predicting a word or character would be impossible—it could be anything. With one character (e.g., *l*) or one word (e.g., *natural*), the number of possibilities is still huge, especially for words. The rules of language do narrow it down for characters: it can be *la* as in *language*, *le* as in *lesson*, or *lo* as in *local*, but few would probably expect it to be *lm* or *lw* (unless it's an abbreviation, of course!). With two previous characters (*la*) or words (*natural language*), the correct prediction becomes easier, and for some long contexts (like *langu*), the possibilities narrow down to one or two options.

This means that the context helps in prediction. That is why we use it and calculate the estimations of probabilities based on it. How far back in context should we look for a reliable prediction, then? It seems like the longer, the better, doesn't it? Well, there is one more factor to consider: language is really creative. If we take only very long expressions for our probability estimations, we'll only be able to predict a few of those and will be missing on many more that are probable but have not occurred in exactly the same long context. This is because we will always see fewer examples for the longer expressions than for the shorter ones. If you've seen *lan* ten times, that means that you've seen any longer sequence at most ten times. In fact, you might have seen *lane* two times, *land* four times, and *language* four times—so, each of these counts is smaller than ten. But now any sequence longer than four characters starting with *lang* will be bound to have counts no greater than four, and so on. Ultimately, your probability estimation based on a very long sequence of previous characters, like *langua*, will return one specific word only. It's reliable but ultimately not very useful for real language generation.

The problem is particularly obvious with words. Say you've seen only one example so far that says "I have been reading this book on natural language processing." If you were to take the whole sentence as the context ("I have been reading this book on natural _____") to predict the next word, you will always predict this particular sentence and nothing else. However, if the book is on natural sciences or natural history, or anything else, you won't be able to predict any of these! At the same time, if you used a shorter context, like "book on natural," your algorithm would be able to suggest more alternatives. To summarize, the goal is to predict what is probable without constraining it to only those sequences seen before, so the tradeoff between more reliable prediction with longer contexts and more diverse one with shorter contexts suggests that something like two previous words or characters is good enough. Figure 1.19 shows roughly how a text prediction algorithm does its job.

Figure 1.19   Text prediction: a user starts typing a word and the algorithm predicts "language" in the end.

As soon as the user starts typing a word (e.g., starting with a letter *l*), the machine offers some plausible continuations. Remember, that for convenience, the most probable one is put in the middle: a text prediction algorithm might suggest *la* (as in *last*), *lo* (as in *love*), or *le* (as in *let's*) as some of the most probable options. The user can then choose the letter that they have in mind. Alternatively, the algorithm can suggest particular words (which most smartphones actually do), like *last*, *love*, or *let's*. We know that reliable prediction with one character as context is really tricky, and quite probably at this point none of the suggestions are the ones that the user has in mind, so they will continue by typing "la." At this point, the algorithm uses these two characters as context and adjusts its prediction. It offers *lan* (or maybe a word like *land*), *las* (or *last*) and *lat* (or *late*) as candidates. The user then chooses *lan* or keeps on typing "lan." At this point, the machine can both try to predict the word based on characters and check the fit with the previous words. If the user has been typing "I've been reading this book on natural lan____," both word context and character context would strongly suggest "language" at this point. Figure 1.20 illustrates this process.

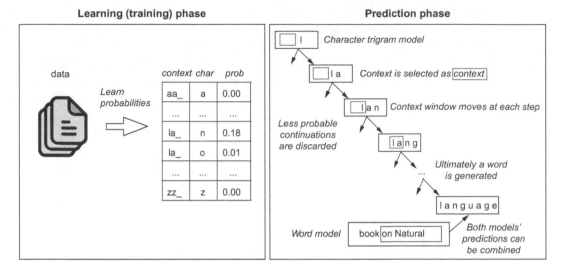

Figure 1.20   Language modeling during the learning and prediction phases

This type of prediction based on the sequences of words and characters in context is known as *language modeling*, and it is at the core of text prediction on your smartphone, or of the Smart Reply technology in your email. It is based on the idea that the sequences of plausible words can be learned in a statistical way—that is, calculating the probabilities on some real data. The data is of paramount importance: both quality and quantity matter. The large quantity of data that became available to the algorithms in the recent decades is one of the strongest catalysts that allowed NLP to move forward and achieve such impressive results. Another is the quality. If you use text prediction on your phone a lot, you might notice that if you had a friend or a colleague named Lang and used this surname quite a lot in messages, your phone will ultimately learn to offer this as the most probable suggestion even if it wasn't part of the original vocabulary—that is, your phone adapts to your personal vocabulary and uses your own data to do that.

Another factor that contributed to the success of conversational agents and predictive text technology is the development of algorithms themselves. This description would not be complete without mentioning that modern text prediction and chatbots increasingly use *neural-based language modeling*. The idea is the same—the algorithm still tries to predict the next character or word based on context, but the use of context is more flexible. For instance, it might be the case that the most useful information for the next word prediction is not two characters or words away, but in the beginning of the sentence or in the previous phrase. The *n*-gram models are quite limited in this respect, whereas more computationally expensive approaches such as neural models can deal with encoding large amounts of information from a wider context and even identify which bits of the context matter more.

Statistical analysis of language, probability estimations, and prediction lie at the core of these and many other applications, including the next ones.

1.2.5 *Spam filtering*

If you use email (and I assume you do), you are familiar with the spam problem. Spam relates to email that is not relevant to you because, for example, it has been sent to many recipients en masse, or it's potentially even dangerous, like spreading malicious content or computer viruses or sending links to unsafe websites. Therefore, it is really desirable that such email does not reach your inbox and gets safely put away in the spam or junk folder.

These days, email agents have *spam filters* incorporated in them, and you might be lucky enough to not see any of the spam emails that are filtered out by these algorithms. Spam filtering is a classic example of an application at the intersection of NLP and machine learning.

To get an idea of how it works, think of something that you would consider to be a spam email. There are several red flags to consider here: an unknown sender, suspicious email address, and unusual message formatting can all be indicative of spam. Ultimately, a lot of what tells you it's spam is its content. Typically, emails that try to sell you products you have no interest in buying, notify you that you have won a large sum of money in a lottery you have not entered, or tell you that your bank account is blocked (and asks you to click links and submit your personal information) are all very strong clues that the email is spam.

Machine-learning algorithms rely on the statistical analysis and vector representations of text. As before with information search, we represent each email as a vector and call it a *feature vector*. Each dimension in this vector, as before, represents a particular word or expression, and each such expression is called a *feature*. The feature occurrences then are counted as before. There is a plethora of machine-learning algorithms, and we will look at some of them in this book, but all they basically do is try to build a statistical model, a *function*, that helps them distinguish between those vectors that represent spam emails and those that represent normal emails (also known as *ham*). In doing so, the algorithms figure out which of the features matter more and should be trusted during prediction. Then, given any new email, the algorithm can tell whether it is likely to be spam or ham (figure 1.21).

Spam filtering is one example of a much wider area in NLP—*text classification*. Text classification aims to detect a class that the text belongs to based on its content. The task may include two classes as with spam filtering (spam versus ham) and sentiment analysis (positive versus negative), or more than two classes: for example, you can try to classify a news article using a number of topics like *politics, business, sports*, and so on. Several applications we will look into in this book deal with text classification: user profiling (chapters 5 and 6), sentiment analysis (chapters 7 and 8) and topic classification (chapter 9), and your first practical NLP application in chapter 2 will be spam filtering.

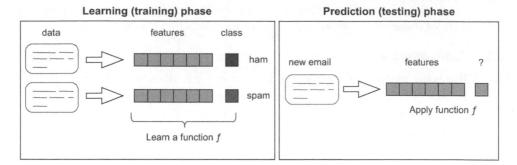

Figure 1.21 **Learning (training) and prediction phases of spam filtering**

1.2.6 *Machine translation*

Another popular application of NLP is machine translation. Whether you tried to check some information from an international resource (e.g., an unfamiliar term or something reported on the news), tried to communicate with an international colleague, are learning a foreign language, or are a non-native English speaker, you might have relied on machine translation in practice, such as using Google Translate.

As you've learned earlier in this chapter, this classic application of NLP has originally been approached in a rule-based manner. Imagine we wanted to translate the text in table 1.1 from English to French and knew how to translate individual words.

Table 1.1 **Word-for-word translation between English and French**

applications	applications
of	de
Natural	naturel
Language	langue
Processing	traitement

Can we just put the words together as "applications de naturel langue traitement" to translate a whole phrase? Well, there are several issues with such an approach.

First, when we check the French translations for "language" (as indeed for "applications"), we see several options (figure 1.22). Which one should we choose—is it *langue* or *langage*? Second, the translation for *natural* is not straightforward either. The words seem to have two forms, according to figure 1.23. Again, which one is it? Finally, when we check the translation for the whole phrase, we actually get the one with a different word order (figure 1.24)!

We see that several of our assumptions from before were incorrect. First, among the two translations for *language,* it is *langage* that should be chosen in this context. Second, French unlike English distinguishes between different genders of words, so if

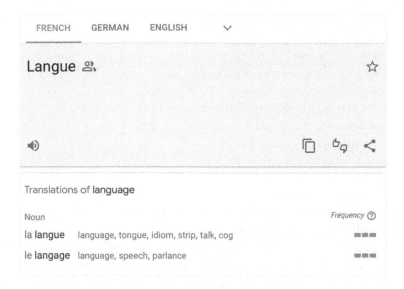

Figure 1.22   Several translations for the English word *language* to French (Google Translate)

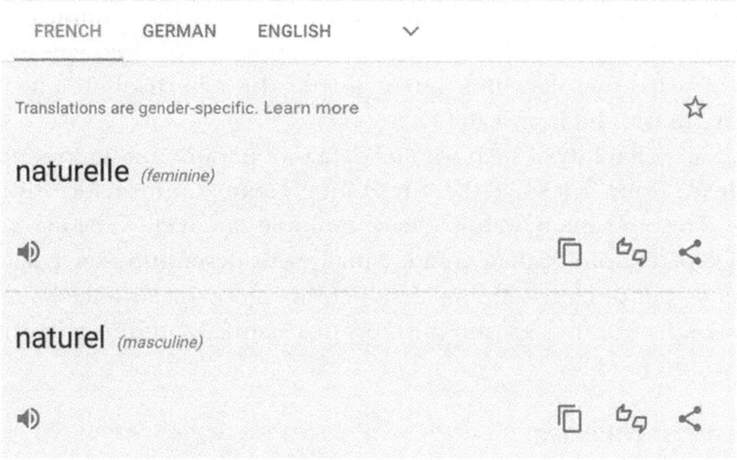

Figure 1.23   The translation of the English word *natural* to French has two forms, "naturel" and "naturelle" (Google Translate).

Figure 1.24   Phrase translation between English and French for "applications of natural language processing"

we wanted to choose a form of *natural* with *la langue* ("the language"), we'll have to say *naturelle*, but with *le langage* ("the language"), as here, *naturel* is used. Third, whereas in English adjectives (the words denoting qualities of nouns) like *natural* come before nouns (the words denoting objects or concepts) like *language*, in French they follow, thus *langage naturel* and not *naturel langage*. Finally, French doesn't permit saying "natural language processing" and instead requires us to say "processing of natural language," thus *traitement du langage naturel*. And, if you are wondering what *du* means, it is a merger of the words *of* (*de*) and *the* (*le*).

Now, imagine having to write rules for translating each of these cases from English to French, and then trying to expand the system to other language pairs as well. It would simply not scale! That is why the early rule-based approaches to machine learning took a long time to develop and did not succeed much.

The field, as with other applications, benefited from two things: the spread of statistical approaches to the NLP tasks and the availability of large amounts of data. Around the 1990s, statistical machine translation (SMT) replaced the traditional rule-based approaches. Instead of trying to come up with ad hoc rules for each case, SMT algorithms try to learn from large amounts of parallel data in two languages—that is, the data where the phrases in one language (e.g., *natural language* on the English side) are mapped to the translated phrases in another language (e.g., *langage naturel* on the French side). Such mapped parallel data is treated as the training data for the algorithm to learn from, and after seeing lots of phrases of this type in English–French pairs of texts, the algorithm learns to put the adjective after the noun in French translations with high probability.

Obviously, the availability of such parallel data is of paramount importance for the algorithm to learn from, but since there is so much textual information available on the web these days, and many websites have multiple language versions, some of it might be easier to get hold of than before. Finally, this description once again would not be complete without mentioning that neural networks advanced the field of machine translation even further, and the most successful algorithms today use neural machine translation (NMT).

1.2.7   *Spell- and grammar checking*

One final familiar application of NLP that is worth mentioning is spell- and grammar checking. Whether you are using a particular application, like Microsoft Word, or typing words in your browser, quite often the technology corrects your spelling and grammar for you (try typing "spleling miskates"!). Sometimes it even advises you on how to better structure your sentences by suggesting word order changes and finds better word replacements.

There is a reason we look into this application last: there is a whole bunch of different approaches one can address it with, using a range of techniques that we discussed in this section, so it is indeed a good one to conclude with. Here are some of such approaches:

- *Rule-based with the use of a dictionary*—If any of the words are unknown to the algorithm because they are not contained in a large dictionary of proper English words, then the word is likely to be a misspelling. The algorithm may try to change the word minimally and keep checking the alternatives against the same dictionary, counting each change as contributing to the overall score or "edit distance." For example, *thougt* would take one letter insertion to be converted into *thought* or one letter substitution to become *though*, but it will take one insertion and one substitution to become *through*, so in practice the algorithm will choose a cheaper option of correcting this misspelling to either *though* or *thought* (figure 1.25).

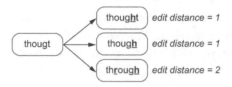

Figure 1.25   Possible corrections for the misspelling *thougt* with the assigned edit distances

- *Use of machine learning*—Of course, whether it should be *though, thought,* or *through* will depend on the context. For example, "I just *thougt* that even *thougt* it was a hard course, I'd still look *thougt* the material" will require all three corrections in different slots. And indeed, one can use a machine-learning classifier to predict the subtle differences in each of the three cases.
- Even better, one can treat it as a machine-translation problem, where the machine has to learn to translate between "bad" English sentences like "I just *thougt* that even *thougt* it was a hard course, I'd still look *thougt* the material" and good ones like "I just *thought* that even *though* it was a hard course, I'd still look *through* the material." The machine then has to establish the correct translation in each context.
- *Use of language modeling*—After all, "I just *thougt*," "I just *though*," and "I just *through*" are all ungrammatical English and are much less probable than "I just *thought*." All you need is a large set of grammatically correct English to let the language-modeling algorithm learn from it.

Now I hope you are convinced that (1) natural language processing is all around you in many applications that you already use on a daily basis; (2) it can really improve your work, in whatever application area you are working in—it's all about smart information processing; (3) you are already an active user of the technology and, by virtue of speaking language, an expert; and (4) the barrier to entry is low; what might look like a black box becomes much clearer when you look under the hood.

Summary

- Natural language processing is a key component of many tasks.
- NLP has seen a huge boost of interest in the recent years thanks to the development of algorithms, computer software and hardware, and the availability of large amounts of data.
- Anyone working with data would benefit from knowing about NLP, as a lot of information comes in a textual form.
- Knowing about NLP practices will help your application in whatever area you work in. This book will address examples from multiple domains—news, business, social media—but the best way to learn is to identify the project you care about and see how this book helps you solve your task.
- Without consciously thinking about it, you are already an expert in language domain, as anyone speaking language is. You will be able to evaluate the results of the NLP applications, and you don't need any further knowledge to do that. Furthermore, you have been actively using NLP applications on a daily basis for a long time now!
- One of the key approaches widely used in NLP is "translating" words into numerical representations—vectors—for the machine to "understand" them. In this chapter, you have learned how to do that in a very straightforward way.
- Once "translated" into a numerical form, words, sentences, and even whole documents can be evaluated in terms of their similarity. We can use a simple cosine similarity measure for that.

Solution to exercise 1.1

First, calculate the length of each vector using Euclidean distance between the vector coordinates and the origin $(0,0)$:

```
length(A) = square_root((4-0)² + (3-0)²) = 5
length(B) = square_root((5-0)² + (5-0)²) ≈ 7.07
length(C) = square_root((1-0)² + (10-0)²) ≈ 10.05
```

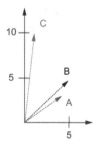

Next, calculate the dot products between each pair:

```
dot_product(A, B) = 4*5 + 3*5 = 35
dot_product(B, C) = 5*1 + 5*10 = 55
dot_product(C, A) = 1*4 + 10*3 = 34
```

Finally, for each pair of vectors, take the dot product and divide by the product of their lengths. You have all the components in place for that (figure 1.26):

Figure 1.26   The graph shows that vectors A and B are very close to each other, and C is more distant from either of them.

```
cos(A,B) = dot_prod(A,B)/len(A)*len(B) = 35/(5*7.07) ≈ 0.99
cos(B,C) = dot_prod(B,C)/len(B)*len(C) = 55/(7.07*10.05) ≈ 0.77
cos(C,A) = dot_prod(C,A)/len(C)*len(A) = 34/(10.05*5) ≈ 0.68
```

Your first NLP example

This chapter covers

- Implementing your first practical NLP application from scratch
- Structuring an NLP project from beginning to end
- Exploring NLP concepts, including tokenization and text normalization
- Applying a machine learning algorithm to textual data

In this chapter, you will learn how to implement your own NLP application from scratch. In doing so, you will also learn how to structure a typical NLP pipeline and how to apply a simple machine-learning algorithm to solve your task. The particular application you will implement is spam filtering. We overviewed it in chapter 1 as one of the classic tasks on the intersection of NLP and machine learning.

2.1 Introducing NLP in practice: Spam filtering

In this book, you use spam filtering as your first practical NLP application, as it exemplifies a widely spread family of tasks—*text classification*. Text classification comprises several applications that we discuss in this book, including user profiling (chapters 5 and 6), sentiment analysis (chapters 7 and 8), and topic classification (chapter 9), so this chapter will give you a good start. First, let's see what exactly *classification* addresses.

We apply classification in our everyday lives pretty regularly: classifying things simply implies that we try to put them into clearly defined groups, classes, or categories. In fact, we tend to classify all sorts of things all the time. Here are some examples:

- Based on our level of engagement and interest in a movie, we may classify it as interesting or boring.
- Based on temperature, we classify water as cold or hot.
- Based on the amount of sunshine, humidity, wind strength, and air temperature, we classify the weather as good or bad.
- Based on the number of wheels, we classify vehicles into unicycles, bicycles, tricycles, quadricycles, cars, and so on.
- Based on the availability of the engine, we may classify two-wheeled vehicles into bicycles and motorcycles.

Figure 2.1 combines the two types of classification for vehicles into one illustration:

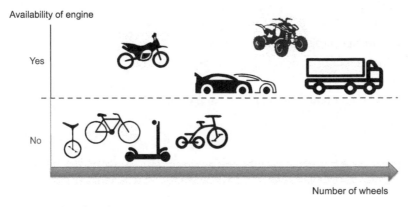

Figure 2.1   Classification of vehicles by two parameters: number of wheels and availability of an engine

Classification is useful because it makes it easier for us to reason about things and adjust our behavior accordingly. For example, there might be more subtle characteristics to a movie than it being just interesting or just boring, but by defining our attitude toward a movie very concisely using these two categories we might save a friend (provided we have similar taste in movies) a lot of time. By defining water as hot, we know that we should be careful when we use it, without the need to think about the precise temperature value and whether it is tolerable. Or take different types of vehicles: once we've done the grouping of vehicles, it becomes much easier to deal with any *instance* of each class. When we see a particular bicycle, we know what typical speed it can travel and what types of actions can be performed with bicycles in general. We know what to expect and don't need to reconsider any of these facts for each bicycle in question because the class of bicycles defines the properties of each instance in particular, too. We refer to the name of each class as a *class label.*

When classifying things, we often go for simple contrasts—good or bad, interesting or boring, hot or cold. When we are dealing with two labels only, it is called *binary classification.* For example, if we classify two-wheeled vehicles on the basis of whether they have an engine or not, we perform a binary classification and end up with two groups of objects—unmotorized two-wheeled vehicles like bicycles and kick scooters, and motorized two-wheeled vehicles like electric bicycles, motorcycles, mopeds, and so on. But if we classify all vehicles based on the number of wheels, on size, or on any other characteristic, we will end up with multiple classes, such as two-wheeled unmotorized vehicles, two-wheeled motorized vehicles, three-wheeled unmotorized vehicles, and so on (figure 2.2). Classification that implies more than two classes is called *multiclass classification.*

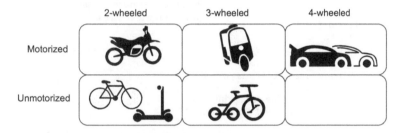

Figure 2.2 Multiclass classification of vehicles based on two parameters

Finally, how do we actually perform classification? We rely on several characteristics of the classified concepts, which in some cases may include one type of information only; for example, to classify water into cold or hot, we may rely on a single value of water temperature, and, say, call anything above 45°C (113°F) hot and anything below this value cold. The selection of such characteristics will depend on the particular task; for example, to classify weather into good or bad, we may need to rely on a number of characteristics, including air temperature, humidity, wind strength, and so on, rather than any single one. In machine-learning terms, we call such characteristics *features.*

Classification

Classification refers to the process of identifying which category or class among the set of categories (classes) an observation belongs to based on its properties. In machine learning, such properties are called *features* and the class names are called *class labels.* If you classify observations into two classes, you are dealing with *binary classification*; tasks with more than two classes are examples of *multiclass classification.*

As we are used to classifying things on a regular basis, we can usually easily define the number of classes, the labels, and the features. This comes from our wide experience with classification and from our exposure to multiple examples of concepts from different classes. Machines can learn to classify things as well, with a little help from humans. Sometimes a simple rule would be sufficient; for example, you can make the machine print out a warning that water is hot based on a simple threshold of 45°C (113°F), as listing 2.1 suggests. In this code, you define a function `print_warning`, which takes water temperature as input and prints out water status. The `if` statement checks if input temperature is above a predefined threshold and prints out a warning message if it is. In this case, since the temperature is above 45°C, the code prints out `Caution: Hot water!`

Listing 2.1   Simple code to tell whether water is cold or hot

The if statement checks if temperature is above the threshold.

The print_warning function takes water temperature as input and prints out water status.

```
def print_warning(temperature):
    if temperature>=45:
        print ("Caution: Hot water!")
    else:
        print ("You may use water as usual")
print_warning(46)
```

The code prints out "Caution: Hot water!"

However, when there are multiple factors to consider and these multiple factors may interact in various ways, a better strategy is to make the machine learn such rules and infer their correspondences from the data rather than hardcode them—after all, what the machines are good at is detecting the correspondences and patterns! This is what machine learning is about: it states that machines can learn to solve the task if they are provided with a sufficient number of examples and with the general outline of the task. For example, if we define the classes, labels, and features for the machine, it can then learn to assign concepts to the predefined classes based on these features. Using the cold or hot water example, we can provide the machine with the samples of water labeled `hot` and samples of water labeled `cold`, tell it to use temperature as the predictive factor (feature), and this way let it learn independently from the provided data that the boundary between the two classes is around 45°C (113°F), as figure 2.3 shows. This type of machine-learning approach, when we supervise the machine while it is learning by providing it with the labeled data, is called *supervised machine learning*.

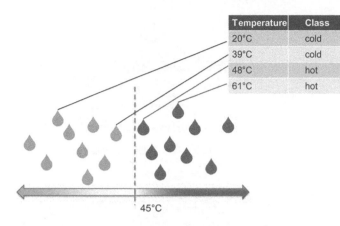

Temperature	Class
20°C	cold
39°C	cold
48°C	hot
61°C	hot

45°C

Figure 2.3   Provided with enough labeled examples of hot and cold water, the machine-learning algorithm can establish the threshold of 45°C independently.

Supervised machine learning

Supervised machine learning refers to a family of machine-learning tasks in which the algorithm learns the correspondences between an input and an output based on the provided labeled examples. Classification is an example of a supervised machine-learning task, where the algorithm tries to learn the mapping between the input data and the output class label.

Now that you are familiar with the ideas behind classification tasks, you are all set to implement your first NLP classification algorithm in practice. Before you move on, test your understanding of the task with exercise 2.1.

Exercise 2.1

Spam filtering is an example of text classification, which is usually addressed with supervised machine-learning techniques. Look at the examples of two emails in the figure and answer the following questions:

1 What labels do we assign in the spam-filtering task in the figure?
2 How many classes are there? What type of classification is this, binary or multiclass?
3 What features will help you distinguish between classes?

Try solving this exercise yourself. Then compare your answers with the solution at the end of the chapter.

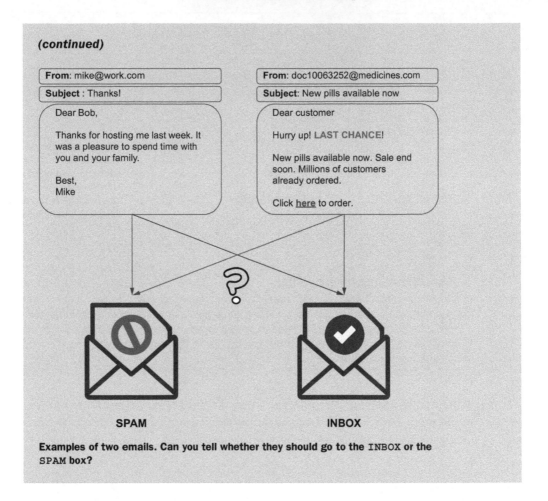

(continued)

From: mike@work.com

Subject : Thanks!

Dear Bob,

Thanks for hosting me last week. It was a pleasure to spend time with you and your family.

Best,
Mike

From: doc10063252@medicines.com

Subject: New pills available now

Dear customer

Hurry up! LAST CHANCE!

New pills available now. Sale end soon. Millions of customers already ordered.

Click here to order.

SPAM   INBOX

Examples of two emails. Can you tell whether they should go to the INBOX or the SPAM box?

2.2   *Understanding the task*

Consider the following scenario: you have a collection of spam and normal emails from the past. You are tasked with building a spam filter, which for any future incoming email can predict whether this email is spam or not. Consider these questions:

- How can you use the provided data?
- What characteristics of the emails might be particularly useful, and how will you extract them?
- What will be the sequence of steps in this application?

In this section, we will discuss this scenario and look into the implementation steps. In total, the pipeline for this task will consist of five steps, visualized as a flow chart in figure 2.4. Now let's look into each of these steps in more detail.

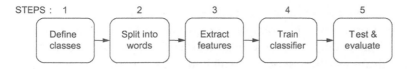

Figure 2.4   Five steps of a machine learning–based text classification project

2.2.1   Step 1: Define the data and classes

First, you need to ask yourself what format the email messages are delivered in for this task. For instance, in a real-life situation, you might need to extract the messages from the mail agent application. However, for simplicity, let's assume that someone has extracted the emails for you and stored them in text format. The normal emails are stored in a separate folder—let's call it Ham, and spam emails are stored in a Spam folder.

> **NOTE**   If you are wondering why "normal" emails are sometimes called "ham" in the spam-detection context, check out the history behind the term *spam* (e.g., at www.merriam-webster.com/dictionary/spam).

If someone has already predefined past spam and ham emails for you (e.g., by extracting these emails from the INBOX and SPAM box), you don't need to bother with labeling them. However, you still need to point the machine-learning algorithm at the two folders by clearly defining which one is ham and which one is spam. This way, you will define the class labels and identify the number of classes for the algorithm. This should be the first step in your spam-detection pipeline (and in any text-classification pipeline), after which you can preprocess the data, extract the relevant information, and then train and test your algorithm (figure 2.5). You can set step 1 of your algorithm as follows: Define which data represents "ham" class and which data represents "spam" class for the machine-learning algorithm.

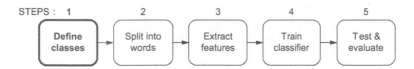

Figure 2.5   In Step 1 (highlighted), define the classes for the machine-learning algorithm.

2.2.2   Step 2: Split the text into words

Next, you will need to define the features for the machine to know what type of information, or what properties of the emails to pay attention to, but before you can do that, there is one more step to perform. As we've just discussed in the previous exercise, email content provides significant information as to whether an email is ham or spam. How can you extract the content? One solution is to read in the whole email as a single textual property—for example, use "Minutes of the meeting on Friday, June 20 [the rest of the email body]" as a single feature for ham emails, and "Low-cost prescription medications [the rest of the email body]" as a single feature for spam emails. This will definitely help the algorithm identify the emails that contain *all* of the included phrases from these two emails as either spam or ham, but how often would you expect to see precisely the same text of the email again? A change in any single character may change the whole feature! This suggests that a better candidate for a feature in this task would be a smaller chunk of text, such as a word. In addition, words are likely to carry spam-related information (e.g., *lottery* might be a good clue that an email is spam), while being repetitive enough to occur in multiple emails. Before moving further, try solving exercise 2.2.

Exercise 2.2

For a machine, the text comes in as a sequence of symbols, so the machine does not have an idea of what a word is.

- How would you define what a word is from the human perspective?
- How would you code this for a machine?

For example, how will you split the following sentence into words? "Define which data represents each class for the machine learning algorithm."

Let's discuss possible solutions to exercise 2.2. The first solution might be "Words are sequences of characters separated by whitespaces." This will work well for some examples, including "Define which data represents each class for the machine learning algorithm." Let's write simple code that uses whitespaces to split text into words, as follows.

Listing 2.2   Simple code to split text string into words by whitespaces

```
text = "Define which data represents each class for the machine learning
    algorithm"
text.split(" ")      ◁──|  You can rely on Python's functionality
                          to split strings of text by whitespaces.
```

The code from this listing will print out the list of words from the input sentence, one per line:

```
['Define',
 'which',
 'data',
 ...
 'algorithm']
```

So far, so good. However, what happens to this strategy when we have punctuation marks? For example: "Define which data represents "ham" class and which data represents "spam" class for the machine learning algorithm."

Now you will end up with the words like [..., "ham", ..., "spam", ..., algorithm.] in the list of words. Are ["ham"], ["spam"], and [algorithm.] any different from [ham], [spam], and [algorithm]? That is, the same words but without the punctuation marks attached to them? The answer is, these words are exactly the same, but because you are only splitting by whitespaces at the moment, there is no way of taking the punctuation marks into account. However, each sentence will likely include one full stop (.), question (?), or exclamation mark (!) attached to the last word, and possibly more punctuation marks inside the sentence itself, so this is going to be a problem for properly extracting words from text. Ideally, you would like to be able to extract words and punctuation marks separately.

Taking this into account, you might update your algorithm with a splitting strategy by punctuation marks. There are several possible ways to do that, including using Python's regular expressions module re. (If you have never used re module and regular expressions before, you can find more information about it on https://docs.python .org/3/library/re.html.) However, if you have never used regular expressions before, you may apply a simple iterative algorithm that will consider each character in the text string and decide whether it should be ignored (if it is a whitespace), added to a word list (if it is a punctuation mark), or added to the current word (otherwise). In other words, the algorithm may proceed as follows:

ALGORITHM 1

1 Store words list and a variable that keeps track of the current word—let's call it current_word for simplicity.
2 Read text character by character:
   – *If* a character is a whitespace, add the current_word to the words list and update the current_word variable to be ready to start a new word.
   – *Else if* a character is a punctuation mark:
      ▪ *If* the previous character is not a whitespace, add the current_word to the words list; then add the punctuation mark as a separate word token, and update the current_word variable.
      ▪ *Else if* the previous character is a whitespace, just add the punctuation mark as a separate word token.
   – *Else if* a character is a letter other than a whitespace or punctuation mark, add it to the current_word.

Figure 2.6 shows how this algorithm will process the string represents "ham".

Listing 2.3 shows how you can implement this algorithm in Python. You start by initializing a list of delimiters and populating it with some punctuation marks (this list is kept short for the sake of simplicity; you will see more comprehensive lists later in this chapter). Note the use of single quotes (') in code around the double quote (") as a delimiter; an alternative to this would be using an escape sequence '\"'. Then you introduce variables words to keep the list of processed words and current_word to keep track of the word that is currently being processed. Next, you iterate through

	Action	current_word	words
START	Initialization	_	[]
r	Add letter to current_word	r	[]
e	Add letter to current_word	re	[]
p	Add letter to current_word	rep	[]
r	Add letter to current_word	repr	[]
e	Add letter to current_word	repre	[]
s	Add letter to current_word	repres	[]
e	Add letter to current_word	represe	[]
n	Add letter to current_word	represen	[]
t	Add letter to current_word	represent	[]
s	Add letter to current_word	represents	[]
	Add to words; update current_word	_	[represents]
"	Add punctuation mark to words	_	[represents, "]
h	Add letter to current_word	h	[represents, "]
a	Add letter to current_word	ha	[represents, "]
m	Add letter to current_word	ham	[represents, "]
"	Add current_word and punctuation mark to words	_	[represents, ", ham, "]

Figure 2.6   Processing of the string `represents "ham"` with a tokenization algorithm

text character by character and apply the algorithm just discussed: if the character is a whitespace and the current_word is not empty, you add it to the words list and re-initialize current_word to keep track of the upcoming words. If the character is one of the punctuation marks and there is nothing stored in the current_word yet, you add this punctuation mark to the words list. If the character is one of the punctuation marks and there is information stored in current_word, you add both the current_word and the punctuation mark to the words list and re-initialize current_word to keep track of the upcoming words. Finally, if the character is any other letter (not specified as a delimiter and not a whitespace), you add it to the current_word.

Listing 2.3   Code to split text string into words by whitespaces and punctuation

```
text = 'Define which data represents "ham" class and which data represents
    "spam" class for the machine learning algorithm.'
delimiters = ['"', "."]
words = []
current_word = ""

for char in text:
    if char==" ":
```

Initialize a list of delimiters and populate it with some punctuation marks.

The current_word variable keeps track of the word currently being processed.

The words variable keeps the list of processed words.

Iterate through the text character by character.

```
        if not current_word=="":
            words.append(current_word)
            current_word = ""
    elif char in delimiters:
        if current_word=="":
            words.append(char)
        else:
            words.append(current_word)
            words.append(char)
            current_word = ""
    else:
        current_word += char

print(words)
```

Check if the character is a whitespace and the current_word is not empty.

Check if the character is one of the punctuation marks and there is nothing stored in the current_word yet.

Check if the character is one of the punctuation marks and there is information stored in current_word.

Check if the character is any other letter; that is, not specified as a delimiter and not a whitespace.

This code will produce the following list of words for our example, as required: ['Define', 'which', 'data', 'represents', '"', 'ham', '"', 'class', 'and', 'which', 'data', 'represents', '"', 'spam', '"', 'class', 'for', 'the', 'machine', 'learning', 'algorithm', '.']. At the same time, it will also split examples like *i.e.* and *e.g.* into ['i', '.', 'e', '.'] and ['e', '.', 'g', '.'], and *U.S.A.* and *U.K.* into ['U', '.', 'S', '.', 'A', '.'] and ['U', '.', 'K', '.']. This is problematic, since if the algorithm splits these examples in this way, it will lose track of the correct interpretation of words like *i.e.* or *U.S.A.*, which should be treated as one word token rather than a combination of characters. How can this be achieved?

This is where the NLP tools come in handy: the tool that helps you split the running string of characters into meaningful words is called *tokenizer*, and it takes care of the cases like the ones we've just discussed—that is, it can recognize that ham. needs to be split into ['ham', '.'] while U.S.A. needs to be kept as one word ['U.S.A.']. Normally, tokenizers rely on extensive and carefully designed lists of regular expressions, and some are trained using machine-learning approaches.

NOTE   For an example of a regular expressions-based tokenizer, you can check the Natural Language Processing Toolkit's regexp_tokenize() to get a general idea of the types of the rules that tokenizers take into account: see Section 3.7 on www.nltk.org/book/ch03.html. The lists of rules applied may differ from one tokenizer to another.

While the steps outlined in algorithm 1 and attempted in code listings 2.2 and 2.3 showed you what is under the hood of a tokenization algorithm, you can see that even this first preprocessing step is not trivial. Therefore, to perform tokenization on text, you can develop your own tokenizer by extending the regular expressions beyond those overviewed earlier and making sure that your algorithm handles the exceptions. However, in the practical examples in this book, we will be relying on the tokenization algorithms available via NLP toolkits: such tokenizers are highly optimized for the task, and they not only perform splitting by whitespaces and punctuation marks, but they also keep track of the cases that should not be split by such methods. This helps make sure that the tokenization step results in a list of appropriate English words.

Tokenization

Tokenization is the process of word token identification or extraction from the running text. It is often the first step in text preprocessing. Whitespaces and punctuation marks often serve as reliable word separators; however, simple approaches are likely to run into exceptions like "U.S.A." and similar. *Tokenizers* are NLP tools that are highly optimized for the task of word tokenization, and they may rely on carefully crafted regular expressions or may be trained using machine-learning algorithms.

To check your understanding of what tokenization step achieves, try manually tokenizing strings of text in exercise 2.3 before looking into the solution at the end of the chapter. Later, you will also be able to check whether your solutions coincide with those returned by a tokenizer:

Exercise 2.3

How will you tokenize the following strings into words? (Solution can be found at the end of this chapter.)

1 What's the best way to cook a pizza?
2 We're going to use a baking stone.
3 I haven't used a baking stone before.

Let's now define step 2 of your algorithm as follows: apply tokenization to split the running text into words, which are going to serve as features (figure 2.7).

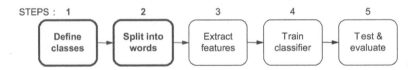

STEPS : 1   2   3   4   5

Define classes → Split into words → Extract features → Train classifier → Test & evaluate

Figure 2.7   In step 2 (highlighted), split the running text into words.

2.2.3   *Step 3: Extract and normalize the features*

Now we look closely into the extracted words and see whether they are all equally good to be used as features—that is, whether they are equally indicative of the spam-related content. Suppose two emails use a different format: one says

```
Collect your lottery winnings
```

while another one says

```
Collect Your Lottery Winnings
```

The algorithm that splits these messages into words will end up with different word lists because, for instance, *lottery ≠ Lottery*, but is it different in terms of the meaning? To get rid of such formatting issues like uppercase versus lowercase, you can put all the extracted words into lowercase using Python functionality. Therefore, step 3 in your algorithm should be defined as follows: extract and normalize the features; for example, by putting all words to lowercase (figure 2.8).

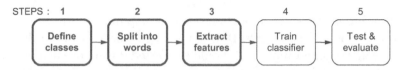

Figure 2.8   In step 3 (highlighted), extract and normalize your features (e.g., words).

2.2.4   *Step 4: Train a classifier*

At this point, you will end up with two sets of data—one linked to the spam class and another one linked to the ham class. Each data is preprocessed in the same way in steps 2 and 3, and the features are extracted. Next, you need to let the machine use this data to build the connection between the set of features (properties) that describe each type of email (spam or ham) and the labels attached to each type. In step 4, a machine-learning algorithm tries to build a statistical model, a *function*, that helps it distinguish between the two classes. This is what happens during the learning (training) phase. Figure 2.9 is a refresher visualizing the training and test processes.

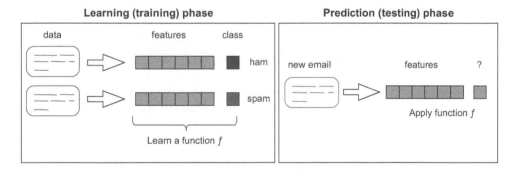

Figure 2.9   Learning (training) and prediction phases of spam filtering

So, step 4 of the algorithm should be defined as follows: define a machine-learning model and train it on the data with the features predefined in the previous steps (figure 2.10).

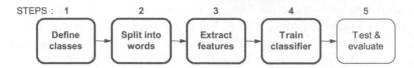

Figure 2.10   In step 4 (highlighted), define a machine-learning model and train it on the data.

Your algorithm has now learned a function that can map the features from each class of emails to the spam and ham labels. During training, your algorithm will figure out which of the features matter more and should be trusted during prediction; for example, it might detect that the occurrence of a word *lottery* in an email should be strongly associated with the label spam, while the occurrence of the word *meeting* should strongly suggest the ham label. The final step in this process is to make sure the algorithm is doing such predictions well. How will you do that?

Remember that you were originally provided with a set of emails prelabeled for you as spam and ham. This means you know the correct answer for these emails. Why not use some of them to check how well your algorithm performs? In fact, this is exactly how it is done in machine learning—you use some of your labeled data to test the classifier's performance. This bit of data is predictably called *test set*. There is one caveat, though: if you've already used this data to train the classifier (i.e., to let it figure out the correspondence between the features and the classes), it already knows the right answers. To avoid that, you need to make sure that the bit of data you used in step 4 for training is separate and not overlapping with the test set. This bit of data is called *training set*. Therefore, before training your classifier in step 4, you need to split your full dataset into training and test sets. Here is the set of rules for that (figure 2.11):

- Shuffle your data to avoid any bias.
- Split it randomly into a larger proportion for the training phase and set the rest aside for the test phase. The typical proportions for the sets are 80% for training and 20% for testing.
- Train your classifier in step 4 using the training set only. Your test set is there to provide you with a realistic and fair estimate of your classifier's performance, so don't let your classifier peek into it. Use it at the final step for evaluation only.

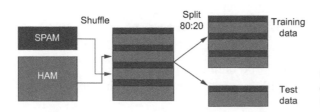

Figure 2.11   Before training the classifier, shuffle the data and split it into training and test sets.

Data splits for supervised machine learning

In supervised machine learning, the algorithm is trained on a subset of the labeled data called *training* set. It uses this subset to learn the function mapping the input data to the output labels. *Test set* is the subset of the data, disjointed from the training set, on which the algorithm can then be evaluated. The typical data split is 80% for training and 20% for testing. Note that it is important that the two sets are not overlapping. If your algorithm is trained and tested on the same data, you won't be able to tell what it actually *learned* rather than memorized.

2.2.5 *Step 5: Evaluate the classifier*

Suppose you trained your classifier in step 4 and then applied it to the test data. How will you measure the performance? One approach would be to check what proportion of the test emails the algorithm classifies correctly—that is, assigns the spam label to a spam email and classifies ham emails as ham. This proportion is called *accuracy*, and its calculation is pretty straightforward:

$$Accuracy = \frac{num(\text{correct predictions})}{num(\text{all test instances})}$$

Now check your understanding with exercise 2.4.

Exercise 2.4

Suppose your algorithm predicts the following labels for some small dataset of test examples. (Solution can be found at the end of this chapter.)

Correct label	Predicted label
Spam	Ham
Spam	Spam
Ham	Ham
Ham	Spam
Ham	Ham

1. What is the accuracy of your classifier on this small dataset?
2. Is this a good accuracy? That is, does it suggest that the classifier performs well? What if you know that the ratio of ham to spam emails in your set of emails is 50:50? What if it is 60% ham emails and 40% spam—does it change your assessment of how well the classifier performs?
3. Does it perform better in identifying ham emails or spam emails?

Let's discuss the solutions to this exercise (note that you can also find more detailed explanations at the end of the chapter). The prediction of the classifier based on the distribution of classes that you came across in this exercise is called *baseline*. In an equal class distribution case, the baseline is 50%, and if your classifier yields an accuracy of 60%, it outperforms this baseline. In the case of 60:40 split, the baseline, which can also be called the *majority class baseline*, is 60%. This means that if a dummy "classifier" does no learning at all and simply predicts the ham label for all emails, it will not filter out any spam emails from the inbox, but its accuracy will also be 60%—just like your classifier that is actually trained and performs some classification! This makes the classifier in the second case in this exercise much less useful because it does not outperform the majority class baseline.

In summary, accuracy is a good overall measure of performance, but you need to keep in mind (1) the distribution of classes to have a comparison point for the classifier's performance, and (2) the performance on each class, which is hidden within a single accuracy value but might suggest what the strengths and weaknesses of your classifier are. Therefore, the final step, step 5, in your algorithm is applying your classifier to the test data and evaluating its performance (figure 2.12).

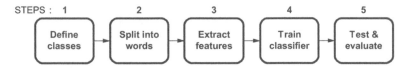

Figure 2.12   In step 5, test and evaluate your classifier.

2.3   *Implementing your own spam filter*

Now let's implement each of the five steps. It's time you open Jupyter and create a new notebook to start coding your own spam filter.

> **NOTE** A reminder: we are using Jupyter Notebooks, as they provide practitioners with a flexible environment in which the code can be easily added, run, and updated and the outputs can be easily observed. Alternatively, you can use any Python IDE for the code examples from this book. See https://jupyter.org for the installation instructions. In addition, see the appendix for installation instructions and the book's repository (https://github.com/ekochmar/Getting-Started-with-NLP) for both installation instructions and all code examples.

2.3.1   *Step 1: Define the data and classes*

Quite often when working on NLP and machine-learning applications, you might find out that the problem has been previously described or someone has already collected some data that you may use to build an initial version of your algorithm. For example, if you want to build a machine-learning classifier for spam detection, you need to provide your algorithm with a sufficient number of spam and ham emails. The best way to build such a classifier would be to collect your own ham and spam emails and train your algorithm to detect what you personally would consider spam. That would tune your classifier toward your needs, as you might consider certain content spam even when other users might see it as a harmless, although unsolicited, email. However, if you don't have enough examples in your own spam box (e.g., many mail agents automatically empty spam folders on a regular basis), there exist some datasets of spam and ham emails collected from other users that you can use to train your classifier. (It should be noted, however, that in practical applications, high-quality annotated data is hard to come by. Privacy is one of the issues when working with such sensitive data as emails.)

One of such publicly available collections is Enron email dataset. (You can read more about the dataset at www.cs.cmu.edu/~enron/, and download the subsets of the data at http://mng.bz/WxYg. The subsets and data collection process are described in more detail at http://www2.aueb.gr/users/ion/docs/ceas2006_paper.pdf.) This is a dataset of emails, including both ham (extracted from the original Enron dataset using personal messages of three Enron employees) and spam emails. To make processing more manageable, we will use a subset of this large dataset, although you can use the full dataset later if you wish. For your convenience, this subset of the data is available together with the code for the book (https://github.com/ekochmar/Getting-Started-with-NLP). We are going to use the `enron1/` folder for training. All folders in the Enron dataset contain spam and ham emails in separate subfolders, so you don't need to worry about predefining them. Each email is stored as a text file in these subfolders. Let's read in the contents of these text files in each subfolder, store the spam emails' contents and the ham emails' contents as two separate data structures, and point our algorithm at each, clearly defining which one is spam and which one is ham.

To that end, let's define a function `read_in` that will take a folder as an input, read the files in this folder, and store their contents as a Python list data structure, as listing 2.4 shows. In this code, you rely on Python's `os` module functionality to list all the files in the specified folder, and then you iterate through them, skipping hidden files that are sometimes automatically created by the operating systems. Such files can be easily identified because their names start with ".". Next, you read the contents of each file. The `encoding` and `errors` arguments of `codecs.open` function will help you avoid errors in reading files that are related to text encoding. You add the content of each file to a list data structure, and in the end, you return the list that contains the contents of the files from the specified folder.

Listing 2.4 Code to read in the contents of the files

```
import os
import codecs

def read_in(folder):
    files = os.listdir(folder)
    a_list = []
    for a_file in files:
```

Import Python's os module that helps iterate through the folders.

Import Python's codecs module that helps with different text encodings.

Iterate through the files in the folder.

Using os functionality, list all the files in the specified folder.

Skip hidden files.

```
if not a_file.startswith("."):
    f = codecs.open(folder + a_file,
        "r", encoding = "ISO-8859-1", errors="ignore")
    a_list.append(f.read())
    f.close()
return a_list
```

Read the contents of each file.

Add the content of each file to the list data structure.

Close the file after you read the contents.

Return Python list that contains the contents of the files from the specified folder.

Now you can define two such lists—spam_list and ham_list—letting the machine know what data represents spam emails and what data represents ham emails. Let's check if the data is uploaded correctly; for example, you can print out the lengths of the lists or check any particular member of the list. Since you are using a publicly available dataset, you can easily check whether what your code put into the lists is correct: the length of the spam_list should equal the number of spam emails in the enron1/spam/ folder, which should be 1,500, while the length of the ham_list should equal the number of emails in the enron1/ham/, or 3,672. If you get these numbers, your data is uploaded and read in correctly. Similarly, you can check the contents of the very first instance in the spam_list and verify that it is exactly the same as the content of the first text file in the enron1/spam/ folder. Listing 2.5 shows how you can do this.

Listing 2.5 Code to verify that the data is uploaded and read in correctly

```
spam_list = read_in("enron1/spam/")
ham_list = read_in("enron1/ham/")
print(len(spam_list))
print(len(ham_list))
print(spam_list[0])
print(ham_list[0])
```

Initialize spam_list and ham_list.

Check the lengths of the lists: for spam it should be 1,500 and for ham, 3,672.

Print out the contents of the first entry (i.e., the first file in each correspondent subfolder).

Next, you'll need to preprocess the data (e.g., by splitting text strings into words) and extract the features. Wouldn't it be easier if you could run all preprocessing steps over a single data structure rather than over two separate lists? The code in listing 2.6 shows how you can merge the two lists, keeping their respective labels. This time, instead of using for-loop, let's use the compact code style that is provided by Python's list comprehensions.

NOTE Refresher on Python's list comprehensions is available at https://docs .python.org/3/tutorial/datastructures.html.

Instead of lengthy for-loops that do updates to the lists, we are going to update the list contents as we go. In this code, you use list comprehensions to create an all_emails list that will keep all emails with their labels. For each member of the ham_list and spam_list it stores a tuple with the content and associated label. In addition, you will need to split the data randomly into the training and test sets. To that end, let's shuffle the resulting list of emails with their labels, and make sure that the shuffle is reproducible by fixing the way in which the data is shuffled. For the shuffle to be reproducible, you need to define the seed for the random operator, which makes sure that all future runs will shuffle the data in exactly the same way. The code shows how you can define such a seed, using `seed 42` as an example. Finally, the code prints out the size of the dataset (the length of the list), which is equal to 5,172 (1,500 spam and 3,672 ham emails).

Listing 2.6 Code to combine the data into a single structure

Python's random module will help you shuffle the data randomly.

Use list comprehensions to create the all_emails list that will keep all emails with their labels.

```
import random

all_emails = [(email_content, "spam") for email_content in spam_list]
all_emails += [(email_content, "ham") for email_content in ham_list]
random.seed(42)
random.shuffle(all_emails)
print (f"Dataset size = {str(len(all_emails))} emails")
```

Select the seed of the random operator to make sure that all future runs will shuffle the data in the same way.

Check the size of the dataset (length of the list); it should be equal to 1,500 + 3,672 (see Note).

NOTE This kind of string is called *formatted string literals* or f-strings, and it is a new feature introduced in Python 3.6. If you are unfamiliar with this type of string literals, check Python documentation at http://mng.bz/8MBK.

2.3.2 *Step 2: Split the text into words*

Remember that the email contents you've read in so far each come as a single string of symbols. The first step of text preprocessing involves splitting the running text into words.

Several NLP toolkits will be introduced in this book. One of them, Natural Language Processing Toolkit (NLTK), you will start using straightaway. (Install the toolkit from www.nltk.org/install.html and the accompanying data from www.nltk.org/data .html.) One of the benefits of this toolkit is that it comes with a thorough documentation and description of its functionality.

You are going to use NLTK's tokenizer (check the documentation at www.nltk .org/api/nltk.tokenize.html). It takes running text as input and returns a list of words based on a number of customized regular expressions, which help to delimit the text by whitespaces and punctuation marks, keeping common words like *U.S.A.* unsplit. The code in listing 2.7 shows how to import the toolkit and the tokenizer and run it over the examples you've looked into in this chapter. This code defines a `tokenize` function that takes a string as input and splits it into words. The `for-loop` within this function appends each identified word from the tokenized string to the output word list; alternatively, you can use list comprehensions for the same purpose. (Can you see how to present this code in a more compact and elegant way using list comprehensions?) Finally, given the input, the function prints out a list of words. You can test your intuitions about the words and check your answers to previous exercises by changing the input to any string of your choice.

Listing 2.7   Code to run a tokenizer over text

```
import nltk
from nltk import word_tokenize          ◁————  Import nltk library and specifically
nltk.download('punkt')                          import NLTK's word tokenizer (see Note).
                              ◁—————————  Install NLTK's
                                          sentence tokenizer.
def tokenize(input):          ◁—————————  Define a function tokenize to
    word_list = []                        split input text into words.
    for word in word_tokenize(input):
        word_list.append(word)    ◁———  This loop appends each identified word from
    return word_list                    the tokenized string to the output word list.

input = "What's the best way to split a sentence into words?"
print(tokenize(input))    ◁———  Given the input, the function
                                prints out a list of words.
```

NOTE   In addition to the toolkit itself, you need to install NLTK data as explained on www.nltk.org/data.html. Running `nltk.download()` will install all the data needed for text processing in one go; in addition, individual tools can be installed separately (e.g., `nltk.download('punkt')` installs NLTK's sentence tokenizer).

If you run the code from listing 2.7 on the suggested example, it will print out `['What', "'s", 'the', 'best', 'way', 'to', 'split', 'a', 'sentence', 'into', 'words', '?']` as the output.

2.3.3   *Step 3: Extract and normalize the features*

Once the words are extracted from running text, you need to convert them into features. In particular, you need to put all words into lowercase to make your algorithm establish the connection between different formats like *Lottery* and *lottery*.

Putting all strings to lowercase can be achieved with Python's string functionality. To extract the features (words) from the text, you need to iterate through the recognized words and put all words to lowercase. In fact, both tokenization and converting text to lowercase can be achieved using a single line of code with list comprehensions. See if you can come up with this line of code before you look at listing 2.8.

In this code, you define a function `get_features` that extracts the features from the text of email passed in as input. Using list comprehensions, you can combine the two steps—tokenization and converting strings to lowercase—in one line, as the code in listing 2.8 shows. Compare this to a much longer piece of code for tokenization in listing 2.7. Here, you first normalize and then tokenize text, but the two steps are interchangeable. Next, for each word in the email, you switch on the "flag" that the word is contained in this email by assigning it with a `True` value. The list data structure `all_features` keeps tuples containing the dictionary of features matched with the spam or ham label for each email. In the end, the code shows how you can check what features are extracted from an input text and what `all_features` list data structure contains (e.g., by printing out its length and the number of features detected in the first or any other email in the set).

Listing 2.8   Code to extract the features

```
def get_features(text):          ←——  Let's define a function that will extract
    features = {}                       the features from the text input.
    word_list = [word for word in word_tokenize(text.lower())]   ←——  Combine
    for word in word_list:                                             tokenization
        features[word] = True    ←——  For each word in the email,            and converting
    return features                    switch on the "flag" that this        strings to
                                       word is contained in the email.       lowercase in one
all_features = [(get_features(email), label)                               line using list
                 for (email, label) in all_emails]      ←——                 comprehensions.

print(get_features("Participate In Our New Lottery NOW!"))     all_features will keep
print(len(all_features))                                       tuples containing the
print(len(all_features[0][0]))                                 dictionary of features
print(len(all_features[99][0]))          ←——                   matched with the
                                                               label for each email.
Check what features are            Check what
extracted from an input text.      all_features list data
                                   structure contains.
```

With this bit of code, you iterate over the emails in your collection (`all_emails`) and store the features extracted from each email matched with the label. For example, if a spam email consists of a single sentence (e.g., "Participate In Our New Lottery NOW!"), your algorithm will first extract the list of features present in this email and assign a `True` value to each of them. The dictionary of features will be represented using this format: `['participate': True, 'in': True, ..., 'now': True, '!': True]`. Then the algorithm will add this data structure to `all_features` together with the spam label: `(['participate': True, 'in': True, ..., 'now': True, '!': True], "spam")`. Figure 2.13 shows the steps performed in this code listing. Now check your understanding of the data processing with exercise 2.5.

Exercise 2.5

Imagine your whole dataset contained only one spam email ("Participate In Our New Lottery NOW!") and one ham email ("Participate in the Staff Survey"). What features will be extracted from this dataset with the code from listing 2.8? (Solution can be found at the end of this chapter.)

Again, it is a good idea to know how your data is represented, so the code in listing 2.8 uses the `print` function to help you check some parameters of your data; for example,

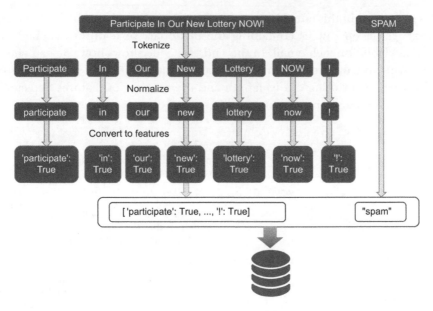

Figure 2.13   Preprocessing and feature extraction steps

you can check how many emails have been processed and put into the feature set (this number should be equal to the number of emails you have started with), as well as the number of features present in each email (i.e., with the `True` flag assigned to them). The data structure that you have just created with the code from listing 2.8, `all_features`, is a list of tuples (pairs), where each tuple represents an individual email, so the total length of `all_features` is equal to the number of emails in your dataset. As each tuple in this list corresponds to an individual email, you can access each one by the index in the list using `all_features[index]`: for example, you can access the first email in the dataset as `all_features[0]` (remember, that Python's indexing starts with 0), and the hundredth as `all_features[99]` (for the same reason).

Let's now clarify what each tuple structure representing an email contains. Tuples pair up two information fields. In this case, a dictionary of features extracted from the email and its label—that is, each tuple in `all_features` contains a pair (`dict_of_features, label`). So if you'd like to access the first email in the list, you call on `all_features[0]`; to access its features, you use `all_features[0][0]`; and to access its label, you use `all_features[0][1]`. Figure 2.14 visualizes the `all_features` data structure and the extraction process.

For example, if the first email in your collection is a spam email with the content "Participate in our lottery now!", `all_features[0]` will return the tuple (`['participate': True, 'in': True, ..., 'now': True, '!': True], "spam"`); `all_features[0][0]` will return the dictionary `['participate': True, 'in': True, ..., 'now': True, '!': True]`, and `all_features[0][1]` will return the value spam.

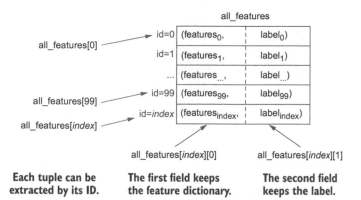

Figure 2.14 The `all_features` data structure

Each tuple can be extracted by its ID.

The first field keeps the feature dictionary.

The second field keeps the label.

2.3.4 *Step 4: Train the classifier*

Next, let's apply machine learning and teach the machine to distinguish between the features that describe each of the two classes. There are several classification algorithms that you can use, and you will come across several of them in this book. But since you are at the beginning of your journey, let's start with one of the most interpretable ones—an algorithm called Naïve Bayes. Don't be misled by the word *Naïve* in its title, though. Despite the relative simplicity of the approach compared to other ones, this algorithm often works well in practice and sets a competitive performance baseline that is hard to beat with more sophisticated approaches. For the spam-filtering algorithm that you are building in this chapter, you will rely on the Naïve Bayes implementation provided with the NLTK library, so don't worry if some details of the algorithm seem challenging to you. However, if you would like to see what is happening "under the hood," this section will walk you through the details of the algorithm.

Naïve Bayes is a probabilistic classifier, which means that it makes the class prediction based on the estimate of which outcome is most likely (i.e., it assesses the probability of an email being spam and compares it with the probability of it being ham), and then selects the outcome that is most probable between the two. In fact, this is quite similar to how humans assess whether an email is spam or ham. When you receive an email that says "Participate in our lottery now! Click on this link," before clicking on the (potentially harmful) link, you assess how likely it is (i.e., what is the probability?) that it is a ham email and compare it to how likely it is that this email is spam. Based on your experience and all the previous spam and ham emails you have seen before, you might judge that it is much more likely (more probable) that it is a spam email. By the time the machine makes a prediction, it has also accumulated some experience in distinguishing spam from ham that is based on processing a dataset of labeled spam and ham emails.

Now let's formalize this step a bit further. In the previous step, you extracted the content of the email and converted it into a list of individual words (features). In this step, the machine will try to predict whether the email content represents spam or ham. In other words, it will try to predict whether the email is spam or ham given or conditioned on its content. This type of probability, when the outcome (class of spam or ham) depends on the condition (words used as features), is called *conditional probability*. For spam detection, you estimate `P(spam | email content)` and `P(ham | email content)`, or generally `P(outcome | (given) condition)`. Then you compare one estimate to another and return the most probable class. For example:

```
If P(spam | content) = 0.58 and P(ham | content) = 0.42, predict spam
If P(spam | content) = 0.37 and P(ham | content) = 0.63, predict ham
```

> **NOTE**   Reminder on the notation: `P` is used to represent all probabilities; `|` is used in conditional probabilities, when you are trying to estimate the probability of some event (that is specified before `|`) given that the condition (that is specified after `|`) applies.

In summary, this boils down to the following set of actions illustrated in figure 2.15.

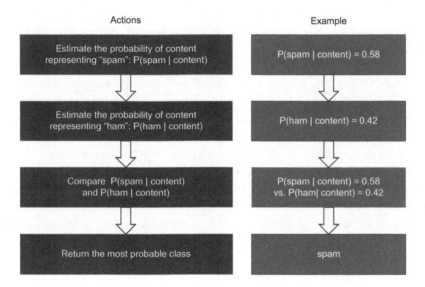

Figure 2.15   Prediction is based on which conditional probability is higher.

How can you estimate these probabilities in practice? Your own prediction of whether an email content like "Participate in our lottery now!" signifies that an email is spam or ham is based on how often in the past an email with the same content was spam or ham. Similarly, a machine can estimate the probability that an email is spam or ham conditioned on its content, taking the number of times it has seen this content leading to a particular outcome:

$$P(spam|\text{"Participate in our lottery now!"}) = \frac{num(\text{spam emails with "Participate in our lottery now!"})}{num(\text{all emails with "Participate in our lottery now!"})}$$

$$P(ham|\text{``Participate in our lottery now!''}) = \frac{num(\text{ham emails with ``Participate in our lottery now!''})}{num(\text{all emails with ``Participate in our lottery now!''})}$$

In the general form, this can be expressed as

$$P(outcome|condition) = \frac{num\_of\_times(\text{condition led to outcome})}{num\_of\_times(\text{condition applied})}$$

You (and the machine) will need to make such estimations for all types of content in your collection, including for the email contents that are much longer than "Participate in our new lottery now!" Do you think you will come across enough examples to reliably make such estimations? In other words, do you think you will see any particular combination of words (that you use as features), no matter how long, multiple times so that you can reliably estimate the probabilities from these examples? The answer is you will probably see "Participate in our new lottery now!" only a few times, and you might see longer combinations of words only once, so such small numbers won't tell the algorithm much and you won't be able to use them in the previous expression effectively.

Additionally, you will constantly get new emails where the words will be used in a different order and different combinations, so for some of these new combinations you will not have any counts at all, even though you might have counts for individual words in such new emails. The solution to this problem is to split the estimation into smaller bits. For instance, remember that you used tokenization to split long texts into separate words to let the algorithm access the smaller bits of information—words rather than whole sequences. The idea of estimating probabilities based on separate features rather than based on the whole sequence of features (i.e., whole text) is rather similar.

At the moment, you are trying to predict a single outcome (class of spam or ham) given a single condition that is the whole text of the email; for example, "Participate in our lottery now!" In the previous step, you converted this single text into a set of features as ['participate': True, 'in': True, ..., 'now': True, '!': True]. Note that the conditional probabilities like P(spam| "Participate in our lottery now!") and P(spam| ['participate': True, 'in': True, ..., 'now': True, '!': True]) are the same because this set of features encodes the text. Therefore, if the chances of seeing "Participate in our lottery now!" are low, the chances of seeing the set of features ['participate': True, 'in': True, ..., 'now': True, '!': True] encoding this text are equally low. Is there a way to split this set to get at more fine-grained, individual probabilities, such as to establish a link between ['lottery': True] and the class of spam?

Unfortunately, there is no way to split the conditional probability estimation like P(outcome | **conditions**) when there are multiple conditions specified; however, it is possible to split the probability estimation like P(**outcomes** | condition) when there is a single condition and multiple outcomes. In spam detection, the class is a

single value (it is spam or ham), while features are a set (`['participate': True, 'in':`
`True, ..., 'now': True, '!': True]`). If you can flip around the single value of class
and the set of features in such a way that the class becomes the new condition and the
features become the new outcomes, you can split the probability into smaller components and establish the link between individual features like `['lottery': True]` and
class values like spam. Figure 2.16 uses this idea to demonstrate how the prediction
can be made in such a case.

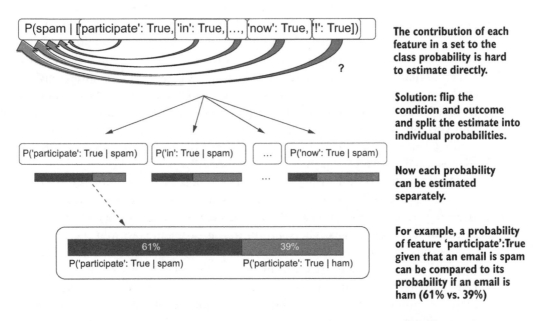

Figure 2.16   Since the conditional probability of class given a whole set of features is hard to estimate directly, flip the condition and outcome around and estimate the probabilities separately.

Luckily, there is a way to flip the outcomes (class) and conditions (features extracted
from the content) around! Let's look into the estimation of conditional probabilities
again: you estimate the probability that the email is spam *given* that its content is "Participate in our new lottery now!" based on how often in the past an email with such
content was spam. For that, you take the proportion of the times you have seen "Participate in our new lottery now!" in a spam email among the emails with this content.
You can express it as

$$P(spam|\text{"Participate in our lottery now!"}) = \frac{P(\text{"Participate in our lottery now!" is in a spam email})}{P(\text{"Participate in our lottery now!" is used in an email})}$$

Let's call this Formula 1. What is the conditional probability of the content "Participate in our new lottery now!" given class spam, then? Similarly to how you estimated

the probabilities earlier, you need the proportion of times you have seen "Participate in our new lottery now!" in a spam email among all spam emails. You can express it as

$$P(\text{"Participate in our lottery now!"}|spam) \quad \frac{P(\text{"Participate in our lottery now!" is in a spam email})}{P(\text{an email is spam})}$$

Let's call this Formula 2. Every time you use conditional probabilities, you need to divide how likely it is that you see the condition and outcome together by how likely it is that you see the condition on its own—this is the bit after |. Now you can see that both Formulas 1 and 2 rely on how often you see particular content in an email from a particular class. They share this bit, so you can use it to connect the two formulas. For instance, from Formula 2 you know that

$$P(\text{"Participate in our lottery now!" is in a spam email}) =$$
$$P(\text{"Participate in our lottery now!"}|spam) \times P(\text{an email is spam})$$

Now you can fit this into Formula 1:

$$P(spam|\text{"Participate in our lottery now!"}) =$$
$$\frac{P(\text{"Participate in our lottery now!" is in a spam email})}{P(\text{"Participate in our lottery now!" is used in an email})} =$$
$$\frac{P(\text{"Participate in our lottery now!"}|spam) \times P(\text{an email is spam})}{P(\text{"Participate in our lottery now!" is used in an email})}$$

Figure 2.17 further illustrates this process.

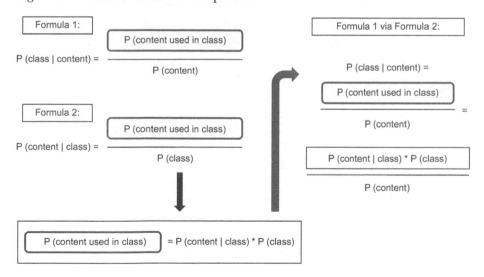

Figure 2.17 The conditional probability for P(class | content) **can be expressed via the conditional probability for** P(content | class)**.**

In the general form,

$$P(class|content) = \frac{P(\text{content in class})}{P(content)} = \frac{P(content|class) \times P(class)}{P(content)}$$

In other words, you can express the probability of a class given email content via the probability of the content given the class. Let's look into these two new probabilities, P(content | class) and P(class), more closely as they have interesting properties:

- P(class) expresses the probability of each class. This is simply the distribution of the classes in your data. Imagine opening your inbox and seeing a new incoming email. What do you expect this email to be—spam or ham? If you mostly get normal emails and your spam filter is working well, you will probably expect a new email to also be ham rather than spam. For example, the enron1/ ham folder contains 3,672 emails, and the spam folder contains 1,500 emails, making the distribution approximately 71:29, or P("ham")=0.71 and P("spam")=0.29. This is often referred to as *prior probability*, as it reflects the beliefs of the classifier about where the data comes from prior to any particular evidence; for example, here the classifier will expect that it is much more likely (chances are 71:29) that a random incoming email is ham.
- P(content | class) is the evidence, as it expresses how likely it is that you (or the algorithm) will see this particular content given that the email is spam or ham. For example, imagine you have opened this new email and now you can assess how likely it is that these words are used in a spam email versus how likely it is that they are used in a ham email. The combination of these factors may in the end change your, or the classifier's, original belief about the most likely class that you had before seeing the content (evidence).

Now you can replace the conditional probability of P(class | content) with P(content | class); for example, whereas before you had to calculate P("spam" | "Participate in our new lottery now!") or equally P("spam" | ['participate': True, 'in': True, ..., 'now': True, '!': True]), which is hard to do because you will often end up with too few examples of exactly the same email content or exactly the same combination of features, now you can estimate P(['participate': True, 'in': True, ..., 'now': True, '!': True] | "spam") instead. But how does this solve the problem? Aren't you still dealing with a long sequence of features?

Here is where the "naïve" assumption in Naïve Bayes helps: it assumes that the features are independent of each other, or that your chances of seeing a word *lottery* in an email are independent of seeing a word *new* or any other word in this email before. Therefore, you can estimate the probability of the whole sequence of features given a class as a product of probabilities of *each* feature given this class:

$$P([\text{'participate'}: \text{True}, \text{'in'}: \text{True}, \ldots, \text{'now'}: \text{True}, \text{'!'}: \text{True}]|\text{"spam"}) =$$

$$P(\text{'participate'}: \text{True} \mid \text{"spam"}) \times P(\text{'in'}: \text{True} \mid \text{"spam"}) \times \ldots \times P(\text{'!'}: \text{True} \mid \text{"spam"})$$

If you express `['participate': True]` as the first feature in the feature list, or f_1, `['in': True]` as f_2, and so on, until f_n = `['!': True]`, you can use the general formula

$$P([f_1, f_2, \ldots, f_n]|class) = P(f_1|class) \times P(f_2|class) \times \ldots \times P(f_n|class)$$

Now that you have broken down the probability of the whole feature set given class into the probabilities for each word given that class, how do you actually estimate them? Since for each email you note which words occur in it, the total number of times you can switch on the flag `['feature': True]` equals the total number of emails in that class, while the actual number of times you switch on this flag is the number of emails where this feature is actually present. The conditional probability `P(feature | class)` is simply the proportion:

$$P(feature|class) = \frac{num(\text{emails in class with feature present})}{total\_num(\text{emails in class})}$$

These numbers are easy to estimate from the training data. Let's try to do that with an example in exercise 2.6. Try solving this exercise yourself. Then compare your answers with the solution at the end of the chapter.

Exercise 2.6

Suppose you have five spam emails and ten ham emails. What are the conditional probabilities for `P('prescription':True | spam)`, `P('meeting':True | ham)`, `P('stock':True | spam)`, and `P('stock':True | ham)`, if

- Two spam emails contain the word *prescription*?
- One spam email contains the word *stock*?
- Three ham emails contain the word *stock*?
- Five ham emails contain the word *meeting*?

(Solution can be found at the end of this chapter.)

Now you have all the components in place. Let's iterate through the classification steps again. First, during the training phase, the algorithm learns prior class probabilities. This is simply class distribution—for example, `P(ham)=0.71` and `P(spam)=0.29`. Secondly, the algorithm learns probabilities for each feature given each of the classes. This is the proportion of emails with each feature in each class—for example, `P('meeting':True | ham) = 0.50`. During the test phase, or when the algorithm is applied to a new email and is asked to predict its class, the following comparison from the beginning of this section is applied:

$$\begin{cases} P(spam|content) \geq P(ham|content) & \Rightarrow \text{spam} \\ otherwise & \Rightarrow \text{ham} \end{cases}$$

This is what we started with originally, but we said that the conditions are flipped, so it becomes

$$\begin{cases} \frac{P(content|spam) \times P(spam)}{P(content)} \geq \frac{P(content|ham) \times P(ham)}{P(content)} & \Rightarrow \text{spam} \\ otherwise & \Rightarrow \text{ham} \end{cases}$$

Note that we end up with P(content) in the denominator on both sides of the expression, so the absolute value of this probability doesn't matter, and it can be removed from the expression altogether. As an aside, since the probability always has a positive value, it won't change the comparative values on the two sides; for example, if you were comparing 10 to 4, you would get 10 > 4 whether you divide the two sides by the same positive number like $(10/2) > (4/2)$ or not. So we can simplify the expression as

$$\begin{cases} P(content|spam) \times P(spam) \geq P(content|ham) \times P(ham) & \Rightarrow \text{spam} \\ otherwise & \Rightarrow \text{ham} \end{cases}$$

P(spam) and P(ham) are class probabilities estimated during training, and P(content | class), using naïve independence assumption, are products of probabilities, so

$$\begin{cases} P([f_1, f_2, \ldots, f_n]|spam) \times P(spam) \geq P([f_1, f_2, \ldots, f_n]|ham) \times P(ham) & \Rightarrow \text{spam} \\ otherwise & \Rightarrow \text{ham} \end{cases}$$

is split into the individual feature probabilities as

$$\begin{cases} P(f_1|spam) \times \ldots \times P(f_n|spam) \times P(spam) \geq P(f_1|ham) \times \ldots \times P(f_n|ham) \times P(ham) & \Rightarrow \text{spam} \\ otherwise & \Rightarrow \text{ham} \end{cases}$$

Figure 2.18 illustrates this classification process.

This is the final expression the classifier relies on, and the code from listing 2.9 applies this idea to practice. This section has discussed step-by-step what goes on "behind the scenes" of the Naïve Bayes classifier. Although you can translate the formulas from this section into code, you do not necessarily have to do this in practice. Many toolkits come with optimized implementations of a range of widely used machine-learning algorithms, and since Naïve Bayes is frequently used for NLP

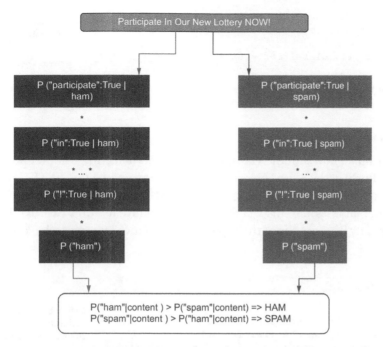

Figure 2.18 Classification process: the conditional probabilities for each feature (word), with some omitted using "..." notation for brevity, are multiplied with each other and with the class probabilities.

tasks, NLTK comes with its own implementation, too. Here you are going to use it. The code in listing 2.9 shows how you can split the data into training and test sets using a predefined proportion *n*% (e.g., 80%) of emails with their features for training and setting the rest aside for testing. It then applies the `train` function using the training set and relying on the `all_features` structure created by the code from listing 2.8.

Listing 2.9 Code to train a Naïve Bayes classifier

Import the classifier implementation from NLTK.

```
from nltk import NaiveBayesClassifier, classify

def train(features, proportion):
    train_size = int(len(features) * proportion)
    train_set = features[:train_size]
    test_set = features[train_size:]
    print (f"Training set size = {str(len(train_set))} emails")
    print (f"Test set size = {str(len(test_set))} emails")
```

Remember that you need to set aside part of the data for testing.

Use the first n% of emails with their features for training and the rest for testing.

Print out simple statistics to make sure the data is split correctly.

```
    classifier = NaiveBayesClassifier.train(train_set)    ◁─┐  Initialize the
    return train_set, test_set, classifier                   │  classifier.
```

```
┌▷  train_set, test_set, classifier = train(all_features, 0.8)
│
│ Apply the train function using 80%
│ (or a similar proportion) of emails
│ for training.
```

2.3.5 Step 5: Evaluate your classifier

Finally, let's evaluate how well the classifier performs in detecting whether an email is spam or ham. For that, let's use the accuracy score returned by the NLTK's classifier. To that end, code in listing 2.10 implements evaluate function. In addition, the NLTK's classifier allows you to inspect the most informative features (words). For that, you need to specify the number of the top most informative features to look into (e.g., 50 here).

Listing 2.10   Code to evaluate classifier's performance

```
def evaluate(train_set, test_set, classifier):        ◁──┐  Define a function to
    print (f"Accuracy on the training set =               │  estimate the accuracy of
     {str(classify.accuracy(classifier, train_set))}")    │  the classifier on each set.
    print (f"Accuracy of the test set = {str(classify.accuracy(classifier,
     test_set))}")
    classifier.show_most_informative_features(50)     ◁──┐  Inspect the most
                                                          │  informative features
evaluate(train_set, test_set, classifier)                 │  (words); here, the top
                                                          │  50 are printed out.
```

Figure 2.19 presents an example of an output returned by the code from listing 2.10.

```
Accuracy on the training set = 0.9613246313753928
Accuracy of the test set = 0.9420289855072463
Most Informative Features
                  forwarded = True          ham : spam     =     198.3 : 1.0
                       2004 = True          spam : ham     =     143.8 : 1.0
  spam                  nom = True          ham : spam     =     125.8 : 1.0
                prescription = True         spam : ham     =     122.9 : 1.0
                       pain = True          spam : ham     =      98.8 : 1.0
                     health = True          spam : ham     =      82.7 : 1.0
                        ect = True          ham : spam     =      76.8 : 1.0
                       2001 = True          ham : spam     =      75.8 : 1.0
  ham              featured = True          spam : ham     =      74.7 : 1.0
                  nomination = True         ham : spam     =      72.1 : 1.0
                medications = True          spam : ham     =      69.9 : 1.0
```

Figure 2.19 Output of the code from listing 2.10. Features indicative of spam and ham are labeled.

One piece of information that this code provides you with is the most informative features—that is, the list of words that are most strongly associated with a particular class. This is functionality of the classifier that is implemented in NLTK, so all you need to do is call on this function as `classifier.show_most_informative_features` and specify the number of words *n* that you want to see as an argument. This function then returns the top *n* words ordered by their "informativeness" or predictive power. Behind the scenes, the function measures "informativeness" as the highest value of the difference in probabilities between `P(feature | spam)` and `P(feature | ham)`— that is, `max[P(word: True | ham) / P(word: True | spam)]` for most predictive ham features, and `max[P(word: True | spam) / P(word: True | ham)]` for most predictive spam features (check out NLTK's documentation for more information: https://www .nltk.org/api/nltk.classify.naivebayes.html). The output shows that such words (features) as *prescription, pain, health,* and so on are much more strongly associated with spam emails. The ratios on the right show the comparative probabilities for the two classes: for instance, `P("prescription" | spam)` is 122.9 times higher than `P("prescription" | ham)`. On the other hand, *nomination* is more strongly associated with ham emails. As you can see, many spam emails in this dataset are related to medications, which shows a particular bias; the most typical spam that you personally get might be on a different topic altogether. What effect might this mismatch between the training data from the publicly available dataset like Enron and your personal data have? You will look into an example of this later in exercise 2.7.

One other piece of information presented in this output is accuracy. Test accuracy shows the proportion of test emails that are correctly classified by Naïve Bayes among all test emails. The preceding code measures the accuracy on both the training data and test data. Note that since the classifier is trained on the training data, it actually gets to "see" all the correct labels for the training examples. Shouldn't it then know the correct answers and perform at 100% accuracy on the training data? Well, the point here is that the classifier doesn't just retrieve the correct answers; during training, it has built some probabilistic model (i.e., learned about the distribution of classes and the probability of different features), and then it applies this model to the data. So, it is actually very likely that the probabilistic model doesn't capture all the things in the data 100% correctly. For example, there might be noise and inconsistencies in the real emails. Note that "2004" gets strongly associated with the spam emails and "2001" with the ham emails, although it does not mean that there is anything peculiar about the spam originating from 2004. This might simply show a bias in the particular dataset, and such phenomena are hard to filter out in any real data, especially when you rely on the data collected by other researchers (see Note). This means that if some ham email in training data contains "2004" and a variety of other words that are otherwise related to spam, this email might get misclassified as spam by the algorithm. Similarly, as many medication-related words are strongly associated with spam, a rare ham email that is actually talking about some medication the user ordered might get misclassified as spam.

NOTE In this particular case, it is related to the fact that emails from Enron employees were collected from earlier years than spam emails (see the dataset description in http://www2.aueb.gr/users/ion/docs/ceas2006_paper.pdf). This might be related to the difficulty of collecting realistic and representative personal ham emails, but despite this difference in the ham versus spam data, the dataset overall is still widely used for training spam-filtering algorithms. This observation, though, should be taken as a word of caution. Datasets often contain certain artifacts, many of which might be difficult to spot or eliminate, so it is often a good idea to get as much diverse data as possible to avoid biases in the data.

Therefore, when you run code in listing 2.10, you will get an accuracy on the training data of 96.13%. This is not perfect (i.e., 100%), but it is very close. This shows that despite certain artifacts in the data (like the association of years to class labels), in general, the classifier gets it right most of the time. When you apply the same classifier to new data—the test set that the classifier hasn't seen during training—the accuracy reflects its generalizing ability. In other words, it shows whether the probabilistic assumptions it made based on the training data can be successfully applied to any other data. The accuracy on the test set in this example is 94.20%, which is slightly lower than that on the training set but is also very high.

Finally, if you'd like to gain any further insight into how the words are used in the emails from different classes, you can also check the occurrences of any particular word in all available contexts. For example, the word *stocks* features as a very strong predictor of spam messages. Why is that? You might be thinking, *Okay, some emails containing "stocks" will be spam, but surely there must be contexts where "stocks" is used in a completely legitimate way?* Let's check this using the code from listing 2.11. This code shows how you can use NLTK's concordancer, a tool that checks for the occurrences of the specified word and prints out this word in its contexts. By default, NLTK's concordancer prints out the `search_word` surrounded by the previous 36 and the following 36 characters, so note that it doesn't always result in full words. Once the use of `concordancer` is defined in the function `concordance`, you can apply it to both `ham_list` and `spam_list` to find the different contexts of the word *stocks*.

Listing 2.11 Code to check the contexts of specific words

```
from nltk.text import Text              ◁————————  Import NLTK's Text
                                                   data structure.
def concordance(data_list, search_word):
    for email in data_list:
        word_list = [word for word in word_tokenize(email.lower())]
        text_list = Text(word_list)
        if search_word in word_list:
            text_list.concordance(search_word)   ◁——  Use NLTK's concordancer to
                                                       print out the search_word
                                                       in context.
print ("STOCKS in HAM:")
concordance(ham_list, "stocks")
```

```
print ("\n\nSTOCKS in SPAM:")
concordance(spam_list, "stocks")
```

← **Apply this function to ham_list and spam_list to search for contexts of "stocks."**

If you run this code and print out the contexts for *stocks*, you will find out that *stocks* features in only four ham contexts (e.g., an email reminder "Follow your stocks and news headlines") as compared to hundreds of spam contexts including "Stocks to play," "Big money was made in these stocks," "Select gold mining stocks," "Little stocks can mean big gains for you," and so on.

Congratulations, you have built your own spam-filtering algorithm and learned how to evaluate it and explore the results!

2.4 *Deploying your spam filter in practice*

Why are the evaluation steps important? We've said before that the machine learns from experience—data that it is provided with—so obviously, the more data the better. You started with about 5,000 emails, but you had to set 20% aside for testing, and you were not allowed to use them while training. Doesn't it mean practically "losing" valuable data that the classifier could have used more effectively?

Well, if you build an application that you plan to use in real life, you want it to perform its task well. However, you cannot predict in advance what data the classifier will be exposed to in the future, so the best way to predict how well it will perform is to test it on the available labeled data. This is the main purpose of setting aside 20% or so of the original labeled data and of running evaluation on this test set. Once you are happy with the results of your evaluation, you can deploy your classifier in practice.

For instance, the classifier that you've built in this chapter performs at 94% accuracy, so you can expect it to classify real emails into spam and ham quite accurately. It's time to deploy it in practice, then. When you run it on some new emails (perhaps, some from your own inbox), you need to perform the same steps on these emails as before:

1 You need to read them in.
2 You need to extract the features from these emails.
3 You need to apply the classifier that you trained before on these emails.

The code from the following listing shows how you can do that. Feel free to type in your own emails as input in the test_spam_list and test_ham_list.

Listing 2.12   Code to apply spam filtering to new emails

```
test_spam_list = ["Participate in our new lottery!", "Try out this new medicine"]
test_ham_list = ["See the minutes from the last meeting attached",
                 "Investors are coming to our office on Monday"]

test_emails = [(email_content, "spam") for email_content in test_spam_list]
test_emails += [(email_content, "ham")
                for email_content in test_ham_list]
```

← **Read the emails extracting their textual content and keeping the labels for further evaluation.**

```
new_test_set = [(get_features(email), label)
                    for (email, label) in test_emails]

evaluate(train_set, new_test_set, classifier)
```

Extract the features.

Apply the trained classifier and evaluate its performance.

The classifier that you've trained in this chapter performs with 100% accuracy on these examples. Good! How can you print out the predicted label for each particular email, though? For that, you simply extract the features from the email content and print out the label; you don't need to run the full evaluation with the accuracy calculation. The code from the following listing suggests how you can do that.

Listing 2.13   Code to print out the predicted label

```
for email in test_spam_list:
    print (email)
    print (classifier.classify(get_features(email)))
for email in test_ham_list:
    print (email)
    print (classifier.classify(get_features(email)))
```

For each email in each list, this code prints out the content of the email and the predicted label.

Finally, let's make the code more interactive and see if the classifier can predict the class label on any input text in real time. For example, how about reading the emails of your choice straight from the keyboard and predicting their label on the spot? This is not very different from what you've just done above. The only difference is that instead of reading the emails from the predefined list, you should allow your code to read them from the keyboard input. Python's `input` functionality allows you to do that. Let's read the emails typed in from the keyboard and stop when no email is typed in. For that, use the `while-break loop` as the following code shows. The code will keep asking for the next email until the user presses Enter.

Listing 2.14   Code to classify the emails read in from the keyboard

```
while True:
    email = input("Type in your email here (or press 'Enter'): ")
    if len(email)==0:
        break
    else:
        prediction = classifier.classify(get_features(email))
        print (f"This email is likely {prediction}\n")
```

Stop when the user provides no text and presses Enter instead.

Print out the predicted label for the email.

Finally, you should try to apply what you have learned in this chapter and test your new skills by attempting exercise 2.7. You can check your solutions against the notebook, but first try to write the code yourself.

Exercise 2.7

Apply the trained classifier to a different dataset; for example to `enron2/` spam and ham emails that originate with a different owner (check *Summary.txt* for more information). For that you need to

- Read the data from the `spam/` and `ham/` subfolders in `enron2/`.
- Extract the textual content and convert it into features.
- Evaluate the classifier.

What do the results suggest? Hint: one man's spam may be another man's ham. If you are not satisfied with the results, try combining the data from the two owners in one dataset. (Solution can be found at the end of this chapter.)

Summary

- Classification is concerned with assigning objects to a predefined set of categories, groups, or classes based on their characteristic properties. There is a whole family of NLP and machine-learning tasks that deal with classification.
- Humans perform classification on a regular basis, and machine-learning algorithms can be taught to do that if provided with a sufficient number of examples and some guidance from humans. When the labeled examples and the general outline of the task are provided for the machine, this is called *supervised learning*.
- Spam filtering is an example of a binary classification task. The machine has to learn to distinguish between exactly two classes—spam and normal email (often called *ham*).
- Classification relies on specific properties of the classified objects. In machine-learning terms, such properties are called *features*. For spam filtering, some of the most informative features are words used in the emails.
- To build a spam-filtering algorithm, you can use one of the publicly available spam datasets. One such dataset is the Enron spam dataset.
- A classifier can be built in five steps: (1) reading emails and defining classes, (2) extracting content, (3) converting the content into features, (4) training an algorithm on the training set, and (5) evaluating it on the test set.
- The data comes in as a single string of symbols. To extract the words from it, you may rely on the NLP tools called *tokenizers* (or use regular expressions to implement one yourself).
- NLP libraries, such as the Natural Language Processing Toolkit (NLTK), come with such tools, as well as implementations of a range of frequently used classifiers.

- There are several machine-learning classifiers, and one of the most interpretable among them is Naïve Bayes. This is a probabilistic classifier. It assumes that the data in two classes is generated by different probability distributions, which are learned from the training data. Despite its simplicity and "naïve" feature independence assumption, Naïve Bayes often performs well in practice and sets a competitive baseline for other more sophisticated algorithms.
- It is important that you split your data into training sets (e.g., 80% of the original dataset) and test sets (the rest of the data), and train the classifier on the training data only so that you can assess it on the test set in a fair way. The test set serves as new unseen data for the algorithm, so you can come to a realistic conclusion about how your classifier may perform in practice.
- Once satisfied with the performance of your classifier on the test data, you can deploy it in practice.

Solutions to miscellaneous exercises

Exercise 2.1

1 We distinguish between spam and normal (ham) emails. Spam emails should end up in the spam box and normal emails should be kept in the inbox.
2 This is an example of binary classification because we distinguish between two classes only.
3 Humans can relatively easily tell a spam email from a normal one, although some spammers use sophisticated techniques to disguise their intentions, and in some cases, it might be tricky to tell the difference. The format of the email (use of unusual fonts and colors), the information about the sender (unusual or unknown email address), the list of addressees (spam emails are often mass emails), and attachments and links are all very indicative of spam. However, some of the strongest clues are provided by the content of the email itself and the language used; for example, you should be wary of emails that tell you that your account is unexpectedly blocked, that you need to provide sensitive personal information for suspicious reasons, or that you have won in a lottery (especially if you haven't participated in one!).

Exercise 2.3

1 You already know that the punctuation marks should be treated as a separate word, so the last bit of text in the sentence "What's the best way to cook a pizza?" should be split into `pizza` and `?`. The first bit, `What's`, should also be split into two words: this is a contraction for *what* and *is*, and it is important that the classifier knows that these two are separate words. Therefore, the word list for this sentence will include [`What`, `'s`, `the`, `best`, `way`, `to`, `cook`, `a`, `pizza`, `?`].

2 The second sentence—"We're going to use a baking stone."—similarly contains a full stop at the end that should be separated from the previous word, and we're should be split into *we* and *'re* ("are"). Therefore, the full word list will be [We, 're, going, to, use, a, baking, stone, .].

3 Follow the same strategy as before. The third sentence—"I haven't used a baking stone before."—will produce [I, have, n't, used, a, baking, stone, before, .]. Note that the contraction of *have* and *not* here results in an apostrophe inside the word *not*; however, you should still be able to recognize that the proper English words in this sequence are *have* and *n't* ("not") rather than *haven* and *'t*. This is what the tokenizer will automatically do for you. (Note that the tokenizers do not automatically map contracted forms like *n't* and *'re* to full form like *not* and *are*. Although such mapping would be useful in some cases, this is beyond the functionality of tokenizers.)

Exercise 2.4

1 Using the following formula for accuracy, we can estimate that the accuracy of this algorithm is 3/5, or 60%. It got 3 out of 5 examples correctly (one case of spam-spam and two of ham-ham, as the table shows), and it made 2 mistakes, mislabeling one spam email as ham and one ham email as spam.

$$Accuracy = \frac{num(\text{correct predictions})}{num(\text{all test instances})}$$

2 An accuracy of 60% doesn't seem very high, but how exactly can you interpret it? Note that the distribution of classes helps you to put the performance of your classifier in context because it tells you how challenging the problem itself is. For example, with the 50–50% split, there is no majority class in the data and the classifier's random guess will be at 50%, so the classifier's accuracy is higher than this random guess. In the second case, however, the classifier performs on a par with the majority class guesser: the 60% to 40% distribution of classes suggests that if some dummy "classifier" always selected the majority class, it would get 60% of the cases correctly—just like the classifier you trained.

3 The single accuracy value of 60% does not tell you anything about the performance of the classifier on each class, so it is a bit hard to interpret. However, if you look into each class separately, you can tell that the classifier is better at classifying ham emails (it got 2/3 of those right) than at classifying spam emails (only 1/2 are correct).

Exercise 2.5

You will end up with the following feature set:

Feature	Spam	Ham
"participate"	True	True
"in"	True	True
"our"	True	False
"new"	True	False
"lottery"	True	False
"now"	True	False
"!"	True	False
"the"	False	True
"staff"	False	True
"survey"	False	True

Exercise 2.6

The probabilities are

- P('prescription':True | spam) = number(spam emails with 'prescription')/ number(spam emails) = 2/5 = 0.40
- P('meeting':True | ham) = 5/10 = 0.50
- P('stock':True | spam) = 1/5 = 0.20
- P('stock':True | ham) = 3/10 = 0.30

Exercise 2.7

Try working on your own solution before checking the code on the book's GitHub page (https://github.com/ekochmar/Getting-Started-with-NLP).

Introduction to information search

3

This chapter covers

- Implementing your information-retrieval algorithm
- Exploring useful NLP techniques, including stemming and stopwords removal
- Assessing importance of different bits of information in a search
- Evaluating the relevance of the documents to the information need

This chapter will focus on algorithms for an information search, which also has a more technical name—*information retrieval*. It will explain the steps in the search algorithm from beginning to end, and by the end of this chapter you will be able to implement your own search algorithm.

You might have come across the term *information retrieval* in the context of search engines; for example, Google famously started its business by providing a powerful search algorithm that kept improving over time. The search for information, however, is a basic need that you may face beyond searching online. For instance, every time you search for the files on your computer, you are performing a sort of information retrieval. In fact, the task predates the digital era. Before computers and the internet became a commodity, one had to manually wade through paper copies of encyclopedias, books, documents, files, and so on. Thanks to the technology, the algorithms these days help you do many of these tasks automatically.

The field of information retrieval has a long history and has seen a lot of development over the past decades. As you can imagine, Google and other search engines are dealing with large amounts of data, which makes their task exceptionally challenging. They have to process billions of pages in a matter of seconds and be able to return the most relevant of those to satisfy the information needs of their users. Truly amazing, if you think about the complexity of the task!

In this chapter, we will break this process into steps. We will look into how the information need is expressed as a query and processed for the computer to understand it, how the documents should be processed and matched to the queries, and how to assess the relevance of the documents to the queries. Search engines, fundamentally, go through all the same steps, albeit they do it on a much larger scale and employ several additional techniques, such as learning from user clicks, linking web content via hyperlinks, using optimization to speed up the processing, storing intermediate results, and so on. Many of these steps are simply outside the scope of this book. Therefore, we include this disclaimer: we are not going to build a new Google competitor algorithm here (although you might consider building one in the future), but we will build a core information search application that you can use in your real-life projects.

3.1   Understanding the task

Let's look at the following scenario, which you might recall from chapter 1. Imagine that you have to search a collection of documents yourself (i.e., without the help of the machine). You have a thousand printed notes and minutes related to the meetings at work, and you only need those that discuss the management meetings. How will you find *all* such documents? How will you identify the *most relevant* among them?

If you were actually tasked with this, you would go through the documents one by one, identifying those that contain keywords like *management* and *meetings* and split all the documents into two piles: those documents that you should keep and look into further and those that you can discard because they do not answer your information need in learning more about the management meetings. This task is akin to filtering, as shown in figure 3.1 (again, you might recall it from chapter 1):

Figure 3.1   Simple filtering of documents into "keep" and "discard" piles based on the occurrence of words

Now, there are a couple of points that we did not discuss before: imagine there are a hundred documents in total and you can quickly skim through them to filter out the most irrelevant ones—those that do not mention either *meetings* or *management*. But what if a high number of documents actually do contain one or the other or even both words? Say, after this initial filtering, you end up with 70 such documents. This is still too much to read through carefully. At the very least, you'd like to sort them in the order of relevance so that you can start by reading the most relevant ones and then stop as soon as you found the information you were looking for. How can you judge whether one of the documents is more relevant than the others, and how can you sort all of them in the order of decreasing relevance?

Luckily, these days we have computers, and most documents are stored electronically. Computers can really help us speed things up here. If we can formulate our information needs for them more or less precisely, they can be much quicker in spotting the keywords, estimating the relevance, and sorting the documents for us; in fact, they can do this in a matter of seconds (think Google). To this end, let's formulate a more technical scenario for this chapter. Imagine that you have to search a collection of documents, this time with the help of a computer. For example, you have a thousand notes and minutes related to the meetings at work stored in an electronic format, and you need only those that discuss the management meetings.

- How will you find *all* such documents? In other words, how can you code the search algorithm, and what characteristics of the documents should the search be based on?
- How will you identify the most relevant of these documents? In other words, how can you implement a sorting algorithm to sort the documents in order of decreasing relevance?

This scenario is only different from the previous one in that it allows you to leverage the computational power of the machine, but the drill is the same as before: get the machine to identify the texts that have the keywords in them, and then sort the "keep" pile according to the relevance of the texts, starting with the most relevant for the user to look at.

Despite us saying just now that the procedure is similar to how humans perform the task (as in the first scenario), there are actually some steps involved in getting the machine to identify the documents with the keywords in them and sorting by relevance that we are not explicitly mentioning here. For instance, humans have the following abilities that we naturally possess but machines naturally lack:

- We know what represents a word, while a machine gets in a sequence of symbols and does not, by itself, have a notion of what a "word" is.
- We know which words are keywords; for example, if we are interested in finding the documents on management meetings, we will consider those containing the words *meeting* and *management*, as well as those containing *meetings* and potentially even *manager* and *managerial*. The machine, on the other hand, does

not know that these words are related, similar, or basically different forms of the same word.

- We have an ability to focus on what matters. In fact, when reading texts, we usually skim over certain words rather than pay equal attention to each word. For instance, when reading the sentence "Last Friday the management committee had a meeting," which words do you pay more attention to? Which ones express the key idea of this message? Think about it—we will return to this question later. The machines, on the other hand, should be specifically "told" which words matter more.

- Finally, we intuitively know how to judge what is more relevant. The machines can make relevance judgments, too, but unlike humans, they need to be "told" how to measure relevance in precise numbers.

That, in a nutshell, represents the basic steps in the search algorithm. Let's visualize these steps in figure 3.2.

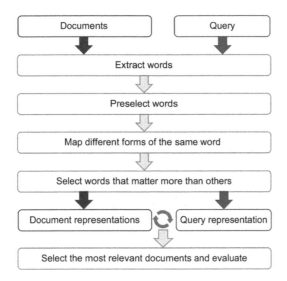

Figure 3.2 Information search algorithm in a nutshell

If you built a spam-filtering application in chapter 2, the first step in this algorithm would be familiar to you. While implementing this algorithm, you learned how to use a tokenizer to extract words from raw text. If you skipped chapter 2, this chapter will briefly explain how this step works, and you can get more details on the process from chapter 2. In this chapter, you will look in more detail into other NLP techniques to preselect words, map the different forms of the same word to each other, and weigh the words according to how much information they contribute to the task. Then you will build an information search algorithm that for any query (e.g., "management meetings") will find the most relevant documents in the collection of documents (e.g., all minutes of the past managerial meetings sorted by their relevance).

Suppose you have built such an application following all the steps. You type in a query and the algorithm returns a document or several documents that are supposedly relevant to this query. How can you tell whether the algorithm has picked out the right documents? When you were building the spam-filtering classifier, you faced the same problem, and we said that before you deploy your spam filter in practice, it is a good idea to get an initial estimate of how well the classifier performs. You can do that if for some data you know the true labels—which emails are spam and which ones are ham. These true labels are commonly referred to as *ground truth* or *gold standard*, and to make sure your algorithm performs well, you first evaluate it against gold standard labels. For that, in the spam-filtering example you used a spam dataset where such gold standard labels were provided, and you are going to do the same in this application. Let's use a dataset of documents and queries, where the documents are labeled with respect to their relevance to the queries. You will use this dataset as your gold standard, and before using the information-search algorithm in practice, you will evaluate its performance against the ground truth labels in the labeled dataset.

> **Gold standard/ground truth**
>
> *Gold standard* (or *ground truth*) refers to the labels that are provided in the annotated data. The goal of the algorithm you are building is to predict such labels; for example, in a supervised machine-learning setting, you train your algorithm using such labels in the training data and evaluate the predictions of your algorithm against gold standard labels in the test data.

3.1.1   *Data and data structures*

As in chapter 2, you will use a publicly available dataset labeled for the task. This means a dataset with several documents and various queries and a labeled list specifying which queries correspond to which documents. Once you implement and evaluate a search algorithm on such data labeled with ground truth, you can apply it to your own documents in your own projects.

There are several datasets that can be used for this purpose (see a list of publicly available datasets at http://ir.dcs.gla.ac.uk/resources/test_collections/). In this chapter, you will use the dataset collected by the Centre for Inventions and Scientific Information (CISI), which contains abstracts and some additional metadata from the journal articles on information systems and information retrieval (you can download the dataset from http://ir.dcs.gla.ac.uk/resources/test_collections/cisi/). Despite the availability of other datasets, there are several reasons to choose the CISI dataset for this chapter, the main of which are the following:

- It is a relatively small dataset of 1,460 documents and 112 queries, which is easy to process and work with. In addition, each document is relatively short, consisting of an article abstract and some additional information, which helps faster processing further.

- It contains gold standard annotations for the relevance of the documents to 76 queries.
- The results are easy to interpret, as the dataset does not include highly technical terms. In contrast, some other widely used benchmark datasets include medical articles or articles on technical subjects such as aerodynamics, which are harder to interpret for non-experts.

Let's first read in the data and initialize the data structures to keep the content. Note that this dataset contains many documents and various queries; for instance, one query in this dataset asks what information science is, while another asks about the methods of information retrieval, and so on. There is a diverse set of 76 questions. Although you might just extract one particular query and focus on, say, searching for the documents in this dataset answering "What is information science?," why not read all of them and store them in some data structure since you have access to so many diverse queries? This way you will be able to search for the matching documents for *any* of the queries rather than for *only one specific query* and check how your algorithm deals with a variety of information needs. For that, it would be good to keep track of different queries; for example, if you assign a unique identifier to each query (e.g., id1 = "What is information science?"; id2 = "What methods do information retrieval systems use?"; and so on), you can then easily select any of the queries by their IDs. You can apply the same approach to storing the documents, too. If each document is assigned a unique ID, it will be easy to identify a particular document by its ID. Finally, the matching between a particular query and documents answering the information need in this query can be encoded as the correspondence between the query ID and documents IDs. This suggests that you can use three data structures for this application:

- A data structure for the documents that will keep document IDs and contents
- A data structure for the queries that will keep query IDs and contents
- A data structure matching the queries to the documents

Exercise 3.1
What would be the best format(s) for representing these three data structures? What type of information do you need to keep in each case?

Let's look into the solution to this exercise together. Information search is based on the idea that the content of a document or set of documents is relevant given the content of a particular query, so a documents data structure should keep the contents of all available documents for the algorithm to select from.

If you have only one query to search for, you can store it as a string of text. However, if you want to use your algorithm to search for multiple queries, you may use a similar queries data structure to keep contents of all queries available in the dataset.

What would be the best way to keep track of which content represents which document? The most informative and useful way would be to assign a unique identifier—an index—to each document and each query. You can imagine, for example, storing content of the documents and queries in two separate tables, with each row representing a single document or query and row numbers corresponding to the documents and queries IDs. In Python, tables can be represented with dictionaries (https://docs .python.org/3/tutorial/datastructures.html).

Now, if you keep two Python dictionaries (tables) matching each unique document identifier (called a *key*) to the document's content (called *value*) in the documents dictionary and matching each unique query identifier to the query's content in the queries dictionary, how should you represent the relevance mappings? You can use a dictionary structure again. This time, the keys will contain the queries IDs while the values should keep the matching documents IDs. Since each query may correspond to multiple documents, it would be best to keep the IDs of the matching documents as lists. Figure 3.3 shows these data structures.

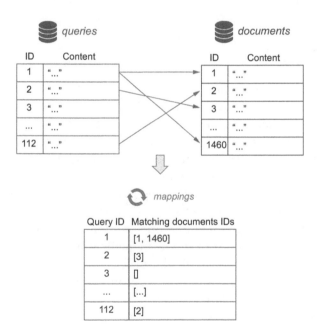

Figure 3.3   Three data structures keeping the documents, queries, and their relevance mappings

As this figure shows, query id 1 matches documents with ids 1 and 1460; therefore, the mappings data structure keeps a list of [1, 1460] for query 1; similarly, it keeps [3] for query 2, [2] for query 112, and an empty list for query 3, because in this example there are no documents relevant for this query.

Now let's look into the CISI dataset and code the data reading and initialization step. All documents are stored in a single text file, CISI.ALL. It has a peculiar format: it keeps the abstract of each article and some additional information, such as the index in the set, the title, the authors' list, and cross-references (a list of indexes for the articles that cite each other). Table 3.1 explains the notation.

> **NOTE** The full texts of the articles are not included in this dataset. However, this is not a problem for your search algorithm application: First of all, abstracts typically summarize the main content of the article in a concise manner, so the abstract content is a more condensed version of the article content. Secondly, the mappings are established between the queries and the documents containing the information summarized in table 3.1.

Table 3.1 Notation used in the CISI dataset for the articles

Notation	Meaning
.I	Document index in the set
.T	Article's title
.A	Authors' list
.W	Text of the abstract
.X	Cross-references list

For the information search application, arguably the most useful information is the content of the abstract: abstracts in the articles typically serve as a concise summary of what the article presents, something akin to a snippet. Are the other types of information included in the dataset useful? Well, you might be interested in the articles published by particular authors, so in some situations you might be interested in searching on the .A field; similarly, if you are interested in articles with particular titles, you might benefit from using the .T field only. For the sake of simplicity, in the application that you will develop in this chapter, we won't distinguish between the .T, .A, and .W lists, and we'll merge them into one "content of the article" field, assuming that the information from each of them is equally valuable. The .X field shows how many other articles refer to a particular article, so it may be used as a credibility rating of an article. This may be quite useful in practice, if you want to rate the articles by how reliable or respected they are (this is what the cross-references show); however, in this application, we won't focus on that and will remove the .X field. Table 3.2 shows the format of information presentation in the CISI.ALL file using an example of the first article in the set.

As you can see, the field identifiers such as .A or .W are separated from the actual text by a new line. In addition, the text within each field (e.g., the abstract) may be spread across multiple lines. Ideally, we would like to convert this format into something like the text in table 3.3. Note that for the text that falls within the same field (e.g., .W), the line breaks ("\n") are replaced with whitespaces, so each line now starts with a field identifier followed by the field content.

Table 3.2   Format used for the articles' representation in the CISI dataset

```
.I 1
.T
```
18 Editions of the Dewey Decimal Classifications
```
.A
```
Comaromi, J.P.
```
.W
```
* The present study is a history of the DEWEY Decimal*
Classification. The first edition of the DDC was published
in 1876, the eighteenth edition in 1971, and future editions
will continue to appear as needed. In spite of the DDC's
long and healthy life, however, its full story has never
been told. There have been biographies of Dewey
that briefly describe his system, but this is the first
attempt to provide a detailed history of the work that
more than any other has spurred the growth of
librarianship in this country and abroad.
```
.X
```
...

Table 3.3   Modified format for the articles' representation in the dataset

```
.I 1
```
.T 18 Editions of the Dewey Decimal Classifications
.A Comaromi, J.P.
.W The present study is a history of the DEWEY Decimal Classification. The first edition of the DDC was published in 1876, the eighteenth edition in 1971, and future editions will continue to appear as needed. In spite of the DDC's long and healthy life, however, its full story has never been told. There have been biographies of Dewey that briefly describe his system, but this is the first attempt to provide a detailed history of the work that more than any other has spurred the growth of librarianship in this country and abroad.

The format in table 3.3 is much easier to work with. You can now read the text line by line, extract the unique identifier for the article from the field .I, merge the content of the fields .T, .A, and .W, and store the result in the documents dictionary as {1: "18 Editions of the ... this country and abroad."}. Code in listing 3.1 implements all these steps in a function read_documents. In this code, you first define the string variable merged, which keeps the result of merging the field identifier (e.g., .W) with its content. Unless a text string starts with a new field identifier, you add its content to the current field separating the content from the previous line with a whitespace; otherwise, you start a new line with the next identifier and field. Next, you define a documents dictionary and populate it with entries. Each entry in this dictionary contains key=doc_id, which specifies the document's unique identifier, and value=content, which specifies the content of the article. The key, doc_id, can be extracted from the line with the .I field identifier. As .X field is always the last in each article, the start of the .X field signifies that you are done reading in the content of the article, so you can put the entry doc_id:content into the documents dictionary. Until you reach .X field, however, you keep extracting the content from other fields (.T, .A, and .W), removing the field identifiers. Finally, as a sanity check, you should print out the size of the dictionary (make sure it contains all 1,460 articles) and print out the content of the first article—it should correspond to the text in table 3.3.

Listing 3.1   Code to populate the documents dictionary

```
def read_documents():
    f = open("cisi/CISI.ALL")          The string variable merged
    merged = ""                         keeps the result of merging the
                                        field identifier with its content

    for a_line in f.readlines():
        if a_line.startswith("."):
            merged += "\n" + a_line.strip()    Updates the
        else:                                   merged variable
            merged += " " + a_line.strip()      using a for-loop

    documents = {}          Initializes the
                            documents dictionary

    content = ""
    doc_id = ""             Each entry in the dictionary contains
                            key=doc_id and value=content.
                                                        doc_id can be extracted
    for a_line in merged.split("\n"):               from the line with the
        if a_line.startswith(".I"):                 .I field identifier.
            doc_id = a_line.split(" ")[1].strip()
        elif a_line.startswith(".X"):
            documents[doc_id] = content    Put the entry
            content = ""                   doc_id:content into the
            doc_id = ""                    documents dictionary.
        else:
            content += a_line.strip()[3:] + " "      Extract the content
    f.close()                                        from fields .T, .A, and
    return documents                                 .W, removing the field
                                                     identifiers.
documents = read_documents()
print(len(documents))            As a sanity check, print out the
print(documents.get("1"))        size of the dictionary and the
                                 content of the very first article.
```

The queries are stored in the CISI.QRY file and follow a very similar format. Half the time, you see only two fields, .I for the unique identifier and .W for the content of the query. Other queries, though, are formulated not as questions but rather as abstracts from other articles. In such cases, the query also has an .A field for the authors' list, a .T field for the title, and a .B field that keeps the reference to the original journal in which the abstract was published. Table 3.4 presents an example of original queries.

We are going to focus only on the unique identifiers and the content of the query itself (fields .W and .T, where available), so the code in listing 3.2 is quite similar to that in listing 3.1, as it allows you to populate the queries dictionary with data. As before, you first merge the content of each field with its identifier and separate different fields with line breaks ("\n"). Next, you define a queries dictionary and store key=qry_id and value=content for each query in the dataset as a separate entry in

Table 3.4   Format used for the queries representation in the CISI dataset

```
.I 88
.T
Natural Language Access to Information Systems.  An Evaluation Study
of Its Acceptance by End Users
.A
Krause, J.
.W
   The question is asked whether it is feasible to use subsets of
natural languages as query languages for data bases in actual applications
using the question answering system "USER SPECIALTY LANGUAGES" (USL).
Methods of evaluating a natural language based information system will
be discussed.  The results (error and language structure evaluation)
suggest how to form the general architecture of application systems which
use a subset of German as query language.
.B
(Inform. Systems, Vol. 5, No. 4, May 1980, pp. 297-318)
```

the dictionary. The start of a new entry is signified with the next `.I` field. Once you encounter an `.I` field identifier in text, you add an entry to the dictionary. Until you encounter an `.I` field identifier, however, you should keep adding content to the current `content` variable. Note that the last query is not followed by any next `.I` field, so the strategy from listing 3.1 won't work—you need to add the entry for the last query to the dictionary using an extra step shown in listing 3.2. Finally, you print out the length of the dictionary (it should contain 112 entries) and the content of the first query (this you can check against the text of the first query in CISI.QRY).

Listing 3.2   Code to populate the queries dictionary

```
def read_queries():
    f = open("cisi/CISI.QRY")
    merged = ""

    for a_line in f.readlines():
        if a_line.startswith("."):
            merged += "\n" + a_line.strip()
        else:
            merged += " " + a_line.strip()
```

Merge the content of each field with its identifier and separate different fields with line breaks.

```
    queries = {}

    content = ""
    qry_id = ""
```

Initialize queries dictionary with key=qry_id and value=content for each query in the dataset.

```
    for a_line in merged.split("\n"):
        if a_line.startswith(".I"):
            if not content=="":
                queries[qry_id] = content
                content = ""
                qry_id = ""
            qry_id = a_line.split(" ")[1].strip()
```

Add an entry to the dictionary when you encounter an .I identifier.

```
        elif a_line.startswith(".W") or a_line.startswith(".T"):
            content += a_line.strip()[3:] + " "        ◄─────    Otherwise, keep
    queries[qry_id] = content    ◄─────                           adding content
    f.close()                                                     to the content
    return queries                                                variable.

                                          This is an extra
queries = read_queries()                  step to add the
print(len(queries))                       entry for the
print(queries.get("1"))    ◄───────       last query to
                                          the dictionary.
                                   Print out the length of the dictionary
                                   and the content of the first query.
```

For the query example in table 3.4, this code will put the unique identifier linked to the query content from the fields .T and .W into the data structure: the particular entry will be represented as {88: "Natural Language Access to Information Systems ... use a subset of German as query language."}.

Finally, you need to know which queries correspond to which documents. This information is contained in the CISI.REL file. This file uses a simple column-based format, where the first column keeps the reference to the query ID, and the second column contains an ID of one of the articles (documents) that matches this query. All you need to do is read this file, split it into columns, and associate to the query ID the list of IDs for the documents that match this query. Listing 3.3 shows how to do this in Python. In this code, you first split each line into columns. Python's split() performs splitting by whitespaces, while strip() helps remove any trailing whitespaces. As the key (query ID) is stored in the first column and the document ID is stored in the second column, you extract this information from the correspondent columns. Next, you check if the mappings dictionary already contains some document IDs for the documents matching the given query. If it does, you need to update the existing list with the current value; otherwise, you just add current value to the new list. Finally, as a sanity check, you can print out some information about the mappings data structure, such as its length (it should tell you that 76 queries have documents associated with them), list of keys (so you can check which queries don't have any matching documents), and the list of IDs for the documents matching the first query (this should print out a list of 46 document IDs, which you can check against CISI.REL).

Listing 3.3 Code to populate the mappings dictionary

```
def read_mappings():
    f = open("cisi/CISI.REL")                     Split each line
                                                   into columns.
    mappings = {}
                                                   Extract the key (query ID)
    for a_line in f.readlines():                   from the first column and
        voc = a_line.strip().split()    ◄─────     the document ID from the
        key = voc[0].strip()                       second column.
        current_value = voc[1].strip()    ◄─────
        value = []                                 Update the entry in the
        if key in mappings.keys():                 mappings dictionary with
            value = mappings.get(key)    ◄─────    the current value.
```

```
        value.append(current_value)
        mappings[key] = value

    f.close()
    return mappings

mappings = read_mappings()
print(len(mappings))
print(mappings.keys())
print(mappings.get("1"))
```

Print out some information about the mappings data structure.

For example, for the first query, the mappings data structure should keep the following list: {1: [28, 35, 38, ..., 1196, 1281]}.

That's it! You have successfully initialized one dictionary for documents with the IDs linked to the articles content, another dictionary for queries linking query IDs to their correspondent texts, and the mappings dictionary, which matches the query IDs to the lists of relevant document IDs. Now you are all set to start implementing the search algorithm for this data.

3.1.2   Boolean search algorithm

Let's start with the simplest approach: the information need is formulated as a query. If you extract the words from the query, you can then search for the documents that contain these words and return these documents, as they should be relevant to the query. Here is the algorithm in a nutshell:

1   Extract the words from the query.
2   For each document, compare the words in the document to the words in the query.
3   Return the document as relevant if any of the query words occur in the document.

Figure 3.4 shows this algorithm.

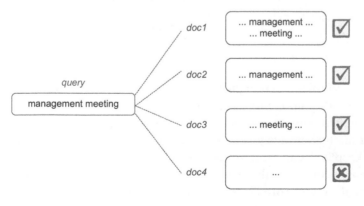

Figure 3.4   Simple search algorithm selects all documents that contain any of the words from the query.

The very first step in this algorithm is extracting the words from both queries and documents. Note that text comes in as a sequence of symbols or characters (recall this from chapter 2), and the machine needs to be told what a word is—you can use a special NLP tool called *tokenizer* to extract words. Let's apply this text-preprocessing step, as listing 3.4 shows. This code uses NLTK's `word_tokenize` (see chapter 2), converts text to lowercase, splits it into words using the tokenizer, and then represents entries in both `documents` and `queries` as word lists. Finally, it prints out the length of the dictionaries (these should be the same as before, 1,460 and 112), and checks what words are extracted from the first document and the first query.

> **NOTE** In addition to the toolkit itself, you need to install NLTK data as explained at www.nltk.org/data.html. Running `nltk.download()` will install all the data needed for text processing in one go; in addition, individual tools can be installed separately; for example, `nltk.download('punkt')` installs NLTK's sentence tokenizer, and `nltk.download('stopwords')` downloads the stopwords list.

Listing 3.4   Preprocess the data in documents and queries

```python
import nltk
from nltk import word_tokenize          # Use NLTK's word_tokenize.
nltk.download('punkt')                   # Install NLTK's sentence tokenizer
                                         # if you haven't used it before.

def get_words(text):
    word_list = [word for word in word_tokenize(text.lower())]   # Text is converted to
    return word_list                                             # lowercase and split
                                                                 # into words.

doc_words = {}
qry_words = {}
for doc_id in documents.keys():
    doc_words[doc_id] = get_words(documents.get(doc_id))
for qry_id in queries.keys():
    qry_words[qry_id] = get_words(queries.get(qry_id))           # Entries in both
                                                                 # documents and
                                                                 # queries are
                                                                 # represented as
                                                                 # word lists.
print(len(doc_words))
print(doc_words.get("1"))
print(len(doc_words.get("1")))          # Print out the length
print(len(qry_words))                   # of the dictionaries
print(qry_words.get("1"))               # and check the first
print(len(qry_words.get("1")))          # document and the
                                        # first query.
```

Now let's code the simple search algorithm just described. We will refer to it as the Boolean search algorithm since it relies on the presence (1) or absence (0) of the query words in the documents (listing 3.5). Specifically, this code iterates through the documents and turns on the `found` flag as soon as any of the query words are found in the document. You keep iterating through the words in the query word list until either of the two conditions is satisfied: either you have reached the end of the word list or one of the words from the query word list is found in the document (`found` flag is on). The `found` flag is turned on as soon as you find any query word in the document. This helps you optimize the search, since as soon as you find one word, you don't need to look any further in this document. Finally, the code helps you check the results. You can select a query by its ID (e.g., query with id 3 here), print out the IDs of the documents that the algorithm found (e.g., the first 100, as there may be many), and check how many there are in total.

Listing 3.5 Simple Boolean search algorithm

```
def retrieve_documents(doc_words, query):
    docs = []
    for doc_id in doc_words.keys():              Iterate through
        found = False                            the documents.
        i = 0
        while i<len(query) and not found:        The index of the query
            word = query[i]                      word in the query word
            if word in doc_words.get(doc_id):    list is represented by i.
                docs.append(doc_id)
                found=True                       Keep iterating through the words
            else:                                in the query word list until one of
                i+=1                             the two conditions is satisfied.
    return docs

docs = retrieve_documents(doc_words, qry_words.get("3"))
print(docs[:100])
print(len(docs))          Check the results.
```

The found flag will be turned on as soon as you find any of the query words in the document.

Turn the found flag on as soon as you find a query word in the document.

If you run this code with a query with id 3 from the queries data structure (the text of this query is "What is information science? Give definitions where possible."), you will get around 1,400 documents returned as relevant. This means that almost each document in the collection of 1,460 documents is considered "relevant" by this algorithm! There is nothing special about query with id 3; in fact, almost any query will return a comparably huge number of "relevant" documents with this approach. This probably means that no truly relevant document escapes such a thorough search, but in practice it is not helpful. In addition to returning a huge number of documents, the algorithm does not provide any relevance sorting for them, and without such sorting, looking through 1,400 documents is not significantly better than looking through 1,460. What exactly went wrong here?

Let's look into how the algorithm decided on the documents relevant for query with id 6 ("What possibilities are there for verbal communication between computers and humans, that is, communication via the spoken word?"). According to the gold standard in mappings data structure, only one document matches this query, but the simple algorithm you applied returns all 1,460 documents as relevant. Figure 3.5 bolds the words by which the match was identified between query 6 and document 1. As it shows, the query is matched to the document based on the occurrence of such words as *there, this, the, and, is,* and even a comma since punctuation marks are part of the word list returned by the tokenizer.

On the face of it, there is a considerable word overlap between the query and the document, yet if you read the text of the query and the text of the document, they

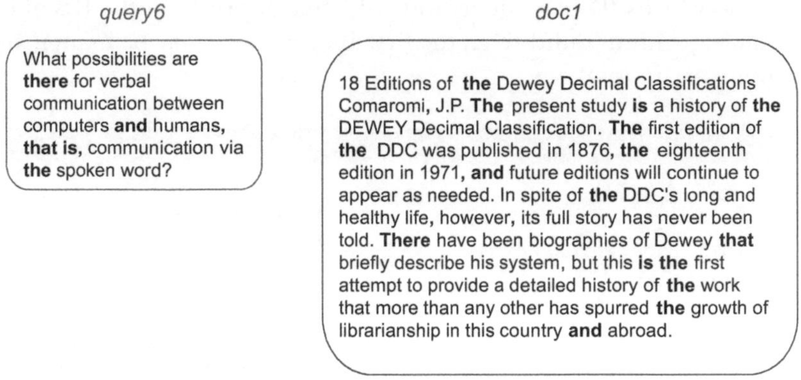

query6

> What possibilities are **there** for verbal communication between computers **and** humans, **that is**, communication via **the** spoken word?

doc1

> 18 Editions of **the** Dewey Decimal Classifications Comaromi, J.P. **The** present study **is** a history of **the** DEWEY Decimal Classification. **The** first edition of **the** DDC was published in 1876, **the** eighteenth edition in 1971, **and** future editions will continue to appear as needed. In spite of **the** DDC's long and healthy life, however, its full story has never been told. **There** have been biographies of Dewey **that** briefly describe his system, but this **is the** first attempt to provide a detailed history of **the** work that more than any other has spurred **the** growth of librarianship in this country **and** abroad.

Figure 3.5   The match between the query and the documents is established based on bolded words.

don't seem to have any ideas in common, so in fact this document is not relevant for the given query at all! It seems like the words on the basis of which the query and the document are matched here are simply the wrong ones—they are somewhat irrelevant to the actual information need expressed in the query. How can you make sure that the query and the documents are matched on the basis of more meaning-ful words?

Exercise 3.2

Another way to match the documents to the queries would be to make it a require-ment that the document should contain *all* the words from the query rather than *any*.

Is this a better approach? Modify the code of the simple Boolean search algorithm to match documents to the queries on the basis of *all* words and compare the results. (Solution can be found at the end of this chapter.)

If you consider an example of any of the queries, you may notice that it is rarely the case that a document, even if it is generally relevant, contains all words from the query (at the very least, it does not have to contain question words like *what* and *which* from the query to be relevant). Therefore, if you run the code from this exercise, which applies the more conservative approach of returning *only* the documents with *all* query words in them, it will work even worse at this stage—it simply will not find any relevant documents for any of the queries.

Before we move on, let's summarize which steps of the algorithm you have imple-mented so far. You have read the data, initialized the data structures, and tokenized the texts (figure 3.6).

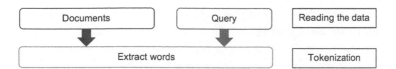

Figure 3.6 At this point, you have read in the data, initialized the data structures, and tokenized the texts.

3.2 Processing the data further

In the previous section, we have identified several weaknesses of the current algorithm. Let's look into further preprocessing steps that will help you represent the content of both the documents and the queries in a more informative way.

3.2.1 Preselecting the words that matter: Stopwords removal

The main problem with the search algorithm identified so far is that it considers all words in the queries and documents as equally important. This leads to poor search results, but on top of that it is also intuitively incorrect. Let's consider an example of query 6: "What possibilities are there for verbal communication between computers and humans, that is, communication via the spoken word?" and identify the words that matter.

Exercise 3.3

Look at the following three queries. Which of the words express the information need most precisely?

1 What possibilities are there for verbal communication between computers and humans?
2 How much do information-retrieval and dissemination systems cost?
3 Testing automated information systems.

Let's discuss the solution to this exercise. While thinking about this exercise, you may notice that not all words are equally meaningful in the sentences. Ask yourself whether you can define in one phrase what a particular word means: for example, what does *the* mean? You can say that *the* does not have a precise meaning of its own, rather it serves a particular function—it signifies that the word following it is defined in the specific context; for example, when you see *the* in "Look at the following queries," you know precisely which queries I am talking about.

You may find that many function words like *for, at, a, the,* and a number of others are less charged with meaning than rarer and longer words like *communication* or *retrieval.* Such short words are very frequent in language. Almost any text you look at contains multiple words like *a* and *the.* You saw an example of that when you ran the simple search algorithm, and it was misled by the presence of such words in all texts.

Most of such words don't have a particular meaning of their own; rather they express a function. Similarly to *the* denoting that the next word or phrase is identifiable in the context, *at* and *in* help specify location or time, and *which* or *what* at the beginning of a sentence suggest that the sentence may be a question. In linguistic terms, such words are called *function words*. You might even notice that when you read a text (e.g., an article or an email), you tend to skim over such words without paying much attention to them.

What happens to the search algorithm when these words are present? You have seen in the example before that they don't help identify the relevant texts, so the algorithm's effort is wasted on them. What would happen if the less meaningful words were not taken into consideration? Figure 3.7 shows an example with the more meaningful words bolded and the less meaningful ones grayed out.

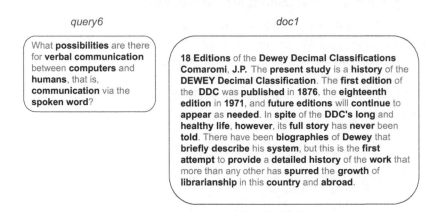

query6

What **possibilities** are there for **verbal communication** between **computers** and **humans**, that is, **communication** via the **spoken word**?

doc1

18 Editions of the **Dewey Decimal Classifications Comaromi, J.P.** The **present study** is a **history** of the **DEWEY Decimal Classification**. The **first edition** of the **DDC** was **published** in **1876**, the **eighteenth edition** in **1971**, and **future editions** will **continue** to **appear** as **needed**. In **spite** of the **DDC's long** and **healthy life**, **however**, its **full story** has **never** been **told**. There have been **biographies** of **Dewey** that **briefly describe** his **system**, but this is the **first attempt** to **provide** a **detailed history** of the **work** that more than any other has **spurred** the **growth** of **librarianship** in this **country** and **abroad**.

Figure 3.7   The more meaningful words in the query and document are bolded.

You can see that if the less meaningful words were removed before matching documents to queries, `document 1` would not stand a chance; there is simply not a single word overlapping between the query and this document. You can also see that the words that are not grayed out concisely summarize the main idea of the text.

This suggests the first improvement to the developed algorithm: let's remove the less meaningful words. In NLP applications, the less meaningful words are called *stopwords*, and luckily you don't have to bother with enumerating them. Since stopwords are highly repetitive in English, most NLP toolkits have a specially defined stopwords list, so you can rely on this list when processing the data, unless you want to customize it. For example, if you believe that it should be extended with more words or that some words that are included in the standard stopwords list should not be there, you can use your own list of stopwords.

> ## Stopwords
>
> *Stopwords* are the words that are very frequently used in language and are mostly devoid of any particular meaning. These include function words—words that mainly express specific grammatical functions rather than certain meanings (e.g., articles like *a* and *the*, prepositions like *in* and *at*, conjunctions like *but* and *so*). There is a more or less standardized stopwords list shared by most machine-learning and NLP toolkits.

In addition to removing stopwords, note that figure 3.7 doesn't have punctuation marks (e.g., periods, commas, and question marks) bolded. Punctuation marks may prove useful in some applications but will unlikely help here. Many queries will contain question marks and documents won't necessarily have any, while all documents will have commas and periods, so punctuation marks are not going to be informative in the matching process. Let's filter them out, too. Listing 3.6 shows how to do that. This code relies on the use of Python's `string` module, which helps remove punctuation marks, as well as on NLTK's tokenizer and stopwords list. NLTK includes stopwords for multiple languages, so you need to specify that you want to use the one for English. You can check which words are included in the stopwords list using `print(stoplist)`. The code shows how you can tokenize text, convert it to lowercase, and only add the words if they are not included in the `stoplist` and are not punctuation marks. Finally, it also shows how to check the results of these preprocessing steps on some documents or queries (e.g., on `document 1`).

Listing 3.6 Preprocessing: Stopwords and punctuation marks removal

```
import nltk
import string                          Import Python's string module that
nltk.download('stopwords')             will help remove punctuation marks.
from nltk import word_tokenize         Install NLTK's
from nltk.corpus import stopwords      stopwords list if you
                                       haven't used it before.
                                                               Specify that you want
def process(text):                                             to use the stopwords
    stoplist = set(stopwords.words('english'))                 list for English.
    word_list = [word for word in word_tokenize(text.lower())
                 if not word in stoplist and not word in string.punctuation]
    return word_list
                                                      Only add the words if they
word_list = process(documents.get("1"))               are not included in the
print(word_list)                                      stoplist and are not
                     Check the results of these       punctuation marks.
                     preprocessing steps on some
                     documents or queries.
```

Import the stopwords list.

NOTE As before, make sure to install NLTK data as explained on www.nltk .org/data.html. Running `nltk.download()` will install all the data needed for text processing in one go. In addition, individual tools can be installed separately; for example, `nltk.download('stopwords')` downloads the stopwords list.

If you run the code from listing 3.6 to preprocess `document 1`, it will return the list of words, including `['18', 'editions', 'dewey', 'decimal', 'classifications', ...]`. As table 3.3 shows, the original text of `document 1` is "18 Editions of the Dewey Decimal Classifications . . .". That is, the preprocessing step helps remove the stopwords like `of` and `the` from the word list.

3.2.2   Matching forms of the same word: Morphological processing

One effect that stopwords and punctuation marks removal has is optimization of the search algorithm; that is, the words that do not matter much are removed, so the computational resources are not wasted on them. In general, the more concise and the more informative the data representation is, the better.

This brings us to the next issue. Look at figure 3.8 illustrating `query 15` and `document 27`, which is a match according to the ground truth mappings.

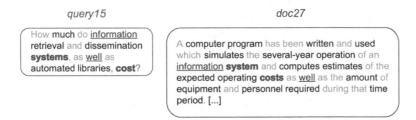

Figure 3.8   The underlined words will be matched between the query and the document; the ones in bold will be skipped.

As figure 3.8 shows, after removing the stopwords and punctuation marks, the algorithm will be able to match the query to the document on some words but will miss others; for instance, it won't be able to tell that `system` and `systems` or `cost` and `costs` essentially represent the same words in different forms. In this particular case, the query and the document will still be matched on such words as *information* or *well*, but the degree to which their contents overlap will be lower. As you will see shortly, such degree matters, as it allows you to reason about the relevance ranking of the document. In addition, in other cases the query–document correspondence might not be established at all, if the only relevant words are used in different forms in the query and the document.

The reason for this mismatch is that words may take different forms in different contexts. Some contexts may require a mention of a single object or concept like *system*, while others may need multiple *systems* to be mentioned. Such different forms of a word that depend on the context and express different aspects of meaning are technically called *morphological forms*, and when you see a word like *systems* and try to match it to its other variant, *system*, you are dealing with morphology. English is relatively "lucky" in that it is not very rich in morphology—that is, it has a limited variety of word forms. Other languages distinguish between many more morphological forms, whereas English forms may be concisely described, as in table 3.5.

Table 3.5 Concise description of English morphological system

Type of word	Example	Type of form
Nouns (words that denote objects, people, animals, concepts)	*system, man, mouse, phenomenon*	Base form: singular form
	*system**s**, men, **mi**ce, phenomen**a***	Plural form
Verbs (words that denote actions, states)	*be, have, retrieve, sing*	Base form: infinitive
	is**, ha**s**, retrieve**s**, sing**s	Third-person form (used with *he/she*)
	***was/were**, ha**d**, retrieve**d**, s**a**ng*	Past tense form
	***been**, ha**d**, retrieve**d**, s**u**ng*	Past participle form (used in phrases like "have been")
	*be**ing**, hav**ing**, retriev**ing**, sing**ing***	Progressive form (as in "I am having a nice time")
Adjectives (words that denote qualities)	*good, bright*	Base form
	better**, bright**er	Comparative form
	best**, bright**est	Superlative form

Morphology

Morphology is a subfield of linguistics that deals with the way words are formed and related to each other in terms of their structure. For example, the word *systems* has a stem, *system,* and a *suffix*, *-s*, denoting multiplicity. English has a relatively simple morphological system.

The base form in table 3.5 is always the most basic form of the word. It is the starting point for any further changes and aspects of meaning, and it is also the word form that you would find in a dictionary. The process of mapping different forms of the word to its most basic one is similar to that of looking words up in a dictionary. Imagine you wanted to know what *sung* meant. Your best strategy would be to look up *sing*. Similarly, the search algorithm would benefit from mapping *sing, sang,* and *sung* to the same word form, by default the most basic one—*sing*. Check your understanding of this processing step with exercise 3.4. First try to solve this exercise yourself, and then you can check the solutions at the end of the chapter.

Such a preprocessing step is quite useful. It results in a more compact search space than the original, with different forms of the same word being mapped together to a single dictionary form. How can a machine perform such a conversion? The solution would be to keep a large dictionary of all known words in a language and try to map the different forms to the known base forms in this dictionary. You might see

Exercise 3.4

What base word forms will you end up with after processing the following text?

"A computer program has been written and used which simulates the several-year operation of an information system and computes estimates of the costs as well as the amount of equipment and personnel required during that time period."

(Solution can be found at the end of this chapter.)

straightaway that there are potential problems with such an approach. To begin with, it is resource intensive, as it has to keep a dictionary for the lookup. Moreover, it would not scale, as it is hard to make sure that a dictionary contains *all* the words in a language. Human languages are creative, and new words tend to crop up on a regular basis, so no dictionary can cover all words in a language, past, present, and future. Can you do better than relying on a dictionary, then?

In fact, there is another option for word form preprocessing that is called *stemming*. Stemming takes word matching one step further and tries to map related words across the board, and this means not just the forms of the same word. For that, stemmers rely on a set of rules that try to reduce the related words to the same basic core. Such rules rely on the idea that even though languages may add new words and borrow words from other languages, they will still apply the same set of rules to build morphological forms for such new additions; for example, the word *selfie* has been relatively recently invented in English, but if you take multiple photos, you will still use the same rules of language and say that you took multiple *selfies*. Similarly, if you use Twitter, you might "tweet" once in a while, or you might be *tweeting* pretty regularly, just like you might write an odd blog post once a year or you might be an active blogger, who is constantly *writing* new blog posts.

Stemming

Stemming refers to the process of mapping multiple forms of related words to the same common core (called a *stem*). This is done using a set of rules that rely on productive word formation patterns in language. Stemmers use these patterns to reverse-engineer what common core multiple related words are derived from.

How does stemming work, then, and what resulting forms does it produce? Take the verb *retrieve* as an example. You can make a whole range of forms out of it, including *retrieving*, *retrieves*, and *retrieved*, as table 3.5 shows. However, if you want to describe the process of retrieving something, you use the word *retrieval*. *Retrieval* is derived from *retrieve*, and the stemmer helps identify this connection by reducing all related words to their common core, their stem, thus the name for the tool. The rule in this particular case will define that the words ending in *-al* can be mapped to the words without *-al*; in fact, forming new words with an addition of *-al* is a productive pattern in English (*remove* + *-al* = *removal*; *approve* + *-al* = *approval*; *deny* + *-al* = *denial*; and so on). The stem in {retrieve, retrieves, retrieved, retrieving, retrieval} is *retriev*. This shows that stemming might result in nonwords; for example, you won't find a word like *retriev* in a dictionary. To provide you with a couple of other examples, the stem for {expect, expects, expected, expecting, expectation, expectations} is *expect* and the stem for {continue, continuation, continuing} is *continu* (figure 3.9).

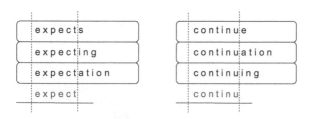

Figure 3.9 Stemming applied to different groups of related words

Note that the stemmer tries to identify which part of the word is shared between the different forms and related words and returns this part as a stem by cutting off the differing word endings.

Now let's implement the stemming preprocessing step using NLTK's stemming functionality. NLTK provides a suite of different stemming tools (check the documentation at www.nltk.org/api/nltk.stem.html), and in this chapter you will use one of the most accurate of them—the Lancaster Stemmer. At the end, the code shows how you can check the results on some document or query; you can also pass in a list of words directly. Do the results correspond to your expectations?

NOTE The source code and the set of rules used by the Lancaster Stemmer can be found at www.nltk.org/_modules/nltk/stem/lancaster.html. As you might guess from the description of the stemming algorithms, they rely on the sets of rules defined by their developers, thus different stemmers can produce different results. Lancaster Stemmer is just one of the algorithms available via NLTK, and we use it here since it shows good results in practice. Note that other stemmers, including ones for other languages, are available at www.nltk.org/api/nltk.stem.html.

Listing 3.7 Preprocessing: Stemming

```
import nltk                                         Import the tools,
import string                                        including the
from nltk import word_tokenize                          stemmer.
from nltk.corpus import stopwords
from nltk.stem.lancaster import LancasterStemmer

def process(text):
    stoplist = set(stopwords.words('english'))      Initialize the
    st = LancasterStemmer()                          LancasterStemmer.
    word_list = [st.stem(word) for word in word_tokenize(text.lower())
```

```
                      if not word in stoplist and not word in string.punctuation]  ◁
          return word_list
```

> **Apply stemming to the preprocessed text.**

```
word_list = process(documents.get("27"))
print(word_list)
word_list = process("organize, organizing, organizational, organ, organic,
     organizer")
print(word_list)    ◁——
```

> **Check the results on some document, query, or on a list of words.**

When you run this code on a particular document (e.g., document 27), the function process receives the following text as input:

```
Input = "Cost Analysis and Simulation Procedures for the Evaluation of Large
     Information Systems ..."    ◁——
```

> **As before, we use "..." to indicate that there are more words in the input and more stems returned in the output.**

As an output, it returns the following list of stems:

```
Output = ['cost', 'analys', 'sim', 'proc', 'evalu', 'larg', 'inform',
     'system', ...]
```

Stem *analys* for "analysis" will help the algorithm to map "analysis" to such words as *analyse* (in British spelling), *analysing, analyst,* and so on; the stem *proc* will help the algorithm group words like *procedure, process, processing,* and so on. Therefore, this step results in an even more compact search space and helps establish useful correspondences between similar words that should help the search algorithm find content related to the information need more effectively.

Now, what happens when you run this function on the input=['organize', 'organizing', 'organizational', 'organ', 'organic', 'organizer']? Intuitively, the words {organize, organizing, organizational, organizer} belong to one group, and you might expect them to be processed as *organiz,* while {organ, organic} belong to another group that should result in something like *organ.* However, the actual output returned by the function process is a list of identical stems for all the words in the input list: ['org', 'org', 'org', 'org', 'org', 'org']. This example is used here as a warning about the way stemmers work: while they are useful in mapping related words to each other, sometimes they might produce an unexpected output and map unrelated words together. This happens because stemmers sometimes go too far in their attempt to establish correspondences. As the stemmer blindly applies a rather general set of rules to all examples, some of these rules overgeneralize. The following list explains how the output for this list of words is produced, step-by-step:

- {organize, organizing, organizational, organizer} may all be reduced to *organiz* by application of the following rules: *-ing* (as in *make → making*), *-ational* (*operate → operational*), and *-er* (*produce → producer*).
- The mapping between *organ* and *organic* is explained by the addition of *-ic* as in *acid → acidic.*

- The less straightforward mapping between *organ* and *organize* is established through the application of ending *-ize*, as in *modern → modernize*.
- Finally, *organ* gets mapped to *org* by the application of *-an*. It is, in fact, applicable in cases like *Italy → Italian* and *history → historian*; that is, to form words describing properties and qualities (such words are called *adjectives*) from words (*nouns*) that describe people in cases when these words are related in meaning.

NOTE This list of rules explaining how the output is arrived at is advanced content. You can consult with this list in case you are interested in what happens "behind the scenes" when you apply the stemming algorithm. However, understanding or knowing these rules is not critical for the application of the stemming algorithm itself.

So, technically, the last two rules should not be applied to map cases like *organ → organize*, because the two words do not mean similar things, and it would be better for the applications like search algorithm to make the distinction between the two groups of words {organize, organizing, organizational, organizer} and {organ, organic}. However, unfortunately, the stemmer algorithm does not take into account what words mean, so once in a while it may make mistakes and connect unrelated words. Figure 3.10 visualizes all the rules that are applied to this set of words, showing the resulting stems and the endings of the words that are cut off by the application of different rules.

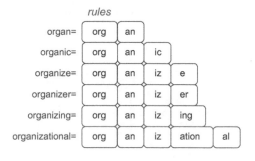

Figure 3.10   The full analysis of rules applied to the example, including *organ* and *organize*

Now, why should you be aware of this peculiarity of the stemmer algorithms? Since in some cases the stemmer would map together words that are not closely related to each other, your search algorithm might consider documents talking about *organic products* somewhat relevant for the query that asks about *organizational skills*. This is something to keep in mind; in general, since the queries are mapped to the relevant documents on the basis of more than one word from the query, such incorrect mappings are usually outweighed by the relevance of other words.

Before we move on, let's summarize which steps of the algorithm you have implemented so far. You have read the data, initialized the data structures, tokenized the texts, removed stopwords, and applied the stemming preprocessing (figure 3.11).

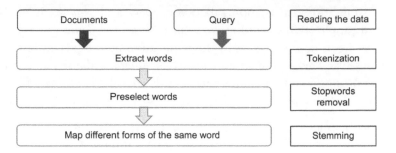

Figure 3.11   At this point, you have read in the data, initialized the data structures, tokenized, and preprocessed the texts.

3.3   *Information weighing*

Another problem with the simple Boolean search algorithm implemented earlier is that it can only return a list of documents that contain some or all of the words from the query, but it cannot tell which of the documents are more relevant. You've seen before that when you run the algorithm from listing 3.5, for most queries it returns a huge number of documents. Stopwords removal helps filter out the less relevant words, while stemming helps find the correspondences between the related words, which alleviates some of these issues. However, your algorithm still returns the relevant documents as an unsorted list. Without some measure of relevance and relevance ordering, it would still be time-consuming to look through all the documents returned by the algorithm. What could serve as such a measure of relevance? Let's look into an example in figure 3.12.

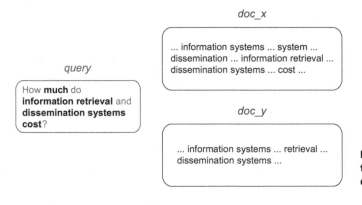

Figure 3.12   An example of the different distribution of query keywords in documents

Suppose you try to find documents most relevant to the given query. After stopwords and punctuation marks removal, you end up with the query words—let's call them *keywords*—consisting of {much, information, retrieval, dissemination, systems, cost}. Which of the two documents appears to be more relevant? As you can see, doc_x contains more keywords than doc_y, and each keyword occurs more times, so it would be reasonable to assume that doc_x is more relevant. Given a choice between these two documents, you should start with doc_x if you want to find the answer to the query. How can we take the factors like more keywords and higher number of occurrences into account?

3.3.1 Weighing words with term frequency

The first requirement, that you should take into account all keywords, suggests that you need to keep track of the words used in the queries and documents. The second requirement, that the number of occurrences of each of the keywords matters, suggests that you need to count the number of occurrences rather than simply register presence or absence of a keyword. You can achieve this by keeping the number of occurrences for the keywords in a table or, translating this into a Python data structure, you can use a dictionary that will allow you to keep track of which counts correspond to which keywords. For instance, the example from figure 3.12 will result in table 3.6.

Table 3.6 The keyword occurrences merged into a shared representation

	much	information	retrieval	dissemination	system(s)	cost
query	1	1	1	1	1	1
doc_x	0	2	1	2	3	1
doc_y	0	1	1	1	2	0

The correspondent Python dictionaries will be as follows:

```
Query={much:1, information:1, retrieval:1, dissemination:1, systems:1, cost:1}
Doc_x={much:0, information:2, retrieval:1, dissemination:2, systems:3, cost:1}
Doc_y={much:0, information:1, retrieval:1, dissemination:1, systems:2, cost:0}
```

This approach, based on calculating the frequency of occurrence, corresponds to the well-known technique in information retrieval called *term frequency* (tf). It relies on the idea that the more frequently the word (term) is used in a document, the more relevant this document becomes to the query. We will use the word *term* instead of *word* from now on following this widely accepted convention. After all, since you apply stemming, not all keywords keep being proper "words" anymore (think of the case of *retriev*). Listing 3.8 shows how to implement this step. Function get_terms helps you preprocess the input text and estimate the counts for each term to populate the dictionary. Using this function, you populate the term frequency dictionaries for all documents and all queries. To check the results, you can print out the length of the resulting data structures (this shouldn't change from before—1,460 for the documents, 112 for the queries), the term frequency dictionaries for a specific document or query (e.g., the first ones in the set), and the length of these dictionaries (it should be 43 terms for document 1 and 14 terms for query 1).

Listing 3.8   Code to estimate term frequency in documents and queries

```
def get_terms(text):
    stoplist = set(stopwords.words('english'))                    Apply all the
    terms = {}                                              preprocessing steps
    st = LancasterStemmer()                                           as before.
    word_list = [st.stem(word) for word in word_tokenize(text.lower())
                 if not word in stoplist and not word in string.punctuation]
    for word in word_list:
        terms[word] = terms.get(word, 0) + 1          ◁        Estimate the counts for
    return terms                                                each term and populate
                                                                the dictionary.
doc_terms = {}
qry_terms = {}
for doc_id in documents.keys():
    doc_terms[doc_id] = get_terms(documents.get(doc_id))
for qry_id in queries.keys():
    qry_terms[qry_id] = get_terms(queries.get(qry_id))    ◁     Populate the term
                                                                frequency dictionaries
                                                                for all documents and
print(len(doc_terms))                                           all queries.
print(doc_terms.get("1"))
print(len(doc_terms.get("1")))
print(len(qry_terms))                    Check the
print(qry_terms.get("1"))                results.
print(len(qry_terms.get("1")))     ◁
```

Now, let's represent all queries and all documents in the same shared space; for example, table 3.6 represents one query and two documents in a space where the columns of the table are shared among all three. In the Python data structure, each of these columns represents a separate dimension. For instance, column 1 keeps the counts of the term *much* across the query and both documents, column 2 keeps the counts for *information*, and so on; similarly, the Python data structures keep these counts in the first two dimensions as

```
Query={much:1, information:1, ...}
Doc_x={much:0, information:2, ...}
Doc_y={much:0, information:1, ...}
```

Now let's add all terms from the data set as columns and keep the counts for each of them in each query and each document as rows. In terms of Python data structures, this means that each document and each query will keep the whole dictionary of terms in the collection with the associated term frequencies. Listing 3.9 presents this step. In this code, you first collect the shared vocabulary of terms used in documents and queries and return it as a sorted list for convenience. You can print out the length of the shared vocabulary (you should end up with 7,775 terms in total if you use the same versions of the tools as suggested in the installation instructions; you might end up with different results, such as 8,881 terms, if you are using different versions of the tools) and check the first several terms in the vocabulary. Now each query and each document can be represented with a dictionary with the same set of keys—the terms from the shared vocabulary. The values will either be equal to the term frequency in the particular query and document or will be 0 if the term is not in the query or document. This functionality is captured by the function `vectorize`: using this function, you can represent all queries and documents in a shared space. Finally, you can print out some statistics on these data structures. You should still have 1,460 `doc_vectors` and 112 `qry_vectors`, with 7,775 terms each.

Listing 3.9 Code to represent the data in a shared space

```
def collect_vocabulary():                    ←──────────
    all_terms = []                                        Collect the shared vocabulary
    for doc_id in doc_terms.keys():                       of terms from documents and
        for term in doc_terms.get(doc_id).keys():         queries and return it as a
            all_terms.append(term)                        sorted list.
    for qry_id in qry_terms.keys():
        for term in qry_terms.get(qry_id).keys():
            all_terms.append(term)
    return sorted(set(all_terms))

all_terms = collect_vocabulary()       Print out the length of the shared
print(len(all_terms))                  vocabulary and check the first
print(all_terms[:10])      ←──────     several terms in the vocabulary.


def vectorize(input_features, vocabulary):
    output = {}
    for item_id in input_features.keys():
        features = input_features.get(item_id)       Represents each query and each
        output_vector = []                           document with a dictionary
        for word in vocabulary:       ←──────        with the same set of keys
            if word in features.keys():
                output_vector.append(int(features.get(word)))
            else:
                output_vector.append(0)
        output[item_id] = output_vector
    return output                                Using the vectorize method,
                                                 you can represent all queries
doc_vectors = vectorize(doc_terms, all_terms)    and documents in this shared
qry_vectors = vectorize(qry_terms, all_terms)  ←─ space.

print(len(doc_vectors))
print(len(doc_vectors.get("1460")))
print(len(qry_vectors))                 Print out some statistics on
print(len(qry_vectors.get("112")))    ←─ these data structures.
```

Another way to think about each of these term dictionaries associated with each document and each query is as vectors—that is, each document and each query is represented as a vector in a shared space, with the number of dimensions equal to the length of the shared vocabulary (7,775) and the term frequencies in each dimension representing the coordinates. This may remind you of the discussion on vectors before (see chapter 1). Figure 3.13 reinterprets the query and two documents from table 3.6 as vectors in two dimensions associated with the terms *system* and *cost*, but you can imagine how these vectors are extended to other dimensions, too (recall that figure 1.7 uses a similar representation for a different example).

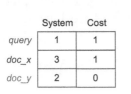

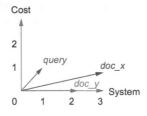

Figure 3.13   Vector representation of the query and two documents along two dimensions

Now you can estimate the relevance, or similarity, of the query and documents using the distance between them in the vector space. But before you do that, there is one more observation due.

3.3.2   Weighing words with inverse document frequency

In a collection of documents you are working with, some terms are much more frequently used across all documents than others. For instance, since this is a collection of articles on information science and information-retrieval systems, such terms as *information* or *system* may occur in many documents while other terms like *cost* may occur in fewer documents. Which ones are more helpful in search, then? Imagine that you were to find the relevant documents for `query 15`, "How much do information retrieval and dissemination systems cost?" If *information* and *system* occur in lots of documents, then you better focus your attention on those documents that contain other terms from the query (e.g., *dissemination* and *cost*) because it is those documents that contain these words that are more relevant. In other words, you would like to give these rarer terms higher weight so that the search algorithm knows it should trust their vote for relevance more. The most straightforward way to assign such weights to the terms is to make it proportionate to the number of documents where the term occurs: the higher the number of documents that contain the term, the lower its discriminative power, and therefore the lower the weight that the term should get.

Take the term *inform* as an example (this is a stem for such words as *inform* and *information*). It occurs in 651 out of 1,460, so its document frequency (`df`) equals $651/1460 \approx 0.45$. On the other hand, the term *dissemin* (stem of *dissemination*) occurs in only 68 documents, so its `df` = $68/1460 \approx 0.05$. *Dissemin* is a more valuable term for the search algorithm because it is rare; if a query contains it, the documents that also contain it should be given preference. To assign a higher weight to *dissemin* than to *inform*, let's take the inverse document frequency (`idf`): `idf("inform")` = $1/0.45 \approx 2.22$, `idf("dissemin")` = $1/0.05 \approx 20$. These weights show that the rare term *dissemin* is almost 10 times more important than the much more frequent term *inform*. There are two more things to take into account here:

- Some terms from the shared vocabulary may not occur in any of the documents, so their `df` will be 0. To avoid division by 0, it is common to smooth the counts. To calculate the idf, take (df+1) rather than df—that is, idf = 1/(df+1)—so you will never have to divide by 0, and the absolute values of idf won't change much.

- It is common to "tone down" the differences in absolute counts, as the difference between very rare and very frequent terms might be huge, especially in large collections. It is assumed that the weight given to the terms should increase not linearly (i.e., by one with each document) but rather sublinearly (i.e., more slowly). Logarithmic function (see https://mathworld.wolfram.com/Logarithm.html) achieves this effect: the relative order of the term's importance doesn't change, while the absolute number does.

To put all the components together, here are the idf values for the terms *inform* and *dissemin* in this collection:

```
idf("inform")   = log₁₀(1460/(651+1))  ≈ 0.35
idf("dissemin") = log₁₀(1460/68+1))    ≈ 1.33
```

As you can see, the difference is still significant, but the counts are more comparable. The general formula then is

$$idf(term) = log_{10}\left(\frac{N}{df(term) + 1}\right)$$

where N is the total number of documents in the collection.

Information weighing

Term frequency (tf) takes into account the frequency of occurrence of the term in a document: the more frequently the word (term) is used in a document, the more relevant this document becomes to the query. Inverse document frequency (idf) takes into account the frequency of occurrence of the term across all documents in the collection: the higher the number of documents that contain the term, the lower its discriminative power.

Exercise 3.5

What are the idf values for the following terms based on the number of documents they occur in:

```
df("system") = 531; df("us" = stem of "use") = 800; df("retriev") = 287;
    df("cost") = 137
```

(Solution can be found at the end of this chapter.)

Try to solve this exercise yourself and then check the solutions at the end of the chapter.

Now, suppose `idf("cost")=1.02` and `idf("system")=0.44`. If a particular document contains two occurrences of the term *cost*, its `idf`-weighed value will be `2*1.02=2.04`, while if it contains two occurrences of the term *system*, its `idf`-weighed value will be `2*0.44=0.88`, so despite the same term frequencies, the more informative term *cost* will get higher overall weight. For instance, table 3.7 shows how `idf` weighing will change the weights of the terms in the documents from table 3.6.

Table 3.7 **Idf weighing applied to the term frequencies in the two documents**

	System(s)	Cost
query	1	1
doc_x	3*0.44=1.32	1*1.02=1.02
doc_y	2*0.44=0.88	0

Listing 3.10 shows how to implement this in Python. In this code, with `calculate_idfs` you estimate `idf` values for each term in the vocabulary by counting how many documents contain it and applying the formula from earlier. You can check the results by printing out `idf` values for selected terms; for example, `idf` values for the terms from exercise 3.5 should coincide with your own estimates. Next, you define a function `vectorize_idf` to apply `idf` weighing to the `input_terms` (in particular, to `doc_terms`) data structure. Specifically, within this function you multiply the term frequencies with the `idf` weights if the term is present in the document; otherwise, its term frequency stays 0. Finally, you apply `idf` weighing to `doc_terms` and print out some statistics: the dimensionality of the data structure should still be 1,460 documents by 7,775 terms.

Listing 3.10 **Code to calculate and apply inverse document frequency weighting**

```
import math

def calculate_idfs(vocabulary, doc_features):      ⟵  Estimate idf values for
    doc_idfs = {}                                      each term in the vocabulary
    for term in vocabulary:                            by counting how many
        doc_count = 0                                  documents contain it.
        for doc_id in doc_features.keys():
            terms = doc_features.get(doc_id)
            if term in terms.keys():
                doc_count += 1
        doc_idfs[term] = math.log(                  Apply the idf
            float(len(doc_features.keys()))/        formula from
            float(1 + doc_count), 10)        ⟵      above.
    return doc_idfs

doc_idfs = calculate_idfs(all_terms, doc_terms)     Check the results: you should
print(len(doc_idfs))                                have idf values for all terms
print(doc_idfs.get("system"))        ⟵             from the vocabulary.
```

```
def vectorize_idf(input_terms, input_idfs, vocabulary):
    output = {}
    for item_id in input_terms.keys():
        terms = input_terms.get(item_id)
        output_vector = []
        for term in vocabulary:
            if term in terms.keys():
                output_vector.append(
                    input_idfs.get(term)*float(terms.get(term)))
            else:
                output_vector.append(float(0))
        output[item_id] = output_vector
    return output

doc_vectors = vectorize_idf(doc_terms, doc_idfs, all_terms)

print(len(doc_vectors))
print(len(doc_vectors.get("1460")))
```

Define a function to apply idf weighing to the input_terms data structure.

Multiply the term frequencies with the idf weights if the term is present in the document.

Apply idf weighing to doc_terms.

Print out some statistics, such as the number of documents and terms.

Let's now summarize what you have implemented so far (figure 3.14).

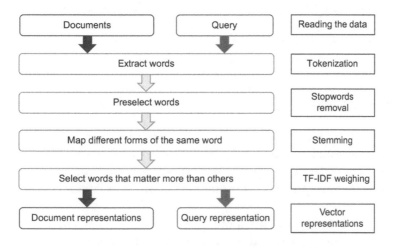

Figure 3.14 At this point, you have read in the data, initialized the data structures, tokenized and preprocessed the texts, and applied information weighing techniques.

3.4 Practical use of the search algorithm

Now that the documents and queries are represented in the shared search space, it's time to run the search algorithm, find the most relevant documents for each query, and evaluate the results.

3.4.1   *Retrieval of the most similar documents*

How can you estimate query to document similarity based on the vector representations? In chapter 1, we discussed that the similarity can be interpreted as distance in space defined by the query and document vectors. Here is a refresher:

- Each document and each query are represented as vectors in a shared space, with the dimensions representing terms and coordinates representing weighted term counts.
- Similarity is estimated using distances in this shared space. To eliminate the effect of different lengths (as queries are traditionally much shorter than documents), it is more reliable to use the cosine of the angle between the vectors, as it normalizes the distance with respect to the different lengths of the vectors. Because of this normalization step, estimating the angle between the vectors of different lengths is equivalent to estimating the distance between the vectors of same length (figure 1.8 in chapter 1 visualizes this idea).
- The higher the cosine, the more similar the query and the document are.
- The cosine can be estimated using the formula

```
cosine(vec1,vec2) = dot_product(vec1,vec2)/(length(vec1)*length(vec2))
```

Let's calculate the cosine between the query and doc_x and doc_y from table 3.6 (using only `tf` and ignoring the `idf` weighing for the sake of simplicity here):

```
cosine(query,doc_x) = (0+2+1+2+3+1)/(sqrt(6)*sqrt(19)) ≈ 0.84
cosine(query,doc_y) = (0+1+1+1+2+0)/(sqrt(6)*sqrt(7))  ≈ 0.77
```

Based on these results, doc_x is more similar to the query than doc_y, so if you apply the cosine similarity estimation for the given query to the set of two documents, you should return them ordered as (doc_x, doc_y). As doc_x is more similar and thus more relevant to the query, if you want more relevant information, you should start with doc_x.

Let's apply cosine similarity to the input queries and documents in the dataset and return the resulting lists of relevant documents ordered by their relevance scores (i.e., cosine similarity values). Listing 3.11 uses `operator`'s `itemgetter` functionality, which helps to sort Python dictionaries by keys or values. The code implements three helper functions that allow you to calculate the length of the input vector, the dot product of two vectors, and cosine similarity between input vectors representing, for example, a query and a document. You initialize the `query` by extracting a query with a particular `qry_id` (e.g., `query 3`). Then, for each document in the set of documents, you calculate cosine similarity between the input query and the document and store the document ID as the key and cosine as the value in the `results` dictionary. Finally, you sort the `results` dictionary by cosine values (key=itemgetter(1) in descending order (reverse=True) and return the top *n* results. This code returns 44 relevant documents for query 3 according to the gold standard, where items[0] returns the document IDs from tuples (document_id, similarity score).

Listing 3.11 Code to run search algorithm for a given query on the set of documents

```
from operator import itemgetter          ◁─┐  The operator's itemgetter
                                             │  functionality helps sort Python
          ┌─▷ def length(vector):            │  dictionaries by keys or values.
Calculate │       sq_length = 0
the length│       for index in range(0, len(vector)):
of the    │           sq_length += math.pow(vector[index], 2)
input     │       return math.sqrt(sq_length)
vector.   │
          │   def dot_product(vector1, vector2):      ◁─┐  Calculate the dot
              if len(vector1)==len(vector2):             │  product of two vectors.
                  dot_prod = 0
                  for index in range(0, len(vector1)):
                      if not vector1[index]==0 and not vector2[index]==0:
                          dot_prod += vector1[index]*vector2[index]
                  return dot_prod
              else:
                  return "Unmatching dimensionality"   │  Calculate cosine similarity between
                                                        │  input vectors (e.g., representing a
          def calculate_cosine(query, document):   ◁──┘  query and a document).
              cosine =  dot_product(query, document) / (
                  length(query) * length(document))
              return cosine

                                             ┌  Initialize the query by selecting
          query = qry_vectors.get("3")    ◁──┤  an example with a particular
          results = {}                        └  qry_id (e.g., query 3).

          for doc_id in doc_vectors.keys():          For each document, calculate
              document = doc_vectors.get(doc_id)      cosine similarity with the query
              cosine = calculate_cosine(query, document)  and store the result in the
              results[doc_id] = cosine    ◁──┘          results dictionary.

          for items in sorted(results.items(), key=itemgetter(1), reverse=True)[:44]:
              print(items[0])   ◁──┐
                                    └  Sort the results dictionary by cosine values in
                                       descending order and return the top n results.
```

This piece of code returns a list of 44 documents identified by the search algorithm as relevant to query 3, ordered by cosine similarity starting with the most relevant one. A quick glance over the first 10 returned documents (that is how many you would see on the first page in the internet browser) shows that 8 out of 10 documents are also included in the gold standard. Perhaps even more importantly, the top 2 documents in the returned list are relevant according to the gold standard—and you might not even need to look any further than the first couple of documents! This looks like a good result, but how can you get a more comprehensive overview of the results across the board (i.e., over multiple queries)?

3.4.2 *Evaluation of the results*

If you are building a search algorithm as part of some application for the users, it is key to the success of your application that the users are satisfied with the results. If you are building an application for your own needs, it is important to be able to measure whether it is doing a good job. How can you measure if the users or you are satisfied with the results?

In the previous step, you added similarity estimation to your search algorithm that allows it to return the results as an ordered list. Suppose you are looking for the documents related to query 3, "What is information science? Give definitions where possible." According to the gold standard, there are 44 documents in this set that match this query. In some situations, you might be interested in an exhaustive search—that is, you will measure the success of your algorithm by its ability to find *all* 44 documents. However, in most situations what you would like is for the algorithm to return the relevant documents at the top of the list: it is more important that the first document returned by the algorithm is relevant than whether the 44th document is relevant. Often, if the first document is relevant to your query, you will read no further; for example, how often do you check the second page of results on Google?

Since the number of relevant documents in the gold standard varies for different queries—for example, it is 44 for query 3 but there is only 1 relevant document for query 6—you may prefer to set the number of top documents to be returned by your algorithm in advance. In addition, it is rarely the case that users are interested in documents after the first several relevant ones, so returning something between top 3 and top 10 documents would be reasonable. The number of documents that are returned by the algorithm among those top 3 (top 10) that are also included as relevant in the gold standard are called *true positives*—they are truly relevant documents actually identified by your algorithm. The proportion of true positives to the total number of documents returned by the algorithm is called *precision*, and if you predefine the number of returned documents to be k, then this measure is called precision@k (e.g., precision@3 or precision@10). For example, listing 3.11 returns 8 relevant documents in the top 10 ones—its precision@10 equals 0.8. That is, precision@10 is defined as

```
precision@10 = (true positives among the top 10 documents) / 10 =
(number of documents that are actually relevant among the top 10) / 10
```

And in the general case, precision@k is

```
precision@k = (true positives among the top k documents) / k =
(number of documents that are actually relevant among the top k) / k
```

The higher the precision, the better the algorithm you have built; however, the results may also depend on the quality of the dataset and the queries themselves. For example, since there are 44 matching documents for query 3 in the dataset and only 1 matching document for query 6, it would be much easier for the algorithm to find relevant documents for query 3. If you want the results to be more objective, it is useful to evaluate precision across all queries. This is called *mean precision* because it takes the mean across all queries. For instance, if the top 3 results for the first query are all relevant, `precision@3=1`; if only 2 are relevant, `precision@3=0.67`; for only one relevant result, `precision@3=0.33`. If you estimate the mean precision across 3 queries with such results, it would be equal to `0.67`, as figure 3.15 shows.

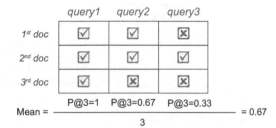

Figure 3.15   Mean `precision@3` per 3 queries

Thus, the mean `precision@k` can be estimated as

$$\text{Mean p@k} = \frac{\sum_{queries} p@k}{num(queries)} = \frac{\sum_{queries} \frac{true\ positives}{k}}{num(queries)}$$

You might also be interested in knowing how often the top results contain at least one relevant document. In the case exemplified in figure 3.15, the user will be able to find at least one relevant document in the top 3 results, which is quite useful; therefore, this ratio will be equal to 1. Listing 3.12 shows how these measures can be implemented in Python. In this code, you define a function to estimate precision, calculating the proportion of relevant documents from the gold standard among the top k results returned by the algorithm. Gold standard is the list of relevant document IDs that can be extracted from the `mappings` data structure. An alternative evaluation gives the algorithm some credit if at least one document in the top k is relevant. Your overall goal is to calculate mean values across all queries. For each document, you estimate its relevance to the query with cosine similarity as before; then you sort the results and consider only top k (e.g., top 3) most relevant documents. In the end, you accumulate evaluation values across all queries and estimate the mean values.

Listing 3.12   Estimate precision@k and ratio of cases with at least one relevant document

```
def calculate_precision(model_output, gold_standard):
    true_pos = 0
    for item in model_output:
        if item in gold_standard:
            true_pos += 1
    return float(true_pos)/float(len(model_output))
```

Define a function to estimate precision.

Calculate the proportion of relevant documents from the gold standard in the top k returned results.

```
def calculate_found(model_output, gold_standard):
    found = 0
    for item in model_output:
        if item in gold_standard:
            found = 1
    return float(found)
```

Alternatively, give the algorithm some credit if at least one document in the top k is relevant.

```
precision_all = 0.0
found_all = 0.0
for query_id in mappings.keys():
    gold_standard = mappings.get(str(query_id))
    query = qry_vectors.get(str(query_id))
    results = {}
    model_output = []
    for doc_id in doc_vectors.keys():
        document = doc_vectors.get(doc_id)
        cosine = calculate_cosine(query, document)
        results[doc_id] = cosine
    for items in sorted(results.items(),
                        key=itemgetter(1),
                        reverse=True)[:3]:
        model_output.append(items[0])
    precision = calculate_precision(model_output, gold_standard)
    found = calculate_found(model_output, gold_standard)
    print(f"{str(query_id)}: {str(precision)}")
    precision_all += precision
    found_all += found

print(precision_all/float(len(mappings.keys())))
print(found_all/float(len(mappings.keys())))
```

Calculate mean values across all queries.

Gold standard is the list of relevant document IDs that can be extracted from the mappings data structure.

Sort the results and consider only top k (e.g., top 3) most relevant documents.

For each document, estimate its relevance to the query with cosine similarity as before.

Accumulate evaluation values across all queries; track the results by a printout message.

In the end, estimate the mean values for all queries.

According to the results, on some queries the algorithm performs very well. For example, a printout message "1: 1.0" shows that all top 3 documents returned for query 1 are relevant, making precision@3 for this query equal to 1. However, on other queries the algorithm does not perform that well—for instance, "6: 0.0"; as there is only one document relevant for query 6 according to the gold standard, the algorithm fails to put it within the first 3 and gets a score of 0 for this query. The mean value of precision@3 for this algorithm is around 0.40, and in about 66% of the cases the algorithm finds at least one relevant document among the top 3.

If you are interested only in the proportion of cases where the top most relevant document identified by the algorithm is actually relevant, you can calculate that by slightly modifying the code in listing 3.12: instead of sorting all the results and then taking the top 3, it simply needs to identify and store a single best result (see exercise 3.6).

Exercise 3.6

Modify the code from listing 3.12 to calculate precision@1; that is, the mean value across the queries when the top 1 document returned by the algorithm is indeed relevant. (Solution can be found at the end of this chapter.)

Finally, you may wish to know how highly, on the average, the algorithm places the relevant document in its ranking. This shows how far into the list of the returned results you should typically look to find the first relevant document. The measure that allows you to evaluate this relies on the use of the highest ranking of a relevant document identified by the algorithm. Since you already sort the returned documents by their relevance scores starting with the most relevant one, position 1 in this list is called *first rank*, position 2 is *second rank*, and so on. Look at the search results from figure 3.15 again (figure 3.16).

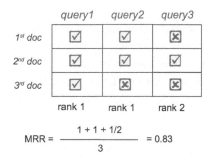

$$MRR = \frac{1 + 1 + 1/2}{3} = 0.83$$

Figure 3.16 Ranks for the first relevant document for each of the three queries and mean reciprocal rank (MRR) across all three results

- The first relevant documents for both query 1 and query 2 in this example are at position 1 in the ordered lists of returned documents, so their ranks are 1; for query 3, the first relevant document is found in the second position, which gives this result rank 2.
- However, returning the first relevant document at rank 1 is better than returning the first relevant document at any further position, so your measure should reflect this by assigning a higher score to the results with rank 1. Just like with the inverse document frequency, if you take the inverse of the ranks, you will end up with exactly such measure: for both query 1 and query 2, the algorithm returns the best possible results by placing the first relevant document at position 1, so it gets a score of 1/1=1 for that; for query 3, it returns an irrelevant document in position 1 and the first relevant document in position 2; for that it gets only half the full score, 1/2. To summarize, to assign a score for the results for each query, take the inverse of the rank of the first relevant document in the ordered list of results. This is called *reciprocal rank*:

```
reciprocal rank = 1 / rank of the first relevant document in the
     ordered list of results
```

- Finally, as before, you want to have a comprehensive overview of the results across all queries, so you need to take a mean reciprocal rank (MRR) for the reciprocal ranks across all queries. For the example from figure 3.16, this will equal to (1 + 1 + 1/2) / 3 = 0.83:

```
MRR = sum of reciprocal ranks across queries / number of queries
```

The best-case scenario is when the algorithm always puts a relevant document at the top of the list, so it assigns rank 1 in all cases. If the first relevant document is always found at rank 2, the mean will equal to $1/2$; for the results at rank 3, the mean will be $1/3$, and so on. The result that you get for the example from figure 3.16, MRR = $(1+1+1/2)/3 = 0.83$, lies between $1/2$ and 1 and is closer to 1. This value shows that, on the average, the ranking of the first relevant document returned by the algorithm is between first and second rank and is in fact more often first than second.

Listing 3.13 shows how to implement this measure in Python. First, as before, you extract the list of gold standard mappings for each query. Next, you sort the documents returned by the algorithm in descending order starting with the most similar one. The position of each document in this sorted list is called *rank*, and you increment the rank with each document in the results list. You only need to find the first relevant document in this list, so you initially set the flag found to False and switch it to True as soon as you encounter the first relevant document or reach the end of the list. In the end, you estimate the inverse of the rank for each query and calculate the mean value across all queries.

Listing 3.13 Code to estimate mean reciprocal rank

```python
rank_all = 0.0
for query_id in mappings.keys():
    gold_standard = mappings.get(str(query_id))          # As before, extract the list
    query = qry_vectors.get(str(query_id))               # of gold standard mappings
    results = {}                                         # for each query.
    for doc_id in doc_vectors.keys():
        document = doc_vectors.get(doc_id)
        cosine = calculate_cosine(query, document)
        results[doc_id] = cosine
    sorted_results = sorted(results.items(),             # Sort the documents returned
                    key=itemgetter(1),                   # by the algorithm in descending
                    reverse=True)                        # order, starting with the most
                                                         # similar one.
    index = 0
    found = False                                        # Set the flag found to False and
    while found==False:                                  # switch it to True when you find
        item = sorted_results[index]                     # the first relevant document.
        index += 1
        if index==len(sorted_results):                  # As before, the document ID is the
            found = True                                 # first element in the sorted tuples of
        if item[0] in gold_standard:                    # (document_id, similarity score).
            found = True
            print(f"{str(query_id)}: {str(float(1) / float(index))}")
            rank_all += float(1) / float(index)          # Estimate the
                                                         # inverse of the rank.

print(rank_all/float(len(mappings.keys())))             # Calculate and print out the
                                                         # mean value across all queries.
```

Increment the index (rank) with each document in the results.

The result—mean reciprocal rank of around 0.58—printed by this piece of code suggests that, on the average, the highest rank of a relevant document identified by this search algorithm is between first and second (i.e., you will often find the relevant results within the first pair of returned documents). This concludes the implementation of the search algorithm, so let's summarize what steps you have implemented (figure 3.17).

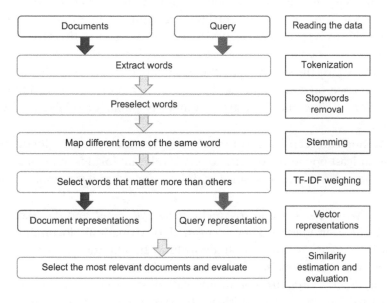

Figure 3.17   The summary of all steps of the search algorithm implemented

3.4.3   Deploying search algorithm in practice

Finally, once you have implemented the algorithm and decided on its components (e.g., the use of stemming, the type of term weighing), you can deploy it in practice. For instance, you may have your own data within your own project, where searching for relevant information is useful (exercise 3.7). If you don't have such a project in mind, try applying the algorithm to another dataset anyway to practice the new skills: you can download one of the datasets from http://ir.dcs.gla.ac.uk/resources/test_collections/.

> **Exercise 3.7**
>
> Apply the search algorithm to your own data. For that, you will need to read in the files one by one as you did for the spam-filtering application in chapter 2.
>
> Alternatively, apply the search algorithm to a different dataset from http://ir.dcs.gla.ac.uk/resources/test_collections/. Among these, the Cranfield dataset uses a similar data format to the CISI dataset and is also relatively small and easy to work with.

Summary

- Search, or information retrieval, algorithms are widely used in many applications, from search in an internet browser to search for the relevant files on your personal computer. In addition, any application where there is a need to efficiently find relevant information in an arbitrarily large collection of documents would benefit from information-retrieval algorithms. The valuable property of these algorithms is that they can sort the results in order of their relevance and ability to answer the information need (typically formulated as a query).

- Before you deploy the search algorithm in practice, it is a good idea to evaluate its performance on some annotated dataset. Such annotation is called *ground truth* or *gold standard*, and there are a number of publicly available datasets that you can use.

- A simple Boolean search algorithm relies on the idea that any document that contains at least one word from the query is relevant for this query. However, it is unable to assess relative relevance of the documents and the results cannot be sorted.

- There is a particular set of words, including *a, the, in, at,* and the like, that are highly frequent in English. They occur in all or virtually all documents, so they are not informative for the search algorithms. In addition, they don't capture the meaning, as they mainly link other words together and fulfill particular functions. Such words are commonly called *stopwords*, and they should be removed so that they do not mislead the algorithm. Many toolkits, including NLTK, contain a standard stopwords list that you can use.

- Words in languages may occur in several different forms. In English, this is relevant for nouns (words denoting objects, people, animals, and abstract concepts), verbs (words denoting actions and states), and adjectives (words denoting qualities). Mapping the different forms of a word to its base (dictionary) form allows the algorithm to establish useful correspondences and optimize the search space. One step further is to apply a set of rules to identify the correspondences across all related words. To link the related words to each other, use an NLP tool called *stemmer* that relies on a set of predefined rules.

- Documents that contain more occurrences of the query terms should be given preference as compared to the documents with a lower number of occurrences. The number of occurrences represents term frequencies (`tf`).

- Not all terms are equally important. Even after the stopwords are removed, there are still terms that are frequently used across all documents. Such terms are less discriminative, and their relative weights should reflect this. Inverse document frequency (`idf`) is used to weigh the terms according to their distribution across the documents.

- To estimate the relevance of the documents to the queries in the collection, one needs to represent them in a shared search space, where each term stands for an individual dimension and term frequencies or `tf-idf` weighted counts are used as the coordinates.

- The relevance in the shared space can be estimated using cosine similarity.
- The search algorithm can be evaluated with the use of one or more popular measures. For example, you can estimate the proportion of the relevant documents returned in the `top k` results. This measure is called `precision@k`. Alternatively, you can measure the average highest rank for the relevant documents returned by the algorithm. This measure is called *mean reciprocal rank*.

Solutions to miscellaneous exercises

Exercise 3.2

First try to code this yourself, and then check the solution in the notebook provided with the book.

> **NOTE**   All the code for this book is available at https://github.com/ekochmar/Getting-Started-with-NLP/.

Exercise 3.4

Conversion of this piece of text to the base forms should result in "A computer program have be write and use which simulate the several-year operation of an information system and compute estimate of the cost as well as the amount of equipment and personnel require during that time period." Base forms of the words from the original sentence are underlined.

Exercise 3.5

```
idf("system") = log₁₀(1460/(531+1)) ≈ 0.44
idf("us") = log₁₀(1460/(800+1)) ≈ 0.26
idf("retriev") = log₁₀(1460/(287+1)) ≈ 0.71
idf("cost") = log₁₀(1460/(137+1)) ≈ 1.02
```

Exercise 3.6

First try to code this yourself, and then check the solution in the notebook provided with the book.

> **NOTE**   All the code for this book is available at https://github.com/ekochmar/Getting-Started-with-NLP/.

Information extraction

This chapter covers

- Extracting information from raw text
- Exploring useful NLP techniques, such as part-of-speech tagging, lemmatization, and parsing
- Building a language-processing pipeline with spaCy

In the previous chapter, you looked into ways of finding texts that talk about particular concepts or facts. You've built an information-retrieval system that can search for texts answering particular questions. For example, if you were wondering what information science is or what methods information-retrieval systems use, you needed to provide your information-retrieval system with the queries like "What is information science?" or "What methods do information-retrieval systems use?" and the system found for you relevant texts that talk about these things.

This system saves you a lot of time: you don't need to manually search for texts that contain *any* relevant information about your question. Moreover, you don't need to assess *how* relevant these texts are as the system can also rank them by relevance. However, this information-retrieval system still has some limitations: if you had a particular question in mind like "What is information science?" and just wanted to know the answer (e.g., "It is an academic field that is primarily concerned with analysis, collection, classification, manipulation, storage, retrieval, movement, dissemination, and protection of information," according to Wikipedia: https://en .wikipedia.org/wiki/Information_science), you probably would not be interested in reading through the whole list of documents in order to find this answer, even if all of them were relevant. In some cases, looking for the exact answer in a collection of documents would be highly impractical. For example, imagine you have access to the whole web, but all you want to know is the definition for information science. If you search for the answer on Google, you would get over $4 * 10^9$ relevant pages for this question. Obviously, looking through even a small portion of those in search for the exact answer would be time-consuming, given that this answer can be summarized in just one sentence. Luckily, Google also provides you with a snapshot of the relevant bit of the web page or even the definition when possible (figure 4.1).

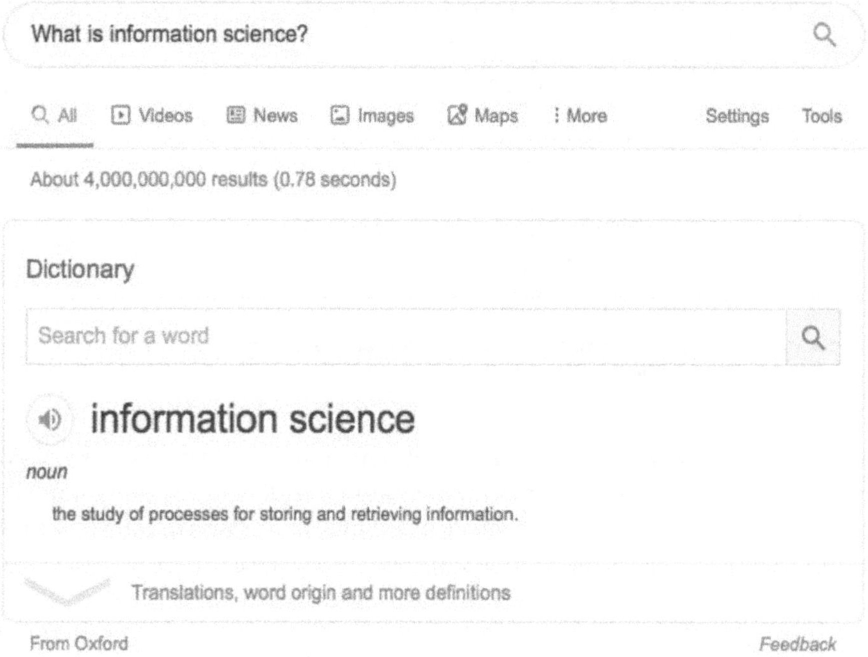

Figure 4.1   In addition to finding the relevant pages, Google returns the exact answer to the question.

The application that is used here is called *information extraction* (or *text analytics* or *text mining*) because it allows you to extract only particular facts or only the relevant information from an otherwise unstructured free-formatted text.

In this chapter, you will build your own system that can extract particular facts of interest from raw text. But first, let's look into some examples of when this is useful.

4.1   Use cases

Here are some real-life applications that can benefit from information extraction.

4.1.1   Case 1

You have a collection of generally relevant documents, but all you need is a precise answer to a particular question. There are many situations where this might occur; for instance, you may be searching for an answer out of curiosity (e.g., "What is the meaning of life?") or for educational purposes ("What temperature does water boil at?"). Perhaps you are collecting some specific information like a list of people present at the last meetings and want to automatically extract the names of all participants from the past meetings minutes. In the general case, your NLP engine might need to first find all relevant documents that talk about the subject of interest, just like you did in chapter 3, and then analyze those texts to identify the relation between the two concepts. Figure 4.2 reminds you of this process, discussed in chapter 1.

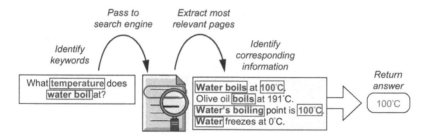

Figure 4.2   To get the answer to the question, you might need to first retrieve all relevant documents and then analyze them.

You are already familiar with the retrieval step, and this chapter will show you how to run the analysis of texts to extract the relevant facts. This case is an example of a popular NLP application—question answering. Question answering deals with a range of queries that might be formulated in a straightforward way, as in the example from figure 4.2, as well as in more convoluted ways. Just to give you a flavor of the task, the exact answer might not always be readily available in text. The question might be formulated as "Where was Albert Einstein born?" while the answer might use wording like "Albert Einstein's birthplace is Ulm, Germany." Despite the words *born* and *birthplace* being related to each other, the exact word matching won't help you find the relevant answer here, and you will need to use further NLP techniques. There are many more examples where finding the correct answer is not trivial (see the examples from the SQuAD, a question-answering dataset and real-time competition, at http://mng .bz/1o5V). In this book, we will look into the extraction of relevant information from explicitly formulated answers, but the overall scope of the task is much wider.

4.1.2 Case 2

You have a collection of relevant documents, and you need to extract particular types of information to fill in a database. For instance, imagine you work in an insurance company, and you have a collection of various companies' profiles. These profiles contain all the essential information about each company (e.g., the size of the company, the type of business it is involved in, its revenue). Many of these factors are critical for determining a suitable insurance policy, so rather than considering the companies one by one, you might want to extract these facts from the profiles and put them in a single database. Alternatively, imagine you work in a human resources division of a company that receives dozens of applications from potential candidates on a daily basis. Again, the types of information that your company would be interested in are easy to define in advance. You need to know about each candidate's education, previous work experience, and core skills. Wouldn't it be helpful if you could extract these bits of information automatically and put them in a single database? Information extraction in this case would help you save time on manually looking through various candidates' CVs.

> **Information extraction**
> *Information extraction* is often defined as a means of imposing structure on otherwise unstructured or only partially structured text.

Databases are one way to structure information. In the candidates' CVs case, you need to fill in specific information fields like `Education`, `Work Experience`, or `Skills` with the details extracted from CVs. One aspect of such documents as CVs and companies' portfolios that may help you in this task is that they typically follow a particular format. A typical CV would contain a section explicitly called `Education`. In the simplest case, it should be possible to automatically identify relevant sections like `Education` and extract the information from such sections in a CV; for instance, everything related to one's studies. Figure 4.3 visualizes this idea.

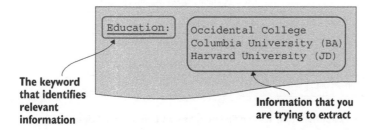

The keyword that identifies relevant information

Information that you are trying to extract

Figure 4.3 CVs are an example of semistructured documents. You may be able to identify where relevant information is located using keywords.

The problem is, not all documents of the same type will be structured in exactly the same way or even contain the same amount of information. To give you one example, imagine you undertook a project dealing with extraction of information about all famous personalities who have a Wikipedia page. A nice fact about Wikipedia is that it contains "infoboxes." An infobox is a fixed-format table that you can see in the upper right corner of a Wikipedia page that summarizes main facts about the subject of that page. This is a good start for your project—infoboxes for people typically contain their name, birthplace, date of birth, reasons they are famous, and so on. This is an example of semistructured information: infoboxes specify the names of the information fields (e.g., Born or Citizenship). However, here is the tricky bit: even though the information is structured, it is not always structured in the same way. Moreover, even the field with the same name might provide you with a different range of information. Figure 4.4 shows an example comparing bits of just two infoboxes, one for Albert Einstein (https://en.wikipedia.org/wiki/Albert_Einstein) and one for Barack Obama (https://en.wikipedia.org/wiki/Barack_Obama).

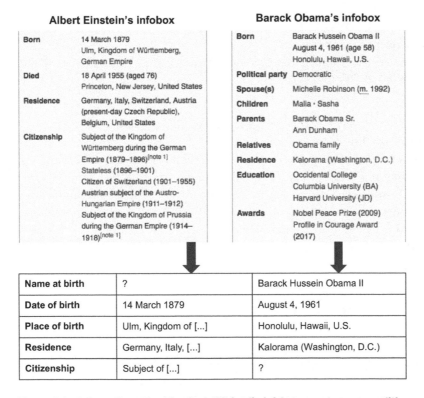

Figure 4.4   Information extraction from Wikipedia infoboxes on two personalities

For space reasons, these are not complete infoboxes. Albert Einstein's infobox contains additional information about his academic work, and Barack Obama's provides more details about his political career. We may expect to see such differences. After all, Albert Einstein was not involved in politics, while Barack Obama is not an academic. However, comparing even the basic information fields, we can see that the format used for the two personalities differs: the Born field contains the name given at birth to Barack Obama, but for Albert Einstein this information is missing. Albert Einstein's entry lists the details of his citizenship, but Barack Obama's doesn't, and so on. This shows that if you were to extract this information automatically, some fields in your database would end up being empty. In addition, even the fields that provide the same type of information sometimes use different formats for the same thing. Note the different date format used in Date of birth and the differences in Residence format—Albert Einstein has a list of countries where he resided, whereas Barack Obama shows only town and state. All these differences are hard to resolve without applying further NLP techniques and allowing more flexibility in the extraction process.

4.1.3 Case 3

You are working on a task not related to information extraction itself, but you expect that adding relevant information or insights would be crucial for the success of this task. Let's take the example with the human resources task of analyzing lots of CVs one step further. Imagine this is an HR department in a large company with multiple open positions. Each position has a job specification: it lists the requirements, job responsibilities, salary level, and so on. In effect, such job specs are themselves examples of semistructured information, so using a very similar approach, one can fill in another database, this time for open job positions. Now, rather than trying to manually match job specifications to the candidates' applications, why not automate this process and try to match relevant information fields between the two databases?

Here is another example: imagine you are a financial analyst in an investment company. It has been shown that certain types of political, financial, or business-related events reported on the news influence trends on stock markets. For instance, a report on a company CEO's death or patent disputes might negatively affect the company's stock prices, while news about a major acquisition or merger might result in a positive trend on the market. As an analyst, you might have to spend your time looking for such signals in the news and trying to connect them with the stock market movements, or you might use the power of data analysis and machine learning. In recent years, there has been a lot of research on the intersection of NLP and financial domains aimed at automatically predicting future stock market movements based on reported news (e.g., check http://mng.bz/N6QE). The key task here is to be able to extract the structured information (i.e., specific facts of interest) from free-formatted text (such as news articles). Apart from these examples, you might use information extraction to

- Learn which types of businesses are riskier and require higher insurance rates by extracting relevant facts from companies' portfolios. For example, there is a higher fire risk in a restaurant than in a convenience store, but a convenience store located in an unsafe neighborhood might have a higher risk for burglary.

- Learn which aspects of your product or service your customers are most happy and most unhappy about by extracting their opinions from customer feedback forms and discussion forums (e.g., customers might find the location of a hotel very pleasant while being unhappy about the cleaning services. See http://mng .bz/DgBy).

- Learn which factors contribute to higher sales of a particular product by extracting features from the product descriptions. For instance, detached houses with gardens might sell better than semidetached ones, while red cars might be more popular than yellow ones, and so on.

These three cases cover diverse areas and scenarios, and in particular examples described under case 3 require you to connect multiple pieces of information across domains, such as from text-based descriptions to financial data. In addition, in many of these cases, the power of NLP techniques combined with machine learning may help you discover new facts about your data and your task. For instance, you don't need to know in advance which aspects of your product or service may be successful or unsuccessful, as this is what NLP techniques help you find in the raw text data. What brings all these case studies together is the need to extract relevant bits of information from fully unstructured (e.g., free-formatted text) or partially structured (e.g., Wikipedia infoboxes) information. NLP techniques that will help you in this task are the subject of this chapter.

4.2   *Understanding the task*

Now that you've looked into some real-life applications of information extraction, it's time to start working on your own information extractor. Let's start with a scenario inspired by one of the use cases we just covered. Imagine that you work as a data analyst. You are planning to investigate how different types of events affect stock market movements. For instance, you have a hunch that the meetings between politicians and other personalities might be important signals for the market. You have a collection of recent news articles. Using information-extraction techniques, extract the facts about all the meetings between politicians and other personalities from this data.

How should you approach this task? Let's first define what represents the core information about the event here. In the meeting events, there are three indispensable bits of information: the *action* of meeting itself and *two participants*, each of whom can be a single person or a group of people. For example, a meeting might take place between two companies, or a president and their administration, and so on. We say that these bits are the core information because one cannot eliminate any of the three: if "X meets Y," saying "X meets," "X Y," or "meets Y" will be nonsensical, as it will raise questions like "Whom X meets?", "What do X and Y do?" and "Who meets Y?" In other words, only the phrase like "X meets Y" contains all the necessary information about who does what and who else is involved. Therefore, at the very least, you'd want to extract these three bits. Once this is done, you may explore the available information further and, if the text mentions it, find out about the time of the meeting ("X meets Y at noon" or "X meets Y on Friday"), the purpose ("X meets Y for coffee"), and so on. Now let's see how you can use Python to do this.

Suppose all the relevant phrases in text were of the form "X meets Y" or "X met Y" (let's ignore the difference between the two different forms of the verb here, *meets* and *met*), as in the title of the movie *When Harry Met Sally* . . . . In these cases, it is very clear who the two participants are and what happened (figure 4.5): the participants can be identified by the questions "Who met Sally?" and "Whom Harry met?" and the action can be identified by the questions like "What did Harry do?" or more generally "What happened with Harry and Sally?"

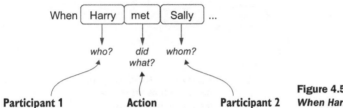

Figure 4.5   Analysis of the phrase *When Harry met Sally . . .*

Such cases are relatively easy to deal with. For instance, you can read the text word by word, and once you see a word, such as *met,* that is of interest to you in this application, you extract the previous word as participant1 and the next word as participant2. Listing 4.1 shows how to implement this in Python. In this code, you first provide the string information that contains met surrounded by the two participants. To extract the names of the participants from it, you split this string by whitespaces and store the result in a list words. Participant1 can be identified by its position immediately before the word met and participant2 by its position immediately after it. Printing the result should return Participant1 = Harry, Action = met, and Participant2 = Sally.

Listing 4.1   Code to extract names of the participants of a meeting

Provide the string information that contains "met" surrounded by the two participants.

Split this text by whitespaces and store the result in the list words.

Participant1 is the word preceding "met," and participant2 is the one following it.

```
information = "When Harry met Sally"
words = information.split()
print (f"Participant1 = {words[words.index('met')-1]}")
print (f"Action = met")
print (f"Participant2 = {words[words.index('met')+1]}")
```

This approach works well in this particular case; however, you're not done with the whole task yet, as the examples that you see in actual data will rarely be as straightforward as that. To begin with, the expressions for participants may span more than one word. For instance, the algorithm from listing 4.1 will fail on `Harry Jones met Sally` and on `Harry met Sally Smith` and `Harry Jones met Sally Smith`, as it will only return partial names for the participants. In addition, there are variations in the wording of the action itself. For official meetings between politicians or personalities, it is more common to say "X met with Y," so once again the algorithm from listing 4.1 is not flexible enough to return the correct names for the participants. Finally, the particular way in which the participants are mentioned in text may differ from the "X met Y" version. The order may be different and the distance between the participants in terms of intervening words may be larger. For instance, in `Sally, with whom Harry met on Friday`, the participants' names are still the same, but the order in which they are mentioned as well as the distance separating them are different. Figure 4.6 shows this idea.

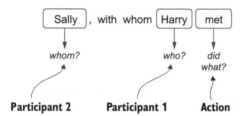

Figure 4.6   A different word order expressing the same idea as in figure 4.5.

Once again, the algorithm from listing 4.1 will not be able to deal with such cases. The problem with this simple code is that it relies too much on the particular template—order and format—which would work in some cases only. After all, we said that sometimes information comes in a semistructured format, so templates are useful in such cases. But in the general case, because language is very creative, there will be multiple ways to express the same idea using different formats, word order, and distance between the meaningful words, so what you actually need is an algorithm that can capture

- Which pieces of information are related to each other
- What role each of them plays
- How they are related

Figure 4.7 illustrates the requirements for such an algorithm.

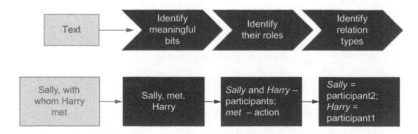

Figure 4.7   An information extraction algorithm in a nutshell

Ideally, your algorithm will take raw text as input and will return tuples consisting of two participants and the action of meeting as a representation of the core information. In the preceding example, (Harry, met, Sally) will be such a tuple. For example, suppose your algorithm can extract the essential information from sentences like "Donald Trump meets with the Queen at D-Day event," "The Queen meets with the Prime Minister every week," and so on, and convert it into a list of tuples of the form (participant1, action, participant2)—that is, [('Donald Trump', 'meets with', 'the Queen'), ('the Queen', 'meets with', 'the Prime Minister')]. Now you can use these tuples in all sorts of applications; for example, you can find answers to questions like "Whom does Donald Trump meet with?" Just consider that you can always convert this question to the same tuple representation ('Donald Trump', 'meets with', ?). Then this question becomes identical to asking, "What are participant2 entries in tuples where action='meet with' and participant1='Donald Trump'?" Figure 4.8 shows this process.

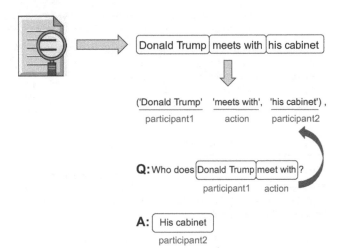

Figure 4.8 Both the input text and the question can be represented as tuples where each bit has a specific role.

The following listing shows how the search for the exact answer, when both questions and potential answers are represented as lists of tuples, becomes just a search on Python lists.

Listing 4.2 Code to search for the exact answer in Python list of tuples

```
meetings = [('Boris Johnson', 'meets with', 'the Queen'),
            ('Donald Trump', 'meets with', 'his cabinet'),
            ('administration', 'meets with', 'tech giants'),
            ('the Queen', 'meets with', 'the Prime Minister'),
            ('Donald Trump', 'meets with', 'Finnish President')
            ]
```

Shows a list of tuples (p1, act, p2) for participant1, action, and participant2 extracted from raw text

```
query = [p2 for (p1, act, p2) in meetings
         if p1=='Donald Trump']
print(query)
```

The resulting list should contain two entries: ['his cabinet', 'Finnish President']

Query looks for all p2 in tuples (p1, act, p2) where p1 ='Donald Trump'.

Obviously, meetings are mutual actions, so if participant1 meets with participant2, then participant2 also meets with participant1. On the news, the order will not always be exactly the same, so in listing 4.3, let's make a minor modification to the preceding code and extract the relevant other participant whenever either participant1 or participant2 is the personality of interest. As with code in listing 4.2, first a list of tuples (p1, act, p2) for participant1, action, and participant2 is extracted from raw text. However, this time the query looks for all p2 in tuples (p1, act, p2) where p1='the Queen' as well as for all p1 in tuples (p1, act, p2) where p2='the Queen'. As a result, you should get a list with two entries: ['the Prime Minister', 'Boris Johnson'].

Listing 4.3   Code to extract information about the other participant of a meeting

```
meetings = [('Boris Johnson', 'meets with', 'the Queen'),
            ('Donald Trump', 'meets with', 'his cabinet'),
            ('administration', 'meets with', 'tech giants'),
            ('the Queen', 'meets with', 'the Prime Minister'),
            ('Donald Trump', 'meets with', 'Finnish President')
           ]
```

Shows a list of tuples (p1, act, p2) for participant1, action, and participant2 extracted from raw text

```
query = [p2 for (p1, act, p2) in meetings if p1=='the Queen']
query += [p1 for (p1, act, p2) in meetings
          if p2=='the Queen']
print(query)
```

Expand the query on tuples (p1, act, p2) so that one of the participants is 'the Queen'.

The resulting list should contain two entries: ['the Prime Minister', 'Boris Johnson'].

Now let's see how you can extract such tuple representations from raw text.

4.3   *Detecting word types with part-of-speech tagging*

This section will show you how to extract the meaningful bits of information from raw text and how to identify their roles. Let's first look into why identifying roles is important.

4.3.1   *Understanding word types*

The first fact to notice about the preceding cases is that there is a conceptual difference between the bits of the expression like [Harry] [met] [Sally]: Harry and Sally both refer to people participating in the event, while met represents an action. When we read a text like this, we subconsciously determine the roles each word or expression plays along those lines. To us, words like Harry and Sally can only represent participants of an action but cannot denote an action itself, while words like met can only denote an action. This helps us get at the essence of the message quickly. We read Harry met Sally and we understand [Harry_WHO] [met_DID_WHAT] [Sally_WHOM].

This recognition of word types has two major effects: the first is that the straightforward, unambiguous use of words in their traditional functions helps us interpret the message. Funnily enough, this applies even when we don't really know the meaning of the words. Our expectations about how words are usually combined in sentences and what roles they usually play are so strong that when we don't know what a word means, such expectations readily suggest what it *might mean*—for example, we might not be able to exactly pin it down, but we still would be able to say if an unknown word means some sort of an object or some sort of an action. This "guessing game" would be familiar to anyone who has ever tried learning a foreign language and had to interpret a few unknown words based on other, familiar words in the context. Even if you are a native speaker of English and never tried learning a different language, you can still try playing a guessing game, such as with nonsensical poetry. Figure 4.9 shows an excerpt from "Jabberwocky," a famous nonsensical poem by Lewis Carroll (https://www .poetryfoundation.org/poems/42916/jabberwocky).

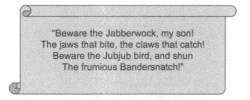

"Beware the Jabberwock, my son!
The jaws that bite, the claws that catch!
Beware the Jubjub bird, and shun
The frumious Bandersnatch!"

Figure 4.9   An example of text where the meaning of some words can only be guessed

Some of the words here would be familiar to anyone, but what do "Jabberwock", "Bandersnatch", and "frumious" mean? It would be impossible to give a precise definition for any of them simply because these words don't exist in English or any other language, so their meaning is anybody's guess. However, one can say with high certainty that "Jabberwock" and "Bandersnatch" are some sort of creatures, while "frumious" is some sort of quality (a blend of *fuming* and *furious*, according to Lewis Carroll). How do we make such guesses? You might notice that the context for these words gives us some clues: we know what "beware" means. It's an action, and as an action it requires some participants. One doesn't normally just "beware"; one needs to beware of someone or something. Therefore, we expect to see this someone or something, and here comes "Jabberwock". Another clue is given away by the word *the*, which normally attaches itself to objects (e.g., "the car") or creatures (e.g., "the dog"), so we arrive at an interpretation of "Jabberwock" and "Bandersnatch" being creatures. Finally, in "the frumious Bandersnatch" the only possible role for "frumious" is some quality because this is how it typically works in language (e.g., "the red car" or "the big dog").

The second effect that the expectations about the roles that words play have on our interpretation is that we tend to notice when these roles are ambiguous or somehow violated, because such violations create a discordance. That's why ambiguity in language is a rich source of jokes and puns, intentional or not. Here is one expressed in a news headline (figure 4.10).

```
Police help dog bite victim
```

Figure 4.10 An example of ambiguity in action

What is the first reading that you get? You wouldn't be the only one if you read this as "Police help a dog to bite a victim"; however, common sense suggests that the intended meaning is probably "Police help a victim with a dog bite" (i.e., someone who was bitten by a dog). News headlines are rich in ambiguities like this because they use a specific format aimed at packing the maximum amount of information in the shortest possible expression. This sometimes comes at a price, as both "Police help a dog to bite a victim" and "Police help a victim with a dog bite (that was bitten by a dog)" are clearer but longer than "Police help dog bite victim" that a newspaper might prefer to use. This ambiguity is not necessarily intentional, but it's easy to see how this can be used to make endless jokes.

What exactly causes confusion here? It is clear that "police" denotes a participant in an event, and "help" denotes the action. "Dog" and "victim" also seem to unambiguously be participants of an action, but things are less clear with "bite." *Bite* can denote an action, as in "Dog <u>bites</u> a victim" or the result of an action, as in "He has mosquito <u>bites</u>." In both cases, what we read is the word "bites," and it doesn't give away any further clues as to what it means. However, in "Dog bites a victim," it answers the question "What does the dog <u>do</u>?" and in "He has mosquito bites," it answers the question "<u>What</u> does he have?" Now, when you see a headline like "Police help dog bite victim," your brain doesn't know straightaway which path to follow:

- *Path 1*—"bite" is an action answering the question "What does one <u>do</u>?" → "Police help dog [bite$_{DO\_WHAT}$] victim"
- *Path 2*—"bite" is the result of an action answering the question "<u>What</u> happened?" → "Police help dog [bite$_{WHAT}$] victim."

Apart from the humorous effect of such confusions, ambiguity may also slow the information processing and lead to misinterpretations. Try solving exercise 4.1 to see how the same expression may lead to completely different readings. You can then check the answers at the end of the chapter.

Exercise 4.1
What interpretations do the following sentences have?

1 I can fish.
2 I saw her duck.

So far, we've been using the terminology quite frivolously. We've been defining words as denoting actions or people or qualities, but in fact there are more standard terms for that. The types of words defined by the different functions the words might fulfill are called *parts of speech,* and we distinguish between a number of such types:

- *Nouns*—Words that denote objects, animals, people, places, and concepts
- *Verbs*—Words that denote states, actions, and occurrences
- *Adjectives*—Words that denote qualities of objects, animals, people, places, and concepts
- *Adverbs*—Those for qualities of actions, states, and occurrences

Table 4.1 provides some examples and descriptions of different parts of speech.

Table 4.1 Examples of words of different parts of speech

Part of speech	What it denotes	Examples
Nouns	Objects, people, animals, places, concepts, time references	*car, Einstein, dog, Paris, calculation, Friday*
Verbs	Actions, states, occurrences	*meet, stay, become, happen*
Adjectives	Qualities of objects, people, animals, places, concepts	<u>red</u> *car,* <u>clever</u> *man,* <u>big</u> *dog,* <u>beautiful</u> *city,* <u>fast</u> *calculation*
Adverbs	Qualities of actions, states, occurrences	*meet* <u>recently</u>*, stay* <u>longer</u>*,* <u>just</u> *become, happen* <u>suddenly</u>
Articles	Don't have a precise meaning of their own but show whether the noun they are attached to is identifiable in context (it is clear what/whom the noun is referring to) or not (the noun hasn't been mentioned before)	*I saw* <u>a</u> *man*—This man is mentioned for the first time ("a" is an indefinite article). <u>The</u> *man is clever*—This suggests that it should be clear from the context which particular man we are talking about ("the" is a definite article).
Prepositions	Don't have a precise meaning of their own but serve as a link between two words or groups of words: for example, linking a verb denoting action with nouns denoting participants, or a noun to its attributes	*Meet* <u>on</u> *Friday*—Links action to time *Meet* <u>with</u> *administration*—Links action to participants *Meet* <u>at</u> *home*—Links action to location *A man* <u>with</u> *a hat*—Links a noun to its attribute

This is not a comprehensive account of all parts of speech in English, but with this brief guide, you should be able to recognize the roles of the most frequent words in text, and this suite of word types should provide you with the necessary basis for the implementation of your own information extractor.

Why do we care about the identification of word types in the context of information extraction and other tasks? You've seen that correct and straightforward identification of types helps information processing, while ambiguities lead to misunderstandings. This is precisely what happens with the automated language processing: machines, like humans, can extract information from text better and more efficiently if they can recognize the roles played by different words, while misidentification of these roles may lead to mistakes of various kinds. For instance, having identified that "Jabberwock" is a noun and some sort of a creature, a machine might be able to answer a question like "Who is Jabberwock?" (e.g., "Someone/something with jaws that bite and claws that catch"), while if a machine processed "I can fish" as "I know how to fish," it would not be able to answer the question "What did you put in cans?"

Luckily, there are NLP algorithms that can detect word types in text, and such algorithms are called *part-of-speech taggers* (or *POS taggers*). Figure 4.11 presents a mental model to help you put POS taggers into the context of other NLP techniques.

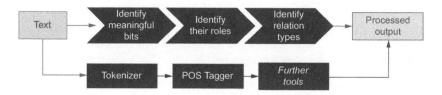

Figure 4.11   Mental model that visualizes the flow of information between different NLP components

As POS tagging is an essential part of many tasks in language processing, all NLP toolkits contain a tagger. You will often need to include it in your processing pipeline to get at the essence of the message. Let's now look into how this works in practice.

4.3.2   *Part-of-speech tagging with spaCy*

In the previous chapters, you used NLTK to process text data. This chapter will introduce spaCy, another very useful NLP library that you can put under your belt. There are several reasons to look into spaCy in this book:

- By the end of this book, you will have worked with many useful toolkits and libraries, including NLTK and spaCy. The two have their complementary strengths, so it's good to know how to use both.
- spaCy is an actively supported and fast-developing library that keeps up-to-date with the advances in NLP algorithms and models.
- There is a large community of people working with this library, so you can find code examples for various applications implemented with or for spaCy on their web page, as well as find answers to your questions on their GitHub page (see various projects using spaCy or developed for spaCy at https://spacy.io/universe).
- spaCy is actively used in industry.
- It includes a powerful set of tools particularly applicable to large-scale information extraction.

NOTE   To get more information on the spaCy library, check https://spacy.io. Installation instructions walk you through the installation process, depending on your operating system: https://spacy.io/usage#quickstart. Note that for this toolkit to work properly, you will also need to install models (e.g., en_core_web_sm, en_core_web_md, and en_core_web_lg) as explained on the web page.

Unlike NLTK, which treats different components of language analysis as separate steps, spaCy builds an analysis pipeline from the very beginning and applies this pipeline to text. Under the hood, the pipeline already includes a number of useful NLP tools that are run on input text without you needing to call on them separately. These tools include, among others, a tokenizer and a POS tagger. You simply apply the whole lot of tools with a single line of code calling on the spaCy processing pipeline, and then your program stores the result in a convenient format until you need it. This also ensures that the information is passed between the tools without you taking care of the input-output formats. Figure 4.12 shows spaCy's NLP pipeline, which we will discuss in more detail next.

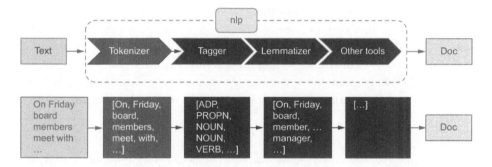

Figure 4.12   spaCy's processing pipeline with some intermediate results. The diagram follows closely the one in the spaCy's documentation (https://spacy.io/usage/processing-pipelines).

In the previous chapters, we've discussed that machines, unlike humans, do not treat input text as a sequence of sentences or words. For machines, text is simply a sequence of symbols. Therefore, the first step that we applied was splitting text into words. This step is performed by a tool called *tokenizer*. Tokenizer uses raw text as an input and returns a list of words as an output. For example, if you passed it a sequence of symbols like "Harry, who Sally met", it would return a list of tokens ["Harry", ",", "who", ...]. Next, we applied a stemmer that converted each word to some general form. This tool takes a word as an input and returns its stem as an output. For instance, a stemmer would return a generic, base form *meet* for both *meeting* and *meets*. A stemmer can be run on a list of words, where it would treat each word separately and return a list of correspondent stems. Other tools, however, will require an ordered sequence of words from the original text. We've seen that it's easier to figure out that Jabberwock is a noun if we know that it follows a word like *the*, so order matters for POS tagging. That means that each of the three tools—tokenizer, stemmer, POS tagger—requires a different type of input and produces a different type of output, so in order to apply them in sequence, we need to know how to represent information for each of them. That is what spaCy's processing pipeline does for you: it runs a sequence of tools and connects their outputs together.

In chapter 3, we mentioned two approaches to getting at the base form of a word. For information retrieval, we opted for stemming that converts different forms of a word to a common core. We said that it is useful because it helps connect words together on a larger scale, but it also produces nonwords: you won't always be able to find stems of the words (e.g., something like *retriev*) in a dictionary. An alternative to this tool is *lemmatizer*, which aims at converting different forms of a word to its base form that can actually be found in a dictionary; for instance, it will return a lemma *retrieval* that can indeed be found in a dictionary. Such base form is called *lemma*. In its processing pipeline, spaCy uses a lemmatizer (more information about spaCy's lemmatizer can be found on the API page: https://spacy.io/api/lemmatizer). Lemmatizers can be implemented in various ways, from lookup approaches, when the algorithm tries to match the word forms to the base dictionary forms; to rule-based approaches, when the algorithm applies a series of rules to process word forms; to machine learning, when the algorithm learns the correspondences from the language data; to a combination of all of the above. Although you can build your own lemmatizer, the benefit of relying on an out-of-the-box lemmatizer (e.g., from spaCy) is that such preprocessing tools are normally highly optimized in terms of speed and performance.

Lemmatization

Lemmatization refers to a preprocessing step, in which word forms are converted into their *lemmas*—the base forms that you would normally find in a dictionary.

The starting point for spaCy's processing pipeline is, as before, raw text. For example, "On Friday board members meet with senior managers to discuss future development of the company." The processing pipeline applies tokenization to this text to extract individual words: ["On", "Friday", "board", ...]. The words are then passed to a POS tagger that assigns POS tags like ["ADP", "PROPN", "NOUN", ...], to a lemmatizer that produces output like ["On", "Friday", ..., "member", ..., "manager", ...], and to a bunch of other tools, many of which we will discuss in this book.

NOTE In the scheme used by spaCy, prepositions are referred to as "adposition" and use a tag ADP. Words like *Friday* or *Obama* are tagged with PROPN, which stands for "proper noun" and is reserved for names of known individuals, places, time references, organizations, events, and such. For more information on the tags, see documentation at https://spacy.io/api/annotation and https://universaldependencies.org/u/pos/.

You may notice that the processing tools in figure 4.12 are comprised within a pipeline called nlp. As you will shortly see in the code, calling on nlp pipeline makes the program first invoke all the pretrained tools and then applies them to the input text in relevant order. The output of all the steps gets stored in a "container" called `Doc`. This contains a sequence of tokens extracted from input text and processed with the tools. Here is where spaCy implementation comes close to object-oriented programming: the tokens are represented as `Token` objects with a specific set of attributes. If you have done object-oriented programming before, you will hopefully see the connection soon. If not, here is a brief explanation. Imagine you want to describe a set of cars. All cars share the list of attributes they have: the car model, size, color, year of production, body style (e.g., sedan, convertible), type of engine, and so on. At the same time, such attributes as wingspan or wing area won't be applicable to cars—they relate to planes. So you can define a class of objects called `Car` and require that each object car of this class should have the same information fields; for instance, `car.model` should return the name of the model of the car, for example `car.model="Volkswagen Beetle"`, and `car.production_year` should return the year the car was made, such as `car.production_year="2003"`, and so on.

This is the approach taken by spaCy to represent tokens in text. After tokenization, each token (word) is packed up in an object `token` that has several attributes. For instance:

- `token.text` contains the original word itself.
- `token.lemma_` stores the lemma (base form) of the word.
- `token.pos_` is its part-of-speech tag.
- `token.i` is the index position of the word in text.
- `token.lower_` is the lowercase form of the word, and so on.

NOTE You may notice that some attributes are called on using an underscore, like `token.lemma_`. This is applicable when spaCy has two versions for the same attribute; for example, `token.lemma` returns an integer version of the lemma, which represents a unique identifier of the lemma in the vocabulary of all lemmas existing in English, while `token.lemma_` returns a Unicode (plain text) version of the same thing. See the description of the attributes on https://spacy.io/api/token.

The `nlp` pipeline aims to fill in the information fields like `lemma`, `pos`, and others with the values specific for each particular token. Since different tools within the pipeline provide different bits of information, the values for the attributes are added on the go. Figure 4.13 shows this process for the words "on" and "members" in the text "<u>On</u> Friday board <u>members</u> meet with senior managers to discuss future development of the company."

Now let's see how this is implemented in Python code. Listing 4.4 provides you with an example. In this code, you rely on spaCy's functionality. The `spacy.load` command initializes the `nlp` pipeline. The input to the command is a particular type of data (model) that the language tools were trained on. All models use the same naming conventions (`en_core_web_`), which means that it is a set of tools trained on

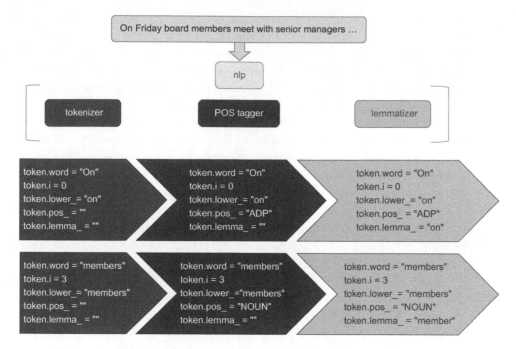

Figure 4.13   Processing of words "On" and "members" within the `nlp` pipeline

English web data; the last bit denotes the size of data the model was trained on, where sm stands for "small."

> **NOTE**   Check out the different language models available for use with spaCy at https://spacy.io/models/en. Small model (en_core_web_sm) is suitable for most purposes and is more efficient to upload and use. However, larger models like en_core_web_md (medium) and en_core_web_lg (large) are more powerful and some NLP tasks will require the use of such larger models. The models should be installed prior to running the code examples with spaCy. You can also install the models from within the Jupyter Notebook using the command !python -m spacy download en_core_web_sm.

Listing 4.4   Code exemplifying how to run spaCy's processing pipeline

```
import spacy          ◁──┤ Start by importing
                            the spaCy library.
nlp = spacy.load("en_core_web_sm")          ◁──
doc = nlp("On Friday board members meet with senior managers " +
          "to discuss future development of the company.")          ◁──

rows = []
rows.append(["Word", "Position", "Lowercase", "Lemma", "POS", "Alphanumeric",
     "Stopword"])          ◁──
```

The spacy.load command initializes the nlp pipeline.

Provide the nlp pipeline with input text.

Print the output in a tabular format and add a header to the printout for clarity.

```
for token in doc:
    rows.append([token.text, str(token.i), token.lower_,
                token.lemma_, token.pos_, str(token.is_alpha),
                str(token.is_stop)])
columns = zip(*rows)
column_widths = [max(len(item) for item in col)
                for col in columns]
for row in rows:
    print(''.join(' {:{width}} '.format(
        row[i], width=column_widths[i])
        for i in range(0, len(row))))
```

Add the attributes of each token in the processed text to the output for printing.

Python's zip function allows you to reformat input from row-wise representation to column-wise.

Calculate the maximum length of strings in each column to allow enough space in the printout.

Use the format functionality to adjust the width of each column in each row while printing out the results.

Once the `nlp` pipeline is initialized, you provide it with input text. The goal of this code is to print out individual words from the input together with all their linguistic attributes assigned by the `nlp` pipeline, so the code shows how you can print the output in a tabular format, add a header to the printout, add the attributes of each token in the processed text to the output, and reformat row-wise representation to column-wise representation using Python's `zip` function (check out documentation on Python's functions at https://docs.python.org/3/library/functions.html). As each column may contain strings of variable lengths, the code shows how you can calculate the maximum length of strings in each column to allow enough space in the printout. Finally, it shows how to print out the results using the `format` functionality to adjust the width of each column in each row (check out string formatting techniques in Python 3 at https://docs.python.org/3/library/string.html).

Table 4.2 shows the output that this code will return for some selected words from the input text. Please note that "..." is used to show that there is more output omitted for space reasons.

Table 4.2   Output from listing 4.4 presented in a table format.

Word	Position	Lowercase	Lemma	POS	Alphanumeric	Stopword
On	0	on	on	ADP	True	True
Friday	1	friday	Friday	PROPN	True	False
...	...	...	...	...	...	...
members	3	members	member	NOUN	True	False
...	...	...	...	...	...	...
to	8	to	to	PART	True	True
discuss	9	discuss	discuss	VERB	True	False
...	...	...	...	...	...	...
.	15	.	.	PUNCT	False	False

This output tells you

- The first item in each line is the original word from text. It is returned by `token.text`.
- The second is the position in text, which starts as all other indexing in Python from 0. This is identified by `token.i`.
- The third item is the lowercase version of the original word. You may notice that it changes the forms of `On` and `Friday`. This is returned by `token.lower_`.
- The fourth item is the lemma of the word, which returns `member` for `members` and `manager` for `managers`. Lemma is identified by `token.lemma_`.
- The fifth item is the part-of-speech tag. Most of the tags should be familiar to you by now. The new tags in this piece of text are `PART`, which stands for `particle` and is assigned to particle `to` in `to discuss`, and `PUNCT` for punctuation marks. POS tags are returned by `token.pos_`.
- The sixth item is a `True/False` value returned by `token.is_alpha`, which checks whether a word contains alphabetic characters only. This attribute is `False` for punctuation marks and some other sequences that don't consist of letters only, so it is useful for identifying and filtering out punctuation marks and other nonwords.
- Finally, the last, seventh item in the output is a `True/False` value returned by `token.is_stop`, which checks whether a word is in a stopwords list. This is a list of highly frequent words in language that you might want to filter out in many NLP applications, as they are likely to not be very informative. For example, articles, prepositions (e.g., *on*), and particles (e.g., *to*) will have their `is_stop` values set to `True` as you can see in the preceding output.

> ### Exercise 4.2
>
> Now run the code on other input texts. For example, use the "Jabberwocky" poem as an input. Does the code recognize the roles words play (i.e., their parts of speech) correctly?
>
> Attempt this exercise before checking the solutions in this chapter's Jupyter Notebook.

If you run the code from listing 4.4 on a text like "Jabberwocky," you will see that even though it contains non-English words, or possibly nonwords at all, this code can tell that "Jabberwock" and "Bandersnatch" are some creatures that have specific names (it assigns a tag `PROPN`, proper noun, to both of them), and that "frumious" is an adjective. How does it do that? Here is a glimpse under the hood of a typical POS tagging algorithm (figure 4.14).

We've said earlier that when we try to figure out what type of a word something like "Jabberwock" is, we rely on the context. In particular, the previous words are important to take into account. If we see *the*, chances that the next word is a noun or an

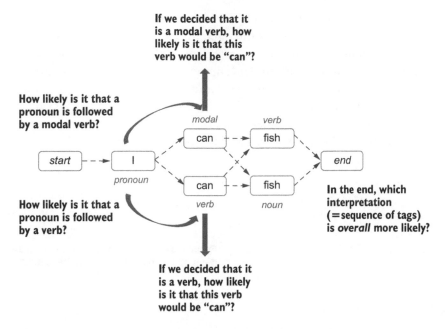

Figure 4.14   A glimpse under the hood of a typical POS tagging algorithm

adjective are very high, but a chance that we see a verb next is minimal—verbs shouldn't follow articles in grammatically correct English. Technically, we rely on two types of intuition: we use our expectations about what types of words typically follow other types of words, and we also rely on our knowledge that words like *fish* can be nouns or verbs but hardly anything else. We perform the task of word type identification in sequence. For instance, in the example from figure 4.14, when the sentence begins, we already have certain expectations about what type of word we may see first—quite often, it will be a noun or a pronoun (like *I*). Once we've established that it is very likely for a pronoun to start a sentence, we also rely on our intuition about how likely it is that such a pronoun will be exactly *I*. Then we move on and expect to see a particular range of word types after a pronoun. Almost certainly it should be a normal verb or a modal verb (as verbs denoting obligations like "should" and "must" or abilities like "can" and "may" are technically called). More rarely, it may be a noun (like "I, Jabberwock"), an adjective ("I, frumious Bandersnatch"), or some other part of speech. Once we've decided that it is a verb, we assess how likely it is that this verb is *can*; if we've decided that it is a modal verb, we assess how likely it is that this modal verb is *can*, and so on. We proceed like that until we reach the end of the sentence, and this is where we assess which interpretation we find overall more likely. This is one possible stepwise explanation of how our brain processes information, on which POS tagging is based.

The POS tagging algorithm, similarly, takes into account two types of expectations: (1) that a certain type of a word (like modal verb) may follow a certain other type of a word (like pronoun), and (2) that if it is a modal verb, such a verb may be *can*. These "expectations" are calculated using the data; for example, to find out how likely it is that a modal verb follows a pronoun, we calculate the proportion of times we see a modal verb following a pronoun in data among all the cases where we saw a pronoun. For instance, if we saw 10 pronouns like *I* and *we* in data before, and 5 times out of those 10 these pronouns were followed by a modal verb like *can* or *may* (as in "I can" and "we may"), what would the likelihood, or probability, of seeing a modal verb following a pronoun be? Figure 4.15 gives a hint on how probability can be estimated.

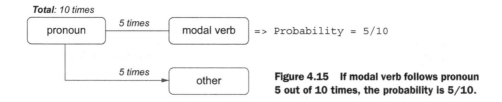

Figure 4.15   If modal verb follows pronoun 5 out of 10 times, the probability is 5/10.

We can calculate it as

```
Probability(modal verb follows pronoun) = 5 / 10
```

or in the general case

$$P(\text{modal verb follows pronoun}) = \frac{how\_often(\text{pronoun is followed by verb})}{how\_often(\text{pronoun is followed by any word, modal verb or not})}$$

NOTE   Recall, *P* is the notation for probability.

Similarly, to estimate how likely (or how probable) it is that the pronoun is *I*, we need to take the number of times we've seen the pronoun *I* and divide it by the number of times we've seen any pronouns in the data. So, if among those 10 pronouns that we've seen in the data before 7 were *I* and 3 were *we*, the probability of seeing a pronoun *I* would be estimated as shown in figure 4.16.

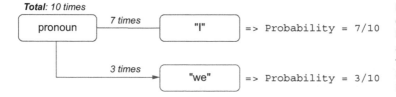

Figure 4.16   If 7 times out of 10 the pronoun is *I*, the probability of a word being *I* given that we know the POS of such a word is pronoun is 7/10.

We can calculate it as

```
Probability(pronoun being "I") = 7 / 10
```

or in the general case

$$P(\text{pronoun being "I"}) = \frac{how\_often(\text{we've seen a pronoun "I"})}{how\_often(\text{we've seen any pronoun, "I" or other})}$$

This description of probability estimation may remind you of the discussion from chapter 2. There, we used a similar approach to estimate probabilities.

In the end, the algorithm goes through the sequence of tags and words one by one and takes all the probabilities into account. Since the probability of each decision (i.e., of each tag and each word) is a separate component in the process, these individual probabilities are multiplied. So, to find out how probable it is that "I can fish" means "I am able / know how to fish," the algorithm calculates

$$
\begin{aligned}
P(\text{"I can fish" is "pronoun modal\_verb verb"}) = {}& P(\text{a pronoun starts a sentence}) \times \\
& P(\text{this pronoun is "I"}) \times \\
& P(\text{a pronoun is followed by a modal verb}) \times \\
& P(\text{this modal verb is "can"}) \times \\
& ... \times \\
& P(\text{a verb finishes a sentence})
\end{aligned}
$$

This probability gets compared with the probabilities of all the alternative interpretations, like "I can fish" = "I put fish in cans":

$$
\begin{aligned}
P(\text{"I can fish" is "pronoun verb noun"}) = {}& P(\text{a pronoun starts a sentence}) \times \\
& P(\text{this pronoun is "I"}) \times \\
& P(\text{a pronoun is followed by a verb}) \times \\
& P(\text{this verb is "can"}) \times \\
& ... \times \\
& P(\text{a noun finishes a sentence})
\end{aligned}
$$

In the end, the algorithm compares the calculated probabilities for the possible interpretations and chooses the one that is more likely (i.e., has higher probability).

4.4 Understanding sentence structure with syntactic parsing

In this section, you will learn how to automatically establish the types of relations that link meaningful words together.

4.4.1 Why sentence structure is important

Now you know how to detect which types the words belong to. Your algorithm from listing 4.4 is able to tell that in the sentence "On Friday, board members meet with senior managers to discuss future development of the company," words like *Friday, board*, *members*, and *managers* are more likely to be participants of some actions as they are nouns, while words like *meet* and *discuss* denote actions themselves as they are verbs. This brings you one step closer to solving the task; however, one bit is still missing: How are these words related to each other, and which of the potential participants are the actual participants of the action in question? That is, who met with whom?

We said before that in the simplest case, returning the words immediately before and immediately after the word that denotes the action works in some cases. However, in the sentence at hand, this doesn't work. POS tagging helps you identify that "meet (with)" is an action, but you would need to return "board members" and "senior managers" as the two participants. So far, the algorithm is only able to detect that *board*, *members*, and *managers* are nouns, while *senior* is an adjective, but it hasn't linked the words together yet. The next step is to identify that *board* and *members* together form one group of words and *senior* and *managers* another group, and these two groups represent the participants in the action as they are both directly related to the verb *meet (with)*. These are not the only words that are related to the action of meeting. In fact, the group of words "On Friday" tells us about the time of the meeting, and "to discuss future development of the company" tells us about the purpose. Ideally, we would like to be able to get all these bits of information. Figure 4.17 demonstrates this idea.

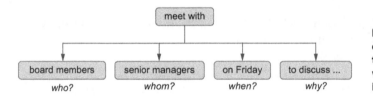

Figure 4.17 **All bits of information related to the action of meeting as we expect them to be identified by a parser**

In this representation, we put the action "meet (with)" at the center or *root* of the whole account of events because it makes it easier to detect other participants that are involved in this action and other bits of information related to it starting from the verb itself.

Word types that we've defined in the previous step help us identify the groups of words and their relations to the main action here. Normally, participants of an action are expressed with groups of words involving nouns, while locations and time references are usually attached to the verb with a preposition (like "<u>on</u> Friday" or "<u>at</u> the office"), and the purpose of the meeting would often be introduced using "to" and a further expression involving a verb (like "discuss"). We rely on such intuitions when we detect which words are related to each other, and machines use a similar approach as well.

Parser
The tool that helps identify which words are related to each other is called a *parser*.

Before we move on to using this tool in practice, here is an example illustrating why parsing and identification of relations between words is not a trivial task and may lead to misunderstandings, just like POS tagging before. This example comes from the joke by Groucho Marx, which went like this: "One morning I shot an elephant in my pajamas. How he got into my pajamas I'll never know." What exactly produces the humorous effect here? It is precisely the identification of relation links between the groups of words! Under one interpretation, "in my pajamas" is attached to "an elephant", and, in fact, because the two groups of words are next to each other in the sentence, this is a much easier interpretation to process, so our brain readily suggests it. However, common sense tells us that "in my pajamas" should be attached to "shot" and that it was "I" who was wearing the pajamas, not an elephant. The problem is that these components are separated from each other by other words, so based on the structure of the sentence, this is not the first interpretation that comes to mind. What adds to ambiguity here is the fact that prepositional phrases (the ones that start with prepositions like *in* or *with*) are frequently attached to nouns ("to a man$_{NOUN}$ with a hammer, everything looks like a nail") and to verbs ("drive$_{VERB}$ nails with a hammer"). Parsers, like humans, rely on the patterns of use in language and use the information about the types of words to identify how words are related to each other; however, it is by no means a straightforward task.

4.4.2 Dependency parsing with spaCy

We said before that as we are interested in the action expressed by a verb, like "meet (with)," and its participants, it is the action that we put at the center or at the root of the whole expression. Having done that, we start working from the verb at the root trying to identify which words or groups of words are related to this action verb. We also say that when the words are related to this verb, they *depend* on it. In other words, if the action is denoted by the verb *meet*, starting from this verb we try to find words that answer relevant questions: "*who* meet(s)?" → "board members," "meet with *whom*?" → "senior managers," "meet *when*?" → "on Friday," and so on. It's as if we are saying that "meet" is the most important, most indispensable, core bit of information here, and the other bits are *dependent* on it. After all, if it wasn't for the verb *meet*, the meeting wouldn't have taken place and there would be no need in extracting any further information! Similarly, in the expression "board members," the core bit is "members" as "board" only provides further clarifications ("*what type* of members?" → "board") but without "members" there would be no need in providing this clarifying information. Figure 4.18 visualizes dependencies between words in this sentence, where the arrows

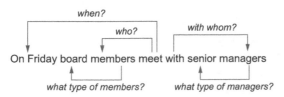

Figure 4.18 Flow of dependencies in "On Friday board members meet with senior managers." Arrows show the direction of the dependency, from the head to the dependent.

explicitly show the direction of relation—they go from the head to the dependent in each pair.

Putting verbs at the root of the whole expression as well as dividing words into groups of more important ones (such words are technically called *heads*) and the ones that provide additional information depending on the heads (such words are called *dependents*) is a convention adopted in NLP. The approach to parsing that relies on this idea is therefore called *dependency parsing*.

Exercise 4.3

To summarize, *heads* are words that express the core bit of information in a group of words; they are the indispensable ones. *Dependents* are the ones that attach themselves to heads providing additional clarifications or complementing the heads. Try to identify heads and dependents in the following expressions. Then you can compare your solutions to those provided at the end of the chapter.

1 senior managers
2 recently met
3 the government
4 talk to the government

Figure 4.12 shows the language-processing pipeline with a number of tools spaCy packs under the hood of `nlp`. Now it's time to add one more tool, parser, to the suite (figure 4.19).

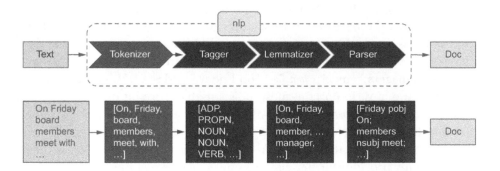

Figure 4.19   A larger suite of spaCy tools

Let's see how spaCy performs parsing on the sentence "On Friday, board members meet with senior managers to discuss future development of the company." First, let's identify all groups of words that may be participants in the meeting event; that is, let's identify all nouns and words attached to these nouns in this sentence. Such groups of words are called *noun phrases* because they have nouns as their heads. As before, you start by importing spaCy library and initializing the pipeline. Note, however, that if you are working in the same notebook, you don't need to do that more than once. Next, you provide the `nlp` pipeline with input text. You can access groups of words involving nouns with all related words (aka noun phrases) by `doc.noun_chunks`. Finally, the code shows how to print out the noun phrase itself (e.g., *senior managers*), followed by the head of the noun phrase (i.e., the head noun, which in this case is *managers*), the type of relation that links the head noun to the next most important word in the sentence (e.g., `pobj` relation links *managers* to *meet with*), and the next most important word itself (e.g., *with*). The code in listing 4.5 uses tabulation in this output.

Listing 4.5   Code to identify all groups of nouns and the way they are related to each other

```
import spacy

nlp = spacy.load("en_core_web_sm")
doc = nlp("On Friday, board members meet with senior managers " +
        "to discuss future development of the company.")

for chunk in doc.noun_chunks:
    print('\t'.join([chunk.text, chunk.root.text, chunk.root.dep_,
                    chunk.root.head.text]))
```

Start by importing spaCy library and initializing the pipeline.

Provide the nlp pipeline with input text.

You can access noun phrases by doc.noun_chunks.

Print out the phrase, its head, the type of relation to the next most important word, and the word itself.

Let's discuss these functions one by one:

- `doc.noun_chunks`—Returns the noun phrases, the groups of words that have a noun at their core and all the related words. For instance, "senior managers" is one such group here.
- `chunk.text`—Prints the original text representation of the noun phrase; for instance "senior managers".
- `chunk.root.text`—Identifies the head noun and prints it out. In "senior managers," it's "managers" that is the main word; it's the root of the whole expression.
- `chunk.root.dep_`—Shows what relates the head noun to the rest of the sentence. Which word is "managers" from "senior managers" directly related to? It is the preposition "with" (in "with senior managers"). Within this longer expression, "senior managers" is the object of the preposition, or prepositional object: `pobj`.
- `chunk.root.head.text`—Prints out the word the head noun is attached to. In this case, it is "with" itself.

To test your understanding, try to predict what this code will produce before running it or looking at the following output. The preceding code will identify the following noun phrases in this sentence:

```
Friday              Friday        pobj    On
board members       members       nsubj   meet
senior managers     managers      pobj    with
future development  development   dobj    discuss
the company         company       pobj    of
```

There are exactly five noun phrases in this sentence: `Friday`, `board members`, `senior managers`, `future development`, and `the company`. Figure 4.20 shows the chain of dependencies in this sentence, this time with the relation types assigned to the connecting arrows (see the description of different relation types at https://spacy.io/api/annotation#dependency-parsing and http://mng.bz/1oeV).

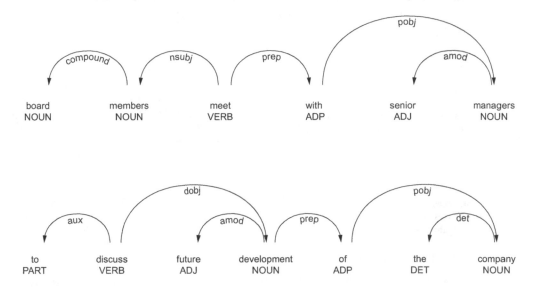

Figure 4.20 Chain of dependencies in "board members meet with senior managers to discuss future development of the company."

In this sentence, "Friday" directly relates to "on"—it's the prepositional object (`pobj`) of *on*. "Board members" has "members" as its head and is directly attached to "meet"—it's the subject, or the main participant of the action (denoted `nsubj`). "Senior members" has "members" as its head, and it's attached to "with" as `pobj`. "Future development" is a direct object (`dobj`) of the verb *discuss* because it answers the question "discuss *what?*" The head of this noun phrase is "development." Finally, "the company" has "company" as its head, and it depends on preposition *of*, thus the relation that links it to *of* is `pobj`.

spaCy allows you to visualize the dependency information and actually print the graphs like the ones in figure 4.20. The code from listing 4.6 will allow you to print out the visualization of the dependencies in input text and store it to a file. If you run it on the sentence "Board members meet with senior managers to discuss future development of the company," this file will contain exactly the graph from figure 4.20. In this code, you rely on the functionality of the spaCy's visualization tool `displacy` to visualize dependencies over the input text, where setting the argument `jupyter=False` tells the program to store the output to an external file, and `jupyter=True` to display it within the notebook. If you select to store the output to an external file, you'll need to import `Path`, which will help you define the location for the file to store the visualization. As the code in listing 4.6 shows, the file the output is stored to simply uses the words from the sentence in its name (e.g., `On-Friday-board-...svg`); however, you can change the file naming in the code. Alternatively, if you want to display the output directly in the Jupyter Notebook, you set `jupyter=True` and you don't need the last three lines of code.

Listing 4.6   Code to visualize the dependency information

Import spaCy's visualization tool displaCy.

Path helps you define the location for the file to store the visualization.

Use displaCy to visualize dependencies over the input text with appropriate arguments.

```
from spacy import displacy
from pathlib import Path

svg = displacy.render(doc, style='dep', jupyter=False)
file_name = '-'.join([w.text for w in doc if not w.is_punct]) + ".svg"
output_path = Path(file_name)
output_path.open("w", encoding="utf-8").write(svg)
```

The file the output is stored to simply uses the words from the sentence in its name.

This line writes the output to the specified file.

NOTE   To find out more about the displaCy tool, see https://spacy.io/usage/visualizers.

Why is it useful to know about the noun phrases and the way they are related to the rest of the sentence? It is because this way your algorithm learns about the groups of words, including nouns and attached attributes (i.e., noun phrases), that are potential participants in the action, and it also learns what these noun phrases are themselves attached to. For instance, note that "board members" is linked to "meet" directly—it is the main participant of the action, the *subject*. "Senior managers" is connected to the preposition "with," which itself is directly linked to the action verb "meet," so it would be possible to detect that "senior managers" is the second participant in the action within one small step.

Before we put these components together and identify the participants of the meeting action, let's iterate through the sentence and print out the relevant information about each word in this sentence. We print the word itself using `token.text`, the relation that links this word to its head using `token.dep_`, the head the word depends on using `token.head.text`, its head's part of speech using `token.head.pos_`, and finally all the dependents of the word iterating through the list of dependents extracted using `token.children`. The code in the following listing shows how you can do this.

Listing 4.7   Code to print out the information about head and dependents for each word

```
for token in doc:
    print(token.text, token.dep_,
          token.head.text, token.head.pos_,
          [child for child in token.children])
```

This code assumes that spaCy is imported and input text is already fed into the pipeline.

This code will produce the following output for the sentence "On Friday board members meet with senior managers to discuss future development of the company."

```
On          prep      meet     VERB    [Friday]
Friday      pobj      On       ADP     []
,           punct     meet     VERB    []
board       compound  members  NOUN    []
members     nsubj     meet     VERB    [board]
meet        ROOT      meet     VERB    [On, ,, members, with, discuss, .]
...
```

This output shows that Friday is the prepositional object of On, which itself has an adposition (ADP) POS tag. Friday doesn't have any dependents, so an empty list [] is returned. Board is dependent on noun members, but it also has no further dependencies itself. Members is a subject of the verb meet and has board as a single dependent. Meet, in its turn, doesn't depend on any other word—it's the ROOT of the whole sentence, and it has a number of dependents, including On (time reference, On Friday), members (head of the subject board members, which is the main participant of the action expressed with the verb meet), with (introducing second participant with senior members), and discuss (indicating the purpose of the meeting, "to discuss the future developments . . .").

4.5   *Building your own information extraction algorithm*

Now let's put all these components together and run your information extractor on a list of sentences to extract only the information about who met with whom. Based on what you've done so far, you need to implement the steps outlined in figure 4.21.

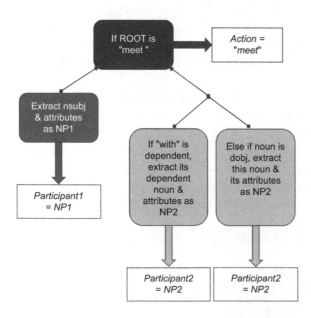

Figure 4.21 Extraction of participant1 and participant2 if the action verb is meet.

To summarize, this means that you need to

1 Identify sentences where "meet" is the main verb (i.e., the ROOT of the sentence).

2 Extract dependents of this verb using `token.children`.

3 Identify `participant1` of the action. It will be a noun linked to the verb with `nsubj` relation.

4 Add all the attributes this noun has (e.g., "board" for "members") to build a noun phrase (NP). This is `participant1`.

5 If the verb has a dependent preposition "with" (e.g., "meet <u>with</u> managers"), extract the noun dependent on "with" together with all its attributes. These will constitute `participant2`.

6 Otherwise, if the verb doesn't have a preposition "with" attached to it but has a directly related noun (as in "meet managers"), extract this noun and its attributes as `participant2`. The directly related noun will be attached to the verb with `dobj` relation.

Now, let's implement this in Python and apply the code to the sentence "On Friday, board members meet with senior managers to discuss future development of the company." Note that if you are working in the same notebook and used this sentence as input before, all the processing outputs are stored in container `Doc`, and you don't need to redefine it. Since this sentence contains preposition "with," let's start with implementing the approach that extracts the noun dependent on "with" together with its attributes and identifies this noun phrase as `participant2`. Listing 4.8 shows this implementation. The code shown here assumes that spaCy is imported and input text is already fed into the pipeline. First, you check that the ROOT of the sentence is a verb with the base form (lemma) "meet"—this verb expresses the action itself. Next, you extract the list of all dependents of this verb using `token.children`. To identify `participant1` of the action, you look for a noun that is the subject of the action verb linked to it with `nsubj` relation. This noun, together with its attributes (`children`), expresses `participant1`. After that, you check if the verb has preposition "with" as one of its dependents and extract the noun that is dependent on this preposition together with its attributes. This is `participant2` of the action. Finally, you print out the results.

> **Listing 4.8 Code to extract participants of the action**

This code assumes that spaCy is imported and input text is already fed into the pipeline.

Check that the ROOT of the sentence is a verb with the base form (lemma) "meet."

This verb expresses the action itself.

Extract the list of all dependents of this verb using token.children.

```
for token in doc:
    if (token.lemma_=="meet" and token.pos_=="VERB"
        and token.dep_=="ROOT"):
        action = token.text
        children = [child for child in token.children]
        participant1 = ""
        participant2 = ""
```

```
                for child1 in children:
                    if child1.dep_ =="nsubj":
                        participant1 = " ".join(
                            [attr.text for attr in child1.children]
                        ) + " " + child1.text
                    elif child1.text=="with":
                        action += " " + child1.text
                        child1_children = [child for child in child1.children]
                        for child2 in child1_children:
                            if child2.pos_ == "NOUN":
                                participant2 = " ".join(
                                    [attr.text for attr in child2.children]
                                ) + " " + child2.text
            print (f"Participant1 = {participant1}")
            print (f"Action = {action}")
            print (f"Participant2 = {participant2}")
```

Find the noun that is the subject of the action verb using nsubj relation.

Check if the verb has preposition "with" as one of its dependents.

Extract the noun that is dependent on this preposition together with its attributes.

Print out the results.

For the input text "On Friday, board members meet with senior managers to discuss future development of the company," this code will correctly return the following output:

```
Participant1 = board members
Action = meet with
Participant2 = senior managers
```

However, what if we provide it with more diverse sentences? For example:

- "Boris Johnson met with the <u>Queen</u> last week." "Queen" is a proper noun, so its tag is PROPN rather than NOUN. Let's make sure that proper nouns are also covered by the code. Note that *met* is the past form of "meet," and since your algorithm uses lemma (base form) of the word, it will be correctly identified here.
- "Donald Trump meets <u>the Queen</u> at Buckingham Palace." Note that "the Queen" is attached to the verb "meet" as dobj. Let's make sure your code covers this case too.

Listing 4.9 shows how to add these two modifications to the algorithm. First, you provide your code with a diverse set of sentences. Note that all but the last sentence contain the verb "meet" and are relevant for your information extraction algorithm. Then you define a function extract_information to apply all the steps in the information extraction algorithm. Note that the code within this function is very similar to listing 4.8. One of the differences is that it applies to participants expressed with proper nouns (PROPN), as well as common nouns (NOUN). Another modification is that it adds the elif branch that covers the direct object (dobj) case. In the end, you apply extract_information function to each sentence and print out the actions and their participants.

Listing 4.9   Code for information extractor

```
sentences = ["On Friday, board members meet with senior managers " +
            "to discuss future development of the company.",
            "Boris Johnson met with the Queen last week.",
```

Provide your code with a diverse set of sentences. ⊢▷

```
                              "Donald Trump meets the Queen at Buckingham Palace.",
                              "The two leaders also posed for photographs and " +
                              "the President talked to reporters."]
```

```
        def extract_information(doc):
            action=""
            participant1 = ""
            participant2 = ""
            for token in doc:
                if (token.lemma_=="meet" and token.pos_=="VERB"
                    and token.dep_=="ROOT"):
                    action = token.text
                    children = [child for child in token.children]
                    for child1 in children:
                        if child1.dep_=="nsubj":
                            participant1 = " ".join(
                                [attr.text for attr in child1.children]
                            ) + " " + child1.text
                        elif child1.text=="with":
                            action += " " + child1.text
                            child1_children = [child for child in child1.children]
                            for child2 in child1_children:
                                if (child2.pos_ == "NOUN"
                                    or child2.pos_ == "PROPN"):
                                    participant2 = " ".join(
                                        [attr.text for attr in child2.children]
                                    ) + " " + child2.text
                        elif (child1.dep_=="dobj"
                            and (child1.pos_ == "NOUN"
                                or child1.pos_ == "PROPN")):
                            participant2 = " ".join(
                                [attr.text for attr in child1.children]
                            ) + " " + child1.text
            print (f"Participant1 = {participant1}")
            print (f"Action = {action}")
            print (f"Participant2 = {participant2}")

        for sent in sentences:
            print(f"\nSentence = {sent}")
            doc = nlp(sent)
            extract_information(doc)
```

Define a function to apply all the steps in the information extraction algorithm. ◁

Extract participants expressed with proper nouns (PROPN) and common nouns (NOUN). ⊢▷

Add the elif branch that covers the direct object (dobj) case. ◁⊣

Apply extract_information function to each sentence and print out the actions and participants. ◁⊣

The preceding code will identify the following actions and participants in each sentence from the set:

```
Sentence = On Friday, board members [...]
Participant1 = board members
Action = meet with
Participant2 = senior managers

Sentence = Boris Johnson met with [...]
Participant1 = Boris Johnson
Action = met with
Participant2 = the Queen
```

```
Sentence = Donald Trump meets [...]
Participant1 = Donald Trump
Action = meets
Participant2 = the Queen

Sentence = The two leaders also [...]
Participant1 =
Action =
Participant2 =
```

Note that the code correctly identifies the participants of the meeting event in each case and returns nothing for the last sentence that doesn't describe a meeting event.

Congratulations! You have built your first information extraction algorithm. Now try to use it in practice.

Exercise 4.4

Apply the information extraction algorithm to your own data to extract the information about all meetings that took place between different participants. Alternatively, apply it to a different type of events expressed with verbs other than "meet."

Summary

- Information extraction is a useful NLP task that helps you impose structure on fully unstructured information or partially structured information. There are multiple scenarios where this is useful, including answering specific questions based on the information provided in the text, filling in a database with the relevant details extracted from text, extracting structured data for further applications, and so on.
- To extract the information from raw text, you need to know which bits are relevant to your information need and how they are related to each other. Bits that are relevant for the description of an event consist of the words defining the action and the words defining its participants.
- Actions, occurrences, and states are typically defined by verbs, and participants are typically defined by nouns. The types of words defined by their typical roles are called *parts of speech*, and the task addressing identification of word types is called *part-of-speech tagging* (or *POS tagging*).
- Since POS tagging is an essential component of many NLP tasks, NLP libraries and toolkits usually include a POS tagger. An industrial-strength NLP library called spaCy performs many processing operations at once and packs all the tools under a single NLP pipeline.
- Nouns tend to attach further attributes (e.g., "fast car"). Such groups of nouns with all related attributes are called *noun phrases*. In addition, nouns that name personalities are called *proper nouns*, and they often come as a sequence of

nouns rather than a single one. Such sequences are also called *noun phrases.* When you are trying to identify participants of events, it is noun phrases rather than single nouns that you are looking for.

- Parser helps you identify relations between all words in a sentence. It is an NLP tradition to consider that the core—the root—of the sentence is the verb that denotes the main action the sentence is talking about. Other components of the sentence depend on the verb. Therefore, this approach is called *dependency parsing.*
- Within dependency parsing, we are talking about the main words, heads of the expression, and their dependents.

Solutions to miscellaneous exercises

Exercise 4.1

These are quite well-known examples that are widely used in NLP courses to exemplify ambiguity in language and its effect on interpretation.

1 "I" certainly denotes a person, and "can" certainly denotes an action. However, "can" as an action has two potential meanings. It can denote ability "I can" = "I am able to" or the action of putting something in cans (when a word has several meanings, it is called lexical ambiguity). "Fish" can denote an animal as in "freshwater fish" (or a product as in "fish and chips"), or it can denote an action as in "learn to fish." In combination with the two meanings of can, these can produce two completely different readings of the same sentence: either "I can fish" means "I am able/I know how to fish" or "I put fish in cans."

2 "I" is a person and "saw" is an action, and "duck" may mean an animal or an action of ducking. In the first case, the sentence means that I saw a duck that belongs to her, while in the second it means that I witnessed how she ducked— once again, completely different meanings of what seems to be the same sentence (figure 4.22)!

Figure 4.22 Ambiguity might result in some serious misunderstanding.

Exercise 4.2

Try working on your own solution before checking the code on the book's GitHub page (https://github.com/ekochmar/Getting-Started-with-NLP).

Exercise 4.3

1 In "senior managers," "managers" is the main bit and "senior" provides further clarification. We ask "What type of managers?" → "senior," so "managers" is the head and "senior" is the dependent.

2 In "recently met," "met" is the main bit and "recently" provides further information about the action. We can ask "Met when?" → "recently," so "met" is the head and "recently" is the dependent.

3 In "the government," "government" is the main bit and "the" tells us that it is some particular government identifiable from the context. "Government" is the head and "the" is the dependent.

4 In "talk to the government," the overall head is "talk"—this is the action that we start with. "Talk" directly attaches "to," so "to" is dependent on the head "talk." "To" in its turn attaches "government," so "to" is the head and "government" is the dependent in this pair. Finally, as before, "the" is the dependent of the head "government" within the pair of words "the government." Figure 4.23 visualizes this chain of heads and dependents where the arrows explicitly show the direction of relation as before.

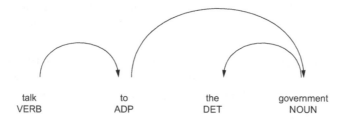

Figure 4.23   The full chain of dependencies in "talk to the government." Arrows show the direction of the dependency, from the head to the dependent.

5
Author profiling as a machine-learning task

This chapter covers

- Implementing your user profiling algorithm
- Exploring NLP techniques with NLTK and spaCy
- Introducing scikit-learn
- Applying `Decision Trees` machine-learning classifier

In this and the next chapter, you will build your own algorithm that can identify the profile or even the precise identity of an anonymous author of a text based solely on their writing. As you will find out over the next two chapters, this task brings together several useful NLP concepts and techniques that were introduced in the previous chapters. You've learned that

- Tokenizers can be applied to split text into individual words.
- Words may be meaningful, or they may simply express some function (e.g., linking other, meaningful words together). In this case, they are called *stopwords*, and for certain NLP applications you will need to remove them.
- Words are further classified into nouns, verbs, adjectives, and so on, depending on their function. Each of such classes is assigned a part-of-speech tag, which can be identified automatically with a POS tagger.

- Words of different functions play different roles in a sentence, and these roles and relations between words with different functions can be identified with a dependency parser.
- Words are formed of lemmas and stems, and you can use lemmatizers and stemmers to detect those.

You have also learned how to use two NLP toolkits to perform these processing steps: NLTK was introduced in chapter 2 and spaCy in chapter 4. This chapter will further exemplify the routines with each of these toolkits and will show how to combine the two.

Chapter 2 also presented you with an example of an NLP task, spam filtering, that is traditionally addressed using machine-learning approaches. Figure 5.1 shows the machine-learning process from chapter 2.

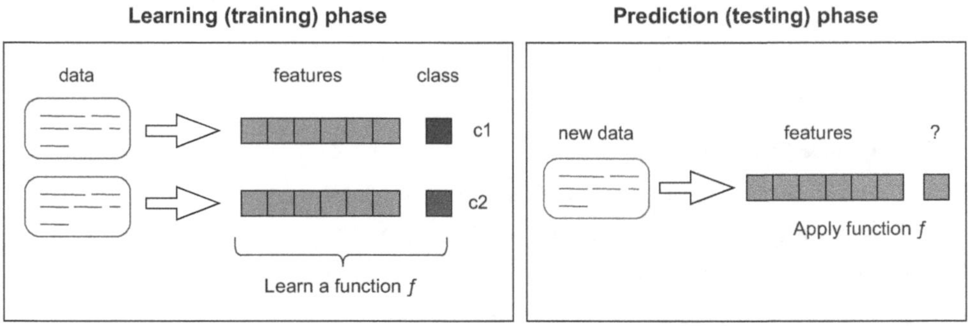

Learning (training) phase   **Prediction (testing) phase**

data   features   class   new data   features   ?

c1

c2

Learn a function *f*   Apply function *f*

Figure 5.1   Text classification using a machine-learning approach

In spam detection, texts are coming from two different sources called *classes*—spam and ham (not spam). Each of these classes can be characterized with a distinctive use of words that helps users tell whether an incoming email is spam or ham, should they happen to read it. In a similar fashion, machines can be taught to distinguish between the two classes based on the words used in spam messages and filter out "bad" emails before they reach the user, thus saving the user precious time and effort.

Machine learning provides you with a whole set of powerful algorithms that can learn from data how to distinguish between classes or how to make predictions; therefore, such algorithms are widely used in NLP. As soon as the task at hand can be presented as a clear set of classes, which can each be characterized with a set of distinguishable properties, you can apply a machine-learning classifier to automatically assign instances to the relevant classes. The set of distinguishable characteristics that uniquely describe each of the classes are called *features* in the machine-learning context, and the process of selecting which type of information represents such useful distinguishable characteristics is called *feature engineering*.

This chapter will show you how to perform feature engineering for an NLP task. It will specifically focus on building a machine-learning (ML) pipeline, following all the steps from data preparation to results evaluation. Chapter 2 relied on the use of a specific ML classifier, Naïve Bayes. Since Naïve Bayes is widely used in practice, many toolkits, including NLTK, have an implementation of this algorithm ready for your use. However, even though NLTK provides you with implementation of some machine-learning algorithms, it is primarily an NLP toolkit. Therefore, in this and the next chapters you will learn how to use an ML toolkit, scikit-learn, which will provide you with a useful set of resources and techniques to apply in an ML project.

As we said, many NLP tasks can be represented as ML tasks. You need three components in place:

- You should be able to define the task in terms of distinguishable classes (e.g., spam versus ham).
- You should be able to tell the machine which types of information are good to use as features (e.g., words in an email are often predictive of its class).
- You should have some labeled data at hand. For example, you may have some previously received normal as well as spam emails, or there may exist some open-source dataset like Enron that we used in chapter 2.

This setup works well for *supervised machine-learning* algorithms, where we know what the classes are and can provide the machine with the data to learn about these classes. In this chapter, we will address a task that is well suited for both practicing your NLP skills and learning how to build an ML project—*user* or *author profiling*. This task helps you identify the profile of an author of a text based solely on their writing. Such a profile may cover any range of characteristics, including age, level of education, and gender, and in some cases may even help you detect the precise identity of an anonymous writer.

5.1 Understanding the task

Let's start with a scenario. Imagine that you have received an anonymous message, and you are certain that the anonymous sender is actually someone from your contacts list, with whom you have previously exchanged correspondence. Using NLP and ML techniques and NLTK and spaCy libraries that you've learned about in the previous chapters, build an algorithm that will help you identify who from your contacts list is the anonymous author, based solely on this piece of writing. To help you with this task, you can use all the previous messages you ever received from any of your contacts. If this algorithm cannot identify the author uniquely, can it at least help you narrow down the set of "suspects"?

It turns out that, if you have a set of texts written previously by each of your contacts, you can train a machine-learning algorithm to detect which of the potential authors the particular piece of writing belongs to. Impressive as it may seem, it relies on the idea that each of us has a distinctive writing style. For example, have you ever noticed that you tend to use *however* rather than *but* (like I do)? Or perhaps you use expressions like *well, sort of,* or *you know* a lot? Have you, perhaps, noticed that you normally use longer and more elaborate sentences than most of your friends? All of these are peculiar characteristics that can tell a lot about the author and may even give away the author's identity. Such writing habits are also behind personalization strategies. For instance, you might notice that a predictive keyboard on your smartphone adapts to your choice of words and increasingly suggests words and phrases that you would prefer to use anyway. Now let's look more closely into two use cases for the task of user/ author profiling.

5.1.1   *Case 1: Authorship attribution*

Perhaps one of the most famous cases for authorship attribution is that of the *Federalist Papers*, which are a collection of 85 articles and essays written by Alexander Hamilton, James Madison, and John Jay in 1787–1788 under the pseudonym "Publius" to promote the ratification of the U.S. Constitution (https://en.wikipedia.org/wiki/The_Federalist_Papers). It is hard to underestimate the importance of these articles for America's history, yet at the time of publication, the authors of these articles preferred to hide their identities. The work of the American historian Douglass Adair in 1944 provided some of the most widely accepted assignments of authorship in this collection, and it has been corroborated in 1964 by computational analysis of word choice and writing style. However, authorship of as many as 12 out of 85 essays in this collection is still disputed by some scholars, which shows that this is by no means an easy task!

Another famous example of authorship attribution studies is the contested authorship of the works by William Shakespeare (http://mng.bz/lx8j). For some time, a theory has been circulating suggesting that the works authored under the name of Shakespeare cover topics and use a writing style that are incompatible with the social status and the level of education that the claimed author, William Shakespeare from Stratford-upon-Avon, possessed. The alternative authorship suggestions included "Shakespeare" being a pseudonym used by some other poet or even a whole group of authors at the time, with William Shakespeare himself simply acting as the cover for this true author or authors. Here, again, computational analysis has been used to prove that the writing style and the word choice in the works authored by William Shakespeare are actually consistent with his identity.

These examples provide you with the historical perspective for the task, but they don't tell you much about the modern application of this task. How is authorship attribution used these days? For a start, it has applications in security and forensics, where there is often a need to detect whether a particular individual is the author of a particular piece of writing, or whether a particular individual is who they claim they are, based on their writing. Another area in which authorship attribution is of help is fake news—a problem that has recently attracted much attention and that is concerned with an attempt of some individuals to spread misinformation, often in order to sway public opinion. As you may expect, authorship attribution is particularly challenging on the web, where the identity of the users can be easily hidden, so this is where computational methods of detecting the potential authors or detecting whether a set of posts are produced by the same author are of most help.

5.1.2 Case 2: User profiling

We all have our particular writing styles and our preferred words that we tend to use more often than other people around us. What explains such phenomena? A lot of it comes from our background: our upbringing, education, profession, and environment have a significant effect on how we speak and write. In addition, words come in and out of fashion, so our word choice can also give away our age. Figure 5.2 shows how the usage of the words *awesome, cool,* and *tremendous* changed over time across a range of books available through Google Books. Note how around 1940 both *tremendous* and *cool* were used with approximately equal frequency, but after then the use of *tremendous* has been declining, while that of *cool* has been on the rise since 1970s, which can be partially explained by it acquiring a new meaning similar to *tremendous* and *awesome* themselves.

> **NOTE** You can explore changes in the word usage with the interactive Google Books Ngram Viewer interface: https://books.google.com/ngrams/. For more information on how to use the interface, check https://books.google.com/ngrams/info.

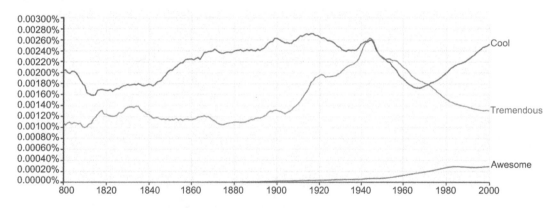

Figure 5.2 **Change in word frequencies between years 1800 and 2000 according to Google Books**

Recent research shows that a number of characteristics, including age, gender, profession, social status, and similar traits can be predicted from the way one tweets. How can this be of further use? Apart from the word choice, people of different social groups have different preferences along various dimensions. Suppose you are providing a particular service or product to a wide and diverse set of users. You don't collect any personal information about them, but you have access to some of their writing (e.g., a set of reviews about your product or a forum where they discuss their experience). Naturally, they may have different opinions about the product or service based on their personal characteristics. But equipped with an algorithm that can distinguish between groups of users of different age, gender, social status, and so on based on their writing, you can further adapt the product or service you provide to the needs of each of these groups.

NOTE There are multiple publications around these topics. Examples include Preotiuc-Pietro et al. (2015), "Studying User Income Through Language, Behaviour, and Affect in Social Media" (http://mng.bz/BMX8); Preotiuc-Pietro et al. (2015), "An analysis of the User Occupational Class through Twitter Content (www.aclweb.org/anthology/P15-1169.pdf); and Flekova et al. (2016), "Exploring Stylistic Variation with Age and Income on Twitter" (www.aclweb.org/anthology/P16-2051.pdf), among others.

Now, how should you approach this task computationally? We have said in the beginning of this chapter that user profiling is a good example of an ML task, so let's define the components: the *classes*, the *features*, and the *data*.

Exercise 5.1

- What classes are there in the authorship attribution case?
- What classes should you distinguish between in the user profiling case?

(Solution can be found at the end of this chapter.)

Figure 5.3 illustrates the two cases of authorship attribution and user profiling.

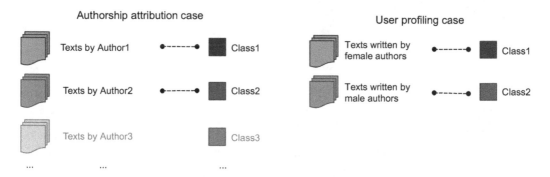

Figure 5.3 **In the authorship attribution case, each author represents a separate class; in the user profiling case, each group of users (e.g., female authors and male authors) forms a separate class.**

Exercise 5.2

Next comes the question of features—what makes one's writing style so distinctive? (Solution can be found at the end of this chapter.)

Finally, you need data. In this case, data refers to a collection of texts that are appropriately labeled with the names of the authors who produced them for authorship attribution, or with the groups of users for user profiling. Then you can apply an ML classifier of your choice and make it learn to distinguish between different authors or groups of authors based on their writing and types of characteristics that you identified for the algorithm as features.

It's now time to define a mental model for the ML pipeline that you are going to build in this chapter. Figure 5.4 presents the mental model.

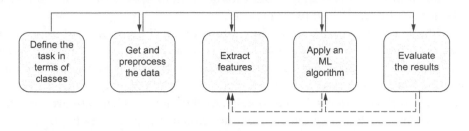

Figure 5.4   Mental model for a supervised machine-learning classification task

We have discussed the first three steps of the pipeline so far. You know how to define the classes and the features and know what the data should contain. This chapter will focus on more informed feature engineering for the task of authorship attribution. In addition, the last two steps in figure 5.4 suggest that once you have extracted features and applied an ML algorithm, you may get back to the feature extraction step and expand the feature set with new types of features. You can also do so and redefine the feature set as well as the ML classifier once you have evaluated the results.

So far, you have looked into one particular example of an ML algorithm applied to an NLP task—Naïve Bayes using NLTK implementation. In this chapter, we will explore in more detail what other classifiers are available for your use, how to apply them to language-related data, and crucially, how to evaluate whether a classifier of your choice with a specific set of features is doing a good job.

5.2   *Machine-learning pipeline at first glance*

Let's now go through the steps in this pipeline one by one. We will start with the question of what represents a good dataset for this task, and then we will proceed with building a *benchmark machine learning model*—something that is relatively straightforward and easy to put together. This benchmark model will set up an important point of comparison for you. Any further model with a different set of features or a different algorithm will have to beat the results of the benchmark model; otherwise, you will know that the task can be easily solved with the algorithm that you've tried first. Finally, we will explore the results and see how the pipeline can be improved to achieve increasingly better results.

5.2.1   *Original data*

In any machine-learning task, data plays a crucial part. Whatever algorithm you are using, the quality of the data decides whether the algorithm will be able to learn how to solve the task. That is, if the data is of poor quality or does not fairly represent the task at hand, it is hard to expect any machine-learning algorithm of any level of sophistication to be able to learn reliably from such data. This is not surprising, if you consider the following: the best learning algorithm known is the human brain, yet even the human brain can get confused if it is provided with conflicting and contradicting evidence. So, for both human learning and machine learning, it is important to define the task from the start and to provide some illustrative examples for the instances of different classes.

Whether you are working on the authorship attribution or on the user profiling variety of the task, good data is not easy to come by. Ideally, you want a set of texts written by different authors or separate sets of authors reliably identified as such. Let's start with a simpler case. Let's use a collection of literary works produced by well-known authors to address the authorship attribution task. There are two clear benefits to that: First, such an experiment does not violate any privacy rights of any users, as famous writers have clearly claimed their authorship on these pieces of writing. Second, texts by famous authors are abundant in quantity, so we can reliably find enough data representing each author (i.e., each class). Exercise 5.3 provides you with an example of the task we will try to solve in this chapter.

Exercise 5.3
Look at the excerpts in figure 5.5 and try to guess who the author of each one of these excerpts is. (Solution can be found at the end of this chapter.)

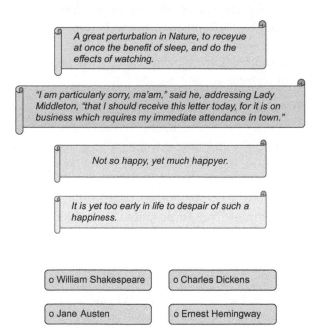

Figure 5.5   **Who wrote these lines?**

The point of this exercise is not to test your knowledge of literary works. It is rather to illustrate a number of points about the task of authorship attribution. First, the word choice and spelling can help you a lot. In this example, Early Modern English (http://mng.bz/BMBv) spelling suggests that a piece comes from a play by Shakespeare; if there happened to be an excerpt with words spelled in an American spelling tradition (e.g., *favorite* versus *favourite, publicize* versus *publicise*), you could have attributed such an excerpt to Ernest Hemingway as the only American writer on the list. Second, you may have noticed that apart from spelling, there are no other obvious clues that could suggest that pieces one and three come from the same author, as do pieces two and four. This is what makes this task challenging, and in what follows you will find out whether words are the only reliable characteristic features that can identify the author.

In this chapter, we will start with a simpler case of two authors, making it a *binary classification task*. First of all, we will look into how to get the data and extract the relevant information from it. For that, we will once again turn to NLTK. One of the useful features of this toolkit is that it provides you with access to a wide range of language resources and datasets. For instance, it contains several literary works that are available in the Project Gutenberg collection (www.gutenberg.org). Listing 5.1 shows how you can access these texts.

NOTE In addition to the NLTK toolkit, you need to install NLTK data as explained at www.nltk.org/data.html. Running `nltk.download()` will install all the data needed for text processing in one go. In addition, individual tools can be installed separately (e.g., `nltk.download('gutenberg')` installs the texts from Project Gutenberg available via NLTK).

Listing 5.1 Code to extract literary works from Project Gutenberg via NLTK

```
import nltk
nltk.download('gutenberg')        ◁─┐ Download NLTK's
from nltk.corpus import gutenberg    Gutenberg collection.
                                  ◁── Import data from the
                                      Gutenberg collection.
gutenberg.fileids()  ◁─┐
                       Print out the
                       names of the files.
```

The code will print out a list of 18 files that contain literary works by 12 authors. In particular, the list contains the following pieces:

```
['austen-emma.txt',
'austen-persuasion.txt',
'austen-sense.txt',
'bible-kjv.txt',
...
'shakespeare-caesar.txt',
'shakespeare-hamlet.txt',
'shakespeare-macbeth.txt',
'whitman-leaves.txt']
```

For instance, the first three entries correspond to Jane Austen's *Emma, Persuasion,* and *Sense and Sensibility.* Despite the fact that NLTK's interface to Project Gutenberg gives you access to only a handful of texts, this is enough for our purposes in this chapter. Let's select two authors that we will use for classification. Jane Austen and William Shakespeare are a natural choice, since three pieces of writing are included in this collection for each of them, which means that we'll have enough data to work with. Our task will be akin to that in exercise 5.3: we will build an algorithm that can attribute a given sentence to `Author1="Jane Austen"` or `Author2="William Shakespeare"`. As you have learned from exercise 5.3, there might be some helpful clues in the writing, such as particular words or characteristic spelling; however, the task is not always straightforward, so let's see how successfully an ML algorithm can deal with it. In general, the main reason we are working with these two authors in this chapter is the availability of the data and, perhaps, in real life we won't be trying to distinguish between this particular pair of authors. However, the techniques overviewed in this and the next chapter are applicable to the task of authorship identification in general and you can easily transfer them to any of your own real-life projects.

Although NLTK's interface gives you access to the full texts of *Emma, Macbeth,* etc., it is sentences that we will try to attribute to authors in this chapter. Why is this more useful in practice? The length of the full text varies a lot across literary works, but it will most typically be a matter of hundreds of thousands or even millions of words and thousands of sentences. It is much longer than what you might want to classify in practice: a typical message that you might try to classify will not run to the length of any of the literary works, so it is more useful to explore which approaches will work at a *sentence level.* This also makes your task more challenging. A sentence outside of its context might be harder to attribute than a whole body of *Macbeth.* Conveniently, NLTK actually allows you to directly access the set of sentences from each of these works, so you don't need to split them into sentences yourself. For that, just use `gutenberg .sents(name_of_file)`.

Now comes the point at which you need to let the algorithm know which data it may use to learn from. You may recall from chapter 2 that the bit of data that is used by the algorithm to learn from is called *training set,* and the bit that is used to evaluate the results (i.e., test how well the algorithm can do the task) is called *test set.* Typically, you would want to provide the algorithm with more data for training, so let's use two out of three works by each of the authors to train the classifier, and the third work to test it. Listing 5.2 shows how to define the training and test sets for the two authors. In this code, you define training sets for the two authors by combining the sentences from two out of three works available for each of them. The test sets then contain the sentences from the third work by each author. You can inspect the data in both sets by printing out some of the uploaded sentences and the length of the sentence lists in the sets.

Listing 5.2   Code to define training and test sets

Define training sets for the two authors.

Install NLTK's sentence tokenizer.

```
nltk.download('punkt')

author1_train = gutenberg.sents('austen-emma.txt') +
    gutenberg.sents('austen-persuasion.txt')
print (author1_train)
print (len(author1_train))

author1_test = gutenberg.sents('austen-sense.txt')
print (author1_test)
print (len(author1_test))

author2_train = gutenberg.sents('shakespeare-caesar.txt') +
    gutenberg.sents('shakespeare-hamlet.txt')
print (author2_train)
print (len(author2_train))

author2_test = gutenberg.sents('shakespeare-macbeth.txt')
print (author2_test)
print (len(author2_test))
```

Inspect the data by printing out some of the uploaded sentences.

Print out the length of the sentence lists in the training set.

Initialize the test set with the sentences from the third work by the author.

The code helps you to initialize the training set for Author1="Jane Austen" with *Emma* and *Persuasion* and the test set with *Sense and Sensibility*. For Author2="William Shakespeare", it uses *Julius Caesar* and *Hamlet* for training and *Macbeth* for testing. When you print out sentences in each of the sets, you will get an output like the following (e.g., for the training set for Author1="Jane Austen"):

```
[['[', 'Emma', 'by', 'Jane', 'Austen', '1816', ']'], ['VOLUME', 'I'], ...]
```

You can see that the training set is essentially a Python list. However, since gutenberg.sents provides you with a list of words in each sentence, the training set is in fact a *list of lists.* The very first sentence in this training set is [Emma by Jane Austen 1816], which, when split into words, becomes a Python list ['[', 'Emma', 'by', 'Jane', 'Austen', '1816', ']']. Since the original sentence itself contains opening and closing brackets, similar to the Python's convention for lists, it might look confusing at first.

When you print out the length of the training and test sets for the two authors, you will find out that the statistics are as follows (note that you might end up with slightly different results if you are using versions of the tools different from those suggested in the installation instructions for the book):

```
Training set for Author1:   11499 sentences
Test set for Author1:        4999 sentences
Training set for Author2:    5269 sentences
Test set for Author2:        1907 sentences
```

In other words, even though we are using the same number of literary works per author for training and testing (two for training, one for testing), the length in terms of the number of sentences is not the same. Jane Austen tends to use a higher number of sentences in her writing than William Shakespeare, which results in more than a double amount of training sentences available for her than for William Shakespeare (11499 versus 5269); and the ratio in the test data is closer to 2.6 (4999 versus 1907). This imbalance may seem unfortunate, but in a real-life ML project, you are much more likely to face challenges of imbalanced datasets than you are to come across a perfectly balanced one, so we'll keep things as they are and see what effect this uneven distribution of data has on our task in due course.

Before moving on, let's run a simple statistical check to see if the two authors indeed have markedly different writing styles. For each literary work by each writer, let's calculate the average length of words in terms of the number of characters, as well as the average length of sentences in terms of the number of words. Finally, let's also calculate the average number of times each word is used in a text by an author. You can estimate this number as the ratio of the length of the *list of all words* used in text to the length of the *set of words*, as a Python set will contain only unique entries. For example, a *list* of words for a sentence like "On the one hand, it is challenging; on the other hand, it is interesting" contains 17 entries, including punctuation marks, but a *set* contains 11 unique word entries; therefore, the proportion for this sentence equals 17/11 = 1.55.

> **NOTE** The list includes all words from the sentence ["On", "the", "one", "hand", ",", "it", "is", "challenging", ";", "on", "the", "other", "hand", ",", "it", "is", "interesting"], while the set includes only non-repeating ones: ["on", "the", "one", "hand", ",", "it", "is", "challenging", ";", "other", "interesting"].

This proportion shows how diverse one's vocabulary is. The higher the proportion, the more often the same words are repeated again and again in text. For comparison, in a sentence like "It is an interesting if a challenging task," each word is used only once, so the same proportion is equal to 1. Listing 5.3 presents the code that will allow you to apply these metrics to any texts of your choice. In this code, you use NLTK's functionality with `gutenberg.raw(work)` for all characters in a literary work, `gutenberg.words(work)` for all words in a work, and `gutenberg.sents(work)` for all sentences. You estimate the number of unique words as the length of a Python set on the list of all words in a work, calculate the average length of words in terms of the number of characters and the average length of sentences in terms of the number of words, and, finally, estimate the uniqueness of one's vocabulary as the proportion of the number of all words to the number of unique words.

Listing 5.3 Code to calculate simple statistics on texts

```
def statistics(gutenberg_data):
    for work in gutenberg_data:
        num_chars = len(gutenberg.raw(work))
        num_words = len(gutenberg.words(work))
        num_sents = len(gutenberg.sents(work))
```

Use NLTK's functionality to calculate statistics over characters, words, and sentences.

Calculate the average length of sentences in terms of the number of words.

Estimate the number of unique words as the length of the Python set on the list of all words in a work.

Calculate the average length of words in terms of the number of characters.

```
num_vocab = len(set(w.lower()
                    for w in gutenberg.words(work)))
print(round(num_chars/num_words),
      round(num_words/num_sents),
      round(num_words/num_vocab),
      work)
gutenberg_data = ['austen-emma.txt', 'austen-persuasion.txt',
                  'austen-sense.txt', 'shakespeare-caesar.txt',
                  'shakespeare-hamlet.txt', 'shakespeare-macbeth.txt']
statistics(gutenberg_data)
```

Calculate the uniqueness of one's vocabulary.

Apply this set of measures to any texts of your choice.

This code will return the following statistics for our selected authors and the set of their literary works:

```
5 25 26 austen-emma.txt
5 26 17 austen-persuasion.txt
5 28 22 austen-sense.txt
4 12 9 shakespeare-caesar.txt
4 12 8 shakespeare-hamlet.txt
4 12 7 shakespeare-macbeth.txt
```

As you can see, there is some remarkable consistency in the way the two authors write: William Shakespeare tends to use, on average, shorter words than Jane Austen (4 characters in length versus 5 characters), while he is also consistent with the length of his sentences (12 words long, on the average), and each word is used 7 to 9 times in each of his works. Jane Austen prefers longer sentences of 25 to 28 words on the average and allows herself more repetition. There is actually a considerable diversity in numbers here. In *Persuasion*, a word is, on the average, used 17 times across the whole text of the work, while in *Emma* the average of a single word usage reaches 26 times. Note that such quantitative differences in writing styles can be used by your algorithm when detecting an anonymous author.

5.2.2 Testing generalization behavior

One of the values of machine learning is its ability to *generalize* from the examples the algorithm sees during training to the new examples it may see in practice. This distinguishes *learning* from *memorizing* the data. For instance, simply memorizing that "Not so happy, yet much happyer" is a sentence written by Shakespeare won't help one recognize any other sentences by Shakespeare, but learning a particular writing pattern (*y* in words like "happyer") might help in recognizing other examples. Therefore, the real test of whether a machine-learning algorithm learns informative patterns rather than memorizes data should look into its *generalization behavior*. That is also why it is important to separate training and test data and make sure there is no overlap between the two.

So far, you have set aside training data consisting of two out of three works by each author, and you put the third work by each of the authors into the test set. Since the training and test sets contain sentences from different literary works (e.g., *Julius Caesar* and *Hamlet* versus *Macbeth*), the only property that relates them to each other is the same authorship. Therefore, they should be well suited for testing authorship identification algorithms. If any set of features is able to distinguish between authors in the test set using an algorithm that is trained on the training set, this set of features must capture something related to the authors themselves; otherwise, there is nothing else in common between the two sets of data.

Now, how do you know that the set of features are indeed capturing the properties that pertain to the authors' writing styles? One way to tell whether the classifier is capturing useful information is to measure its performance under different settings. In chapter 2 we talked about the ways of evaluating the performance of a machine-learning classifier on a binary task of spam detection, and the measure we used was accuracy, which reflects the proportion of correctly classified examples. In the authorship identification case, accuracy would show the following:

```
Accuracy = (number of sentences by Jane Austen that are classified as such
+
number of sentences by William Shakespeare that are classified as such)
/ total number of test sentences
```

We will use accuracy for our task in this chapter as well, but we will look in more detail into the advantages and disadvantages of using this measure. Let's start with the following question:

> **Question 1**
> You have trained the classifier on the training data with some specific set of features; then you tested it on the test data, and you got 80% accuracy. This means that 80% of the sentences in the test set are correctly identified with the author who wrote them. Does that mean that you have come up with a powerful set of features that can distinguish reliably between one author and another?

On the face of it, 80% accuracy seems to be a good performance value, but it doesn't really reflect whether the set of features you applied are really doing the job of distinguishing between the two authors well—for that, you need some point of comparison.

One such point of comparison is looking into how the same algorithm with the same features performs on a portion of the data that has more obvious similarities with the data the algorithm is trained on. For instance, recall how you split the data into training and test sets in chapter 2. Figure 5.6 provides a refresher.

In this case, both training and test sets come from the same data source. In the spam-detection example in chapter 2, you shuffled the data and split it into training

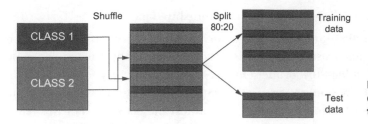

Figure 5.6 Reminder of the data splitting into training and test sets

and test sets using the enron1/ folder. Note that the training and test sets are still separate and not overlapping; however, the data itself might have additional properties that would make the two sets similar in some other ways. For example, if you attempted exercise 2.7 from chapter 2 and applied the spam-filtering algorithm trained on enron1/ to emails from the folder enron2/, you might have noticed a drop in performance, which we described as "One man's spam may be another man's ham." In other words, the data in the two folders originated with different users, and what was marked as spam by one of them might have been considerably different from what another one marked as spam.

By analogy, we are going to use a similar setup with the authorship identification data. We are going to first train and test our algorithm on different subsets of the data originating from the same literary works, and then run a final test on completely different data. To achieve that, let's apply shuffling to the set of texts that are currently labeled as training and split it into "training" and "test" bits (figure 5.7).

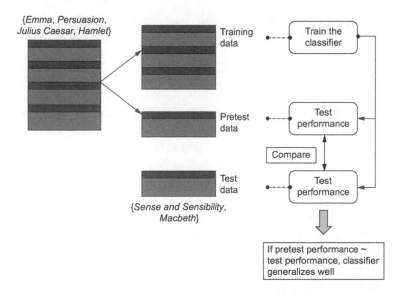

Figure 5.7 By testing the classifier's performance on the data from the same source (*pretest*) and from a different source (*test*), you can tell whether the classifier generalizes well to new test data.

Here is what we are going to do with the authorship data:

1 We will shuffle sentences in the *original* training set consisting of *Emma* and *Persuasion* by Jane Austen, and *Julius Caesar* and *Hamlet* by William Shakespeare.

2 We will set aside 80% of the sentences shuffled this way for the actual training set that you are going to use in the rest of this chapter to train the classifiers.

3 Finally, we will use the other 20% to pretest the classifier. For this reason, let's call this set a *pretest set* (this naming convention will also allow us to avoid confusing the final test set with the intermediate pretest set).

Note that the training and pretest sets contain non-overlapping sentences, so it would be legitimate to train on the training set and evaluate the performance of the classifier on the pretest set. The data, however, even more obviously comes from the same sources. For instance, the sentences in the training and pretest sets will likely contain mentions of the same characters and will follow the same topics. This is the main point of setting such a pretest dataset. By testing on the set that comes from the same source as the training data and comparing the performance to that achieved on the data from a different test set, you should be able to tell whether the algorithm generalizes well.

> **How to tell whether your algorithm generalizes well**
>
> *If the results on both pretest and test sets are similarly good*, and you don't observe a major drop in performance from pretest to test set, this means that the classifier captures the information pertaining to the authors and their writing styles.
>
> *If the results on the pretest set are much better than those on the test set*, you should conclude that the classifier learns something about the data itself rather than about the authors.

Now, there is one more aspect to consider: as we said before, the data in the two classes is not equally distributed, as `Author1="Jane Austen"` having twice as many sentences in the original training set as `Author2="William Shakespeare"`. When you split this data into actual training and pretest sets, you should take care of preserving these proportions as close to the original distribution as possible, since if you split the data randomly, you might end up with even less equally distributed classes and your test results will be less informative. In machine-learning terms, a data split that preserves the original class distribution in the data is called *stratified*, and the approach, which allows you to shuffle and then split the data in such a way, is called *stratified shuffling split*. It is advisable to apply stratified shuffling split whenever the classes in your data are distributed unequally, so you should apply this technique here.

It's time now to introduce scikit-learn, a very useful machine-learning toolkit that provides you with the implementation of a variety of machine-learning algorithms, as well as a variety of data-processing techniques (https://scikit-learn.org/stable/). The first application we will use this toolkit for is to perform stratified shuffling on the data. Listing 5.4 shows you how to do that. Start by importing `random`, `sklearn` (for scikit-learn), and `sklearn`'s function `StratifiedShuffleSplit`. Then you combine all sentences into a single list `all_sents`, keeping the author label. The total length of this list should equal 16,768 (11,499 sentences for Jane Austen + 5,269 for William Shakespeare). You keep the set of labels (authors) as `values`. It is the distribution in these values that you should be careful about. Next, you initialize the `split` as a single stratified shuffle split (thus, `n_splits=1`), setting 20% of the data to the pretest set (thus, `test_size=0.2`). To make sure the random splits you are getting from one run of the notebook to another are the same, you need to set the random state (i.e., random seed) to some value (e.g., `random_state=42`). The `split` defined in this code runs on the `all_sents` data, taking care of the distribution in the `values`, and you keep the indexes of the entries that end up in the training set (`train_index`) and pretest set (`pretest_index`) as the result of this split. Finally, you store the sentences with the correspondent indexes in `strat_train_set` list (for "stratified training set") and `strat_pretest_set` (for "stratified pretest set").

Listing 5.4   Run StratifiedShufflingSplit on the data

Keep the set of labels (authors) as values.

Add imports.

Combine all sentences into a single list called all_sents, keeping the author label.

```
import random
import sklearn
from sklearn.model_selection import StratifiedShuffleSplit

all_sents = [(sent, "austen") for sent in author1_train]
all_sents += [(sent, "shakespeare") for sent in author2_train]
print (f"Dataset size = {str(len(all_sents))} sentences")

values = [author for (sent, author) in all_sents]
split = StratifiedShuffleSplit(
    n_splits=1, test_size=0.2, random_state=42)
strat_train_set = []
strat_pretest_set = []
for train_index, pretest_index in split.split(
    all_sents, values):
    strat_train_set = [all_sents[index] for index in train_index]
    strat_pretest_set = [all_sents[index]
                         for index in pretest_index]
```

Initialize the split as a single stratified shuffle split with 20% of the data in the pretest set.

The split runs on the all_sents data, taking care of the distribution in the values.

Store the sentences with the correspondent indexes in strat_train_set and strat_pretest_set.

Let's now check that, as a result of the stratified shuffling split, you get the data that is split into two subsets following the distribution in the original dataset. That is, if in the original data Jane Austen is the author of around two-thirds of all sentences, after shuffling the data and splitting it into training and pretest sets, both should still have around two-thirds of the sentences in them written by Jane Austen. Listing 5.5 shows how to check if the proportions in the data are preserved after shuffling and splitting. You start by defining a function `cat_proportions` to calculate the proportion of the entries in each class (category) in the given dataset data. Then you apply this function to the three datasets: the original "training" data (marked here as Overall), the training subset that you set aside for actual training (Stratified train), and the pretest subset (Stratified pretest), which were both created using the code from listing 5.4. Finally, you use Python's printout routines to produce the output in a formatted way. This code is similar to what you used to print outputs in a tabulated way in chapter 4.

Listing 5.5   Check the proportions of the data in the two classes

```
def cat_proportions(data, cat):        ◄──┐  Calculate the proportion of the
    count = 0                              │  entries in each class (category)
    for item in data:                      │  in the given dataset data.
        if item[1]==cat:
            count += 1
    return float(count) / float(len(data))

categories = ["austen", "shakespeare"]
rows = []
rows.append(["Category", "Overall", "Stratified train",        Apply this function to
            "Stratified pretest"])          ◄──────────         the three datasets.
for cat in categories:
    rows.append([cat, f"{cat_proportions(all_sents, cat):.6f}",
                f"{cat_proportions(strat_train_set, cat):.6f}",
                f"{cat_proportions(strat_pretest_set, cat):.6f}"])

columns = zip(*rows)
column_widths = [max(len(item) for item in col) for col in columns]
for row in rows:
    print(''.join(' {:{width}} '.format(row[i], width=column_widths[i])
                for i in range(0, len(row))))      ◄──┐  Use Python's printout
                                                      │  routines to produce the
                                                      │  output in a formatted way.
```

The code produces the following output, printed in a tabulated format:

```
Category      Overall    Stratified train   Stratified pretest
austen        0.685771   0.685776           0.685748
shakespeare   0.314229   0.314224           0.314252
```

In other words, this confirms that the class proportions are kept approximately equal to the original distribution. In the original data, around 68.6% of the sentences come from Jane Austen's literary works, and 31.4% from William Shakespeare's plays. Quite similarly to that, with minor differences in the fifth and sixth decimal values, the class distributions in the stratified training and pretest sets are kept at the 68.6% to 31.4% level.

With the code from listing 5.4, you coupled sentences with the names of the authors that produced them and stored them in the all_sents structure that you later used to create your stratified training and pretest sets. Let's use a similar approach and create the test_set structure as a list of tuples, where each tuple maps a sentence to its author. Note that the following code is very similar to that in listing 5.4.

Listing 5.6	Code to create the test_set data structure

```
test_set = [(sent, "austen") for sent in author1_test]
test_set += [(sent, "shakespeare")
             for sent in author2_test]
```
⟵ **Create a list test_set and store tuples mapping sentences to the author names in it.**

It would be good now to check the class distribution in the test set as well.

> **Exercise 5.4**
>
> Check class distributions in the test set modifying the code from listing 5.5 appropriately. (Solution can be found at the end of this chapter.)

5.2.3 Setting up the benchmark

Now that the data is prepared, let's run a classifier to set up a benchmark result on this task. Which classifier and which set of features should you choose for such a benchmark? The rule of thumb is to select a simple and straightforward approach that you would find easy to implement and apply to the task. In chapter 2, when you implemented your first NLP/ML approach for spam filtering, you didn't apply any feature engineering; you simply used all words in the emails as features that can potentially distinguish between the classes, and you've got some reasonably good results with those. Let's use all words from the training set texts by the two authors for the benchmark authorship attribution model. After all, we said that we all have our favorite words that we tend to use more frequently than others, so there is a lot to be learned from the word choice that each writer makes. As for the classifier, the only ML algorithm that you've used so far is Naïve Bayes, which is a reasonable choice here, too: it is easy to apply, it is highly interpretable, and, despite its name, it often performs well in practice.

Let's briefly remind ourselves how feature extraction from chapter 2 works. You start with data structures strat_train_set, strat_pretest_set, and test_set. Figure 5.8 visualizes such a data structure, using strat_train_set as an example. Each of these structures is stored as a Python list of tuples that you created in listings 5.4 and 5.6.

The first element in each tuple corresponds to a sentence from a data set. You can access it as strat_train_set[i][0], where i is the index of any of the sentences from the stratified training set, that is a number between 0 and the size of the data set. In the toy example in figure 5.8, strat_train_set[0][0] corresponds to It is yet too early in life . . . , and strat_train_set[2][0] to Not so happy, yet . . .

> **NOTE** It is a "toy" example, since the sentences from figure 5.8 do not necessarily correspond to the order in which they are stored in the actual datasets, so don't get alarmed if you get different sentences returned by the code.

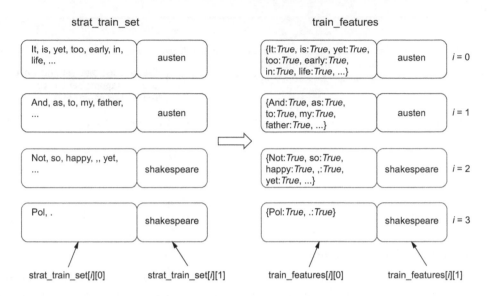

Figure 5.8   Visualization of the data structures with sentences and features mapped to labels

The second element corresponds to the label assigned to the sentence in the data set. You can access it as `strat_train_set[i][1]`, where *i* is the same index pointing to the instance. In the toy example in figure 5.8, `strat_train_set[0][1]` corresponds to austen and `strat_train_set[2][1]` to shakespeare.

To extract features from each instance in these data structures, you need to convert sentences into Python dictionaries that map each word present in a sentence to a `True` flag signifying its presence. This is the way NLTK's Naïve Bayes implementation defines feature representation: all words that are actually present in a sentence will receive a `True` flag, and all words not present in the sentence (but present in other sentences in the training data) will implicitly receive a `False` flag. For example, in `train_features[0][0]`, words It, is, and yet will all be flagged as `True`, because they occur in this sentence, while words like Not, so, happy, and others, not present in this sentence, will all be implicitly flagged as `False`.

The new data structures `train_features`, `pretest_features`, and `test_features` will still be Python lists of tuples, but this time each tuple will map a dictionary of features to the author label. For instance, in the toy example from figure 5.8 `train_features[0][0]` will return {It:True, is:True, yet:True, too:True, early:True, in:True, life:True, ...}, and `train_features[2][0]` will return {Not:True, so:True, happy:True, ,:True, yet:True, ..."}, while `train_features[0][1]` will return austen, and `train_features[2][1]` will return shakespeare.

Listing 5.7 provides a reminder about how you can extract words as features from the data sets. In this code, you set a presence flag to `True` for each word in text. As a result, the code returns a Python dictionary that maps all words present in a particular text to True flags. Next, you extract features from training and pretest sets. Now train_features and pretest_features structures store lists of tuples, where word features rather than whole sentences are mapped to the authors' names. Finally, it's good to run some checks to see what the data contains. For instance, you can print out the length of the training features list, the features for the first entry in the training set (indexed with 0), and any other entry of your choice (e.g., the 101st entry in the code).

Listing 5.7 Code to extract words as features

```
def get_features(text):
    features = {}
    word_list = [word for word in text]
    for word in word_list:
        features[word] = True
    return features

train_features = [(get_features(sents), label)
                    for (sents, label) in strat_train_set]
pretest_features = [(get_features(sents), label)
                      for (sents, label) in strat_pretest_set]

print(len(train_features))
print(train_features[0][0])
print(train_features[100][0])
```

> **For each word in text, set a presence flag to "True" and, in the end, return a Python dictionary.**

> **Extract features from training and pretest sets.**

> **Run some checks to see what the data contains.**

This code should tell you that the length of the train_features list is 13,414. This is exactly how many sentences were stored in the training set after a stratified shuffled split. Now each of these sentences is converted to a dictionary of features and mapped to the author label, but the total number of these entries stays the same. The code will also print out the dictionary of features for the first entry in the training set (thus indexed with 0):

```
{'Pol': True, '.': True}
```

This sentence comes from William Shakespeare, so printing out train_features[0][1] should return shakespeare as the label. Running print(train_features[100][0]) will return

```
{'And': True, 'as': True, 'to': True, 'my': True, 'father': True, ',': True,
... 'need': True, 'be': True, 'suspected': True, 'now': True, '.': True}
```

This is the 101st entry in the training set that corresponds to a sentence from Jane Austen, so printing train_features[100][1] should return austen.

Let's now use the Naïve Bayes classifier from the NLTK suite, train it on the training set, and test it on the pretest set. The code in listing 5.8 should remind you of the code you ran in chapter 2—this is essentially the same routine.

Listing 5.8   Code to train the Naïve Bayes classifier on train and test on pretest set

Import the classifier of your choice—
NaiveBayesClassifier in this case.

```
from nltk import NaiveBayesClassifier, classify

print (f"Training set size = {str(len(train_features))} sentences")
print (f"Pretest set size = {str(len(pretest_features))} sentences")
classifier = NaiveBayesClassifier.train(train_features)

print (f"Accuracy on the training set = {str(classify.accuracy(classifier,
    train_features))}")
print (f"Accuracy on the pretest set = " +
     f"{str(classify.accuracy(classifier, pretest_features))}")
classifier.show_most_informative_features(50)
```

Train the classifier on
the training set.

Print out the most
informative features.

Evaluate the performance on
both training and pretest sets
and print out the results.

The output that this code produces will look like the following:

```
Training set size = 13414 sentences
Pretest set size = 3354 sentences
Accuracy on the training set = 0.9786789920978083
Accuracy on the pretest set = 0.9636255217650567
Most Informative Features
been = True             austen : shakes =    257.7 : 1.0
King = True             shakes : austen =    197.1 : 1.0
thou = True             shakes : austen =    191.3 : 1.0
...
```

This tells you that there are 13,414 sentences in the training set and 3,354 in the pretest set. The accuracy on both sets is pretty similar: approximately 0.98 on the training data and 0.96 on the pretest. The classifier trained on the sentences in the training portion of the data learns how to distinguish between the two authors in the pretest portion of the data, too. The author-specific characteristics that the classifier learns can be seen in the list of the most informative features it relies upon: for Shakespeare, these include words like *King, Lord, Tis, ere, Mark,* while for Austen, they include *she, father, mother, brother,* and *husband,* among others. Note that the preceding printout includes only the first 3 lines of the output, but you can see the full list of the top 50 most informative features printed out in the Jupyter Notebook.

So far, so good. Looks like the classifier learned to distinguish between the two authors with very high, almost perfect accuracy! The small drop in performance between the training and pretest sets suggests that features are mostly portable between the two sets. However, remember that both training and pretest sets cover sentences that come from the same sources—the same set of literary works for the two authors. The real test of generalization behavior is to run the classifier on the test set. The code in listing 5.9 does exactly that.

Listing 5.9   Code to test the classifier on the test set

```
test_features = [(get_features(sents), label) for (sents, label) in test_set]
print (f"Test set size = {str(len(test_features))} sentences")
print (f"Accuracy on the test set = {str(classify.accuracy(classifier,
    test_features))}")          ◁─┐  Test the classifier on the test set
                                   │  and print out the results.
```

The code returns the following results:

```
Test set size = 6906 sentences
Accuracy on the test set = 0.895742832319722
```

This is still quite good performance; however, note that the drop in accuracy is considerable. The accuracy drops from over 0.96 to below 0.90. To help you appreciate the difference in performance on these data sets, figure 5.9 visualizes this drop in accuracy. To make the results more salient, it puts them on the scale from 68% (remember that the data is distributed across the two classes as 68.6% to 31.4%, with over 68% of the sentences originating with Author1="Jane Austen", so 68.6% defines the *lower bound* on your classifier's performance) to 100%—an accuracy that would be returned should you succeed in building a perfect classifier for this task (thus, 100% is the *upper bound* on performance). Before you read on, try answering question 2.

> **Question 2**
> You have trained the classifier on the training data using words as features, and then you tested it on the pretest data that comes from the same source and on the test data that comes from a different source. Accuracy on training and pretest sets is quite similar; however, you notice a considerable drop in performance on the test data. What does it suggest about the algorithm and/or your selection of features?

We said before that a comparative drop in performance for the classifier tested on data coming from a different source suggests that it might not generalize well to the new data. In practice, this means that it might have learned, or memorized, something about the training data itself, rather than learned something useful about the task at hand. Words are strong features in many NLP tasks, but unfortunately, they often tend to capture one particular property of the language data—*the selection of topics*. For instance, listing 5.8 shows some of the most informative features for the training data. They include not only the specific words that are used by the authors due to their personal choice (e.g., *Tis* for William Shakespeare, which you will not see in the works of Jane Austen), but also topics of the literary works. The abundance of family terms like *father*, *mother*, and *husband*, as well the presence of *she* as one of the most informative features in the works of Jane Austen clearly shows that she wrote about family affairs and marriage prospects. At the same time, *Mark* as one of the most informative features for William Shakespeare simply points to one of the characters.

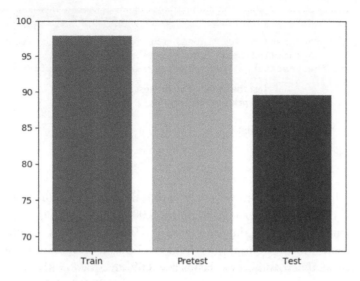

Figure 5.9　Drop in accuracy between training and pretest sets on the one side and test set on the other

The difference between the training and pretest data on the one hand and the test data on the other is that these sets contain references to different characters and might also discuss, even if slightly, different topics. It might be true that certain authors stick to the same selection of subjects throughout their lives, but in reality, one cannot guarantee that a selection of words that describe, for example, only family affairs and marriage prospects would be a reliable set of features to identify the same author in a different testing scenario. The drop in performance in our example already suggests that words do not provide you with a reliable and fully generalizable set of features. If you test your classifier on a different literary work, the performance may drop even further. Can you do better than that and find features that identify the author beyond specific topics and characters, names (i.e., based on their writing style specifically)? To find out if it's possible to do that, let's step away from the benchmark model and try to solve the task using a different set of features.

Before we embark on the quest for finding such generalizable features, here is one more disadvantage of relying on words too much: there are as many as 13,553 various words in the training set covering these two authors (since words haven't been converted to lowercase yet, this number includes different versions of same words, such as *King* and *king*). This is a large feature space; however, each particular sentence will use only a handful of these features. Recall that an average sentence length for Jane Austen is 28 words at most, and for William Shakespeare it is 12 words only. This means that the feature set is very *sparse*: the algorithm relies on comparison of words occurring across the sentences, but even though there are many words in total, only a few of them occur repeatedly in the sentences to help the algorithm decide on the class. This means that a lot of information is stored unnecessarily. This is not a big problem for Naïve Bayes, which can deal with such sparse features, but it will prevent you from efficiently applying some other algorithms. Application of a broader set of algorithms is a topic covered by the next section.

5.3   A closer look at the machine-learning pipeline

Let's revise what you have done so far. You've set a benchmark applying a particular set of features (words) and a particular classifier (Naïve Bayes in the NLTK implementation) to the binary task of authorship attribution. Figure 5.10 summarizes these steps by filling in the details into the mental model for this chapter that we formulated earlier in figure 5.4.

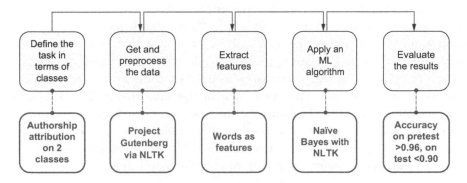

Figure 5.10   Steps of the machine-learning pipeline implemented so far

Now it's time to step back, revise your approach to the features, try to tackle this task with a different classification algorithm, and compare the results to the benchmark model. Let's start with a new classification algorithm.

5.3.1   Decision Trees classifier basics

When we introduced spaCy in the previous chapter, we said that it is beneficial to have several toolkits under your belt, as it broadens your perspective and provides you with a wider choice of useful techniques. The same goes for the selection of machine-learning approaches. In this section, you will learn how your second classification algorithm, `Decision Trees` classifier, works. It takes a different approach to the learning process. Whereas Naïve Bayes models the task in terms of how probable certain facts are based on the previous observations in the training data, the `Decision Trees` classifier tries to come up with a set of rules that can separate instances of different classes from each other as clearly as possible. Such rules are learned on the training data and then applied to the new test instances. Like Naïve Bayes, the `Decision Trees` classifier is highly interpretable. At the same time, conceptually it is quite different from Naïve Bayes. For these reasons, we are looking into this classifier in this chapter.

Let's start with a practical example. In chapter 2, we talked about classification of vehicles into different types based on a small number of features (e.g., availability of an engine and the number of wheels). Suppose that your dataset contains just four classes: two-wheeled bicycles, two-wheeled motorcycles, four-wheeled cars, and six-wheeled trucks (figure 5.11).

Training set:

Figure 5.11   Vehicle classification task with four classes

One way in which you can learn to separate four classes in this data is to first split it by the availability of an engine (i.e., by asking "Is it a motorized vehicle?"). We will call such a question a *decision rule*. This will help you to set bicycles versus all motorized vehicles apart. Next, you can apply a set of decision rules based on the number of wheels (e.g., by asking "Are there two wheels?" "Are there four wheels?" "Are there six wheels?") and gradually separating each of the motorized vehicles from the rest. These rules don't have to include exact numbers and may instead cover bands of values. Depending on the task, it is possible to formulate the rules as "Are there two or less wheels?" or "Are there six or more wheels?" and so on. Figure 5.12 visualizes a decision tree that includes a sequence of such decision rules.

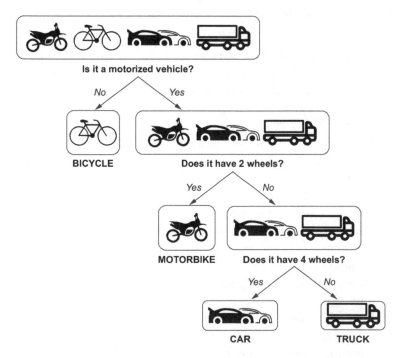

Figure 5.12   A decision tree that applies a sequence of three rules to separate instances of four classes

Is this the only possible sequence of rules that you can apply to separate instances of the four classes in this data? Look at exercise 5.5.

Exercise 5.5

Are there other sequences of rules that you can apply to separate the instances in these four classes? Hint: You can come up with a different set of rules altogether, or you may try applying the same rules in a different order.

Let's discuss the solution together. In fact, there are multiple rules you can formulate, and there are, consequently, multiple orders in which you can apply them to the data. For instance, figure 5.13 demonstrates a tree built using a different sequence in the same set of questions.

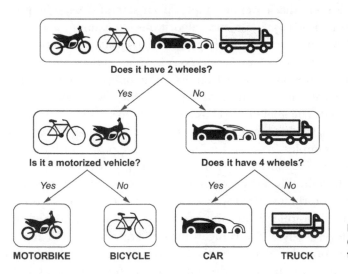

Figure 5.13 An alternative decision tree using the same set of three questions in a different order

Are the trees in figures 5.12 and 5.13 equally good or is one better than another? The tree in figure 5.12 is "taller"—there are three levels at which the rules have to be applied. At the same time, the question on the first level successfully separates one of the classes (bicycles) from the rest of the data. The tree in figure 5.13 is a bit "flatter"—it has only two levels. Each level is binary-branching, and one needs to apply further rules to separate the classes under each branch. However, both trees eventually arrive at the correct solution, as the four classes are clearly separated from each other: the *terminal* (lower) *leaves* of the tree each contain instances of one class only. Let's now discuss how the Decision Trees classifier decides which tree to build.

5.3.2   *Evaluating which tree is better using node impurity*

Generally, the `Decision Trees` classifier uses training data to do two things:

- Come up with a set of rules
- Figure out in which order it is best to apply them

The notion of "best" here means the following: among all available rules at each step, the classifier aims to select the one that will produce the cleanest, purest separation of the classes at the following nodes. The degree of purity (or impurity) of the data separation in the node can be measured quantitatively, and there are several measures that are used in practice. For instance, suppose you have applied a rule and ended up with a leaf that contains instances of one class only. This is a perfect case, in which a node with the purest data is produced. If you introduce some measure of purity, in this case you can assign such a leaf the maximum value (e.g., a value of 1). At the same time, if you applied a rule and ended up with a node that covers examples from several classes, its purity value should be lower than 1. Heads-up: in practice, algorithms often aim to *minimize the impurity* of the nodes rather than to maximize the purity. This is just a convention, as the two measures are really two sides of the same coin. To convert a *purity* measure into an *impurity* measure, just subtract the purity value from its maximum possible value. If a node's purity value is 1, its impurity value is 0. If a node's purity value is less than 1, then its impurity value is larger than 0. The goal of the classifier is then to select a rule that produces nodes with *lowest impurity*, with an impurity of 0 in the ideal scenario.

Let's look at our examples from figure 5.12 again. Suppose you had a set of 100 motorbikes, 100 bicycles, 100 cars, and 50 trucks. To help you visualize this situation, let's say that each vehicle in this set is represented with its toy model, so you have 100 toy bicycles, 100 toy motorbikes, 100 toy cars, and 50 toy trucks. Let's now imagine that when you apply a decision rule and it separates the vehicles into nodes, you put the correspondent toy models of the vehicles into separate boxes. For instance, you apply a rule "Is it a motorized vehicle?" to this set and it puts 100 bicycles (and none of the other vehicles) under the node on the left, as figure 5.12 shows. Therefore, you put all 100 toy bicycles in a single box. This rule also puts 250 of the other vehicles under the node on the right in figure 5.12, so you, too, put all the other toy models in the second box. This is what your first box with the contents of the leftmost node from figure 5.12 contains, if you used array notation to represent it:

```
    num(motorbikes)     num(bicycles)     num(cars)     num(trucks)
  [        0                100               0              0         ]
```

Now suppose you blindly selected one instance of a vehicle from this node—that is, you blindly pick a toy model of a vehicle from the first box. What type would that vehicle be? Since you know that all 100 examples under this node (and in this box) are bicycles, with a 100% certainty you will end up selecting a bicycle every time you blindly pick a vehicle from this node and this box. At the same time, your chances of picking a vehicle of any other type from this node are equal to 0. That is, with a 100%

certainty (or probability) you would expect to select a bicycle from this node, and with a 0% probability you would get anything else.

In chapter 2 we discussed a notion of probabilities. This chance of selecting a vehicle of a particular type when you blindly (or randomly) pick an instance from a node is exactly what we call a *probability* of selecting a vehicle of a particular type. It is estimated as the proportion of instances of a particular class among all vehicles under a particular node (i.e., as the number of instances of a particular class divided by the total number of instances under the node). For brevity, let's call this probability p, and denote the node that we are talking about as *left*. Table 5.1 shows how you can estimate class probabilities for this node, using *class* to denote a type of vehicle in the set of {motorbikes, bicycles, cars, trucks}:

Table 5.1 Probability estimation for the four classes in the left node (first box)

class	num(class)	total(left)	$p_{class,left}$
motorbikes	0	100	0/100 = 0
bicycles	100	100	100/100 = 1
cars	0	100	0/100 = 0
trucks	0	100	0/100 = 0

Now, to estimate how impure this node is, you need one more component: the measure of impurity tries to strike the balance between the chances of picking an instance of a particular class and *the chances that this node contains instances of class(es) other than this particular one.* Let's turn to our boxes and toy models metaphor again. As we said, if you blindly selected a vehicle from the first box (or left node), this vehicle will always be a bicycle. Suppose you blindly picked a vehicle out of the first box, and naturally expected to see a bicycle. What are the chances that when you check what toy model you got it turns out to actually be something other than a toy bicycle?

This might sound trivial—didn't we say earlier that the chances of picking anything else from this box are 0, since there is nothing other than bicycles in this box? That's exactly right, and this argument might seem repetitive to you precisely because the left node is an example of a pure node. If you were to discuss the contents of this node (or the first box, for that matter) with someone else, it might look like what figure 5.14 shows.

To summarize, whenever you select anything from this node, it is a bicycle, and whenever you select a bicycle from this node, you can be sure about this instance's class. This is because the classifier put nothing else under this node. It's not surprising that the probability that the node contains instances of class(es) other than the class in question equals $(1 - p_{class,node})$. Table 5.2 lists the probabilities for all the classes in the left node.

Finally, let's put these two components together. For each node, an impurity measure iterates over all classes in the dataset and considers how probable it is to randomly

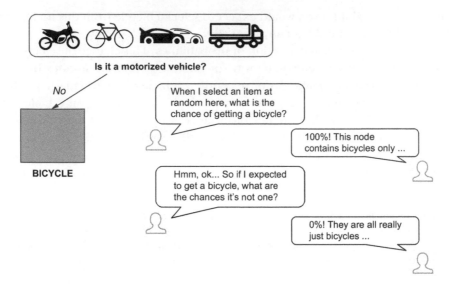

Figure 5.14 The left node is an example of a pure node, so there are no chances of selecting anything else.

Table 5.2 Summary of all class probabilities in the left node (first box)

class	$p_{class,left}$	$1 - p_{class,left}$
motorbikes	0	1
bicycles	1	0
cars	0	1
trucks	0	1

select an instance of a particular class from this node and, at the same time, how probable it is in this case that the instance is actually of any other class than the expected one. Put another way, we are estimating how probable it is that the classifier made a mistake by putting instances of other classes under the same node. Whenever we are talking about a probability of two things happening at the same time, in mathematical terms we mean multiplication. So, to derive the final measure of impurity for the left node, let's apply the following equation:

```
Impurity_of_node =
sum_over_all_classes(probability_of_class_under_node *
                     probability_of_other_classes_under_same_node)
```

Let's apply this formula to the left node:

$$\text{Impurity}_{left} = p_{motorbikes,left} * (1 - p_{motorbikes,left})$$
$$+ \, p_{bicycles,left} * (1 - p_{bicycles,left})$$
$$+ \, p_{cars,left} * (1 - p_{cars,left})$$

$$+ \ \text{p}_{\text{trucks,left}} * (1 - \text{p}_{\text{trucks,left}}) \ =$$
$$= \ 0*1 \ + \ 1*0 \ + \ 0*1 \ + \ 0*1 \ = \ 0$$

We started off saying that the leftmost node presents a case of a clear data separation, so its impurity should be the lowest (i.e., 0). Here we've got mathematical proof that this is indeed the case, as this calculation tells us that this node's impurity indeed equals 0.

Let's now look into the right node at the first level of the tree in figure 5.12. Going back to our boxes and toy models metaphor, let's inspect the contents of the second box. After you applied a rule "Is it a motorized vehicle?" to the full set, it put 250 of the vehicles other than bicycles in the second box (and under the node on the right). This is a more challenging case, as this box contains a combination of 100 motorbikes, 100 cars, and 50 trucks, so we know from the start that it is not pure, and its impurity score should be greater than 0. Let's derive this score step by step. First of all, let's estimate the probability of randomly selecting instances of each class from this node. In other words, randomly pick models of a particular type out of the second box. Table 5.3 presents these probabilities.

Table 5.3   Probability estimation for the four classes in the right node (second box)

class	num(class)	total(right)	$\text{p}_{\text{class,right}}$
motorbikes	100	250	100/250 = 0.40
bicycles	0	250	0/250 = 0.00
cars	100	250	100/250 = 0.40
trucks	50	250	50/250 = 0.20

If you were to blindly pick a vehicle from the second box (or from under the right node), you would expect to end up selecting a motorbike 40% of the time (i.e., with a 0.40 probability), another 40% of the time you will expect to get a car, and in 20% of the cases it will be a truck. Now, say, you have blindly picked a toy model out of the box and expected to see a motorbike. According to the distribution of instances in this box, how often will it turn out to not be a motorbike? Figure 5.15 visualizes this.

As before, this equals to the probability of *any class other than motorbike* under this node, or $(1 - \text{p}_{\text{motorbikes,right}}) = (1 - 0.4) = 0.60$. Let's summarize this for all classes in Table 5.4.

Table 5.4   Summary of all class probabilities in the right node (second box)

class	$\text{p}_{\text{class,right}}$	$1 - \text{p}_{\text{class,right}}$
motorbikes	0.40	0.60
bicycles	0.00	1.00
cars	0.40	0.60
trucks	0.20	0.80

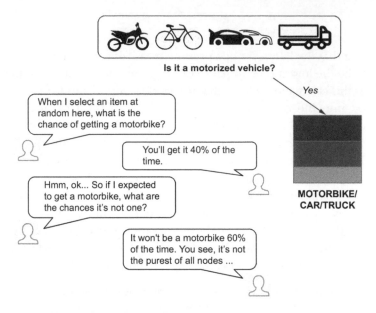

Figure 5.15 **Right node is an example of a less pure node: whenever you expect to get instances of a certain class, there are chances that you get instances of other classes instead.**

Finally, let's calculate impurity of this node as before:

$$
\begin{aligned}
\text{Impurity}_{\text{right}} &= P_{\text{motorbikes,right}} * (1 - P_{\text{motorbikes,right}}) \\
&+ P_{\text{bicycles,right}} * (1 - P_{\text{bicycles,right}}) \\
&+ P_{\text{cars,right}} * (1 - P_{\text{cars,right}}) \\
&+ P_{\text{trucks,right}} * (1 - P_{\text{trucks,right}}) = \\
&= 0.4*0.6 + 0*1 + 0.4*0.6 + 0.2*0.8 \\
&= 0.64
\end{aligned}
$$

If you continue estimating impurity of each of the nodes in the tree from figure 5.12 in the same way, you will end up with the impurity values shown in figure 5.16. It uses a more technical term for the node impurity estimations that we've just run—*Gini impurity.* Gini impurity is widely used in practice, and it is the value that is applied by the scikit-learn implementation of the `Decision Trees` algorithm that you will use for this task. The general formula for Gini impurity (GI) for a particular node *i* (e.g., left or right at a particular level) in a case that contains data from *k* classes (e.g., {motorbikes, bicycles, cars, trucks}) looks like that:

```
GIᵢ = Σₖ,ᵢ probability_of_k_in_node_i * (1 - probability_of_k_in_node_i)
```

Note that this is exactly the set of estimations that we used earlier.

Before we move on, here is a trick that will make estimations somewhat simpler and faster. Let's denote `probability_of_k_in_node_i` as $p_{k,i}$ for brevity. When

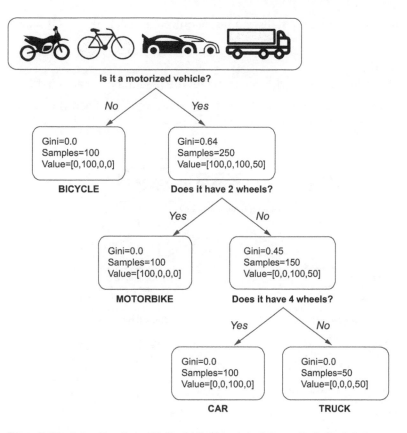

Figure 5.16   Impurity values (Gini impurity) for each of the nodes in the tree from figure 5.12

you calculate the Gini score over all classes in a node, you end up with the following components:

$$GI_i = \Sigma_{k,i} \; (p_{k,i} \; * \; (1 \; - \; p_{k,i})) \; = \; \Sigma_{k,i} \; p_{k,i} \; - \; \Sigma_{k,i} \; (p_{k,i})^2$$

Each node contains instances of some classes of vehicles. For example, the left node contains 100 bicycles out of the 100 instances it has, and the right node has 100 motorbikes and 100 cars out of 250 instances of vehicles it has, and then it also contains 50 trucks. So, whenever you look at the sum of the vehicles of *all* the classes under the same node (i.e., at $\Sigma_{k,i} \; p_{k,i}$), they necessarily cover the total of all the vehicles in this node. There is simply no other way. This means that for the left node $\Sigma_{k,i}$ $p_{k,i} = \Sigma_{k,left} \; p_{k,left} = 0 \; + \; 1 \; + \; 0 \; + \; 0 \; = \; 1$, and for the right node $\Sigma_{k,i} \; p_{k,i} = \Sigma_{k,right}$ $p_{k,right} = 0.4 \; + \; 0.0 \; + \; 0.4 \; + \; 0.2 \; = \; 1$ (i.e., you always end up with 1). So, you can rewrite the formula from earlier as

$$GI_i = \Sigma_{k,i} \; (p_{k,i} \; * \; (1 \; - \; p_{k,i})) \; = \; \Sigma_{k,i} \; p_{k,i} \; - \; \Sigma_{k,i} \; (p_{k,i})^2 \; = \; 1 \; - \; \Sigma_{k,i} \; (p_{k,i})^2$$

Now it's time to practice the skills you just acquired and calculate a GI score yourself.

> **Exercise 5.6**
>
> What is the Gini impurity of the nodes in the tree presented in figure 5.13?
>
> First try to calculate the Gini impurity of the nodes yourself. Then you can compare your solution to the solution presented in figure 5.17.

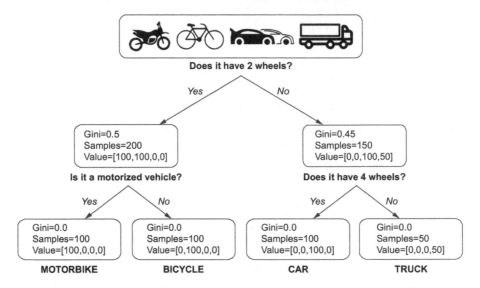

Figure 5.17   Impurity values (Gini impurity) for each of the nodes in the tree from figure 5.13 (solution to exercise 5.6)

5.3.3   *Selection of the best split in Decision Trees*

Now that you have estimated the impurity of each node in each of the trees, how can you compare whole trees, and which one should the algorithm select? The answer is, at each splitting point, the `Decision Trees` algorithm tries to select the rule that will *maximally decrease the impurity of the current node*. In both cases, you start with the original dataset of 100 examples for 3 classes plus 50 examples for the fourth class. What is the original impurity of the topmost node, then?

```
GI(topmost node) = 1 - (3*(100/350)² + (50/350)²) ≈ 1 - 0.265 = 0.735
```

The tree from figure 5.12 produces two nodes at the first step. The left node of 100 out of 350 (2/7 of the dataset) instances with the GI of 0 and the right node of 250 out of 350 instances (5/7 of the dataset) with the GI of 0.64. The total impurity for this split (let's call it `split1`) can be estimated as a weighted average where the weight is equal to the proportion of instances covered by each node:

```
GI(split1) = (2/7)*0 + (5/7)*0.64 ≈ 0.46
```

Similarly, the tree in figure 5.13 produces two nodes at the first step. The left node of 200 out of 350 (4/7 of the dataset) instances with the GI of 0.5 and the right node of 150 out of 350 instances (3/7 of the dataset) with the GI of 0.45. The total impurity for this split (let's call it split2) is then

$$GI(split2) = (4/7)*0.5 + (3/7)*0.45 \approx 0.48$$

Here is what happens when you apply the rule for split1: the impurity of the original set of instances drops from 0.735 down to 0.46. For split2, the impurity drops from 0.735 to 0.48. See figure 5.18 for a visualization.

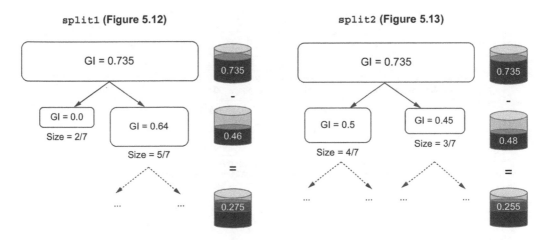

Figure 5.18 split1 **contributes to a comparatively larger gain in GI (0.275) than** split2 **(0.255).**

Comparatively, split1 contributes to a larger gain. The difference between the original node impurity and the impurity of the produced nodes after split1 is 0.275 (i.e., 0.735 − 0.46), which is larger than the difference of 0.255 (i.e., 0.735 − 0.48) for split2. Even though the difference in this small example is not strikingly large, the classifier will prefer split1—the sequence of rules from figure 5.12 because they contribute to larger purity of the subsequent nodes. After all, the first rule applied in the tree in figure 5.12 successfully separates one of the classes (bicycles) from the rest of the data.

There are further parameters of the Decision Trees algorithm that you can control for. For instance, the tree in figure 5.13 is flatter than the one in figure 5.12, which will be selected based solely on the Gini impurity score. You can constrain the algorithm to build a tree of a particular depth, as well as containing up to a maximum number of nodes/leaves, which will also impact the order in which the rules are applied.

5.3.4   Decision Trees on language data

Now, let's apply a Decision Trees algorithm to language data. See exercise 5.7 for another toy example based on authorship identification task. As before, try solving this exercise yourself before checking the solution, which is discussed immediately after the exercise.

Exercise 5.7

What is the Gini impurity of the nodes in the part of a decision tree presented in figure 5.19?

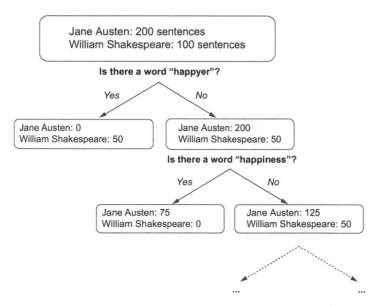

Figure 5.19   An example of a decision tree built for a hypothetical set of 200 sentences from Jane Austen and 100 sentences from William Shakespeare. Only two rules are shown in this bit.

Let's discuss the solution to this exercise. In this example, you start with a set of some 200 sentences from Jane Austen and 100 sentences from William Shakespeare. Application of the first rule, "Is there a word 'happyer'?" allows you to set aside 50 sentences by William Shakespeare. But, as the word is spelled in the Early Modern English tradition, it doesn't occur in any of the sentences by Jane Austen, so all 200 of them are shuffled to the right node at the first level of the tree. The second rule, "Is there a word 'happiness'?" helps you identify 75 sentences from Jane Austen; however, none written by William Shakespeare contain a word with such a spelling. For brevity, only part of the whole tree is presented in this figure, so you can assume that there are many more rules applied at the later steps to the remaining set of 125 sentences by Jane Austen and 50 sentences by William Shakespeare. What are the Gini impurity scores for the nodes that are presented here? As before, you need to apply the Gini impurity calculation to each node using the formula

$$GI_i = \Sigma_{k,i} \ (p_{k,i} \ * \ (1 \ - \ p_{k,i})) = \Sigma_{k,i} \ p_{k,i} \ - \ \Sigma_{k,i} \ (p_{k,i})^2 = 1 \ - \ \Sigma_{k,i} \ (p_{k,i})^2$$

This should give you the scores as presented in figure 5.20.

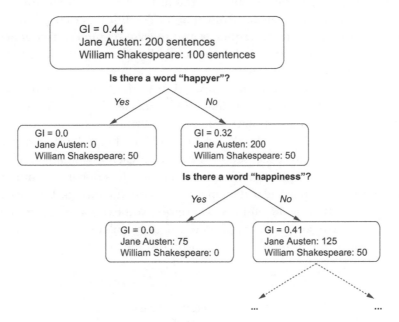

Figure 5.20   Gini impurity scores calculated for the tree from figure 5.19

This exercise may give you an idea as to why applying a `Decision Trees` classifier with all words as features and using thousands of rules in the form of "Is there a word X in this sentence?" would not be very efficient. With over 13,000 words in the vocabulary between the two authors, trees built that way would grow prohibitively large. From the algorithm's efficiency point of view, there are two particular problems for decision trees: the prohibitively high number of features, and the fact that many words among this large number of features are very rare and will occur only in a few texts. This problem is called *feature sparsity*, and it means that the classifier will waste a lot of resources on features that are not very useful because they occur too rarely. This does not mean that the `Decision Trees` classifier is not applicable to this task; it only means that one needs to select appropriate features.

To wrap this chapter up, let's apply the `Decision Trees` classifier to our task and compare the results to the benchmark model. NLTK has its own implementation of the `Decision Trees` algorithm, which you are going to use here. Since using all 13,553 words as features will slow the classifier down a lot, let's select a smaller range of words that would make for promising features. This will be your first attempt at *feature selection*. A simple heuristic that works with selecting words as features is that those words that occur across most texts are not very informative, as they do not help distinguish between classes. At the same time, words that occur only in a few texts are not helpful either—even if they identify the author uniquely, they don't occur frequently enough, so you might never see them again in any other text and thus they won't help in practice. (This may remind you of the discussion on word importance based on word frequency from chapter 3—differences in word distributions are the motivation for term frequency and inverse document frequency measures.) Therefore, the best approach is to consider the middle range of word frequencies to generate the features.

Let's start by estimating how often each word from the training set occurs across texts in this set—that is, let's estimate document frequencies for all 13,553 words. Listing 5.10 shows how to do that. You start by importing Python's Counter (https://docs .python.org/3/library/collections.html), which provides helpful frequency estimation functionality. Then you extract sets of words from each document. You need to use sets, since all you care about is whether a word occurs in a document and not how many times it occurs in a particular document. The "documents" in this task are, in fact, the sentences written by the authors. Therefore, you extract words from all sentences in the strat_train_set and apply Counter to calculate document frequency for each word in the training set. Finally, you print out the results.

Listing 5.10 Code to estimate document frequencies for all words in the training set

```
from collections import Counter        ◁──┐  Import Python's
                                           │  Counter.
words = []

def extract_words(text, words):                        Extract sets of words
    words += set([word for word in text])   ◁──┐       from each document.
    return words                                │
                                          Extract words from
                                          all sentences in the
for (sents, label) in strat_train_set:    strat_train_set.
    words = extract_words(sents, words)   ◁──┘

counts = Counter(words)       ◁──┐  Apply Counter to calculate
print(counts)    ◁──┐              document frequency for each
                    │              word in the training set.
      Print out the output.
```

If you print out the results returned by this code, you will get a Python dictionary, where each word is assigned with its document frequency (i.e., the number of sentences in the training set, where it occurs). Here are the first few entries from this dictionary:

```
Counter({'.': 9108, ',': 7126, 'to': 4382, 'the': 4119, 'and': 3996,...
```

As you can see, the most frequent word (full stop) occurs in 9,108 sentences in the training data, the next most frequent one (comma) in 7,126 sentences, and then the number of occurrences starts dropping quite quickly. In fact, if we visualize the number of document occurrences for all words, starting with the most frequent one (such word is technically said to be at *rank 1* in the frequency table) and following with the descending order of frequencies (higher ranks), we will see a sharp drop, as the left plot in figure 5.21 shows. In practice, logarithmic function is often applied to raw frequencies to make the curve smoother and the changes in frequencies clearer. The right plot in figure 5.21 shows the same trend, but with the logarithm with base 10 applied to the absolute numbers.

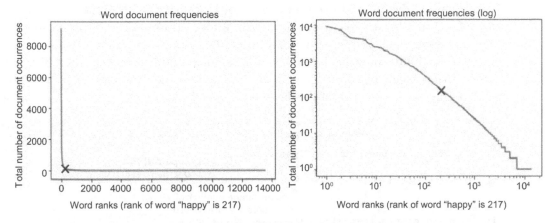

Figure 5.21 Document frequencies for all words from the training set plotted against their ranks. The results for the word "happy" are marked with a cross on each graph.

To give you a more precise example, figure 5.21 also shows the position at which word *happy* can be found: it is the 217th most frequent word (thus, it has a rank of 217) and it occurs in 154 sentences in the training set. Document distribution of words in the training set is quite sparse. As many as 13,355 words occur in less than 0.0125% of the sentences (i.e., in less than 168 sentences each).

This skew in the distribution is not something specific to this particular task or dataset. It is an example of a common phenomenon in language data known as *Zipf's law* (https://en.wikipedia.org/wiki/Zipf%27s_law). It was formulated by George Kingsley Zipf, and it states that the frequency of any word is inversely proportional to its rank in the frequency table. Originally, it states that the most frequent word will occur approximately twice as often as the second most frequent word, three times as often as the third most frequent word, and so on. The particular proportion is a rough estimate and depends on the data (e.g., in this case, you are looking into document rather than total word frequencies, so the ratio between the first and the second ranks is not exactly 1:2), but what matters is that the rank-frequency distribution is an inverse relation. In plain terms, this means that a small amount of very frequent words will occur in most documents, and a much larger number of words (so-called long tail of the word distribution) will be seen very rarely. This is exactly why you should apply frequency-based feature selection if you don't want to overload your classifier with many relatively rare features.

Listing 5.11 selects words as features based on their distribution. It applies a threshold for the minimum and the maximum number of occurrences. For the minimum number of occurrences, a threshold of 200 sentences is used (i.e., a word is required to occur in at least 200 sentences to become a feature). The maximum threshold of 20% of the sentences is used in this code—that is, a word is required to occur in at most 20% (2,683) of all the sentences to be used as a feature. You may consider changing these thresholds, as they are used for the sake of the example only. Note that the maximum number of sentences in which a word may occur is 13,414, since this is the size of the training set. You store the words, whose distribution falls within the predefined range, in the selected_words list, and then you extract features from the sentences by including only the words that are contained in the selected_words list. This procedure is applied to all three datasets. Finally, you train the classifier and report the accuracy scores on each of the datasets.

Listing 5.11   Code to run DecisionTreeClassifier with the selected features

```
from nltk import DecisionTreeClassifier          ◁──┐  Import NLTK's
                                                      DecisionTreeClassifier.
maximum = float(13414)          ◁──┐
                                    The maximum number of
selected_words = []                 sentences in which a word
for item in counts.items():         may occur is 13,414.
    count = float(item[1])
    if count > 200 and count/maximum < 0.2:   ◁──┐  Select words based on the
        selected_words.append(item[0])              minimum and the maximum
print(len(selected_words))                          occurrence thresholds.

def get_features(text, selected_words):   ◁──┐  Extract features from the sentences
    features = {}                               by including only the words from
    word_list = [word for word in text]         the selected_words list.
    for word in word_list:
        if word in selected_words:
            features[word] = True
    return features

train_features = [(get_features(sents, selected_words), label)
                   for (sents, label)
                   in strat_train_set]
pretest_features = [(get_features(sents, selected_words), label)
                    for (sents, label)
                    in strat_pretest_set]
test_features = [(get_features(sents, selected_words), label)
                 for (sents, label)
                 in test_set]          ◁──┐  Extract features from
                                              all three datasets.
                                                                    Train the
classifier = DecisionTreeClassifier.train(train_features)   ◁──┘    classifier.

print (f"Accuracy on the training set = {str(classify.accuracy(classifier,
    train_features))}")
print (f"Accuracy on the pretest set = {str(classify.accuracy(classifier,
    pretest_features))}")
print (f"Accuracy on the test set = " +                     Report the accuracy
     f"{str(classify.accuracy(classifier, test_features))}")   ◁──┤  scores on each of
                                                                    the datasets.
```

This code returns an accuracy of around 81.00 on the training set, around 79.60 on the pretest, and around 80.70 on the test set. Figure 5.22 visualizes these results.

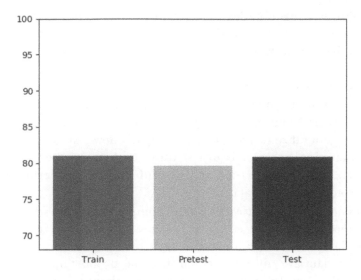

Figure 5.22 Accuracy scores on the training, pretest, and test sets with the `Decision Trees` classifier

Even though these results are lower than those obtained with the benchmark model, the model is remarkably consistent across all three datasets. This shows that the `Decision Trees` classifier generalizes well across the three datasets. In addition, it achieves relatively good results with a small subset of features. In fact, there are only 166 words that are selected as features by the code in listing 5.11, which is a much more compact feature space than the one that contains all of the 13,553 words as features. Chapter 6 will focus on the question of how you can find more informative and compact sets of features for language tasks.

Summary

- Authorship attribution is concerned with identification of the precise identity of an anonymous author, while user profiling is concerned with profiling a broader set of users from various groups based on their writing. These two applications represent varieties of essentially the same task: our writing styles and word choices are typically very consistent, making it possible for automated algorithms to solve these tasks based on the characteristic features in writing.
- Authorship attribution and user profiling are examples of tasks typically addressed with machine learning (ML) classifiers. Many NLP applications can be represented as supervised ML classification tasks, provided that you can define classes and features and provide high-quality data for the algorithms to learn from.
- High-quality data is the key ingredient of a successful ML application. In case of authorship attribution and user profiling, we need texts annotated with

the particular authors (or groups of authors). While such data may be hard to come by, literary works by famous writers are readily available, such as via Project Gutenberg.

- The first steps in a machine learning pipeline include initialization of the data, extraction of the initial set of features, and setting up of the benchmark model. Naïve Bayes with words as features can be used as one of such benchmark models.

- The true goal of machine learning is for the classifier to identify a set of characteristics pertaining to the task rather than the data. This helps ensure that the classifier learns about the task rather than memorizes the facts from the data, so it can generalize its knowledge well to any new test data. One way to check generalization behavior is to test your classifier on the data coming from the same source as the training data and compare its performance to that on the completely new data.

- The ML toolkit scikit-learn provides you with implementations of a wide variety of classifiers and data processing techniques. In particular, it can be used to split the data into subsets representing a fair distribution of classes. If classes in your data are not represented in equal proportions, you need to apply the stratified shuffle split technique to learn about the actual, unbiased performance of your algorithm.

- Unlike Naïve Bayes, the `Decision Trees` classifier tries to learn a sequence of rules that can split the data into pure sets of classes. Purity (or impurity) of the split can be measured quantitatively; for example, using Gini impurity score. In addition, purity scores are used across the board in machine learning, such as to select informative features for machine-learning classification other than decision trees.

- One of the approaches to feature selection relies on the idea that the most informative words are neither very frequent, nor very rare. The results from the `Decision Trees` classifier show that it generalizes well, but there is still some room for improvement in terms of its performance.

Solutions to miscellaneous exercises

Exercise 5.1

Suppose you had only two people on your contacts list. This means you have two "suspects" as the authors of the anonymous message you received. Each of them represents a particular class: `Author1` or `Author2`, each with their own writing style. This makes it a binary task: the message is either produced by `Author1` or `Author2`. This case can further be extended to as many authors (classes) as you have entries on your contacts list. In the case of user profiling, each class can be defined based on the particular groups of authors considered. For example, you can represent this as a binary problem for male versus female writers, or split the users into age groups—for instance 10–20, 20–30, 30–40 years old, and so on.

Exercise 5.2

Chapter 2 presented an earlier example of an NLP task addressed with an ML approach that relied on word choice as features. Words are a good start. In the case of spam filtering, certain words like *lottery* signaled that the topic of the email is likely to be inappropriate for a work-related email. Words are useful as features in authorship attribution and user profiling, too—as we all have our favorites that we frequently use, they can signal who the author is. We will start with words as features in this task, and then we will explore the potential of other linguistic features.

Exercise 5.3

You might notice that the first excerpt contains a word "receyue" that looks like a misspelled English word. This is actually how the word *receive* was spelled in Early Modern English, which might help you attribute the first piece of writing to William Shakespeare as the only author from this period of time. This sentence comes from his play *Macbeth*.

The second excerpt contains modern spelling of "receive," so it is unlikely to originate from Shakespeare. However, unless you know about the favorite topics of the other writers or the names of the characters in their works, you might find this question challenging, so don't worry if you didn't get it right. This piece comes from Jane Austen's *Sense and Sensibility*.

Now, what about the other two pieces? Do they come from any of the same authors, or are any of these pieces written by the other two writers? Can you see any similarities between the third and the fourth sentences and the first two?

In fact, the third piece also comes from *Macbeth* and the fourth from *Sense and Sensibility*, but don't worry if you were not able to tell that. You may have spotted, however, an unusual spelling of "happyer" with *y* instead of *i*, which is another trait of Early Modern English. Note how in the fourth piece "happiness" is spelled in the more usual way.

Exercise 5.4

Before you check the solution in the notebook, try coding it yourself. You need to apply the method `cat_proportions` to the `test_set` and add one more column to the results table. You might find out that the class proportions are not exactly the same in the test set as they are in the training and pretest sets; however, they are relatively similar and follow the same distribution trend. In real-life applications, you need to make sure that the training and test data have similar distributions, but it is hard to guarantee *exactly the same* class proportions.

Linguistic feature engineering for author profiling

This chapter covers

- Improving the implementation of your user profiling algorithm

- Discovering strategies for linguistic feature engineering

- Exploring other useful NLP techniques with NLTK and spaCy

- Applying a `Decision Tree` classifier with sklearn

- Evaluating a machine-learning classifier in application to an NLP task

The last chapter introduced the task of author (user) profiling and focused on authorship identification. We said that it is a good example of how machine learning can be applied to build an NLP application. This works because

- We can clearly define *classes* for this task. In particular, you were detecting which of the two authors, Jane Austen (`class1`) or William Shakespeare (`class2`), produced a piece of writing. This is a binary task, as there are two classes to distinguish between.

- We can get good-quality *data* to work with. Chapter 5 showed how you could access literary texts using NLTK's interface to Project Gutenberg. Literary works by famous writers are widely and often freely available, and we can rely on the author assignment in this data—there is no doubt as to who the author of *Macbeth* or *Sense and Sensibility* is.
- We can define *features*. For instance, one of the strongest characteristics of individual writing style is the selection of words, as we all have our own favorite words that we tend to use more frequently than other people around us.

You built your benchmark model for this task using words as features and NLTK's implementation of Naïve Bayes classifier, and you found out that, in addition to capturing one's writing style, words also encode topics of the literary works, so the performance of your algorithm drops when it is applied to the new set of texts. This means that the classifier does not generalize well, and one of the challenges that lie ahead in this task is to identify the set of features that can capture one's writing style in a more focused way. Another problem with the use of words as features is their number: there are over 13,000 words in the combined works of Jane Austen and William Shakespeare in your training set, and many of them will occur very rarely and will not be informative. What is more, some classifiers will find it difficult to deal with such a large number of features. Chapter 5 introduced another interpretable and easy-to-use classifier, `Decision Trees`, which would benefit from having a more compact set of features to build decision rules from.

The process of identifying such a smaller and more informative set of features is called *feature engineering*. It is an important step in an NLP project, since for many tasks, it is not known in advance which features are most informative, while feature engineering involves comparative experiments that allow you to find this out. This process is the main focus of this chapter. Figure 6.1 is a reminder of our mental model for this task.

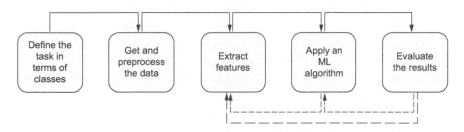

Figure 6.1　Mental model for a supervised machine-learning classification task

In particular, you are going to focus on and iterate over the last three steps of the pipeline: you will investigate which features should be extracted, how the ML algorithm uses them, and what results this produces. As you continue working with the same task, you will rely on the preprocessing done in chapter 5, so open the Jupyter Notebook that you worked on for the previous chapter and let's get started!

6.1   *Another close look at the machine-learning pipeline*

Before you start experimenting with the new classifier (Decision Trees) and various features in search of a more compact, informative, and generalizable set of those, there is one more aspect of the machine-learning pipeline implementation that we need to look into in more detail: *evaluation of your algorithm's performance.*

6.1.1   *Evaluating the performance of your classifier*

So far, you have evaluated the performance of your algorithm using one specific metric—*accuracy*. It's time now to further discuss its informativeness.

> **Question 1**
> You have trained a classifier using some set of features, and then you tested it on the test data. Accuracy on the test set is 0.60. Would you call this accuracy high? How can you interpret this number?

This question may remind you of a similar discussion in chapter 2: to interpret whether accuracy is high or low, you need to know what the distribution of classes is. In isolation, 0.60 does not seem like a high number. If this accuracy is achieved by an algorithm on a set with a 50:50 distribution between two classes, an accuracy of 0.60 does not seem to be very impressive. Worse still, if the distribution of the two classes is closer to 60:40, such an algorithm performs hardly better than a majority baseline algorithm that always selects the majority class without doing any learning. However, on a ten-class problem with an equal distribution of data between the classes (i.e., 10% each), an accuracy of 0.60 would not seem to be as low.

Let's look further into the accuracy measure for the binary case. Suppose you have two classes labeled as class1="Jane Austen" and class2="William Shakespeare", with the actual distribution between these classes being 60:40: there are 60 sentences written by Jane Austen and 40 sentences by William Shakespeare. Figure 6.2 presents you with three scenarios of how you can get an accuracy of 0.60 on this data. In this figure, Act stands for the actual number of sentences, and the actual numbers are provided for both authors in the rows of the tables. Pred stands for the number of sentences predicted to be in each of the two classes by the classification algorithm. You can find the number of the sentences predicted to be written by each of the authors in the columns. For brevity, class1="Jane Austen" is denoted as J.A. and class2="William Shakespeare" as W.S. The rightmost columns and bottom rows present the total counts in rows and columns: the rightmost columns tell you that 60 sentences are actually written by Jane Austen and 40 are written by William Shakespeare.

Tables presented in figure 6.2 are called *confusion matrices*. They show confusions between the actual labels and the labels predicted by the classifier. Under the first scenario, the algorithm fails to identify any sentences written by William Shakespeare and achieves an accuracy of 0.60 by simply predicting that all sentences belong to Jane

	Pred J.A.	Pred W.S	Σ
Act J.A.	**60**	0	60
Act W.S	40	**0**	40
Σ	100	0	100

Scenario 1: better performance on J.A.

	Pred J.A.	Pred W.S	Σ
Act J.A.	**40**	20	60
Act W.S	20	**20**	40
Σ	60	40	100

Scenario 2: mixed case

	Pred J.A.	Pred W.S	Σ
Act J.A.	**20**	40	60
Act W.S	0	**40**	40
Σ	20	80	100

Scenario 3: better performance on W.S.

Figure 6.2 Three possible scenarios in which the algorithm's predictions achieve an accuracy of 0.60

Austen. Since class1="Jane Austen" is the majority class, this works correctly 60% of the time. In the case presented in scenario 2 in figure 6.2, the same accuracy value of 0.60 is achieved by correctly classifying 40 out of 60 sentences from Jane Austen and half of the sentences by William Shakespeare. Finally, in scenario 3, the same accuracy is achieved by correctly classifying all of the sentences by William Shakespeare and some (20 out of 60) sentences by Jane Austen. Now, here is the problem with results evaluation according to the accuracy measure only: accuracy score hides all these details under the hood of a single number. This means that you have no way of telling what your algorithm does correctly and how it can be further improved. This, in its turn, calls for an application of a different measure or a set of measures.

6.1.2 *Further evaluation measures*

Here is one more example for you. Suppose your algorithm was tasked with classifying balls of two colors. In the test set, you have 10 balls, 6 of which belong to class1="light color" and 4 to class2="dark color" (thus, the class distribution, like in the preceding examples, is 0.60:0.40). Suppose you trained your algorithm on some training data and applied it to this test set of 10 balls. The algorithm comes back predicting that 4 actually light colored balls and 1 actually dark colored ball belong to class1 ("light color"), and 3 actually dark colored balls and 2 actually light colored balls belong to class2 ("dark color"). Figure 6.3 shows this situation.

What can you say about the predictions this algorithm makes? First of all, you can estimate its accuracy as 4 correctly predicted instances of class1="light color" and

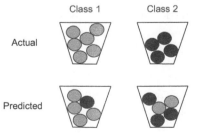

Figure 6.3 A classification example with some actual distribution of classes and predicted results: according to the actual distribution of the two classes (top row) there are 6 balls in class1 (light color) and 4 balls in class2 (dark color); the predictions (bottom row), however, misclassify some of the balls.

3 correctly predicted instances of class2="dark color" (i.e., 0.70 accuracy). However, this doesn't tell you *how the classifier performs on each class.* In the future, should you try to improve performance of this classifier on the light colored class or on the dark colored class?

One way to approach class-based evaluation is to look into *how many instances of each class were correctly identified.* There are 6 balls of class1 that the classifier should have correctly identified (of which it identified only 4), and 4 balls of class2 (of which it identified only 3). The measure that tells you about the proportion of instances of each class correctly found by the classifier is called *recall.* This measure expresses the coverage of the algorithm.

> **Recall**
> *Recall* is the proportion of instances of each class that are correctly identified as belonging to the correspondent class. This shows the coverage of your algorithm.

In other words, recall on class c is estimated as follows:

```
Recall(class c) = number of instances of class c correctly identified as
     class c / total number of actual instances of class c in the set
```

Table 6.1 provides recall values for our example from figure 6.3. From the recall point of view, the classifier performs better on class2. It achieves higher recall; therefore, if you wanted to improve the classifier's performance in terms of recall, it is class1 that you should take more care of.

Table 6.1   Recall values for the example from figure 6.3

	class1	class2
Recall	4/6 = 0.67	3/4 = 0.75

However, the flip side to this measure is that the instances that are responsible for lower recall in class1 are the ones that are incorrectly put by the classifier in the bucket for class2, making it less homogeneous. Therefore, there is another measure, called *precision,* that shows the proportion of instances that are predicted by the classifier to belong to a particular class that are actually instances of this class. This shows reliability of your classifier. If it says something is a dark colored ball, how often would this actually be a dark colored ball?

> **Precision**
> *Precision* is the proportion of instances predicted by the algorithm to belong to a particular class that are actually from this class. This shows reliability of your algorithm.

In other words, precision on `class c` is estimated as follows:

```
Precision(class c) = number of instances of class c correctly identified as
    class c / total number of instances the classifier identifies as class c
```

In the case of `class1`, 4 out of 5 balls that are predicted by the algorithm to be light colored are actually light colored, and in case of `class2`, 3 out of 5 balls predicted to be dark colored are actually dark colored. This means that the classifier's precision on the two classes is as table 6.2 shows.

Table 6.2 Precision values for the example from figure 6.3

	`class1`	`class2`
Precision	4/5 = 0.80	3/5 = 0.60

It turns out, in terms of precision, the classifier performs better on `class1`. This is not surprising; in fact, the two measures are complementary. For instance, the simplest way for an algorithm to perform with a 100% recall on `class1` is to put all 10 balls in the bucket for `class1`, which would lower the precision on this class to 0.60 (as 4 out of 10 balls will actually be dark colored). The third measure that combines precision and recall together is called *F1 measure* or *F1 score*, and it is a harmonic mean between the other two measures, thus showing how the two perform in combination. A harmonic mean is used instead of an arithmetic mean to estimate F1 because this measure tries to strike the balance between two measures (precision and recall), which express proportions estimated at different scales. Precision is the proportion of the correctly identified instances of a class among those that the classifier believes belong to this class, while recall is the proportion of correctly identified instances of a class among those that actually belong to this class. In cases where proportions originating from different scales need to be combined, harmonic mean is more appropriate than a simple arithmetic mean.

> **F1 measure (F1 score)**
> *F1* is a harmonic mean between precision and recall, thus showing how the algorithm performs in terms of both.

Specifically, F1 is estimated as follows:

```
F1 = 2*precision*recall / (precision + recall)
```

Table 6.3 summarizes all these measures on our toy example with the balls. This shows that, on balance, performance of the classifier is better on `class1`, and if you wanted to increase overall performance, you should look into the examples that are misclassified as `class2` while being of `class1`, thus significantly lowering precision on `class2`.

Table 6.3   Recall, precision, and F1 values for the example from figure 6.3

	class1	class2
Recall	0.67	0.75
Precision	0.80	0.60
F1	0.73	0.67

Now that you are equipped with further knowledge about machine-learning algorithms and ways to evaluate the results, let's get back to the task of authorship attribution and see how we can improve previous results.

6.2   *Feature engineering for authorship attribution*

You have so far implemented a benchmark algorithm (Naïve Bayes with words as the only types of features), and we said that there were some problems with this approach. Let's summarize them once again:

- The Naïve Bayes algorithm that uses *all* words as features shows similar results on the datasets that come from the same source (training and pretest sets), but there is a considerable drop in performance on the data coming from a different source (test data). We are looking for a better generalization performance. Preliminary experiments with the Decision Trees classifier at the end of chapter 5 showed much better generalization behavior, but this classifier works more efficiently if the feature set is compact and informative.
- Accuracy measure doesn't tell us much about the algorithm's performance on each of the classes. At the same time, it is important that the algorithm performs well on both majority (Jane Austen) and minority (William Shakespeare) classes. We are looking for an ML model that can deal with both classes equally well.

In this section, we are going to look into *feature engineering*—that is, we are going to try out different types of features that can be applied to this task. Then we are going to train the classifier using these features, test it on the pretest and test sets, and evaluate the results. If we still find the results unsatisfactory (e.g., the classifier's performance on the two sets suggests that it is not generalizing well, or its performance on the minority class is poor as compared to that on the majority class), we will add more features to our feature set and run the whole process again. Figure 6.4 summarizes this process, using input to denote training, pretest, and test datasets with the sentences mapped to their author labels, as produced by the code you've been working with so far. Let's start looking into other, potentially informative types of features and identify an optimal set of such features.

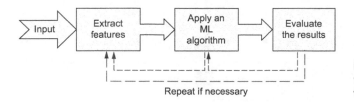

Figure 6.4   The ML routine we are going to run through in this section

6.2.1   Word and sentence length statistics as features

In listing 5.3 in chapter 5, you estimated the average length of words in terms of the number of characters, and the average length of sentences in terms of the number of words. Here is a reminder: it turns out that William Shakespeare consistently uses shorter words than Jane Austen (4 characters in length against 5 characters), as well as shorter sentences (12 words long as opposed to 25–28 words, on the average, for Jane Austen). These figures seem to reflect the authors' distinctive style well, so why not use them as features.

Let's start by defining a function `avg_number_chars` to extract the relevant statistics regarding the average word length in a sentence and `number_words` to calculate sentence length in terms of the number of words, as the following listing shows. If you apply these functions to the example sentence used in this listing, you should get 3.5714 as the average number of characters per word and 7.0 as the length of the sentence in terms of the number of words.

Listing 6.1   Code to extract word and sentence length statistics

```
def avg_number_chars(text):
    total_chars = 0.0
    for word in text:
        total_chars += len(word)
    return float(total_chars)/float(len(text))        Estimate the average
                                                       length of words in the
                                                       sentence in terms of the
                                                       number of characters.

def number_words(text):                  Calculate the sentence
    return float(len(text))              length in terms of the
                                         number of words.

print(avg_number_chars(["Not", "so", "happy", ",", "yet", "much", "happyer"]))
print(number_words(["Not", "so", "happy", ",", "yet", "much", "happyer"]))
```

Try it out on some sentences of your choice.

Next, you need to apply these functions to convert your datasets into sets of features. At the moment, your datasets are represented as sets of tuples where each sentence is mapped to its author label. What you would like instead is a *feature vector*—an array containing the average number of characters per word and the total number of words in a sentence for each sentence in each set mapped to the author label. Figure 6.5 visualizes this idea.

Listing 6.2 shows how to do that. We are going to call feature vectors `feature_list` to keep with the idea that it is essentially a Python list filled with relevant numbers,

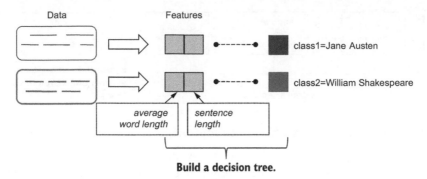

Figure 6.5   In order to build a decision tree, convert the data into feature vectors mapped with labels.

and we will map these lists with `targets` for author labels, which we will represent numerically. There is a simple reason for representing labels numerically. From now on, we will be using scikit-learn for all machine-learning routines, and scikit-learn algorithms expect numerical values. To keep with Python traditions, let's start indexing from 0, and use `0` if the author is Jane Austen and `1` if the author is William Shakespeare.

Listing 6.2   Code to extract features and map them to the labels

```
def initialize_dataset(source):          ◁─── Argument source denotes the
    all_features = []                          dataset you are applying the
    targets = []                               feature extraction to.
    for (sent, label) in source:
        feature_list=[]
        feature_list.append(avg_number_chars(sent))    Fill in feature vector feature_list
        feature_list.append(number_words(sent))        with the features and add them
        all_features.append(feature_list)         ◁── to all_features.
        if label=="austen": targets.append(0)
        else: targets.append(1)     ◁───┐  Append the relevant author label
    return all_features, targets           (0 or 1) to the list of targets.
```

Iterate through all (sent, label) pairs in the given dataset.

```
train_data, train_targets = initialize_dataset(strat_train_set)
pretest_data, pretest_targets = initialize_dataset(strat_pretest_set)
test_data, test_targets = initialize_dataset(test_set)     ◁──┐ Apply this function
                                                               to all datasets to
print (len(train_data), len(train_targets))                    initialize feature
print (len(pretest_data), len(pretest_targets))    Print out   structures mapped
print (len(test_data), len(test_targets))     ◁──  the length  with their labels
                                                   of the      (targets).
                                                   structures.
```

In this code, you first define a function `initialize_dataset` with a single argument `source`, which denotes the dataset you are applying feature extraction to. For example, `strat_train_set`, `strat_pretest_set`, or `test_set`. Within this function, you iterate through all `(sent, label)` pairs in the given dataset and fill in feature vector feature_list with the features for the given sentence, also adding these features to the overall structure all_features that keeps track of all feature vectors in the dataset. Finally, you append the relevant author label (0 or 1) to the list of targets. Then you apply this function to all datasets to initialize training, pretest, and test feature structures mapped with their labels (targets). In the end, you print out the length of the structures. In this case, you end up with a list of 13,414 feature vectors mapped with a list of 13,414 targets for the training set, 3,354 feature vectors and targets for the pretest, and 6,906 feature vectors and targets for the test set.

> **NOTE** Here and for the other listings in this chapter, you might end up with slightly different results if you are using versions of the tools different from those suggested in the installation instructions for the book.

Figure 6.6 shows how this step converts two sentences from a dataset into feature vectors mapped with the correspondent targets.

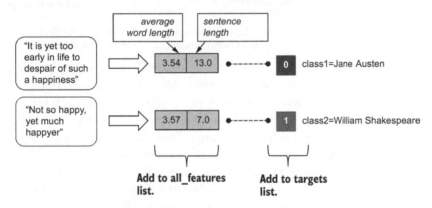

Figure 6.6 An example of feature vectors and target labels for two sentences in the dataset

Now that the data is converted into sets of features mapped to the target labels, let's train a Decision Trees classifier with scikit-learn and apply it to our task. A nice feature of this toolkit is that the machine-learning routine is easy and consistent across all types of classifiers. In particular, with scikit-learn, there are three steps that you need to apply, as figure 6.7 shows.

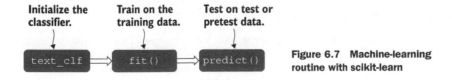

Figure 6.7 Machine-learning routine with scikit-learn

In particular, you need to

- Initialize the classifier and store it in a variable (e.g., `text_clf`).
- Train it on the training data using a method called `fit`.
- Test it on the test (or pretest) data using a method called `predict`.

Listing 6.3 shows how to apply all these steps to our data. Start by uploading the classifier from scikit-learn's suite of classifiers. Then, initialize it and set the random state to a particular value—this helps ensure that you get the same classifier setup every time you run your code. Finally, train the classifier using the `fit` method and test it using the `predict` method.

Listing 6.3   Code to train and test a classifier with sklearn

```
from sklearn.tree import DecisionTreeClassifier        ◁──┐  Upload the classifier from
                                                            sklearn's suite of classifiers.

text_clf = DecisionTreeClassifier(random_state=42)    ◁──┐  Initialize the classifier and
text_clf.fit(train_data, train_targets)          ◁──┐      set the random state.
predicted = text_clf.predict(pretest_data)    ◁──┐
                    Test the classifier using       Train the classifier
                     the predict method.            using the fit method.
```

You may notice that we fix the `random_state` to a particular value. When training, scikit-learn's `Decision Trees` classifier runs over all features and tries out various values that can split the current node into the purest possible nodes underneath. Depending on the number of features and the range of values each one takes, the range of possibilities may be prohibitively large. Therefore, in scikit-learn's implementation, the classifier doesn't try out all possible orders of the features; it randomly selects one, tries to come up with a set of the best possible splitting rules (according to the Gini impurity) based on this randomly selected feature, and then randomly selects the next one, and so on. To get the classifier to select the features and create the rules in the same order each time you run your code, you need to set the `random_state` parameter. This helps you get comparable results every time you run your code.

Finally, let's evaluate the classifier's performance. To do that, let's report accuracy, precision, recall, and F1 measures, and print out the confusion matrix. Listing 6.4 shows how to do that. It relies on `numpy` and scikit-learn's `metrics` functionality. For instance, it shows how to use `numpy.mean` to estimate how often the predicted class coincides with the original target (i.e., how to calculate the accuracy of the classifier). In addition, it shows how to use `metrics.confusion_matrix` to print out the confusion matrix for the class predictions and `metrics.classification_report` to report precision, recall, and F1 values for each class and for the whole dataset. The same routine can be applied to all datasets.

Listing 6.4   Code to evaluate the classifier

```
import numpy as np                          Import numpy and sklearn's
from sklearn import metrics      ◁──┘       metrics functionality.
```

```
def evaluate(predicted, targets):
    print(np.mean(predicted == targets))
    print(metrics.confusion_matrix(targets, predicted))
    print(metrics.classification_report(targets,
                                          predicted))

evaluate(predicted, pretest_targets)

predicted = text_clf.predict(test_data)
evaluate(predicted, test_targets)
```

You can use numpy.mean to estimate the accuracy of the classifier.

Use metrics.confusion_ matrix to print out the confusion matrix for the class predictions.

Apply the same routine to the test set.

metrics.classification_ report returns precision, recall, and F1 values.

The listing's code will print out the results as shown and explained in figure 6.8.

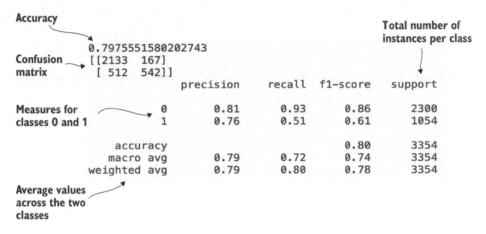

Figure showing:

Accuracy

Confusion matrix

Total number of instances per class

```
           0.7975551580202743
          [[2133  167]
           [ 512  542]]
                     precision    recall  f1-score   support

                0       0.81      0.93      0.86      2300
                1       0.76      0.51      0.61      1054

         accuracy                           0.80      3354
        macro avg       0.79      0.72      0.74      3354
     weighted avg       0.79      0.80      0.78      3354
```

Measures for classes 0 and 1

Average values across the two classes

Figure 6.8 Summary of the results achieved on the pretest set with a feature set of two features

These results show that, overall, the classifier performs with an accuracy of about 0.7976. This is the proportion of sentences in the pretest set that are correctly classified by this algorithm. Class 0 represents Jane Austen, with 2300 sentences in total, as support values show. Per confusion matrix, 2133 of those sentences are correctly classified as class 0, and 167 are incorrectly classified as belonging to class 1 (or, William Shakespeare). This results in a precision value of 0.81 (2133 sentences out of the 2133 + 512 = 2645 sentences identified as written by Jane Austen are indeed written by Jane Austen), recall of 0.93 (2133 sentences out of the total of 2133 + 167 = 2300 by Jane Austen found), and f1-score of 0.86 on class 0. At the same time, the pretest set contains 1054 sentences from class 1, and it correctly identifies 542 of those, while misclassifying 512 as class 0. This results in a precision value of 0.76 (542 sentences out of the 542 + 167 = 709 sentences identified as written by William Shakespeare are indeed written by William Shakespeare), recall of 0.51 (542 sentences out of the total of 542 + 512 = 1054 by William Shakespeare found), and f1-score of 0.61. On the average, between the two classes, the pretest set contains 3354 sentences, and the classifier achieves precision of 0.79, recall of 0.80, and f1-score of 0.78 on this set.

Figure 6.9 highlights the relevant values in the confusion matrices and connects them to the estimation of precision and recall values. It may remind you of the discussion in figure 6.2. Class 0 corresponds to Jane Austen (J.A. in figure 6.9) and class 1 to William Shakespeare (W.S. in figure 6.9).

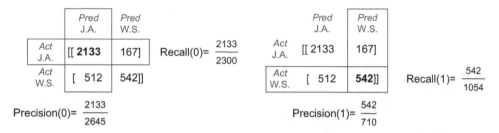

Figure 6.9   Interpretation of the confusion matrices and precision and recall values for two classes

What about the test set? On the test set, the classifier shows the following results:

```
0.8049522154648132
[[4605  394]
 [ 953  954]]
              precision    recall   f1-score    support
          0        0.83      0.92       0.87       4999
          1        0.71      0.50       0.59       1907

avg / total        0.80      0.80       0.79       6906
```

Let's visualize the accuracy scores as before using bar charts. In particular, let's compare the performance of the benchmark model from chapter 5 on the pretest and test sets to your new model that uses two new types of features: average word length (let's denote this feature type as F1 on the graph) and sentence length (F2). Figure 6.10 visualizes the results.

Several observations are due:

- With the benchmark model, we were achieving quite different accuracy scores on the pretest and test sets. With features and the classifier we are using here, all measures, including accuracy, precision, recall, and F1 on both classes and overall are quite similar on both sets. This means that the classifier generalizes much better with this set of features, and therefore characteristics related to the length of words and sentences are more reliable as author-specific characteristics.
- The overall performance is quite a bit lower than that achieved with the benchmark model. Classifying with words achieved an accuracy of 0.96 on the pretest set (as opposed to 0.80 here) and about 0.90 on the test set (as opposed to

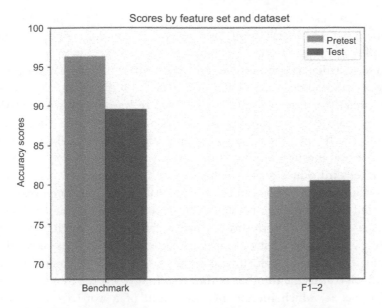

Figure 6.10 **Accuracy scores of a new model relying on average word length (F1) and sentence length (F2) compared to the benchmark model's performance from chapter 5**

0.80 here). However, note that here our classification algorithm relies on a very small feature set of just 2 features. As a reminder, the benchmark model based on the Naïve Bayes classifier and all words as features used over 13,000 features! The Decision Trees classifier from chapter 5, which showed quite similar performance to the one we observe here, used a smaller set of features selected according to their frequency, but was still relying on as many as 166 features.

- Performance on the minority class (class 1, William Shakespeare) is much lower than that on the majority class (class 0, Jane Austen). On both pretest and test sets, only about half of the instances belonging to class 1 are correctly identified, resulting in recall values around 0.50-0.51.

Therefore, we are not done yet, and we should continue looking into other features.

6.2.2 *Counts of stopwords and proportion of stopwords as features*

You came across the notion of stopwords several times in this book. *Stopwords* are words that are used frequently in language, and most of the time, they don't have a meaning of their own. Usually, they connect other meaningful words to each other or express some other function rather than meaning. For instance, articles like *a* and *the* are stopwords. They are very frequent, and their main goal in language is to express whether you came across a mention of a particular object before (definite article *the*) or not (indefinite article *a*). Prepositions like *at, on, about,* and others usually connect meaningful words to the notions of location (*stay* at *home*), time (*meet* on *Friday*), topic (*talk* about *politics*), and so on. In many applications they can be disposed of, as they don't contribute much to the task itself. You've seen an example of such an application in chapter 3.

However, one's particular writing style is a whole different matter. As it turns out, different authors use function words of different types with different frequencies. For instance, if you prefer using the word *but* whenever I use *however*, our writing styles will differ with respect to the use of these stopwords even if we otherwise use absolutely the same set of words. If you notice that you tend to use expressions like *well, sort of,* or *you know,* these are also mostly composed of stopwords.

To this end, let's introduce a new feature type that will estimate the number of times each stopword is used in a sentence and a feature estimating the proportion of stopwords in a sentence. As opposed to calculating the number of times various words are used in texts, in the case of stopwords, we are talking about a much more compact set of words (e.g., the spaCy's list of stopwords contains 305 words only) that frequently occur across sentences. Listing 6.5 shows how to implement a function word_counts, which counts the number of times each word occurs in text, and a function proportion_words, which increments the count of a word from a particular wordlist each time you see it in text and estimates the proportion of the words from the wordlist against all other words in the end.

> **Listing 6.5   Code to calculate the number and proportion of times certain words occur**

```
def word_counts(text):
    counts = {}
    for word in text:
        counts[word.lower()] = counts.get(
            word.lower(), 0) + 1          ◁    Each time you see a particular
    return counts                              word in text, simply increment
                                               the counter.
def proportion_words(text, wordlist):
    count = 0
    for word in text:
        if word.lower() in wordlist:          Estimate the proportion of
            count += 1                         the words from the wordlist
    return float(count)/float(len(text))   ◁  against all other words.
```

Now let's calculate the number of times we see each of the stopwords in sentences written by each of the authors, as well as the proportion of stopwords in their sentences using these functions. We are going to use the stopwords list from spaCy, and for each of the 305 words we are going to add one feature to the feature set representing the number of times this particular stopword occurs in a particular sentence, and then add one extra feature representing the proportion of *all* stopwords as opposed to all words used in each sentence by each writer. This means that our feature set at this point will contain 308 features. For instance, one of the new features in this new feature set corresponds to the count of the stopword 'a': for the sentence "It is yet too early in life to despair of such a happiness", this count equals 1.0, while for the sentence

"Not so happy, yet much happier", it is 0.0. At the same time, for the feature representing the count for the stopword 'not', the feature values are exactly the opposite: 0.0 and 1.0. Nine out of the total of 13 words in the sentence "It is yet too early in life to despair of such a happiness" are stopwords (all underlined); therefore, the stopwords proportion for this sentence equals 0.69. There are 7 words (including the comma) in the sentence "Not so happy, yet much happyer" in total, and 4 of them (underlined) are stopwords, making the proportion for this sentence equal to 0.57, as figure 6.11 illustrates.

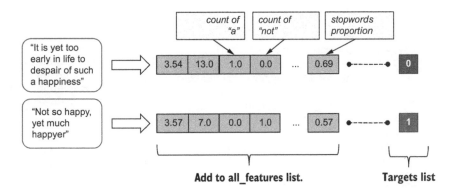

Figure 6.11 An updated `all_features` list (compared to the previous version of the `all_features` list in figure 6.6), now containing 308 features, including average length of words, word count, counts of all stopwords, and overall stopwords proportion

Listing 6.6 shows how to add the new 306 features to the feature set. You start by adding spaCy's functionality to the code and upload the stopwords list. Then you add the previous features to the set, and for each stopword from the stopwords list, you either add the count to the feature list or add 0 if the stopword doesn't occur in the sentence. You calculate the proportion of all stopwords combined as opposed to all words used in a sentence and add this as another feature, and, as before, you append the target labels. Finally, you extract the features from the datasets and print out the length of the feature lists and targets lists, which, as before, should equal to 13,414, 3,354, and 6,906 for the training, pretest, and test sets, respectively.

> **NOTE** Check out the different language models available for use with spaCy: https://spacy.io/models/en. Small model (en_core_web_sm) is suitable for most purposes and is more efficient to upload and use. However, larger models like en_core_web_md (medium) and en_core_web_lg (large) are more powerful, and some NLP tasks will require the use of such larger models. The models should be installed prior to running the code examples with spaCy. You can also install the models from within the Jupyter Notebook using the command !python -m spacy download en_core_web_md.

Listing 6.6   Code to add stopword counts and proportion as features

```python
import spacy
from spacy.lang.en.stop_words import STOP_WORDS

nlp = spacy.load('en_core_web_md')          ◁─┐  Add spaCy's functionality
                                              │  to the code and upload
def initialize_dataset(source):               │  the stopwords list.
    all_features = []
    targets = []
    for (sent, label) in source:
        feature_list=[]
        feature_list.append(avg_number_chars(sent))      ┐  Add the previous
        feature_list.append(number_words(sent))    ◁─────┤  features to the set.
        counts = word_counts(sent)
        for word in STOP_WORDS:                            ┐  For each stopword,
            if word in counts.keys():                      │  either add the count to
                feature_list.append(counts.get(word))      │  the feature list or add 0
            else:                                          │  if the stopword doesn't
                feature_list.append(0)            ◁────────┘  occur in the sentence.
        feature_list.append(proportion_words(
            sent, STOP_WORDS))               ◁──┐  Calculate the proportion of all
        all_features.append(feature_list)       │  stopwords combined as opposed
        if label=="austen": targets.append(0)   │  to all words used in a sentence.
        else: targets.append(1)
    return all_features, targets

train_data, train_targets = initialize_dataset(strat_train_set)
pretest_data, pretest_targets = initialize_dataset(strat_pretest_set)
test_data, test_targets = initialize_dataset(test_set)     ◁─┐  Initialize datasets
                                                            │  with the new
print (len(train_data), len(train_targets))                 │  features.
print (len(pretest_data), len(pretest_targets))
print (len(test_data), len(test_targets))     ◁──┐  Print out the length of the
                                                 │  feature lists and targets lists.
```

As before, append the target labels.

Finally, let's evaluate the results using the following code (which, you may notice, is very similar to listing 6.4).

Listing 6.7   Code to evaluate the results

```python
text_clf = DecisionTreeClassifier(random_state=42)     ┐  Train the classifier on
text_clf.fit(train_data, train_targets)          ◁─────┘  the training data.
predicted = text_clf.predict(pretest_data)
evaluate(predicted, pretest_targets)      ◁──┐  Print out accuracy, precision, recall,
                                             │  F1 scores, and the confusion matrix.
predicted = text_clf.predict(test_data)
evaluate(predicted, test_targets)      ◁──┐  Apply the same routine
                                          │  to the test set.
```

Test on the pretest set.

With this new set of features, the classifier achieves a slightly better accuracy of up to and above 0.81 on both pretest and test sets—that is, the classifier performs almost equally well on the two various datasets. These results are still a long way away from the result we got using all 13,000 words as features, as figure 6.12 demonstrates.

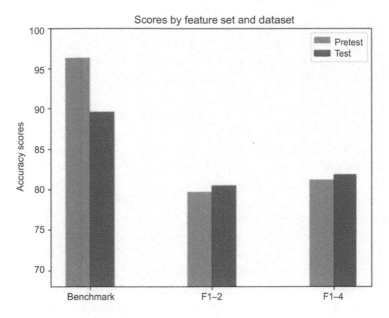

Figure 6.12 Accuracy scores after adding new types of features—counts of stopwords (F3) and their proportion in a sentence (F4)—compared to the previous models

However, the main contribution of these types of features is that they actually improve performance of the classifier on the minority class quite a lot. They help identify over 700 out of 1054 sentences by Shakespeare in the pretest set (resulting in a recall and f1-score values of 0.70 and above; this is a 20-point and an almost 10-point improvement above the recall and f1-score values with just 2 features), and over 1300 out of 1907 sentences by Shakespeare in the test set (resulting in a recall value above 0.70 and an f1-score above 0.67, an improvement similar to the pretest set results). Figure 6.13 shows confusion matrices for the pretest and test sets, with the sample results on the minority class highlighted.

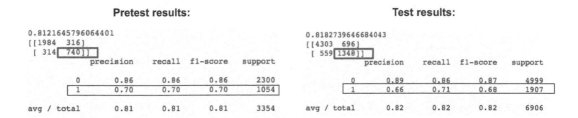

Figure 6.13 Confusion matrices with the sample performance on the minority class highlighted

6.2.3   *Distributions of parts of speech as features*

So far, you have applied quite "shallow" (i.e., superficial) features to address this task. It is time now to apply deeper linguistic analysis to better model each writer's style. Chapter 4 introduced spaCy, a toolkit that provides you with rich linguistic representations of words. Let's use some of these representations here.

For instance, one topic that we discussed was types of words, or parts of speech. Recall that words denoting objects, people, or facts are called *nouns*; words denoting actions and states are called *verbs*; words denoting qualities of objects, people, and facts are called *adjectives*; and so on. People are remarkably different in their choice of words even when they talk about relatively similar things. Action-oriented accounts would contain more verbs (e.g., one may say "I *booked* the hotel"); stories with more facts would contain more nouns (alternatively, one could say "I made the *booking*" to express the same idea); and if one wants to provide more details, adjectives and adverbs would be added in (as in "It was *easy* to make this booking"). The way different parts of speech are distributed in one's writing would make a promising type of feature.

To get POS tags of the words, let's use a tagger from spaCy's suite, which provides each word token with an extended set of linguistic information. Word tokens are analyzed and assigned with word forms (original words), lemmas (dictionary forms), POS tags, and grammatical relations, among other things (for the full description of all attributes, see https://spacy.io/api/token). It would be impractical to run a spaCy pipeline on the same sentences multiple times if you decided to use any of the other attributes as features at a later point, so let's apply the spaCy pipeline once and store the results in some external data structure. For instance, let's create a Python dictionary `source_docs` and map each sentence to a spaCy's token "container," which will contain all linguistic information pertaining to the tokens in this sentence. This way, you can extract any linguistic information you need at any later point. Figure 6.14 visualizes this idea.

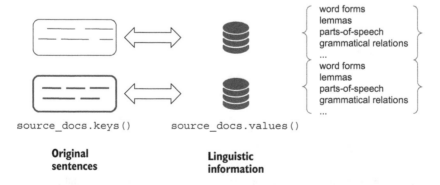

word forms
lemmas
parts-of-speech
grammatical relations
...
word forms
lemmas
parts-of-speech
grammatical relations
...

`source_docs.keys()`   `source_docs.values()`

Original   **Linguistic**
sentences   **information**

Figure 6.14 Within `source_docs`, original sentences are mapped to "containers" with linguistic information.

Let's implement a function preprocess that will create such a mapping. As listing 6.8 shows, you will need to provide the preprocess function with the original sentences from the datasets. Since spaCy needs a full grammatical sentence to apply the preprocessing steps, and in our data, sentences are already split into individual words, you'll need to merge them back together using whitespaces as word separators. As a result, the code adds the processed linguistic information to the source_docs dictionary. Since in this step spaCy performs all preprocessing operations and applies them to the full dataset, this step may take a bit of time. However, you will only need to run this code once, and in the rest of the chapter rely on the features extracted and stored in this step. To keep track, you can add a printout message that notifies you every time another 2,000 sentences have been processed. Finally, you apply the preprocess function to the three original datasets—strat_train_set, strat_pretest_set, and test_set—and store the results in the correspondent data structures.

Listing 6.8   Code to apply spaCy preprocessing

Provide the preprocess function with the original sentences from the datasets.

Merge the sentences back together using whitespaces.

Add the processed linguistic information to the source_docs dictionary.

```
def preprocess(source):
    source_docs = {}
    index = 0
    for (sent, label) in source:
        text = " ".join(sent)
        source_docs[text] = nlp(text)
        if index>0 and (index%2000)==0:
            print(str(index) + " texts processed")
        index += 1
    print("Dataset processed")
    return source_docs

train_docs = preprocess(strat_train_set)
pretest_docs = preprocess(strat_pretest_set)
test_docs = preprocess(test_set)
```

Let's add a printout message that notifies you every time another 2000 sentences have been processed.

Apply the preprocess function to the three original datasets.

Next, let's implement a function that will count words of specific parts of speech in each sentence. spaCy uses a variety of tags to distinguish between different forms of verbs (e.g., *done* and *doing* will receive different tags to express the idea that one denotes a finished action and another a continuous one), nouns (proper nouns like *Google* will receive a tag different from common nouns like *company*), and so on (you can see the full list of tags and their descriptions on https://spacy.io/usage/linguistic-features#pos-tagging). This will add a great variety of features, but if all we want to know is the distribution of nouns, verbs, and so on *in general* (i.e., without the finer distinctions between the *types* of nouns, verbs, etc.), using the first letter of the tag will typically be enough. Under the annotation scheme used by spaCy, all types of nouns are annotated with tags starting with N, all verbs are annotated with V, and so on. We will take into account 14 such coarse-grained POS tags. Table 6.4 provides more information about the correspondence of this coarse-grained notation to the actual parts of speech.

Table 6.4   Correspondence of the coarse-grained notation to the parts of speech

Notation	Part of speech	Example
C	Conjunctions	*and, but, or*
D	Determiners	*the, a, an*
E	Existential "there"	*there ("there is")*
F	Foreign words	*inter alia*
I	Prepositions	*in, at, during*
J	Adjectives	*big, bigger, biggest*
M	Modal verbs	*could, should, ought*
N	Nouns	*car, Google, Smiths, cars*
P	Pronouns	*I, his, somebody*
R	Adverbs	*fast, faster, very*
T	Particle "to"	*to ("to do")*
U	Interjections	*hello, bravo, ouch*
V	Verbs	*do, did, done, doing*
W	Wh-determiners and pronouns	*what, who, when*

This will add 14 new features to our feature set, making it a total of 322. Figure 6.13 shows how the feature vectors for the two example sentences from Jane Austen and William Shakespeare should be changed with the addition of these features. There is one adjective ("early") in the sentence "It is yet too early in life to despair of such a happiness" and two nouns ("life" and "happiness"), so given that this sentence contains 13 words in total, the proportion of adjectives (tag J) would be $1/13 = 0.08$ and the proportion of nouns (tag N) would be $2/13 = 0.15$. There are two adjectives ("happy" and "happyer") and no nouns in the sentence "Not so happy, yet much happyer", which consists of 7 words in total, so the proportions would be $2/7 = 0.29$ and $0/7 = 0$, as shown in figure 6.15.

In practice, though, NLP tools, including those that are part of the spaCy toolkit, are built with the standard modern language in mind. This means that occasionally they will make mistakes on texts written in a less usual style (e.g., poems, plays, and other types of literary works) and older versions of English language itself (like Early Modern English). Such occasional mistakes are to be expected. Many of these tools, including POS taggers, are built using machine learning, and you've seen in this and the previous chapters that machine-learning algorithms trained on one type of data cannot always be expected to do well on another type of data. For instance, a POS tagger trained on modern English does not learn how to process a word like "happyer" and therefore may assign it a different POS tag. In particular, here is how spaCy's tagger analyses the sentence containing "happyer": "Not$_{RB}$ so$_{RB}$ happy$_{JJ}$,

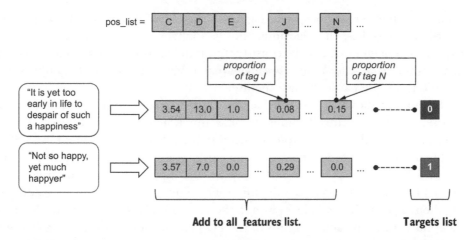

Figure 6.15   Addition of part-of-speech distribution features further expands the feature set.

yet$_{CC}$ much$_{JJ}$ happyyer$_{NN}$", or "Not$_{adverb}$ so$_{adverb}$ happy$_{adjective}$, yet$_{conjunction}$ much$_{adjective}$ happyyer$_{noun}$". From the linguistic point of view, there are two errors here: "happyyer" should be annotated as adjective, not noun, and "much" is an adverb rather than adjective. Why does the tool make these errors here?

Mistagging of "happyyer" occurs precisely because the POS tagger has been built on modern English texts, where it has never seen, and never learned how to process, the word "happyyer," so in this sentence it makes an assumption that such an unfamiliar word is most likely to be a noun. In fact, the sentence "Not so happy, yet much happyyer" doesn't contain any nouns, which is very unusual for a normal English sentence, so the tagging algorithm's assumption is not unreasonable: typically, an English sentence would have a noun, and if there is any candidate in this sentence for the role of a noun, it is the unfamiliar word "happyyer." What about the mistagging of "much", then? This is where one error leads to another one: having identified "happyyer" as a noun, the algorithm now needs to decide how to tag the previous word "much." This is because the POS tagger tries to make sense of the sentence as a whole and is trained to assign a plausible combination of tags in sequence, rather than analyzing each word in isolation (which would lead to many more errors!). Which tag is likely to precede a noun "happyyer"? Adverbs (tag RB) do not typically come in combination with nouns, but adjectives (tag JJ) do so all the time, so that is how the algorithm ends up assigning a tag JJ to the word "much", and that is how "much" ends up being an adjective rather than an adverb in this sentence.

What can one do with such errors, and will they impact performance of our authorship identification algorithm? If one's goal is to get accurate and high-quality POS tags assignment on a specific type of text (e.g., plays written in Early Modern English), the best solution would be to adapt the POS tagging algorithm to the specific type of data, such as by retraining it on this specific type of data. However, this is not the focus of our application here. In the context of authorship identification, even an imperfect part-of-speech tagging is still helpful. First of all, despite making occasional mistakes, the algorithm mostly analyzes texts correctly; second, we can expect such tagger errors to be consistent with the texts written by a particular author, and it is the *patterns of the tag distributions* that are informative for the authorship identification, not the particular tags themselves.

Listing 6.9 shows how to add the 14 part-of-speech features to the feature set. As before, you rely on the Python's `Counter` functionality to simplify counting procedures. As this code suggests, you first need to provide a coarse-grained list of POS tags that you'd like to extract (note that you can modify this list at any point). Then you define a function `pos_counts` and apply it to the input sentences (argument `text`) by extracting their POS tags from the linguistic containers in `source_docs` and comparing them against the set of tags given in the `pos_list`. Next, you populate `pos_counts` dictionary using the actual counts of the POS tags if they occur in the given sentence or `0` if a POS tag does not occur. Finally, you extract the previous 308 features as before and add the new 14 features by calculating the proportion of words with each of the 14 POS tags in the sentence (i.e., by dividing the part-of-speech counts by the total number of words in the sentence).

Listing 6.9   Code to add distribution of part-of-speech tags as features

Import Python's Counter functionality to simplify counting procedures.

Provide a coarse-grained list of part-of-speech tags that you'd like to extract.

Extract part-of-speech tags from the linguistic containers and compare them to predefined tags.

You only need the first letter from the actual part-of-speech tag.

Populate the pos_counts dictionary using the counts of the part-of-speech tags or inserting 0.

```python
from collections import Counter
pos_list = ["C", "D", "E", "F", "I", "J", "M",
            "N", "P", "R", "T", "U", "V", "W"]

def pos_counts(text, source_docs, pos_list):
    pos_counts = {}
    doc = source_docs.get(" ".join(text))
    tags = []
    for word in doc:
        tags.append(str(word.tag_)[0])
    counts = Counter(tags)
    for pos in pos_list:
        if pos in counts.keys():
            pos_counts[pos] = counts.get(pos)
        else: pos_counts[pos] = 0
    return pos_counts

def initialize_dataset(source, source_docs):
    all_features = []
    targets = []
    for (sent, label) in source:
        feature_list=[]
        feature_list.append(avg_number_chars(sent))
        feature_list.append(number_words(sent))
        counts = word_counts(sent)
        for word in STOP_WORDS:
            if word in counts.keys():
                feature_list.append(counts.get(word))
```

```
        else:
            feature_list.append(0)
    feature_list.append(proportion_words(
        sent, STOP_WORDS))
    p_counts = pos_counts(sent, source_docs, pos_list)
    for pos in p_counts.keys():
        feature_list.append(
            float(p_counts.get(pos))/
            float(len(sent)))
    all_features.append(feature_list)
    if label=="austen": targets.append(0)
    else: targets.append(1)
return all_features, targets
```

Extract the previous **308 features** as before.

Add the new **14 features** by calculating the proportion of words with each of the 14 part-of-speech tags.

Finally, let's train, test, and evaluate the classifier based on these new features, as we did before. Here is one modification that we will make to the code. From now on, the code that trains and tests the algorithm and evaluates the results is not going to change, so we can simply pack it up under a method called run() and apply this method every time we need the train-test-evaluate routine. The following code does exactly that.

Listing 6.10 Code to run the train-test-evaluate routine

```
def run():
    train_data, train_targets = initialize_dataset(strat_train_set, train_docs)
    pretest_data, pretest_targets = initialize_dataset(strat_pretest_set,
     pretest_docs)
    test_data, test_targets = initialize_dataset(
        test_set, test_docs)

    print (len(train_data), len(train_targets))
    print (len(pretest_data), len(pretest_targets))
    print (len(test_data), len(test_targets))
    print ()

    text_clf = DecisionTreeClassifier(random_state=42)
    text_clf.fit(train_data, train_targets)
    predicted = text_clf.predict(pretest_data)
    evaluate(predicted, pretest_targets)

    predicted = text_clf.predict(test_data)
    evaluate(predicted, test_targets)

run()
```

Initialize the datasets.

As a sanity check, print out the sizes of the datasets.

Train on the training set.

Test and evaluate on the pretest set.

Test and evaluate of the test set.

The results printed out by this code show that the addition of these 14 features improves the performance even further. Now the classifier performs with 0.82–0.83 accuracy on both pretest and test sets, showing good generalization behavior. For example, you may get results similar to the ones presented in figure 6.16.

NOTE Don't be alarmed if you get slightly different results from one run to another. Minor deviations are possible, since spaCy introduces its own random seed.

Pretest results: **Test results:**

```
0.8208109719737626                                  0.8284100781928757
[[1999  301]                                        [[4326  673]
 [ 300  754]]                                        [ 512 1395]]
              precision    recall  f1-score   support              precision    recall  f1-score   support

           0       0.87      0.87      0.87      2300           0       0.89      0.87      0.88      4999
           1       0.71      0.72      0.72      1054           1       0.67      0.73      0.70      1907

    accuracy                          0.82      3354    accuracy                          0.83      6906
   macro avg       0.79      0.79      0.79      3354   macro avg       0.78      0.80      0.79      6906
weighted avg       0.82      0.82      0.82      3354weighted avg       0.83      0.83      0.83      6906
```

Figure 6.16   Sample results on the pretest and test sets with the addition of the part-of-speech features

Moreover, precision, recall, and F1 scores improve on both minority and majority classes: now the classifier reaches very balanced precision, recall and F1 at and above 0.87 on class 0 (Jane Austen) on the pretest set, and similar values on the test set. Performance on the minority class—class 1 (William Shakespeare)—is also consistent: precision, recall, and F1 are all around 0.70 and above, bringing the average performance across classes to 0.82–0.83 across the runs of the classifier. This is great news. The results keep improving, and they are very stable across the pretest and test sets, showing that the set of features we are applying represents the task well, as it generalizes between the data sets. However, there is still a considerable gap in performance between the majority and minority classes, and in terms of absolute numbers, the results are not yet at the level we got with the benchmark model, as figure 6.17 shows. Let's add some additional features.

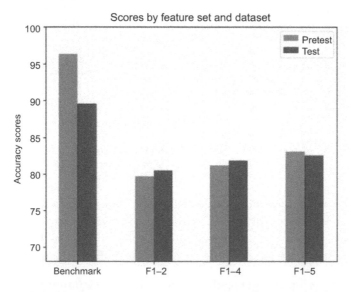

Figure 6.17   Accuracy scores after adding a new type of feature— distribution of parts of speech (F5) compared to the previous models

6.2.4 *Distribution of word suffixes as features*

Words are excellent source of features: they tell us about author's individual preferences, choices, and topics covered in one's writing. The caveat with the words used as features is that they tend to represent the training dataset a bit too precisely, so such things as topics and characters from the training set might get memorized rather than used to learn informative patterns, and as the same character names and topics do not necessarily occur in the test set, the classifier performs less well on the test data if it uses only words. The problem is, the classifier has no way to distinguish between those words that relate to topics and particular literary works and those that reflect the author's distinctive writing style.

A solution to this problem is to use *parts of words* rather than full words. Why is this useful? In fact, bits of words encode the full set of words much more compactly, which helps the classifier's performance as it creates a much smaller feature space. At the same time, they capture spelling conventions that pertain to one's writing *across* the words. For instance, if I used British spelling, many of the words would end with *–ise* as in *initialise*, rather than with *–ize* as in *initialize*. Finally, bits of words would, once again, reflect what types of words an author prefers using—are those adjectives ending with *–able*, as in *remarkable, unmistakable*, and so on? Or are those nouns ending with *–tion*, as in *reflection, composition*, and so on?

With spaCy, you can extract the final three letters of a word, called *suffixes*. This is one of the linguistic features of a token that we stored at the previous step. Let's use suffixes as features. To make our feature space more compact, let's focus on the distribution of the most frequent *n%* of the suffixes in our data. You can select your own cutoff point, as the following code suggests. Here, we are using 40% most frequent suffixes from the data.

Listing 6.11 Code to collect the most frequent suffixes from the data

Import Python's operator functionality, which is useful when sorting dictionaries.

Implement a function to select a certain proportion of the most frequent suffixes in the data.

Suffixes can be directly accessed for each word in each sentence using word.suffix__.

Iterate through the list of values in the train_docs.values().

```python
import operator

def select_suffixes(cutoff):
    all_suffixes = []
    for doc in train_docs.values():
        for word in doc:
            all_suffixes.append(str(word.suffix_).lower())
    counts = Counter(all_suffixes)
    sorted_counts = sorted(counts.items(), key=operator.itemgetter(1),
                           reverse=True)
    selected_suffixes = []
    for i in range(0, round(len(counts)*cutoff)):
        selected_suffixes.append(sorted_counts[i][0])
    return selected_suffixes
```

First, store the frequency of all the suffixes in the counts dictionary, and then sort it in descending order.

Use some of the most frequent suffixes only; the suffixes can be accessed with sorted_counts[i][0].

```
selected_suffixes = select_suffixes(0.4)
print(len(selected_suffixes))
print(selected_suffixes)        ◄──────────
```

Apply this function to extract and print out the most frequent 40% of the suffixes.

In this code, you rely on Python's operator functionality, which is useful when sorting dictionaries. You implement a function select_suffixes to select a certain proportion (defined by cutoff) of the most frequent suffixes in the data. For that, you iterate through the list of values in the train_docs.values(). These are linguistic containers for all the sentences from the training set. From these containers, you extract suffixes, which can be directly accessed for each word in each sentence using word.suffix_. You store the frequency of all the suffixes in the counts dictionary and then sort this dictionary according to the number of times each suffix occurs in the training data—thus, key=operator.itemgetter(1) in descending order, starting with the most frequent suffixes (i.e., reverse=True). To make the feature space more compact, the code shows how you can use only some of the most frequent suffixes. You can control the proportion of the most frequent suffixes with the cutoff argument. For the sorted_counts entries within this range, you need only the suffix, which can be accessed with sorted_counts[i][0]. Finally, you apply this function to extract and print out the most frequent 40% of the suffixes.

The code in listing 6.11 will print out a list of 577 suffixes. As we don't restrict the length of the words, whenever the word itself is shorter than 3 characters in length, the full word is returned by this method by default, so you might see some words like was, as, or even punctuation marks like ? in this list. At the same time, word fragments such as ing (as in *interes*ting and *mov*ing), ion (as in *celebrat*ion and *un*ion), uld (as in *sho*uld and *wo*uld), ess (as in *selfl*ess and *darkn*ess), and many others feature on this list.

Let's now use these suffixes as features, which will increase the size of our feature set from 322 up to 899 features. As before, we will extract features from each of the sentences by using the counts for each of the suffixes in a particular sentence and using a count of 0 whenever a suffix does not occur in any of the words in a sentence. We will then add these features to our feature set, and we will train, test, and evaluate the classifier.

Listing 6.12 runs through all of these steps. First, the suffix_counts function returns the counts of suffixes from the suffix_list in the given sentence (text). You need to add source_docs as an argument because source_docs store the linguistic containers with the suffixes for all the words in the sentence. For each suffix from the suffix_list, you use its count in the sentence as the feature value if it occurs, and you use 0 otherwise. Next, you extract the previous 322 features as before and add the new 577 suffix distribution features by calculating the proportion of words containing each of the suffixes in the sentence—that is, by dividing the suffix counts by the total number of words in the sentence. Finally, you apply the train-test-evaluate routine as before.

Listing 6.12 Code to add new, suffix-based features, then train and test the classifier

```
def suffix_counts(text, source_docs, suffix_list):

    suffix_counts = {}
    doc = source_docs.get(" ".join(text))
    suffixes = []
    for word in doc:
        suffixes.append(str(word.suffix_))
    counts = Counter(suffixes)
    for suffix in suffix_list:
        if suffix in counts.keys():
            suffix_counts[suffix] = counts.get(suffix)
        else: suffix_counts[suffix] = 0
    return suffix_counts

def initialize_dataset(source, source_docs):
    all_features = []
    targets = []
    for (sent, label) in source:
        feature_list=[]
        feature_list.append(avg_number_chars(sent))
        feature_list.append(number_words(sent))
        counts = word_counts(sent)
        for word in STOP_WORDS:
            if word in counts.keys():
                feature_list.append(counts.get(word))
            else:
                feature_list.append(0)
        feature_list.append(proportion_words(sent, STOP_WORDS))
        p_counts = pos_counts(sent, source_docs, pos_list)
        for pos in p_counts.keys():
            feature_list.append(
                float(p_counts.get(pos))/
                float(len(sent)))
        s_counts = suffix_counts(sent, source_docs, selected_suffixes)
        for suffix in s_counts.keys():
            feature_list.append(
                float(s_counts.get(suffix))/
                float(len(sent)))

        all_features.append(feature_list)
        if label=="austen": targets.append(0)
        else: targets.append(1)
    return all_features, targets

run()
```

The suffix_counts function returns the counts of suffixes from the suffix_list in the given sentence (text).

For each suffix from the suffix_list, use its count in the sentence if it occurs or 0 otherwise.

Add the previous 322 features as before.

Add the new 577 suffix distribution features by calculating the proportion of words containing the suffixes.

Apply the train-test-evaluate routine as before.

This code will print out accuracy values over 0.95 for both pretest and test sets! That is, you've reached performance comparable to that of the benchmark model on the pretest set, and you've also significantly improved performance of the classifier on the test set, as figure 6.18 shows. Now the performance on both sets is almost equally good, proving that the set of features is generalizable and captures the author's style

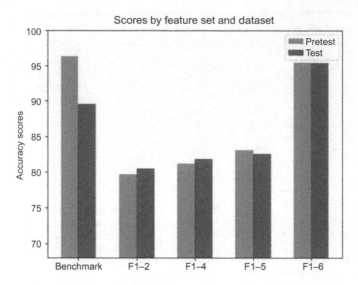

Figure 6.18 Accuracy scores after adding suffixes distribution (F6) compared to the previous models

rather than topics or any other phenomena in the data. Moreover, the classifier uses a much smaller feature set of under 1,000 features as opposed to over 13,000-word features with the benchmark model.

What about performance on each of the classes? All class-related measures (precision, recall, and F1 score) reach around 0.96–0.97 on both pretest and test sets for class 0 (Jane Austen), as figure 6.19 shows. This is by itself an improvement of almost 10 points over the previous results. What is more, on the minority class, class 1 (William Shakespeare), the classifier reaches precision, recall, and F1 score in the range of 0.90–0.93 on both pretest and test sets. This is not only a significant improvement of 20 points over the previous results but it also makes performance on both majority and minority classes sufficiently similar.

Pretest results: **Test results:**

```
0.9543828264758497                         0.9501882421083117
[[2218   82]                               [[4815  184]
 [  71  983]]                               [ 160 1747]]
          precision  recall  f1-score  support              precision  recall  f1-score  support

       0      0.97     0.96     0.97      2300          0      0.97     0.96     0.97      4999
       1      0.92     0.93     0.93      1054          1      0.90     0.92     0.91      1907

accuracy                        0.95      3354   accuracy                        0.95      6906
macro avg      0.95     0.95     0.95      3354   macro avg      0.94     0.94     0.94      6906
weighted avg   0.95     0.95     0.95      3354   weighted avg   0.95     0.95     0.95      6906
```

Figure 6.19 Sample results with the addition of suffix-based features

6.2.5 *Unique words as features*

Finally, to round off the discussion, let's revisit the notion of words as features once again. We said that words create a very sparse feature set without providing for the good generalizability of the classifier. Is there any more compact and useful subset of words to use as features?

If each author has their favorite words to use, can we simply use the unique vocabularies each author has for classification? That is, if William Shakespeare repeatedly uses words like *nephewes, suppresse, poysoner, wildenesse,* and *eternall* (all Early Modern English spellings of otherwise familiar words) that do not occur in Jane Austen's literary works, while Jane Austen repeatedly uses words like *Mr., Mrs., family, business,* and *handsome,* which William Shakespeare does not use, then can't these words represent some useful features in our task? Let's try adding them to our feature set. As with suffixes, let's start by collecting the set of words to work with. This time we want to extract all words that occur in Jane Austen but not in William Shakespeare, and vice versa. Next, to make sure we don't end up with very rare words than occur only once or twice in the training set, let's apply a cutoff again and consider, say, the top 50% of the unique vocabularies from each author. The following code collects unique words in that way.

> **Listing 6.13 Code to collect 50% most frequent unique words per author**

```
def unique_vocabulary(label1, label2, cutoff):       ◁─┐  Implement a function
                                                         │  that selects a certain
    voc1 = []                                            │  proportion of the most
    voc2 = []                                            │  frequent unique words
    for (sent, label) in strat_train_set:               │  for each author.
        if label==label1:
            for word in sent:
                voc1.append(word.lower())
        elif label==label2:                      Collect full vocabularies
            for word in sent:                    (all words used) for
                voc2.append(word.lower())   ◁─┘  each author.
    counts1 = Counter(voc1)
    sorted_counts1 = sorted(counts1.items(), key=operator.itemgetter(1),
      reverse=True)
    counts2 = Counter(voc2)
    sorted_counts2 = sorted(counts2.items(), key=operator.itemgetter(1),
      reverse=True)                                 ◁─┐  Count the number of
                                                       │  times each word occurs
    unique_voc = []                                    │  with each author and
    for i in range(0, round(len(sorted_counts1)*cutoff)):  sort them in descending
        if not sorted_counts1[i][0] in counts2.keys():     order.
            unique_voc.append(sorted_counts1[i][0])
    for i in range(0, round(len(sorted_counts2)*cutoff)):  The unique_voc list
        if not sorted_counts2[i][0] in counts1.keys():     stores the most frequent
            unique_voc.append(sorted_counts2[i][0])   ◁─┘  words for each author if
                                                           they are never used by
    return unique_voc                                      the other author.
```

```
unique_voc = unique_vocabulary("austen", "shakespeare", 0.5)
print(len(unique_voc))
print(unique_voc)     ◁———|  Print out the unique_voc list
                              using 50% as the cutoff.
```

In this code, you implement a function `unique_vocabulary` that selects a certain proportion (defined by `cutoff`) of the most frequent unique words for `author1` (`label1`) and `author2` (`label2`). Within this function, you first collect full vocabularies—that is, all words used, for each author. Then you count the number of times each word occurs with each author and sort them in descending order. The `unique_voc` list stores only the most frequent words (defined by `cutoff`) for each author if they never occur in the other author's vocabulary. You can access the words themselves using `sorted_counts[i][0]`. In the end, you can print out the `unique_voc` list using 50% as the `cutoff`.

The code will print out a list of 4,435 words. This constitutes about one-third of the total set of over 13,000 words occurring in the training set. Given that we are using only 50% of the unique words, we can tell that about two-thirds of the total number of words used in the training set are unique. They occur in the works by one author but not the other. This partially explains high accuracy values achieved with the benchmark model. Given that the vocabularies of the two authors are so diverse and there is, relatively speaking, not much overlap, it is easier for the classifier to separate the sentences produced by these two authors. However, the main problem with the words as features only is that they don't produce reliably good results. Is this selected set of words better?

Inspecting the `unique_voc` list printed out by the code from listing 6.13, you may notice several character names on this list, like `emma`, `harriet`, `hamlet`, and `polonius`. As you know by now, such features won't help much in classification of any new test data. At the same time, the `unique_voc` list also contains words that use Early Modern English spelling and should help in identifying William Shakespeare, as well as words like `agreeable`, `amiable`, and `desirable` from the works by Jane Austen, that confirm our earlier hypotheses that the use of adjectives or the use of words ending in `ble` can be characteristic of a particular author.

Let's add the count of unique words as another type of feature. This time, we will be adding extra 4,435 features, making our whole feature set as large as 5,334 features. Listing 6.14 shows how to add these new features and run the train-test-evaluate routine. In this code, the `unique_counts` function returns the counts of unique words from the `unique_voc` list in the given sentence (`text`). For each word from the `unique_voc`, it uses its count in the sentence as the feature value if it occurs and 0 otherwise. The previous 899 features are extracted as before and complemented with the new 4,435 unique word count features. Finally, the train-test-evaluate routine is applied as before.

NOTE   This final set of features is still considerably smaller than the one that you used with the benchmark model in chapter 5. It is also less sparse than the set of all words in the data, which helps the `Decision Trees` classifier deal with this task efficiently. Finally, scikit-learn's implementation of the algorithm ensures optimal performance of the classifier.

Listing 6.14 Code to add new word-based features, then train and test the classifier

```
def unique_counts(text, unique_voc):

    unique_counts = {}
    words = []
    for word in text:
        words.append(word.lower())
    counts = Counter(words)
    for word in unique_voc:
        if word in counts.keys():
            unique_counts[word] = counts.get(word)
        else: unique_counts[word] = 0

    return unique_counts

def initialize_dataset(source, source_docs):
    all_features = []
    targets = []
    for (sent, label) in source:
        feature_list=[]
        feature_list.append(avg_number_chars(sent))
        feature_list.append(number_words(sent))
        counts = word_counts(sent)
        for word in STOP_WORDS:
            if word in counts.keys():
                feature_list.append(counts.get(word))
            else:
                feature_list.append(0)
        feature_list.append(proportion_words(sent, STOP_WORDS))
        p_counts = pos_counts(sent, source_docs, pos_list)
        for pos in p_counts.keys():
            feature_list.append(float(p_counts.get(pos))/float(len(sent)))
        s_counts = suffix_counts(sent, source_docs, selected_suffixes)
        for suffix in s_counts.keys():
            feature_list.append(
                float(s_counts.get(suffix))/
                float(len(sent)))
        u_counts = unique_counts(sent, unique_voc)
        for word in u_counts.keys():
            feature_list.append(u_counts.get(word))
        all_features.append(feature_list)
        if label=="austen": targets.append(0)
        else: targets.append(1)
    return all_features, targets

run()
```

The unique_counts function returns the counts of unique words from the unique_voc list in the given sentence.

For each word from the unique_voc, use its count in the sentence if it occurs or 0 otherwise.

Add the previous 899 features as before.

Add the new 4,435 unique word counts features.

Apply the train-test-evaluate routine as before.

The results returned by this code show that a further small improvement is achieved with these new features. Now accuracy on both pretest and test sets is around 0.96;

precision, recall, and F1 score on the majority class (class 0, Jane Austen) is reliably at 0.97 on both sets, while performance on the minority class (class 1, William Shakespeare) is further improved by 1 percentage point, reaching around 0.91 to 0.94 in terms of precision, recall, and F1 score on both datasets. Average precision, recall, and F1 scores per two classes on both pretest and test sets reach 0.96, which is a remarkably consistent behavior. Figure 6.20 summarizes the results you've got with various models, with F7 representing the final group of features you've added—counts of unique words per author.

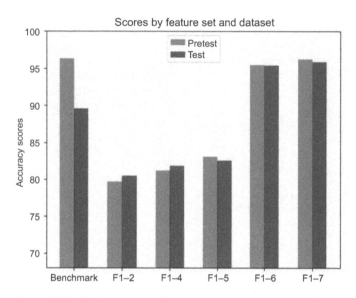

Figure 6.20   Final summary of accuracy scores across all models

6.3   *Practical use of authorship attribution and user profiling*

Congratulations! You have now implemented your second machine learning and natural language processing application! What is more, you have learned about linguistic feature engineering, and the machine-learning pipeline you've built over the course of the past two chapters can be applied to any language-related task as soon as you can represent it as a classification problem with a clear set of classes.

Now that you have acquired new skills—you know how to use two NLP toolkits, how to apply two ML classification algorithms, and how to properly evaluate the results—it's time to put your skills to practice. For further practice, consider working on the open-ended exercises 6.1–6.3. Since these tasks are open-ended (e.g., in exercise 6.1, you may consider working on any pair of authors, and exercise 6.2 invites you to work on your own data), it would be impossible to give you any precise solutions for these exercises. However, I hope the material of this and the previous chapter will guide you in your own practical applications.

Exercise 6.1

Jane Austen and William Shakespeare have quite different writing styles, which might have considerably helped the classification algorithm to distinguish between the two. The reason we selected those two authors was the availability of the data through the NLTK interface. At the same time, Project Gutenberg contains a much larger number of literary works for a wide variety of authors. Use texts from Project Gutenberg to create training and test sets for the authors of your choice; then apply the machine-learning pipeline to get new results.

Hint: You can access texts using the following code:

```
from urllib.request import urlopen
in_text = ""
with urlopen('https://www.gutenberg.org/files/521/521-0.txt') as response:
    for line in response:
        line = line.decode('utf-8')
        in_text += line
```

Check out the IDs of the literary works of your favorite authors: 521 in the code here stands for *The Life and Adventures of Robinson Crusoe*. Note that the texts come in untokenized, so you will need to first split them into sentences and words.

Exercise 6.2

If you have your own set of texts (e.g., blog posts or forum posts) produced by users with different characteristics (e.g., age, occupation, status, or gender), adapt the authorship attribution algorithm that we built in this chapter to classify users according to these characteristics instead of authorship.

Exercise 6.3 (Advanced)

If you would like more practice with real-life NLP and ML tasks, check datasets and projects available on the Kaggle platform (www.kaggle.com/) and in the UCI Machine Learning Repository (https://archive.ics.uci.edu/ml/index.php).

Explore user- and author-profiling datasets available on these platforms. For example:

- Detect an author of a tweet based on the text of a tweet in "Hillary Clinton and Donald Trump Tweets" (www.kaggle.com/benhamner/clinton-trump-tweets) dataset. *Possible extension*: the dataset contains other characteristics about author behavior and statistics on Twitter, which can be added to the feature set and combined with linguistic features.
- Detect an author of an article from the Reuters dataset (https://archive.ics .uci.edu/ml/datasets/Reuter_50_50). Note that this dataset contains articles from as many as 50 different authors. You can either select two authors to keep with the binary classification task, or extend the machine-learning pipeline to 50 classes.

Summary

- An advanced author profiling algorithm uses a more compact and informative set of linguistic features with the `Decision Trees` classifier.

- Accuracy is one of the most widely used measures for performance evaluation, but as a single score, it hides away how the classifier performs on each of the classes. If you want to know how to improve the results of your algorithm further, look into class-wise performance and use precision, recall, and the F1 measure/score. In addition, it is always helpful to print out the confusion matrix, which shows the distribution of predicted class instances against the actual class instances.

- Linguistic feature engineering is a process that helps you identify which types of information represent informative characteristics of the classes and can be used as features. This process is an important part of an NLP project. Often, it is not known in advance which features should be used, and you need to run comparative experiments to find this out. For the author-profiling task, words do not provide for good generalization behavior; therefore, other features ranging from "shallow" (e.g., word and sentence length) to "deep" linguistic features (e.g., suffixes or part-of-speech distributions in texts) may be more informative. Such linguistic features can be extracted using spaCy. The feature engineering experiments presented in this chapter can be extended and the effect that some other features (e.g., phrases or word order in the author's writing) may have on the results can be further investigated.

- `Decision Trees` is one of the many classifiers available via scikit-learn. The toolkit makes it easy to experiment with other classifiers further.

- The authorship attribution application achieves equally good results on various sets of data and on both majority and minority classes and beats the results of the benchmark model. This application can be adapted to identify authors and groups of users in other datasets. Moreover, the machine-learning pipeline from this section can be applied to *any* NLP application that can be represented as a supervised machine-learning task.

7

Your first sentiment analyzer using sentiment lexicons

This chapter covers

- Discussing sentiment analysis in depth
- Implementing a sentiment analyzer using a lexicon-based approach
- Using spaCy to apply linguistic pipeline and linguistic concepts

The last two chapters discussed implementation of an authorship-attribution algorithm using NLP approaches and machine-learning techniques. You can now apply your authorship-attribution application whenever you want to identify the actual author of a particular piece of writing. The previous chapters also introduced several new ideas. Let's summarize them here before we attempt a new NLP application:

- You've learned that machine learning is used quite a lot across NLP tasks. So far, you have applied it to authorship attribution in chapters 5 and 6 and to spam filtering in chapter 2. In particular, whenever you can enumerate the desired outcomes, you can present the task as that of classification. In spam filtering, you classified an email as class1="spam" or class2="ham", and in authorship attribution your goal was to assign sentences to class1="Jane

Austen" or class2="William Shakespeare". In addition, whenever you have access to data where classes were reliably identified in the past, you can use this class-annotated past data to teach a machine-learning algorithm to identify more instances of the same classes in the future. Such an approach is called *supervised learning*. So far, you have worked with binary classification since both authorship attribution and spam filtering included two classes only, but the tasks can easily be extended to multiclass settings. For example, if you attempted exercise 6.3 from chapter 6, you might have already worked with multiple authors as classes. Similarly, in your email inbox you might want to distinguish between "spam," "urgent," and "normal" emails, making email filtering a three-class rather than a two-class task.

- Previous chapters taught you how to use two popular classification algorithms—Naïve Bayes and Decision Trees. You have used them via different toolkits, scikit-learn and NLTK. We said that since scikit-learn is specifically built for the use in machine-learning applications, from now on we will rely on its functionality and learn how to use it across multiple scenarios.

- You have also learned how to use two NLP toolkits—NLTK and spaCy, and above all, how functionalities of the two can be combined. Both are built with NLP practitioners in mind, and previous chapters taught you how to leverage their capabilities to access linguistic resources and tools, and how to extract relevant linguistic information that can be used by a machine-learning classifier as features. You have learned that various types of such linguistic information may be relevant for the task at hand. For instance, in chapter 2 you built a spam filter that relied on word content of emails only, but as chapter 5 showed, words on their own are not enough to distinguish between various authors' writing styles. For that, you also needed to take the distribution of specific types of words (e.g., function words like articles or prepositions) or parts of words (e.g., suffixes) into account. You have learned that feature selection depends on the task.

- Finally, now you know how to build a machine-learning pipeline, from beginning to end. Typically, here's what you will need to do:
  1 Select relevant data, where classes can be reliably identified.
  2 Proceed by preprocessing it.
  3 Split it into separate sets for training and testing.
  4 Extract the selected set of features.
  5 Train the classifier of your choice on the training set.
  6 Apply the trained model to a separate (pretest or test) set and evaluate the results.
  7 Depending on the results, you may wish to change the set of features or the algorithm itself, and iterate over the previous steps.

Figure 7.1 visualizes the machine-learning pipeline you built and used in the previous chapters.

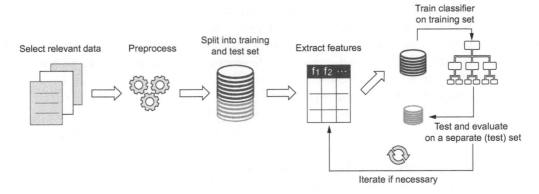

Figure 7.1 Machine-learning pipeline for a supervised classification task. The figure visualizes all steps in the pipeline.

> **NOTE** The best strategy to test generalization behavior of your machine-learning application is to split your data into three sets: a training set, on which you train your algorithms; a separate validation set, on which you can repeatedly test different settings of your algorithm and select the best ones; and the final test set, to which you apply the best model, once you selected it on the basis of the results on the validation set, to measure the ultimate algorithm's performance. In chapters 5 and 6, you used a pretest set for validation. In this and the next chapter, you will use a simplified version of this procedure using only training and test sets.

It's time to practice your new skills and improve them further! In this chapter, you will be working on another very popular NLP task, *sentiment analysis*. Sentiment analysis is concerned with automatic detection of whether a particular text—for example, a review of a new phone, an app that you are about to install, a restaurant that you are planning to go to this evening, or a movie that you are about to watch in a cinema—is *positive* or *negative*.

7.1 Use cases

Having an opinion about various events and products is natural for humans. Typically, once we try something new, be that reading a new book, watching a new TV show, or going to a new restaurant, we form an opinion about that, which most of the time falls within one of the two categories: if we like it, we feel and talk positively about it and we might recommend it to our friends. In contrast, if the experience was not satisfactory, we feel the urge to share this with others and warn them so that they don't repeat our mistakes and don't waste their time and money. One can be sure that people felt the need to share their positive and negative emotions about various types of experience with their family and friends from the very onset of social interaction; however, the development of the internet and technology over the past decades enabled us to share our opinions with anyone in the world. For instance, how often do you read reviews about a newly released movie on IMDb (Internet Movie Database; www.imdb.com/) before buying your cinema ticket? Or how often do you check reviews of a new restaurant on Tripadvisor (www.tripadvisor.com) before making a reservation? Our reliance on ratings and reviews provided by a large number of absolute strangers is so ingrained in us these days that many would check the opinions of others even before taking a new job! (See the popular Glassdoor platform that allows former and current employees to anonymously review companies: www.glassdoor.com/.)

This particular situation is created and supported by the technology. What makes us trust the opinion of (often anonymous) others? At the core of this process lies the idea of collective intelligence (http://mng.bz/95j0), which suggests that a large group of people can make more accurate predictions and better decisions than a few individuals, often even when those few are experts in their field. It is this idea that is behind our trust in the information presented by online sources (e.g., Quora or Stack Overflow). It is also behind such self-regulating platforms as Uber and Airbnb, that rely solely on the opinion of their users, and it is also widely used by crowdsourcing and crowdfunding platforms. What matters for us in this and the next chapters is that it is also at the core of sentiment analysis: when a number of people express their opinion in writing, we can extract this opinion and analyze the sentiment with the help of NLP and ML techniques. Let's look into some specific examples:

- There are multiple scenarios where you, as an individual user, would like to rely on collective intelligence to help you make your own decisions. As we just discussed, it has become a common practice to check movie reviews before buying tickets to the cinema, read what people say about a restaurant before planning your evening or what they say about a resort before planning your whole holiday, read other users' reviews before buying a new phone or installing a new app, and so on. Typically, you would want to know what other people thought in general. For instance, if you are selecting between two different phones, you might be interested in comparing their overall quality to each other. At the same time, you might also want to know about particular strengths and weaknesses of a product that other users already spotted: you might be inclined to buy a phone with a longer lasting battery and not the one with a better camera, even if overall it has less positive reviews (e.g., because other users were primarily looking for one with a better camera).

- Oftentimes, you can rely on star rating. For instance, IMDb aggregates reviews and provides a single star rating averaged across all users who left a review. So, if you are making plans for tonight and choosing between two movies, you might just compare this aggregated star rating. However, this is not always possible (e.g., some websites might not use star rating at all) or reliable. To see why star rating might not always be reliable, just ask yourself what a 7-star rating (on a scale of 1 to 10) for a movie means for you. How good or how bad should a movie be to get such a rating? Once you've formulated the requirements for yourself, ask a friend of yours the same question. Now, do you think the two of you will always give 7 stars to exactly the same movies? The point is, numerical scales are subjective, while what people write about their experience or opinion is more reliable for the general (i.e., positive versus negative) sentiment detection. However, wading through lots of reviews in order to extract relevant opinion-bearing information is a laborious task! Sentiment analysis uses NLP techniques to distill text down to such valuable opinion-bearing information. Figure 7.2 shows how sentiment is expressed in a review on a hotel with positive sentiment words and expressions (marked with a plus sign), negative comments (marked with a minus), and expressions that can go either way depending on context but are actually used with a positive sentiment in this particular review (marked with a question mark).

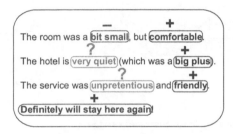

Figure 7.2   A positive review on a hotel with positive (+), negative (−), and other sentiment-bearing expressions (?) highlighted

- If you've developed your own product, or you work for a company that has a specific product or provides a service, you might also benefit from knowing what your users or customers think. In fact, companies often use sentiment analysis in their market analysis strategies. For instance, a company may run sentiment analysis on the posts from social media and forums to find out what users like or dislike about their product/service and how it compares to their competitors' products/services.

- Moreover, sentiment analysis can help optimize other aspects of business. For instance, in 2016 a British online grocery company Ocado started using a sentiment analysis algorithm to automatically analyze and interpret customers' complaints, praise, and requests for assistance. The company noticed that on a normal day they would receive about 2,000 emails from their customers, but on days when, for example, bad weather or traffic accidents lead to delivery delays, the number of emails could rise up to 6,000—an enormous amount for a human to analyze! Among those emails, there would be positive ones that simply say "My order was perfect. Thank you for your service!" but there might also be ones with complaints, saying things like "The delivery was one hour late, and it's my son's birthday party this afternoon." Finally, another category of emails would ask for assistance and practical advice, such as how to complete an online order. While the positive emails do not always require immediate response—an automated acknowledgment from the company may be enough—it is the negative ones and the ones asking for assistance that might need urgent attention and action on the part of the company. So, the company's solution was to train a sentiment analysis classifier on around 3 million emails that they received over the previous 3 years and that were analyzed by their customer service in the past, and then to automate the analysis and response action chain. Figure 7.3 visualizes such an analysis-and-response chain.

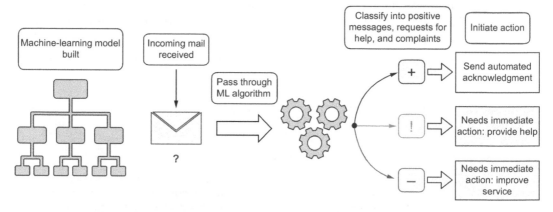

Figure 7.3   An automated analysis-and-response chain for customer service

Now that you've got the general perspective of the task and the benefits of running an automated sentiment analyzer, let's look into how you can implement one yourself.

7.2   Understanding your task

Let's start with a scenario. Suppose you are planning an evening out with some friends, and you'd like to go to a cinema. Your friends' preferences seem to have divided between a superhero movie and an action movie. Both start around the same time, and you like both genres. To choose which group of friends to join at the cinema, you decide to check what those who have already seen these movies think about them. You visit a movie review website and find out that there are hundreds of reviews about both movies. Reading through all these reviews would not be feasible, so you decide to apply a sentiment analyzer to see how many positive and negative opinions there are about each of these movies and then make up your mind. How can you implement such a sentiment analyzer?

Before you start implementing an algorithm to solve the task, it is always a good idea to analyze how we humans solve it. For instance, what makes a review positive?

> **Exercise 7.1**
>
> Look at the two short reviews in figure 7.4. One is positive and one is negative. Which one is which? Can you name some distinguishing characteristics of the positive and the negative review? (Solution can be found at the end of this chapter.)

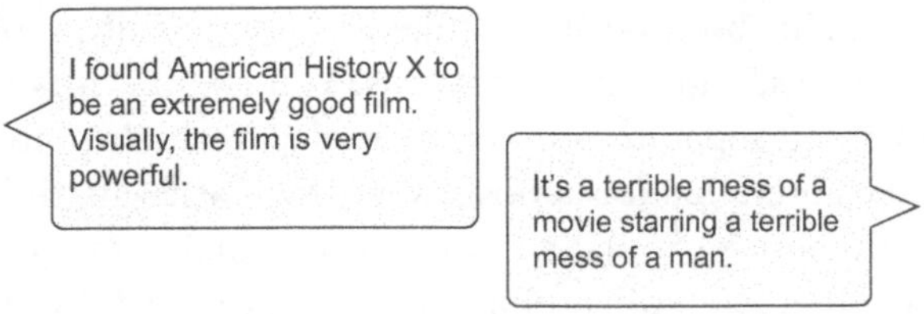

I found American History X to be an extremely good film. Visually, the film is very powerful.

It's a terrible mess of a movie starring a terrible mess of a man.

Figure 7.4   Examples of a positive review and a negative one

7.2.1 Aggregating sentiment score with the help of a lexicon

Let's now formulate the first approach you can apply to detect sentiment in text automatically.

> **Approach 1**
>
> If a review contains positive words, it should be classified as a positive review; if it contains negative words, it should be classified as negative.

How do you know if words themselves are positive or negative? Imagine someone actually compiled a comprehensive list of positive and negative words for you so you can simply rely on that list. In fact, this is exactly the case, and there exist lists of words that typically express positive or negative sentiment; these are called *sentiment lexicons*, and approach 1 is indeed one of the most basic and straightforward approaches to sentiment analysis that you can apply. We'll refer to it as the *sentiment lexicon-based approach* and we will use it as our baseline model. This approach is similar to saying that an email should be flagged as spam as soon as a spam filter detects that the word *lottery* occurs in it, while the word *meeting* should signal that it is a normal email.

So far, so good. Let's assume that our lexicon contains all English words that can ever express any sentiment, and we detect the sentiment in text based on the presence of words in the positive and negative lists within such a comprehensive lexicon. Figure 7.5 shows an example of a review with positive and negative words highlighted in bold. This is not the full review, and ellipses (. . .) show that there are some sentences in between. However, based on this excerpt, can you tell whether it is a positive or a negative review?

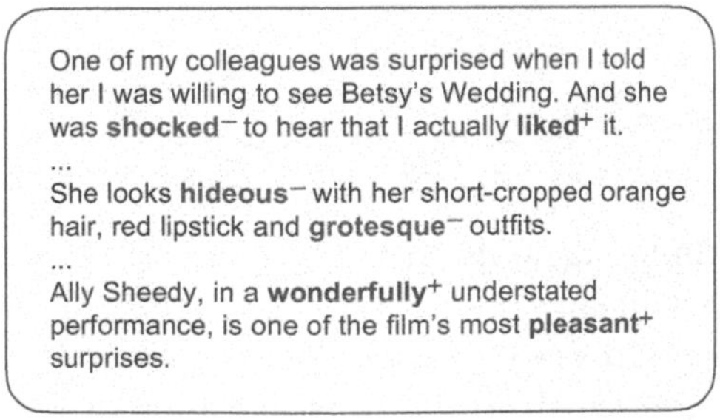

One of my colleagues was surprised when I told her I was willing to see Betsy's Wedding. And she was **shocked**[-] to hear that I actually **liked**[+] it.
...
She looks **hideous**[-] with her short-cropped orange hair, red lipstick and **grotesque**[-] outfits.
...
Ally Sheedy, in a **wonderfully**[+] understated performance, is one of the film's most **pleasant**[+] surprises.

Figure 7.5   An example of a review with positive (+) and negative (−) words highlighted

As you can see, the review contains both positive ("liked," "wonderfully," "pleasant") and negative ("shocked," "hideous," "grotesque") words. Yet, overall, it is actually a positive one: even based on these separate sentences, some of which point out the weaknesses of the movie, you can tell that it is a positive review—after all, the reviewer says that she "actually liked" the movie! So, let's refine our original approach. It's not always true that an overall positive review will contain *only* positive words. A review may contain a combination of words with different sentiments, but among those some might have more weight than others. For instance, "hideous" and "grotesque" may point out minor weaknesses of the movie, but if a reviewer says that they "actually liked" the movie, this should outweigh the rest of it.

> ## Approach 1 (refined)
> If a review contains positive words that together outweigh all negative words, it should be classified as a positive review. If, on the other hand, the negative words outweigh the positive ones, the review should be classified as negative.

Let's assume that our comprehensive sentiment words lexicon doesn't just list the words as positive or negative, but it also has some weights assigned to them. Then a simple algorithm can estimate the overall sentiment of a review as a sum of the individual words' sentiment weights. For instance, let's say that some sentiment lexicon assigns sentiment weights to the six words from our review, as shown in table 7.1. Then at each step, the algorithm updates the total sentiment score with each word's sentiment weight, as the rightmost column of the table shows. In the end, the algorithm will accumulate 0.96 as the final score, which, being a positive number, suggests an overall positive sentiment for the given review.

Table 7.1   Aggregation of the total sentiment score from individual words' sentiment weights

Word	Sentiment weight	Total
shocked	−1.47	0 − 1.47 = −1.47
liked	+2.18	−1.47 + 2.18 = 0.71
hideous	−3.33	0.71 − 3.33 = −2.62
grotesque	−2.16	−2.62 − 2.16 = −4.78
wonderfully	+3.61	−4.78 + 3.61 = −1.17
pleasant	+2.13	−1.17 + 2.13 = **0.96**

Figure 7.6 visualizes another way of thinking about this aggregation process using the following metaphor. Imagine a review being some sort of a container, originally of a neutral temperature (e.g., 0). Every positive word makes the temperature of the container's contents warmer by the degree equal to the word's sentiment weight (e.g.,

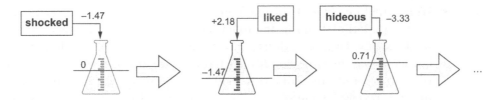

Figure 7.6   Imagine that the total sentiment is expressed by the temperature of the contents. Each positive word warms the content up, while each negative word cools it down according to sentiment weights.

"liked" adds 2.18), while each negative word makes the contents cooler by the degree equal to its sentiment weight (e.g., "shocked" cools it down by 1.47 and "hideous" by 3.33).

7.2.2   *Learning to detect sentiment in a data-driven way*

Great! Now you have an algorithm that measures the "positiveness" of a review in a somewhat similar way to how a thermometer measures the temperature: each positive word adds some degree(s) to the overall temperature, while each negative one takes some away. This approach would have worked perfectly, if two conditions were satisfied:

- A comprehensive sentiment lexicon containing all the words of English—past, present, and future—could be created.
- Language was less creative (i.e., each word meant the same thing in all of its possible contexts).

Let's look into the first problem—coverage of the lexicon. Imagine someone was actually determined enough to collect absolutely all words of English that can ever possibly express any sentiment and assigned a sentiment (and the sentiment weight) to all of them. Immediately, several questions would arise that should be answered: Who is this someone assigning sentiments and weights to words, and how subjective would such judgment be? Is it possible to cover absolutely all words in any particular language? Words are added to language all the time, and they also change meaning quite regularly. For instance, words like *cool* ("This is a cool movie!"), *terrific* ("Terrific experience!"), and *sick* and *wicked* all used to mean negative things but are regularly used with a positive sentiment these days. So, how can this be taken into account in a lexicon?

To make things worse, it is not always possible to predict what a word would mean in context. Here are some of the most typical problems:

- Each word in isolation might be neutral, but together they might express some sentiment, like in the positive review that says "Just go see the movie" or the negative review that says "How could anyone sit through this movie?" Note that the first statement doesn't contain any overtly positive words, while the second one doesn't contain a single negative one.

- Words might change their sentiment polarity in wider context, as the negative words (underlined) do in the following positive review: "It makes me wonder what, exactly, Tony Kaye disliked about the final version of his film. Perhaps this last scene was the problem. It's hard to imagine any director not being at least partially pleased with a film this good"; or as positive words do in the following negative review: "If you're in the mood for a good suspense film, though, stake out something else."

- Negative words like *no, not, neither, nothing,* and so on are a real problem for a word-based analysis, as they flip the sentiment of the whole expression. Consider the negative reviews where the sentiment of positive words is negated, as in "*Nine Months* is a predictable cookie-cutter movie with no originality in humor or plot"; "There weren't even nine laughs in *Nine Months*"; "Neither super nor standard, *8MM* is shocking only in its banality"; "The characters and acting is nothing spectacular"; and so on.

- Finally, irony, sarcasm, and metaphorical use of words present another big problem for lexicon-based approaches. For instance, "Otherwise, it's pretty much a sunken ship of a movie" expresses a really negative sentiment, but how would one break it down to individual words?

To summarize, it is really hard to rely on individual words when it comes to predicting sentiment. Instead of using any resources like lexicons, it might be more effective to learn sentiment in a data-driven way. After all, when you implemented a spam filter, you didn't just rely on occurrence of words like *lottery* and *click* to detect spam. You learned to distinguish spam from ham based on some emails that were previously detected as being spam or ham. Let's formulate our second approach as a data-driven one and learn the intricacies of sentiment from actual positive and negative reviews.

> **Approach 2**
>
> Take a collection of positive and negative reviews. Set up a machine-learning pipeline, as you did for the applications in the previous chapters. This pipeline should rely on the dataset of reviews previously determined to be positive and negative. You should split this set into training and test data, define the set of features to learn the sentiment from, train a classifier of your choice on the training data with the selected set of features, and evaluate it on the test set.

Figure 7.7 illustrates the machine-learning pipeline as applied to the sentiment data. Does this approach sound familiar? In essence, it relies on the same routine you used in the previous chapters. Let's formulate a mental model for this task. As figure 7.8 visualizes, in these two chapters you will implement and compare two approaches to sentiment analysis.

Let's now open your Jupyter Notebook and start implementing your first sentiment analyzer!

Machine-learning pipeline

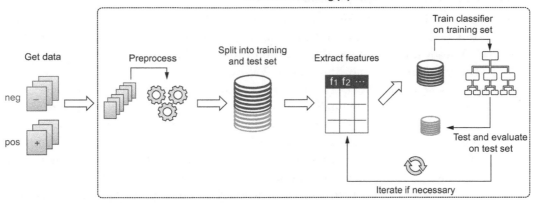

Figure 7.7 **Machine-learning pipeline applied to the sentiment data**

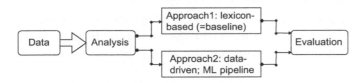

Figure 7.8 **Mental model for this task: two ways of implementing a sentiment analyzer**

7.3 *Setting up the pipeline: Data loading and analysis*

Your present task at hand—detecting positive and negative sentiment in movie reviews—may remind you of the other two applications you've attempted before: spam filtering from chapter 2 and authorship attribution from chapters 5 and 6. There are certain conceptual similarities between all three. In spam filtering, your goal was to detect emails that should be flagged as "spam" and those that should be flagged as "ham"; in authorship attribution, you tried to assign a text to one of the two authors; and in sentiment analysis, you are trying to label reviews as "positive" or "negative." This suggests that you can reuse some of the methods you applied before. In particular, you can treat sentiment analysis as a binary classification problem and apply similar machine-learning routines to the ones you used before.

One of the most important components in a supervised machine-learning application is data labeled with the classes that you will be predicting. For spam filtering, you used an open access Enron dataset, and for authorship attribution you relied on the literary works written by specific authors. What data can you use for sentiment analysis?

7.3.1   Data loading and preprocessing

One of the early attempts at sentiment analysis, which at the same time introduced and popularized it as an NLP task, is presented in the paper from 2002 called "Thumbs up? Sentiment Classification using Machine Learning Techniques," by Bo Pang, Lilian Lee, and Shivakumar Vaithyanathan (www.cs.cornell.edu/home/llee/papers/sentiment.pdf). This paper presented for the first time a machine-learning approach to sentiment analysis, practically defining and framing the task of sentiment analysis as that on the intersection of natural language processing and machine learning. The paper was published together with the dataset consisting of 700 positive and 700 negative reviews that the authors collected from IMDb and annotated with the sentiment polarity labels using the star rating assigned to reviews. Shortly after that, the dataset was expanded, and it is version 2.0 of this `polarity dataset`, containing 1,000 positive and 1,000 negative reviews, that you will be using in this chapter (the `polarity dataset` v2.0 can be downloaded from http://mng.bz/Wxnd).

When you download the dataset, a quick look into the folder (as well as the included **README** file) will tell you that the positive and negative reviews have been extracted from their html sources and stored as plain text files in two subfolders, helpfully called `pos/` and `neg/` for the two types of sentiment expressed in them. This means that it will be easy to extract the sentiment polarity labels from this annotated data.

Let's start by reading in the data, as shown in listing 7.1. This code relies on Python's `os` functionality, which helps you list all the files in a given folder. You iterate through the files in each folder, and unless the file name starts with "`.`" (which is used by some operating systems for hidden files, so none of those will be a review of interest to us here), you read the contents of the file. Since each filename is of the format `unique_id.txt`, you extract the `unique_id` bit and use it as the unique identifier for the contents of the review. Finally, you return a Python dictionary, `a_dict`, where the review's unique identifier is mapped to the review's content.

Listing 7.1   Code to read in the positive and negative movie reviews

```
import os, codecs

def read_in(folder):
    files = os.listdir(folder)        ◁── List all the files in a given
    a_dict = {}                            folder using Python's os
    for a_file in sorted(files):           functionality.
        if not a_file.startswith("."):
            with codecs.open(folder + a_file,
                             encoding='ISO-8859-1',
                             errors ='ignore') as f:
                file_id = a_file.split(".")[0].strip()   ◁── Extract the unique_id
                a_dict[file_id] = f.read()                    bit and use it as the
            f.close()                                         unique identifier for
    return a_dict                                             the contents of
                                                              the review.
```

Unless a file name starts with ".", read the contents of the file.

Return a Python dictionary a_dict, where the review's unique identifier is mapped to the review's content.

We will apply this code to the two subfolders that contain positive and negative reviews, thus creating two Python dictionaries: pos_dict for all positive reviews and neg_dict for all negative ones. Listing 7.2 shows you how to do that. Note that unless you've renamed the folder after downloading the data, all the reviews will be stored in review_polarity/txt_sentoken/. Once you've applied the read_in function to the two subfolders, you can print out the length of the dictionary with positive reviews, pos_dict, as well as the first positive review, which can be identified using Python iterator on the dictionary and extracting the first entry with next(iter(dictionary)). Then you can print out similar information on the neg_dict.

> **Listing 7.2 Code to initialize two Python dictionaries for the reviews of different polarity**

```
folder = "review_polarity/txt_sentoken/"        ◁──┐  All the reviews are stored in
pos_dict = read_in(folder + "pos/")                 │  review_polarity/txt_sentoken/.
print(len(pos_dict))
print(pos_dict.get(next(iter(pos_dict))))       ◁──┐  Print out the length of the pos_dict
neg_dict = read_in(folder + "neg/")                 │  and the very first positive review.
print(len(neg_dict))
print(neg_dict.get(next(iter(neg_dict))))       ◁──┐  Similarly, print out the length of the
                                                    │  neg_dict and the first review in it.
```

This code will print the following output (with [...] used to save space, as you will see much longer texts printed out when you run this code in the notebook):

```
1000
films adapted from comic books have had plenty of success , whether they're
about superheroes ( batman , superman , spawn ) , [...]

1000
plot : two teen couples go to a church party , drink and then drive .
they get into an accident . [...]
```

This output shows that the length of each of the two dictionaries equals 1000 because there are exactly 1,000 positive and 1,000 negative reviews in this dataset. How is the data stored in the two Python dictionaries?

The first entry in the positive dictionary, pos_dict, has a unique identifier (key in the Python dictionary) cv000_29590, as the text comes from the file cv000_29590.txt in the review_polarity/txt_sentoken/pos/ subfolder. The following content (value in the Python dictionary) is associated with this key:

```
films adapted from comic books have had plenty of success , whether they're
about superheroes ( batman , superman , spawn ) , or geared toward kids (
casper ) or the arthouse crowd ( ghost world ) , but there's never really
been a comic book like from hell before .
```

NOTE We are keeping the filenames as unique identifiers for the sole reason of being able to track them back to the dataset if needed. Don't worry about the filenaming conventions in this dataset, but if you're interested to know how the files were named, the bit before "_" is the unique ID within the folder (pos/ or neg/), while the bit after refers to the name of the original html file from which the content was extracted.

Figure 7.9 visualizes how the read_in function extracts the data from the original files and stores it in two Python dictionary structures.

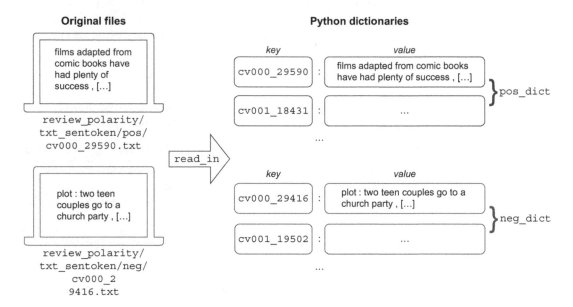

Figure 7.9 The read_in **function extracts reviews from the original files and stores them in Python dictionaries.**

Now, if you open cv000_29590.txt in the review_polarity/txt_sentoken/pos/ sub-folder, which is the first file there, you should see the same content in the file. The first negative entry in the negative dictionary, neg_dict, corresponds to the contents of the file review_polarity/txt_sentoken/neg/cv000_29416.txt, as both the code output and figure 7.9 show:

```
plot : two teen couples go to a church party , drink and then drive .
they get into an accident .
one of the guys dies , but his girlfriend continues to see him in her life ,
and has nightmares .
```

The checks that you've just run are essentially "sanity checks"—they help you make sure that all data is uploaded correctly and that you understand how it is represented. Look at exercise 7.2 and try to analyze what you have learned about the data and the task so far.

Before you move on to the sentiment detection step itself, let's take a closer look into the data and analyze it a bit further.

> ### Exercise 7.2
> What can you say about the data at this point? In particular:
>
> 1. How are the classes in this data distributed?
> 2. How much processing will you need to apply to this data?
> 3. Are there any obvious differences between this pair of positive and negative reviews? In other words, if you didn't know whether a review came from the pos/ or the neg/ subfolder, will you be able to easily detect its polarity, and what clues would help you then?
>
> (Solution can be found at the end of this chapter.)

7.3.2 A closer look into the data

Let's run a set of standard quantitative checks on the two sets of reviews. For instance, in chapter 5, you checked for the length of sentences, length of words, and lexical diversity of language used by the two authors and found out that Jane Austen tended to use longer sentences and longer words. Some of these characteristics could serve as distinguishable features and help you understand the task at hand better.

This time, let's measure for each of the polarity review collections:

- Average length of a review in terms of words.
- Average sentence length.
- Vocabulary size, or the number of distinct words (often called word *types* in NLP lingo).
- Lexical diversity (also called *type-token ratio*), which is the ratio of the overall number of words used (*tokens*) to the number of distinct words (*types*) used. You used lexical diversity in chapter 5 to measure the difference between the two authors' writing styles. Lexical diversity shows how often, on average, each word occurs in a collection of texts. If each word was used only once (i.e., each word was unique), this measure would equal 1.

Listing 7.3 calculates all these statistics on the data. Note that since the texts are already tokenized, all you need to do to extract words is to split texts by whitespaces. In this code, you initialize the following variables: length to store the overall length of the reviews, sent_length for the length of the sentences, num_sents for the number of sentences, and vocab for the list of distinct words. Then you calculate the average length of a review (avg_length) by dividing the overall length in a collection of reviews by its size and average sentence length (avg_sent_length) by dividing the length of all sentences combined by their number. Next, you estimate vocabulary size as the length of the set of distinct words and diversity as the average number of times each word occurs in texts of a particular sentiment. Finally, you use the printing routine from earlier chapters and print out the statistics for the positive and negative reviews.

Listing 7.3   Code to calculate statistics on the review dataset

```
def tokenize(text):
    text.replace("\n", " ")
    return text.split()

def statistics(a_dict):
    length = 0
    sent_length = 0
    num_sents = 0
    vocab = []
    for review in a_dict.values():
        length += len(tokenize(review))
        sents = review.split("\n")
        num_sents += len(sents)
        for sent in sents:
            sent_length += len(tokenize(sent))
        vocab += tokenize(review)
    avg_length = float(length)/len(a_dict)
    avg_sent_length = float(sent_length)/num_sents
    vocab_size = len(set(vocab))
    diversity = float(length)/float(vocab_size)
    return avg_length, avg_sent_length, \
            vocab_size, diversity

categories = ["Positive", "Negative"]
rows = []
rows.append(["Category", "Avg_Len(Review)", "Avg_Len(Sent)", "Vocabulary Size",
    "Diversity"])
stats = {}
stats["Positive"] = statistics(pos_dict)
stats["Negative"] = statistics(neg_dict)
for cat in categories:
    rows.append([cat, f"{stats.get(cat)[0]:.6f}",
                f"{stats.get(cat)[1]:.6f}",
                f"{stats.get(cat)[2]:.6f}",
                f"{stats.get(cat)[3]:.6f}"])

columns = zip(*rows)
column_widths = [max(len(item) for item in col) for col in columns]
for row in rows:
    print(''.join(' {:{width}} '.format(row[i], width=column_widths[i])
                for i in range(0, len(row))))
```

To tokenize texts, simply split them by whitespaces.

Initialize length, sent_length, num_sents, and vocab variables.

Calculate avg_length and avg_sent_length and estimate vocabulary size and diversity.

Use the printing routine from before and print out the statistics for the positive and negative reviews.

This code will print out the results shown in table 7.2.

Table 7.2   Results from listing 7.3

Category	Avg_Len(Review)	Avg_Len(Sent)	Vocabulary Size	Diversity
Positive	787.051000	23.191531	36805.000000	21.384350
Negative	705.630000	21.524266	34542.000000	20.428174

These figures suggest that, on average, positive reviews in this dataset tend to be longer (around 787 words as opposed to around 706 words in negative reviews), with slightly longer sentences (around 23 words as opposed to around 22 for negative reviews) and a considerably larger vocabulary (36,805 distinct words used as opposed to 34,542 on the negative side). As a result, each word gets to be used a bit more frequently in the collection of positive reviews (on the average, around 21 times) than in negative ones (around 20 times). To summarize, it appears that in this dataset, positive reviews are overall "wordier," while larger vocabulary size suggests that some words occur only in the positive subset of reviews.

What effect does this have on the word choice in each part? In other words, do positive reviews use the same set of 34,542 words as negative ones plus an additional set of 2,263 words, or are there more differences between the two sets? Let's find out!

Listing 7.4 demonstrates how to measure the difference between two sets of words used in the reviews of different polarity. As a result, you can print out the number of words that occur in positive reviews but not in negative ones, and vice versa; you can also print out the full list of such non-overlapping words or some selected bits of it. Specifically, in this code, you first collect vocabularies from each type of reviews by "tokenizing" the reviews, content (splitting text by whitespaces as before), and then you return the list of elements that are in one vocabulary but not in another. Note that contents of the reviews can be extracted from sentiment dictionaries by accessing values(). As a result, you can print out full lists of non-overlapping words (caution: this will result in quite long lists!) or some selected parts. Here, I've chosen to print out 100 words from each list, from 1500th to 1600th—a randomly selected span, really, so feel free to use your own range. Finally, you can also print out the length of each list of non-overlapping words.

Listing 7.4   Code to measure the difference between two lists of words

```
def vocab_difference(list1, list2):
    vocab1 = []
    vocab2 = []
    for rev in list1:
        vocab1 += tokenize(rev)          Collect vocabularies from reviews
    for rev in list2:                    and return the list of words that
        vocab2 += tokenize(rev)     ◁──  are in one vocabulary but not in
                                         another.

    return sorted(list(set(vocab1) - set(vocab2)))

pos_wordlist = pos_dict.values()         Contents of the reviews can
neg_wordlist = neg_dict.values()    ◁──  be extracted from sentiment
                                         dictionaries by accessing values().

print(vocab_difference(pos_wordlist, neg_wordlist)[1500:1600])
print(vocab_difference(neg_wordlist, pos_wordlist)[1500:1600])   ◁────
print()                                                               Print out
print(str(len(vocab_difference(pos_wordlist, neg_wordlist)))          full lists of non-
    + " unique words in positive reviews only")                      overlapping words or
                                                                      some selected parts.
```

```
print(str(len(vocab_difference(neg_wordlist, pos_wordlist))) + " unique words
    in negative reviews only")
```

Finally, print out the length of each
list of non-overlapping words.

This code will print out the following results for the lengths of the two non-overlapping
wordlists:

```
16378 unique words in positive reviews only
14115 unique words in negative reviews only
```

In other words, there are 16,378 words that occur in positive reviews but not in negative ones, and 14,115 that occur only in negative but never in positive reviews (in this
dataset). Both are impressively high numbers. If you also printed out some of these
words, you will see words like "atmospheric" and "attention-grabbing" on the positive
side and "baffling" and "bamboozled" on the negative side. However, you will also see
many neutral words or names on both sides (e.g., "attendees" and "Aurelien" on the
positive side and "barbeque" and "Barrie" on the negative side). This is because not all
words used on the positive side necessarily contribute to the positive sentiment, just as
not all words on the negative side contribute to the negative sentiment. This nature of
different words used in reviews with certain polarity is something to keep in mind
when you get to select the features for your sentiment analyzer.

Figure 7.10 shows the findings from the previous two code listings. If you consider that the full vocabulary of positive words contains 36,805 words and 16,378 of
them do not occur in the negative words vocabulary, this leaves you with a shared
vocabulary of 20,427 (you can arrive at the same number considering that the negative vocabulary contains 34,542 words in total, 14,115 of which occur only on the
negative side).

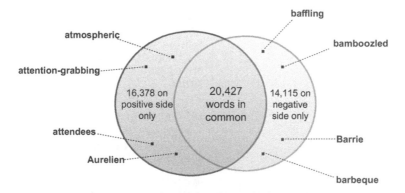

**Figure 7.10   The two sentiment vocabularies share many words, but the lists
of non-overlapping words are also quite large.**

Exercise 7.3
What else makes the size of the vocabularies, both in the full wordlists (36,805 and 34,542 words, as returned by the code in listing 7.3) and in non-overlapping parts (16,378 and 14,115 here), so large? Do you need to take all these words into consideration when detecting sentiment, or are there ways to make the vocabularies more compact and possibly more informative? (Solution can be found at the end of this chapter.)

To this end, let's extract such information as lemmas and part-of-speech tags from reviews. Luckily, you can use spaCy's linguistic pipeline to do all linguistic processing in one go. You are going to process each review from a specific input dictionary of reviews and store the related linguistic analysis in a special spaCy container. You may recall now that you applied a similar step in chapter 6 to the literary works for the two authors. The benefit of running the linguistic pipeline here is that all the information within it will from now on be available to your sentiment analyzer on demand.

Listing 7.5 shows how to run spaCy's pipeline. First of all, you need to import spacy and initialize the pipeline with the particular set of tools available in spaCy's model called en_core_web_md (check the different models available with spaCy: https://spacy.io/usage/models). The "container" with the linguistic information will be represented with a Python dictionary, source_docs, where each review's unique identifier will be mapped to its linguistic information. Such linguistic information includes lemmas, POS tags, grammatical relations, and so on. To facilitate processing, you can merge all sentences in the review in one line of text, since in the original review's sentences are separated by line breaks. To further speed up processing, you can disable the ner (named-entity recognition) module of spaCy. As linguistic processing of thousands of reviews takes a bit of time, it is helpful to print out some tracking messages after a batch of each 200 reviews is processed. In the end, the code returns the linguistic containers for the two types of reviews.

Listing 7.5 Code to run spaCy's linguistic pipeline and store the results

```
import spacy                                    Import spacy and initialize
nlp = spacy.load("en_core_web_md")         ◁── the pipeline with the
                                               particular set of tools.
def spacy_preprocess_reviews(source):
    source_docs = {}                    ◁─── The "container" source_docs maps
                                             each review's unique identifier to
                                             its linguistic information.
    index = 0
    for review_id in source.keys():
        source_docs[review_id] = nlp(
            source.get(review_id).replace("\n", ""),
            disable=["ner"])            ◁──┐
        if index>0 and (index%200)==0:      To facilitate processing,
          ▷ print(str(index) + " reviews processed")    merge all sentences in the
        index += 1                          review in one line of text
                                            and disable "ner".
```

Print out some tracking messages after a batch of each 200 reviews is processed.

```
    print("Dataset processed")
    return source_docs

pos_docs = spacy_preprocess_reviews(pos_dict)
neg_docs = spacy_preprocess_reviews(neg_dict)
```

Return the linguistic containers for the two types of reviews.

This code will put information in the specific spaCy containers as figure 7.11 shows.

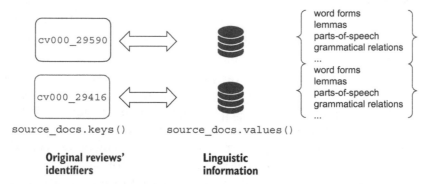

source_docs.keys()   source_docs.values()

Original reviews'   **Linguistic**
identifiers   **information**

Figure 7.11   Run spaCy's pipeline and store the results in the `source_docs` **Python dictionaries.**

Now with very minor modifications to the code in listings 7.3 and 7.4, you can extract similar statistics using lemmas rather than word forms and predefined sets of words (e.g., adjectives and adverbs only) rather than all words. For example, the code in the following listing shows how to calculate similar statistics taking word lemmas rather than original words into account, with the key differences between listings 7.3 and 7.6 highlighted.

Listing 7.6   Code to calculate statistics on word lemmas

```
def statistics_lem(source_docs):
    length = 0
    vocab = []
    for review_id in source_docs.keys():
        review_doc = source_docs.get(review_id)
        lemmas = []
        for token in review_doc:
            lemmas.append(token.lemma_)
        length += len(lemmas)
        vocab += lemmas
    avg_length = float(length)/len(source_docs)
    vocab_size = len(set(vocab))
    diversity = float(length)/float(vocab_size)
    return avg_length, vocab_size, diversity

categories = ["Positive", "Negative"]
rows = []
```

Input linguistic containers, source_docs, instead of original review dictionaries.

Lemmas can be accessed using the lemma_ field.

```
rows.append(["Category", "Avg_Len(Review)", "Vocabulary Size", "Diversity"])
stats = {}
stats["Positive"] = statistics_lem(pos_docs)
stats["Negative"] = statistics_lem(neg_docs)
for cat in categories:
    rows.append([cat, f"{stats.get(cat)[0]:.6f}",
                f"{stats.get(cat)[1]:.6f}",
                f"{stats.get(cat)[2]:.6f}"])

columns = zip(*rows)
column_widths = [max(len(item) for item in col) for col in columns]
for row in rows:
    print(''.join(' {:{width}} '.format(row[i], width=column_widths[i])
                for i in range(0, len(row))))
```

> The rest of the code is very similar to what you did in listing 7.3.

This code will produce the output shown in table 7.3.

Table 7.3   Results from listing 7.6

Category	Avg_Len(Review)	Vocabulary Size	Diversity
Positive	818.960000	24424.000000	33.530953
Negative	737.666000	22811.000000	32.338170

> **NOTE**   As in other examples, you might end up with slightly different results if you are using versions of the tools different from those suggested in the installation instructions for the book. In such cases, you shouldn't worry about the slight deviations in the numbers, as the general logic of the examples still holds.

Note that the average lengths of the reviews on both sides increased: positive reviews, still being longer than negative ones, have around 818–819 lemmas against around 737–738 lemmas in negative reviews (as opposed to the average of 787 and 705–706 word forms in the two types of reviews). What is responsible for this increase in the average review length?

If you've taken a closer look into the original reviews provided as preprocessed (e.g., already tokenized) text, you might have spotted such word forms as they've, there's, and similar. In other words, the tokenization wasn't very consistent, as such forms should be split into they and 've, there and 's, and so on. Since now you have preprocessed data with spaCy, such cases are dealt with properly, and thus you get slightly higher numbers for the average length.

At the same time, vocabulary size figures clearly show how much more compact the lemma space is compared to the full word forms space, while still preserving same trends as the original space. Positive reviews have 24,424 lemmas (as compared to 36,805 distinct word forms), which is about 1,600 lemmas more than what the vocabulary for the negative reviews contains (22,811), which in turn is a much smaller number than the full list of word forms used in negative reviews (34,542). Since multiple word forms result in the same lemma, each lemma gets to be used more frequently: over 33 times, on the average, for positive reviews (as opposed to 21 times for each word form) and just over 32 times for negative reviews (as opposed to 20 times for each word form).

What about the non-overlapping lemmas then? The following listing is a modification of the code from listing 7.4, but instead of using word forms, it takes lemmas into account.

Listing 7.7   Code to detect the non-overlapping lemmas between two types of reviews

```
def vocab_lem_difference(source_docs1, source_docs2):
    vocab1 = []
    vocab2 = []
    for rev_id in source_docs1.keys():
        rev = source_docs1.get(rev_id)
        for token in rev:
            vocab1.append(token.lemma_)          ◁── Most of this code is
                                                     similar to the code from
    for rev_id in source_docs2.keys():               listing 7.4. The difference
        rev = source_docs2.get(rev_id)               is that you need to use
        for token in rev:                            lemma_.
            vocab2.append(token.lemma_)
    return sorted(list(set(vocab1) - set(vocab2)))

print(str(len(vocab_lem_difference(pos_docs, neg_docs))) + " unique lemmas in
    positive reviews only")
print(str(len(vocab_lem_difference(neg_docs, pos_docs))) + " unique lemmas in
    negative reviews only")
```

Here are the results that you will get with this code:

```
9213 unique lemmas in positive reviews only
7600 unique lemmas in negative reviews only
```

As you can see, this is indeed a much more compact space: under 10,000 non-overlapping lemmas on each side as opposed to over 16,000 and over 14,000 for word forms. To finish this set of experiments, try to solve exercise 7.4 before checking the solutions in the Jupyter Notebook and at the end of this chapter.

Exercise 7.4
Calculate the statistics (similar to listings 7.3 and 7.6) and estimate the number of non-overlapping adjectives and adverbs between the two types of reviews (similar to listings 7.4 and 7.7).

Hint: You can access part-of-speech information using `token.pos_==pos`, where pos is the POS code (tag) (e.g., `ADJ` for adjectives or `ADV` for adverbs). (Reminder: you can check the POS tags on https://spacy.io/usage/linguistic-features#pos-tagging.) Before you move on to building a sentiment analyzer, let's summarize what we have learned about the data and the task so far:

- The vocabularies used in the positive and negative reviews are large, with the positive reviews having more unique words used in them, as well as being longer overall. That means that even though you are working with a balanced dataset of 1,000 reviews in each class, positive reviews provide more information than negative ones.

- If you want to make the word (feature) space more compact, you may prefer to use lemmas or words of selected parts of speech only. For instance, adjectives and adverbs are good candidates for sentiment-bearing words. Their distribution follows the same trends as you observe with all word forms and lemmas, with the positive reviews having more unique items (around 2,000 unique adjectives and over 500 unique adverbs on the positive side as opposed to under 2,000 unique adjectives and under 500 unique adverbs on the negative side). This might provide you with a stronger sentiment-related signal; however, note that the number of items is quite small, which might make the resulting adjective- and adverb-based feature space too sparse. We will investigate these questions in the course of this chapter and the next one.

- We've found out that there is a considerable overlap between the vocabularies used in the positive and negative reviews. Presence of such words on both sides might make them less effective as features. In addition, both positive and negative vocabularies seem to include neutral words, so one should apply feature selection to make sure the most informative words are used.

7.4 Aggregating sentiment scores with a sentiment lexicon

Now that you are familiar with the task and the dataset, let's turn to sentiment analysis itself and build the baseline analyzer. Earlier, we said that the most straightforward way to detect the overall sentiment of a review is to aggregate its sentiment score through the words in the review. Figure 7.12 shows how far you've got with the mental model for this task.

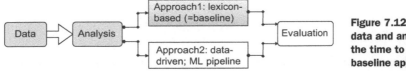

Figure 7.12 You've got the data and analyzed it. Now is the time to implement the baseline approach.

We've discussed two variants of such an approach. Here is a reminder: you can either count which side the majority of words is on, positive or negative (approach 1); or you can use the sentiment "weight" of each word and aggregate the score this way (approach 1—refined).

We said that both variants of this approach rely on the idea that there is some ground truth about words' sentiments—that is, out there, there is some comprehensive list of words that someone has reliably annotated for sentiment polarity (i.e., at the very minimum, identified whether each word on the list is generally positive or negative) or even assigned relative sentiment strength (weight) to each such word. Such resources, called *sentiment lexicons*, help build competitive baselines for machine-learning approaches. Are the lexicon-based and the machine learning–based approaches completely separate? Figure 7.13 highlights the differences.

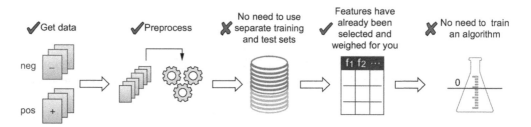

Figure 7.13   Lexicon-based approach mapped onto the machine-learning pipeline

In essence, the two approaches are similar to a point, with the following core difference: with the lexicon-based approach, your features have already been selected and weighed for you. One could have done that manually or applied a machine-learning algorithm trained on some other data. That means you don't have to train the classifier yourself, which in turn means that you don't need to separate the data into different subsets. You can *use the whole dataset,* treat the words from the sentiment lexicon as your *features,* and apply *a simple heuristic algorithm* that outputs sentiment label based on the aggregated score from all such "features." This provides for a competitive baseline, which is why we are applying this approach first. Let's find out how competitive the results are.

7.4.1   *Collecting sentiment scores from a lexicon*

Earlier in this chapter we discussed that there are several possible issues with a lexicon-based approach. They can be summarized by the statement "A single lexicon is too static in its nature to be able to capture the intricacies and changes of the word use." In particular:

- Words' sentiments change over time, so it would never be possible to register any word's sentiment once and forever. For instance, words like *wicked* and *sick* are quite often used these days to express the sentiment similar to (and of a more extreme degree than) that of the word *cool,* as used in "This movie is so cool!"
- Words' sentiments depend a lot on the context, so it would never be feasible for a single lexicon to cover all possible uses of a word in all domains. For example,

using *cool* in combination with *temperature* or *wind* might mean that the weather, for example at a resort where someone spent their vacation, was not as nice as expected (i.e., expressing a negative sentiment), while saying that a movie is "cool" would mean that a movie is rather good.

Thus, a sentiment lexicon should somehow take at least these two aspects—the one of *time* and the one of the *subject domain*—into account. Luckily, there is a sentiment lexicon that answers these two criteria.

A group of researchers from Stanford University developed an algorithm that can collect in an automated way sentiment-bearing words and assign weights to them. Most importantly, they released the lexicons they collected on the SocialSent project web page for anyone to make use of them. What is of particular interest to us in this respect is that the data released contains historical lexicons covering 150 years of English (1850 to 2000), which reflect how words changed their sentiment from one decade to another (e.g., the researchers note that more than 5% of sentiment-bearing words switched their polarity from 1850 to 2000!), as well as community-specific sentiment lexicons for 250 "subreddit" communities from reddit.com (here, the researchers note that the sentiment of certain words changes drastically from one community to another).

> **NOTE** The lexicons can be downloaded from the project web page: https://nlp.stanford.edu/projects/socialsent/. Also, if you want to learn more about this research, check https://arxiv.org/pdf/1606.02820.pdf.)

The historical lexicons contain mean sentiment scores for the top 5,000 non-stopwords in each decade from 1850 to 2000, as well as mean sentiment scores for the adjectives that occurred more than 100 times in the data. The community-specific (i.e., domain-specific) lexicons contain sentiment values for up to 5,000 most frequent non-stopwords that occur in each "subreddit" community posts, using public comment data from the year 2014. We are going to use the following sentiment lexicons in our experiments in this chapter:

- Since adjectives bear a lot of sentiment information, we will use *adjectives lexicons*. The review data was extracted from IMDb in the beginning of the 2000s. It is possible that the expressions used reflect sentiments typical of either the 1990s or 2000s. To this end, let's experiment with the adjectives and their sentiment values from both these decades.
- Since some words of other parts of speech may also express sentiment of a particular polarity, let's use the *frequent words lexicons* from the 1990s and 2000s as well.
- Finally, let's use a domain-specific lexicon from the *movies* subreddit community.

Each lexicon is stored in a distinct tab-separated file with one word per line mapped to its mean sentiment score and standard deviation for that score. Let's read in the data from these files and store the scores in sentiment lexicon dictionaries, as the code in listing 7.8 shows. In this code, you read the tab-separated file line by line and split each line by tabs, accessing the word as the first element and its mean sentiment score as the second element in the resulting list. You can read in the data from the sentiment lexicons of your choice, using the paths to the files where the lexicons are stored. In my case, the files are located in `sentiment_words/folder_name/file_name.tsv`. These files can be found in the book's code repository together with the notebook. As usual, it's a good idea to run some checks (e.g., print out the scores for some selected words, as well as the total length of a particular lexicon).

Listing 7.8   Code to populate sentiment word dictionaries with sentiment values

```
def collect_wordlist(input_file):
    word_dict = {}
    with codecs.open(input_file, encoding='ISO-8859-1', errors ='ignore') as f:
        for a_line in f.readlines():
            cols = a_line.split("\t")          ◁── Read the tab-separated
            if len(cols)>2:                          file line by line and split
                word = cols[0].strip()               each line by tabs.
                score = float(cols[1].strip())
                word_dict[word] = score        ◁── The first element corresponds
        f.close()                                    to a word and the second to its
        return word_dict                             mean sentiment score.

adj_90 = collect_wordlist("sentiment_words/adjectives/1990.tsv")
print(adj_90.get("cool"))
print(len(adj_90))
adj_00 = collect_wordlist("sentiment_words/adjectives/2000.tsv")
print(adj_00.get("cool"))
print(len(adj_00))
all_90 = collect_wordlist("sentiment_words/frequent_words/1990.tsv")
print(len(all_90))
all_00 = collect_wordlist("sentiment_words/frequent_words/2000.tsv")
print(len(all_00))
movie_words = collect_wordlist("sentiment_words/subreddits/movies.tsv")
print(len(movie_words))     ◁── Feel free to explore your own selection of words or
                                 even use different lexicons from the original source!
```

Read in the data from the sentiment lexicons of your choice and run some checks.

If you run the code from this listing unmodified, here is what you will learn: *cool* hasn't changed its polarity between the 1990s and the 2000s; it has stayed quite a positive word throughout. Its sentiment strength, though, did drop slightly, from 1.28 in the 1990s to 1.19 in the 2000s. There are 1,968 adjectives in the 1990s adjectives lexicon and 2,041 in the 2000s one. As for the *all frequent words* data, both the 1990s and 2000s lexicons contain 4,924 words—that is how many words are left of the most frequent 5,000 ones once the stopwords are filtered out (the selection of 4,924 and the sentiment weights are quite different though!). Finally, the movies lexicon contains 4,981 words in total. Again, this is the result of filtering out stopwords among the most frequent 5,000 words used in the movies community. Recall from the data exploration in section 7.3 that the total size of positive and negative vocabulary is within the range of 34,000 to 37,000 words (i.e., much larger than these lexicons contain). At the same time, the sizes of the adjective vocabularies are comparable to the sizes of the adjective lexicons. The idea behind using lexicons is that they contain smaller but more informative sets of words. Let's see if this helps with detecting review polarity.

7.4.2 Applying sentiment scores to detect review polarity

We've discussed two types of a lexicon-based approach, which are illustrated in figure 7.14.

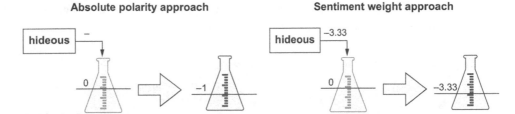

Figure 7.14   The difference between taking the absolute polarity and sentiment weight approaches is in the degree to which the overall sentiment of the review changes when the word is considered.

The difference between these two types of approaches can be summarized as follows:

- Let's imagine that sentiment is a quality of a movie review akin to temperature. The more positive a review is, the "warmer" the feelings of a user are toward a particular movie. Then your sentiment analyzer is some sort of a thermometer: it measures the degree of a review on the negative to positive temperature scale. Under the most straightforward approach, each positive word may add exactly one degree to the overall temperature, and each negative word may take exactly one away.
- Since sentiment lexicons provide you with the absolute sentiment polarity of the words (e.g., positive versus negative) and with relative values (i.e., how strongly positive or negative a word is), you can also say that each positive word may add more than one degree (or less than one degree) to the overall "temperature" of the review, just as each negative word may take away more than one degree or less than one degree.

Let's now implement the two variations of this approach. First, let's implement a method `bin_decisions` for binary decisions (i.e., taking absolute polarity into account). Under this variation of the approach, every positive word will contribute exactly +1 point and each negative word will contribute exactly –1 point. In the end, let's measure the aggregated score on the whole review and predict a positive sentiment if this aggregated score is positive (i.e., simply above 0) and a negative sentiment if it is negative (i.e., strictly below 0). The second variant of the approach, `weighted decisions`, will take into account the relative positivity and negativity of each word.

Finally, let's measure how often such prediction, based on the aggregated scores from the words in a review, leads to correct labeling. Recall that a measure that evaluates how often an algorithm's prediction coincides with the correct prediction is called *accuracy*, and you've used it in the course of this book before. Here is the formula:

```
Acc = correct_predictions / all_predictions
```

You can estimate the number of correct predictions as the sum of all those cases where the lexicon-based approach predicts a positive sentiment for actually positive reviews and all those cases where the lexicon-based approach predicts a negative sentiment for actually negative reviews. Figure 7.15 illustrates this idea.

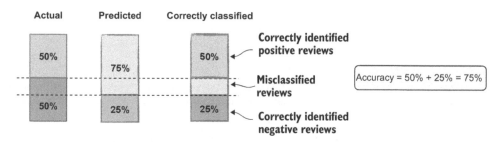

Figure 7.15   The accuracy score is composed of the proportion of correctly classified positive and correctly classified negative reviews.

Finally, listing 7.9 walks you through the steps we just discussed. In this code, you first implement the `bin_decisions` function, which aggregates the score for each review in the binary way: each positive word contributes +1, and each negative word contributes −1. You take word forms into account as the lexicons distinguish between different word forms with the same lemma (e.g., *dislike* and *disliked* have different entries with different scores). In the end, you convert all aggregated positive scores to 1 and all aggregated negative scores to −1, and you populate the `decisions` list with tuples where each aggregated score is mapped to the actual sentiment label. With the second function, `weighted_decisions`, each positive and each negative word from the lexicon that occurs in a review contributes some sentiment score according to its weight in this lexicon. As before, you populate the `decisions` list with tuples where the predicted scores are mapped with the actual sentiment labels. Next, you calculate accuracy for both `bin_decisions` and `weighted_decisions` functions: you estimate the proportion of reviews with the correctly identified sentiment in the positive and negative subsets of reviews, as well as in the whole collection, and based on this, you can estimate accuracies for each of the word lexicons of interest. Finally, you use the printing routine from the previous code listings to print out the results in one nice table.

Listing 7.9 Code to apply and evaluate the sentiment lexicon-based approach

```
def bin_decisions(a_dict, label, sent_dict):
    decisions = []
    for rev_id in a_dict.keys():
        score = 0
        for token in a_dict.get(rev_id):
            if token.text in sent_dict.keys():
                if sent_dict.get(token.text)<0:
                    score -= 1
                else:
                    score += 1          ◁──   With the bin_decisions function,
        if score < 0:                          for each review you aggregate
            decisions.append((-1, label))       the score in the binary way.
        else:                                   Convert all aggregated
            decisions.append((1, label))   ◁──  scores and store them
    return decisions                            in the decisions list.

def weighted_decisions(a_dict, label, sent_dict):
    decisions = []
    for rev_id in a_dict.keys():                      With the
        score = 0                                      weighted_decisions
        for token in a_dict.get(rev_id):               function, each word from
            if token.text in sent_dict.keys():         the lexicon contributes a
                score += sent_dict.get(token.text) ◁── sentiment score.
        if score < 0:
            decisions.append((-1, label))        Populate the decisions
        else:                                    list with tuples of the
            decisions.append((1, label))    ◁──  predicted scores and the
    return decisions                             actual sentiment labels.

def get_accuracy(pos_docs, neg_docs, sent_dict):
    decisions_pos = weighted_decisions(pos_docs, 1, sent_dict)
    decisions_neg = weighted_decisions(
        neg_docs, -1, sent_dict)          ◁─────        Calculate accuracy for
    decisions_all = decisions_pos + decisions_neg       both the bin_decisions
    lists = [decisions_pos, decisions_neg, decisions_all]  and weighted_decisions
    accuracies = []                                     functions.
    for i in range(0, len(lists)):
        match = 0
        for item in lists[i]:                    Calculate the proportion
            if item[0]==item[1]:                 of reviews with the
                match += 1                       correctly identified
        accuracies.append(                       sentiment.
            float(match)/float(len(lists[i]))) ◁─┘
    return accuracies

categories = ["Adj_90", "Adj_00", "All_90", "All_00", "Movies"]
rows = []
rows.append(["List", "Acc(positive)", "Acc(negative)", "Acc(all)"])
accs = {}
accs["Adj_90"] = get_accuracy(pos_docs, neg_docs, adj_90)
accs["Adj_00"] = get_accuracy(pos_docs, neg_docs, adj_00)
accs["All_90"] = get_accuracy(pos_docs, neg_docs, all_90)
accs["All_00"] = get_accuracy(pos_docs, neg_docs, all_00)
```

```
accs["Movies"] = get_accuracy(
    pos_docs, neg_docs, movie_words)
for cat in categories:
    rows.append([cat, f"{accs.get(cat)[0]:.6f}",
                f"{accs.get(cat)[1]:.6f}",
                f"{accs.get(cat)[2]:.6f}"])
columns = zip(*rows)
column_widths = [max(len(item) for item in col) for col in columns]
for row in rows:
    print(''.join(' {:{width}} '.format(row[i], width=column_widths[i])
                  for i in range(0, len(row))))
```

Estimate accuracies for each of the word lexicons of interest.

Use the printing routine to print out the results in one nice table.

The code from this listing will return the results shown in table 7.4 for the *binary method*.

Table 7.4   Results for the binary method from listing 7.9

List	Acc(positive)	Acc(negative)	Acc(all)
Adj_90	0.889000	0.267000	0.578000
Adj_00	0.825000	0.354000	0.589500
All_90	1.000000	0.000000	0.500000
All_00	0.965000	0.086000	0.511000
Movies	0.014000	0.995000	0.504500

And table 7.5 shows the results for the *weighted method*.

Table 7.5   Results for the weighted method from listing 7.9

List	Acc(positive)	Acc(negative)	Acc(all)
Adj_90	0.788000	0.507000	0.647500
Adj_00	0.818000	0.424000	0.621000
All_90	0.984000	0.017000	0.500500
All_00	0.805000	0.373000	0.589000
Movies	0.008000	0.997000	0.502500

Exercise 7.5

What can you say about the performance of this approach? In particular:

1 Are these accuracy figures high?
2 Which list is most suitable for the task?
3 Which approach—binary or weighted—works better?

(Solution can be found at the end of this chapter.)

Congratulations! You have successfully built the first version of a sentiment analyzer that achieves competitive results even before you apply machine learning and train your algorithm. The next chapter will look into how to improve these results with a data-driven approach.

Summary

- As with some previous tasks in this book, sentiment analysis on the publicly available dataset of movie reviews annotated with positive and negative sentiment can be framed as a binary classification task.
- This is a challenging task. It seems like some words, including, to a large extent, adjectives and adverbs, carry a lot of sentiment-related information. At the same time, other types of words may still be useful. However, words may change sentiment over time and may have different meanings and, therefore, may have different sentiment polarity and sentiment weight in different domains; in addition, context matters a lot.
- Positive reviews in the inspected dataset are overall longer and contain more unique words and more unique adjectives. Vocabularies for both positive and negative reviews are quite large, with many words being used on both sides. This may have implications for sentiment detection with the use of these words. At the same time, if you want to make the word (feature) space more compact, you can consider only certain types of words (e.g., adjectives and adverbs), which typically carry more sentiment-related information, or lemmatize texts.
- A sentiment analysis algorithm may rely on the use of sentiment lexicons—comprehensive word lists covering a wide range of sentiment-bearing words with sentiment weights assigned manually or through application of some algorithm. With such lexicons, one can aggregate the overall sentiment in a review either in a binary way, taking only the absolute polarity of words into account, or in a weighted sentiment way, taking relative weights into account as well. With this type of approach, competitive results, considerably above the majority class baseline, can be achieved without any actual training, which means that the whole dataset can be used without the need of splitting it into training and test sets, and the algorithm can be applied instantaneously. The best results obtained with this method put accuracy values in the range of 0.62-0.65 on the given dataset. This is informative, as your goal with the more sophisticated data-driven approaches in the next chapter will be to outperform this baseline approach.

Solutions to exercises

Exercise 7.1

The review on the left is positive, while the one on the right is negative. What exactly helps you identify the review on the left as positive and the one on the right as negative? The first thing that you might notice is that the positive review contains words like "good" and "powerful," which by themselves can be considered positive. More-over, the positive sentiment is intensified further by addition of such words as "extremely (good)" and "very (powerful)." Here's a reminder: words that denote qual-ities are called *adjectives* ("good" and "powerful" here are adjectives), while qualities of qualities are expressed by adverbs (such are "extremely" and "very" here). So, you may start with an assumption that adjectives and adverbs are reliable clues (features) that help you identify sentiment of the text. Indeed, the negative review on the right con-tains a negative adjective, too—it is hard to imagine anyone using "terrible" to denote a positive thing. However, in addition to the negative adjective "terrible," the review on the right contains quite a negative noun, "mess." So, it is generally true that, since adjectives and adverbs typically denote qualities, they are your first reliable source of information when it comes to sentiment; however, other words, including nouns (like "mess") and verbs (e.g., "Avoid this film at all costs") might be very informative, too. Figure 7.16 highlights words that help sentiment detection in exercise 7.1.

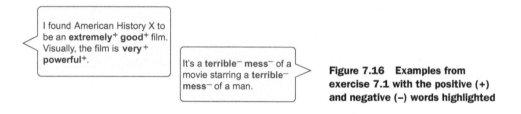

I found American History X to be an **extremely**+ **good**+ film. Visually, the film is **very**+ **powerful**+.

It's a **terrible**− **mess**− of a movie starring a **terrible**− **mess**− of a man.

Figure 7.16   Examples from exercise 7.1 with the positive (+) and negative (−) words highlighted

To summarize, the sentiment in these two reviews can be identified by the presence of specific sentiment-bearing words: note that the positive review contains only positive words, while the negative review only negative ones.

Exercise 7.2

1   It is important to note the distribution of classes in the data because this gives you a rough idea of the difficulty of the task. If the algorithm blindly predicted polarity of a new review relying on how often a review is positive or negative, based on the observations made on this data, what would such a blind predic-tion be? Since in this data you are working with 1,000 positive and 1,000 nega-tive reviews, this prediction will be completely unbiased—50:50 for two classes. This may remind you of the majority class baselines in the previous tasks where the data was less fairly distributed between the classes (e.g., Jane Austen had more sentences than William Shakespeare in the data you used in chapters 5 and 6).

2   A quick glance over the texts in this dataset reveals that the data has been pre-processed. In particular, all words were converted to lowercase and texts were tokenized (i.e., each word is separated from its neighbors by whitespaces). This should make some further processing of the data easier. A closer look into the data may also reveal that not all words are properly tokenized. For instance,

they're, there's, and similar are kept as single tokens. We'll deal with such inconsistencies later by applying our own tokenizer through spaCy's pipeline.

3 The last question is quite open-ended, and it's up to your judgment and interpretation whether you can detect the sentiment of a review by reading through it. Both positive and negative reviews provide a brief summary of the plot, as well as opinionated analysis. Both contain positive as well as negative words, which complicates sentiment detection further. It is no wonder, then, that the authors of the paper, who put the original dataset together, noted that sentiment analysis is far from being a trivial task! In particular, they note that "Document polarity classification poses a significant challenge to data-driven methods, resisting traditional text-categorization techniques" (www.cs.cornell.edu/home/llee/papers/cutsent.pdf).

Exercise 7.3

There are two observations to be made at this point:

- First, you may have noticed, when you were inspecting the wordlists, that they include words like *attendees* as well as *attendee*. They also include both *film* and *films*, *see* and *saw*, and so on. That is, every word form is counted as a separate word token, thus the number of distinct words is quite high. From chapter 3 on, you've been working with more compact representations of a word—word stems and lemmas, which bring such different forms of a word to the same common representation. For instance, both *attendees* and *attendee* have a lemma *attendee*, while *see*, *saw*, and *seen* can all be converted to *see* by lemmatization. The number of lemmas in positive and negative reviews, as opposed to the total number of words, may tell you how many various concepts are discussed in these reviews.

- Secondly, as we noted earlier in this chapter, some words are more expressive in terms of sentiment or opinion. Words like *good* and *awful*, *audience-friendly* and *baldly* are more expressive than words like *film* and *saw*. The difference between the two groups of words lies in their parts of speech: adjectives (*good*, *awful*) and adverbs (*audience-friendly*, *baldly*) typically express qualities and therefore may bear more sentiment-related information than nouns (*film*) or verbs (*see*).

Exercise 7.4

Your code should produce an output similar to the results in table 7.6 (note that you may get slightly different results with different versions of spaCy):

Table 7.6 Results from listing 7.7

Category	Unique adj's	Unique adv's
Positive	2051	535
Negative	1620	456

Exercise 7.5

Recall from previous chapters that one way to tell whether an accuracy score that you are getting on the task with your algorithm is "good" or not is to compare it to the majority class distribution—that is, if the classifier had to predict labels simply based on how data is distributed, what would the result be?

1 In this dataset, the two classes are equally distributed, so the majority baseline is, in fact, 0.50. Many of the accuracy figures, especially with the binary approach, hardly outperform this baseline. Accuracies in the range of 0.62–0.65 are the highest values obtained with the lexicon-based methods. This level of performance is not surprising, if you think about the following: the algorithm is not learning anything about your specific task or data at hand; instead, it relies on a static resource, and the sentiment scores in your data might actually differ from those provided in the lexicon. On the plus side, accuracies in the range of 0.62–0.65 are considerably above the majority baseline, and it's important to note that this simple baseline algorithm is able to achieve these results on the basis of a small set of words (much smaller, as we noted, than the full vocabularies) and without any training.

2 The results confirm that adjectives are the most informative words for this task. The results with both binary and weighted methods are higher when you use adjective sentiment values than when you use any other lists. It seems like both 1990s and 2000s lists of adjective sentiment scores are useful. Among the two all frequent words lists, the 2000s one shows better results with both types of methods. Finally, surprisingly, the movies words list extracted from the subreddit community proves to not be very helpful, as it hardly gets you over the 0.50 accuracy threshold. One possible explanation for this result is that a word list from the movie domain collected in 2014 (as this particular movies sentiment lexicon was) is not exactly suitable for classifying sentiment in the movie reviews from as far back as early 2000s.

3 Finally, among the two methods—binary and weighted—the weighted one performs better for the majority of the word lists. It's also worth noting that the proportions of reviews with the correctly identified sentiment in the positive and negative parts of the dataset are radically different with the binary approach. It looks like certain lists cover specific sentiment better than others. For instance, adjectives and all frequent words lists do much better on the positive sentiment side, while the movies word list achieves almost perfect accuracy on the negative reviews. Sadly, this doesn't translate in the overall good performance. The weighted method, on the other hand, strikes a much better balance, at least with the adjectives list.

Sentiment analysis with a data-driven approach

This chapter covers

- Implementing improved algorithms for sentiment analysis
- Introducing several machine-learning practices and techniques with scikit-learn
- Applying linguistic pipeline and linguistic concepts with spaCy
- Combining use of spaCy and NLTK resources

In the previous chapter, you started looking into sentiment analysis and implemented your first sentiment analyzer using a lexicon-based approach. Recall that sentiment analysis is concerned with the automated detection of sentiment (usually along two dimensions of *positive* and *negative* sentiments) for a piece of text. It is a popular task to apply to such opinionated texts as, for example, reviews on movies, restaurants, products, and services. A good sentiment analyzer may help save the user a lot of time!

Let's remind ourselves of the scenario addressed with this application: suppose you are planning an evening out with some friends, and you'd like to go to a cinema. Your friends' preferences seem to have divided between a superhero movie and an action movie. Both start around the same time, and you like both genres. To choose which group of friends to join at the cinema, you decide to check what those who have already seen these movies think about them. You visit a movie review website and find out that there are hundreds of reviews about both movies. Reading through all these reviews would not be feasible, so you decide to apply a sentiment analyzer to see how many positive and negative opinions there are about each of these movies and then make up your mind. How can you implement such a sentiment analyzer? Here is a brief summary of what you've done to solve this task so far:

- To implement a sentiment analyzer, you first looked into how humans understand what the overall sentiment of a piece of text is (often after one quick glance at a text!). The minimal unit bearing sentiment information is a word. While a text may contain a combination of positive and negative opinions (e.g., a review on a new phone may highlight that it has a good camera but battery life is poor), in the simplest case you can detect the overall sentiment as the balance between the number of positive and negative words. If the review contains more positive than negative words, it is considered overall positive, and it is considered negative if negative words prevail.

- If you'd like to be more precise about the sentiment, you can take the strength of the sentiment in words into account. For instance, both *good* and *amazing* are positive words, but the latter suggests that the user feels more strongly about their positive experience.

- The most straightforward way in which you can identify that individual words are positive or negative is to rely on some comprehensive database of sentiment-bearing words. Such databases exist and are called *sentiment lexicons*. In the previous chapter, you built your first baseline approach using sentiment lexicons and aggregating the overall sentiment scores for reviews using either absolute polarity or weights.

The results showed that you can achieve better performance when you use sentiment lexicons that cover adjectives (words like *amazing, awful,* etc.), as such words typically describe qualities. A weighted approach, in which you take into account the strength of the sentiment expressed by a word, worked better than absolute polarity scores. The results for the weighted approach with adjective lexicons ranged between 62% and 65% on the combined set of positive and negative reviews, and, remarkably, this approach worked better on the positive reviews (79% to 82% identified) than on negative ones (42% to 51% identified), proving detection of negative sentiment more challenging.

This approach is not only the most straightforward, but it is also easy to implement and fast to run; it doesn't require any machine training or expensive calculations. Being the baseline approach, it sets up the benchmark on the task—with any further, more sophisticated, or more expensive approaches that you apply, you'll need to make sure your baseline is outperformed (i.e., the new approach is worth the effort). The current baseline set up by the sentiment lexicon-based approach is at 65%, suggesting you can do significantly better.

Figure 8.1 Mental model for the improved sentiment analysis implementation

In the list that follows, let's summarize what might have gone wrong with the simple lexicon-based approach and what can be improved (figure 8.1 visualizes the mental model for this chapter).

- Words may change their polarity and strength of sentiment across domains as well as over time. For instance, *soft* is not a very positive quality to have in sports (e.g., *soft player*), but it would sound positive in many other domains (e.g., when talking about clothes as in *soft pajamas*). The SocialSent lexicons that you used in the previous chapter solve these issues to a certain extent, as there is a range of lexicons built per domain and decade. However, one remaining problem is that the same word can have several meanings, which may in turn be associated with different sentiments. For instance, *terrific* has gradually changed its meaning and sentiment from negative (something scary and terrifying) to pretty positive (something impressive and on a grand scale) sometime between 1800 and the 2000s, so the more up-to-date versions of the lexicons contain a positive score for it. At the same time, the lexicons contain a single score for each word only, but a resource that can help you distinguish between more subtle differences in meaning and associated sentiment scores might provide you with better results. After all, there is always a chance that someone would still use *terrific* in this very old negative sense. We will refer to this case as *multiple senses of the word* issue and will look into how to improve this aspect of the system.
- A lot depends on the surrounding context of the word. We've talked about examples of contexts that are overall positive (e.g., "Just go see this movie") or negative (e.g., "How could anyone sit through this movie?") without containing a single strong polarity word. It's the combination of words, then, that makes the whole phrase or sentence sentiment-bearing. We will refer to this case as a *dependence on context* issue. A static resource like a sentiment lexicon cannot make subtle context-specific distinctions, and here is where a data-driven approach, with the classifier learning directly from the data, is more promising. In this chapter, you will put this hypothesis to the test.
- Sometimes, looking at the words on their own is not enough. For instance, a *cheap rate* may express a positive sentiment, while a *cheap trick* denotes something quite negative. Related to this is the observation that it would be hard to spot irony, sarcasm, and metaphorical use of a word (as in "Otherwise, it's pretty much a *sunken ship of a movie*") if you always looked at a single word at a time.

We will refer to this as *the length of the sentiment-bearing unit* issue and will look into how to handle this in a machine-learning classifier.

- The final issue, which is in a way related to the previous one, is the case of *negation*. In the previous chapter, we identified a group of words that have a special effect on the surrounding context—specifically, they have the ability to change the sentiment of what follows. For instance, *neither super nor standard* or *nothing spectacular* convert positive phrases into negative ones, while *not bad* puts the description on the positive scale.

Using the results of the sentiment lexicon-based system built in chapter 7 as the benchmark and involving machine-learning techniques and data-driven approaches, in this chapter you will try to improve your sentiment analyzer step-by-step.

8.1   Addressing multiple senses of a word with SentiWordNet

Our discussion about the sentiment detection based on a sentiment resource wouldn't be complete without talking about SentiWordNet, a lexical database where *different senses* of a word are assigned with *different sentiment scores*. Since language is diverse and creative, using a resource that accounts for the sentiment difference of various instances of the word use is preferable to relying on a single score resource. In what cases should you care about that?

In previous chapters, we talked about parts of speech and how identification of the part of speech helps make (the right) sense of expressions like "I saw her duck" (figure 8.2 shows a reminder).

Figure 8.2   The two senses of the word *duck*, as a verb (to move downward) and as a noun (bird)

In this case, applying part-of-speech tagging, as you did in various previous applications, would help distinguish between the two options. In other situations, things go a step further: a classic, widely used example in NLP domain is the case of *bank*. How many possible readings of the word *bank* can you think of? Here are the two most common contexts of use:

- I need to go to the *bank* today to get some money.
- The water erodes the *bank* as it flows along.

In the first case, one is talking about a bank as a financial institution, while in the second it is the riverbank that one has in mind. Both cases of *bank* belong to the same part of speech (they are nouns), and the best clues as to what is meant in each sentence are the words surrounding *bank*: such as the references to money in the first sentence, and the references to water in the second. So far so good, but what about such sentences as "I went to the bank"? In which sense is *bank* used here? Our intuition tells us that, most probably, in everyday life we'd hear this statement from someone who is going to a bank to get some money. However, in general, this sentence is naturally ambiguous and may well mean that someone went fishing on a riverbank. Language is full of such ambiguities.

Why is this relevant to our task at hand? If a word may mean different things, each of these things may be positive or negative to a different extent independently of other senses of the same word. A resource that can tell you about such differences in meaning and sentiment is of a great value. Luckily, such a resource exists: it is called SentiWordNet (http://mng.bz/YG4Q) by analogy with a widely used lexical database called WordNet (https://wordnet.princeton.edu), to which it is closely related.

WordNet is a lexical database created at Princeton University, and it is an invaluable resource to use with any application that recognizes that words can be ambiguous between various senses. Essentially, WordNet is a huge network containing various nouns, verbs, adjectives, and adverbs grouped into sets of *cognitive synonyms* (i.e., words that mean similar things in the same context, as in *interesting* film = *interesting* movie or *fast* car = *fast* automobile). Such groups of cognitive synonyms in WordNet are called *synsets*. For instance, one such synset in WordNet would contain both words {film, movie} (and another one both words {car, automobile}) and that suggests that the words within each of these groups can be used interchangeably in various contexts. In total, there are 117,000 such groups of interchangeable words—that is, 117,000 synsets—and they also hold certain further relations among themselves. For instance, WordNet imposes a hierarchy on concepts, so you can also link them via the IS-A relation; for example, {car, automobile} is a type of *vehicle* (*i.e.*, car/automobile IS-A vehicle), and {film, movie} is a type of *show* (*i.e.*, film/movie IS-A show), which is, in turn, a type of *event*, and so on. We are not going to discuss such other relations in detail in this chapter, since it is the *synonymy* relation, the one that holds the words within each synset together, that is most relevant for sentiment analysis.

To use a concrete example, let's look into how *terrific* is represented in WordNet. WordNet distinguishes between three senses of the word:

- Very great or intense, as in "a terrific noise."
- Extraordinarily good or great, as in "The film was terrific!"
- Causing extreme terror as in "a terrific wail."

Figure 8.3 visualizes the three synsets and includes definitions, further words belonging to each of these synsets, and examples of use (the WordNet interface, where you can search for words and their synsets, is available at http://mng.bz/Pnw9).

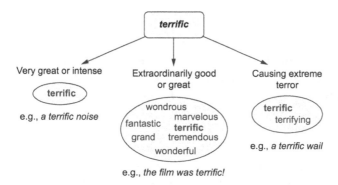

Figure 8.3 Three synsets for *terrific*, with definitions, other words from the same synset, and examples

One would expect the first two synsets (i.e., each of the words covered by these synsets) to carry a positive sentiment, and the third one to be negative. This is, in essence, the motivation behind SentiWordNet (https://github.com/aesuli/SentiWordNet), a sentiment-oriented extension to WordNet, developed by the researchers from the Text Learning Group at the University of Pisa.

SentiWordNet closely follows the structure of WordNet itself. That is, the same synsets are included in SentiWordNet, and each one is assigned with three scores: a positive score, a negative score, and an objective (neutral) score. The scores are assigned by a "committee" of classifiers—a combination of eight different machine-learning classifiers, where each one votes for one of the three polarity dimensions (find more details on implementation at http://mng.bz/GE58). In the end, the votes for each dimension (positive, negative, and objective) are aggregated across the classifiers and the scores represent the proportion of the classifiers among the eight that vote for the score of a particular polarity.

A nice fact about these two resources is that they are easily accessible through an NLTK interface. You used NLTK resources earlier in this book, such as when you accessed the texts from Project Gutenberg in chapters 5 and 6. You are going to use a similar approach here. Open your Jupyter Notebook that you worked on in chapter 7. You will add to that throughout this chapter.

Listing 8.1 shows how to access SentiWordNet via NLTK and check how two words, *joy* and *trouble*, are represented in WordNet. First, import sentiwordnet from NLTK and give it a shortcut for brevity. Next, you check which synsets words of your choice belong to. In this example, I check *joy* and *trouble*.

NOTE In addition to the toolkit itself, you need to install NLTK data as explained at www.nltk.org/data.html. Running nltk.download() will install all the data needed for text processing in one go; in addition, individual tools can be installed separately; for example, nltk.download('sentiwordnet') installs SentiWordNet.

Listing 8.1 Code to access SentiWordNet and check individual words

```
import nltk
nltk.download('wordnet')          ⎱ Install NLTK's interfaces
nltk.download('sentiwordnet')  ⎰ to WordNet and
                                      SentiWordNet.
from nltk.corpus import sentiwordnet as swn   ⎤ Import sentiwordnet
                                               ⎥ from NLTK and give it
print(list(swn.senti_synsets('joy')))        ⎦ a shortcut for brevity.
print(list(swn.senti_synsets('trouble')))

                 Check which synsets words
                 of your choice belong to.
```

The code produces the following output:

```
[SentiSynset('joy.n.01'), SentiSynset('joy.n.02'), SentiSynset('rejoice.v.01'),
    SentiSynset('gladden.v.01')]
[SentiSynset('trouble.n.01'), SentiSynset('fuss.n.02'),
    SentiSynset('trouble.n.03'), SentiSynset('trouble.n.04'),
    SentiSynset('worry.n.02'), SentiSynset('trouble.n.06'),
    SentiSynset('disturb.v.01'), SentiSynset('trouble.v.02'),
    SentiSynset('perturb.v.01'), SentiSynset('trouble_oneself.v.01'),
    SentiSynset('trouble.v.05')]
```

This shows that *joy* may be a noun (the synset 'joy.n.01', meaning the "emotion of great happiness," or the synset 'joy.n.02', meaning "something/someone providing a source of happiness as in "a joy to behold"). Alternatively, *joy* may be a verb, and as a verb, it can mean "rejoice" ("feel happiness or joy" [synset 'rejoice.v.01']) or "gladden" ("make glad or happy" [synset 'gladden.v.01']). You can tell which part of speech is involved by the abbreviations: e.g., n for noun and v for verb.

Trouble is a more complex case, with as many as six different meanings as a noun. For instance, it can mean a particular event causing pain, as in "heart trouble," or a difficulty, as in "he went to a lot of trouble," and as many as five senses for the verb. The differences may be quite subtle, yet leading to different interpretations, potentially with sentiments of different strength.

Let's check this out. With the code from listing 8.2, you can check the positive and negative scores assigned in SentiWordNet to various senses of the words you choose. The following code accesses two synsets for *joy* and two synsets for *trouble*. With this code, you can access specific synsets (senses) for each of the input words (feel free to use different words) and use the printout routine from the previous chapters to print the results as a table. Each synset has a positive and a negative score assigned to it. You can access them with pos_score() and neg_score().

Listing 8.2   Code to explore the differences in the sentiment scores for word senses

```
joy1 = swn.senti_synset('joy.n.01')          Access specific synsets
joy2 = swn.senti_synset('joy.n.02')          (senses) for each of
                                             the input words.
trouble1 = swn.senti_synset('trouble.n.03')
trouble2 = swn.senti_synset('trouble.n.04')


categories = ["Joy1", "Joy2", "Trouble1", "Trouble2"]     Use the printout
rows = []                                                 routine from the
rows.append(["List", "Positive score", "Negative Score"]) previous chapters
accs = {}                                                 to print the results
accs["Joy1"] = [joy1.pos_score(), joy1.neg_score()]       as a table.
accs["Joy2"] = [joy2.pos_score(), joy2.neg_score()]
accs["Trouble1"] = [trouble1.pos_score(), trouble1.neg_score()]
accs["Trouble2"] = [trouble2.pos_score(), trouble2.neg_score()]
for cat in categories:                          Each synset has a positive
    rows.append([cat, f"{accs.get(cat)[0]:.3f}",  pos_score() and a negative
                f"{accs.get(cat)[1]:.3f}"])        neg_score() assigned to it.

columns = zip(*rows)
column_widths = [max(len(item) for item in col) for col in columns]
for row in rows:
    print(''.join(' {:{width}} '.format(row[i], width=column_widths[i])
                  for i in range(0, len(row))))      Print positive and negative
                                                     scores for each synset.
```

Table 8.1 shows the results.

Table 8.1   Results printed out by the code from listing 8.2

List	Positive score	Negative score
Joy1	0.500	0.250
Joy2	0.375	0.000
Trouble1	0.000	0.625
Trouble2	0.000	0.500

In other words, despite both senses of *joy* (as an emotion and as a source of happiness) being overall positive, the first one, the emotion, is more ambiguous between the positive and negative uses, as 50% of the classifiers (4 out of 8) voted for the positive sentiment, and 25% (2 out of 8) voted for the negative sentiment, with the rest voting for the neutral sentiment for this sense of the word. The second sense of *joy* is more markedly positive, with 37.5% (3 out of 8 of the classifiers) voting for the positive sentiment, and the rest for the neutral one. Note that the two senses of trouble (as an event causing pain or as a difficulty) are decidedly negative, but even here the degree of negativity is different.

As you can see, different senses of the same word are indeed marked with sentiments of different strength, if not of different polarity. Ideally, when encountering a word in text, you would like to first detect which sense it is used in and then access the sentiment scores for that particular sense. In practice, this first step, called *word sense disambiguation* (see Section 18.4 in https://web.stanford.edu/~jurafsky/slp3/18.pdf) is a challenging NLP task in its own right. Short of attempting full-scale word sense disambiguation, in this chapter we are going to detect the part of speech for the word (e.g., *trouble* as a noun) and extract the sentiment scores pertaining to the senses of this word when it is used as this part of speech (i.e., only noun-related sentiment scores for *trouble* will be taken into account). This will help you eliminate at least one level of word ambiguity.

Listing 8.3 shows how to access synsets related to the specific part of speech for a given input word. For example, nouns can be accessed with tag n or wn.NOUN, verbs with v or wn.VERB, adjectives with a or wn.ADJ, and adverbs with r or wn.ADV. As this code shows, you can access synsets for a given word (e.g., *terrific*) of a specific part of speech (e.g., adjective) using an additional argument with the senti_synsets function. In the end, you print out positive and negative scores for each synset, using + and – in front of the scores for clarity, as by default all scores are returned as absolute values without indication of their polarity.

Listing 8.3   Code to access synsets of a specific part of speech

```
synsets = swn.senti_synsets('terrific', 'a')          ⟵  Access synsets for a given word
for synset in synsets:                                     of a specific part of speech using
    print("pos: +" + str(synset.pos_score()) +            an additional argument in
        " neg: -" + str(synset.neg_score()))              senti_synsets.
```

Print out positive and negative scores for each synset.

This code produces the following output:

```
pos: +0.25 neg: -0.25
pos: +0.75 neg: -0.0
pos: +0.0 neg: -0.625
```

That is, out of the three senses of *terrific*, the second one associated with "extraordinarily good or great" is strongly positive (+0.75 for positive), the third one associated with "causing extreme terror" is strongly negative (–0.625 for negative), and the first one associated with "very great or intense" is ambiguous between the two polarities—it can be treated both as positive (+0.25) and negative (–0.25). It looks like intensity may not always be welcome; after all, something like "a terrific noise" may elicit negative or positive emotions, and SentiWordNet captures this idea. Figure 8.4 visualises this further.

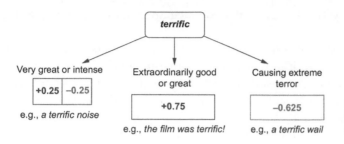

Figure 8.4   Three synsets of *terrific* with different sentiment scores assigned to them

Now let's see how you can incorporate the SentiWordNet information with your sentiment analyzer. As in listing 8.3, let's make sure that you are accessing the right type of synsets—that is, let's extract the synsets for the specific part of speech. Remember that you have previously (i.e., while building your baseline classifier in chapter 7) processed the reviews with spaCy and saved the results in the linguistic containers `pos_docs` and `neg_docs`. These containers, among other information, contain POS tags for all words in the reviews. You don't need to run any further analysis to detect parts of speech, but the particular tags used to denote each part of speech differ between spaCy and NLTK's interface to SentiWordNet. Here is the summary of the differences:

- Nouns have tags starting with `NN` in spaCy's notation and are denoted as `wn.NOUN` in NLTK's interfaces to WordNet and SentiWordNet. (For the full tag description, check the English tab under Part-of-Speech Tagging at https://spacy.io/usage/linguistic-features#pos-tagging.)
- Verbs have tags starting with `VB` or `MD` in spaCy and are denoted as `wn.VERB` in NLTK.
- Adjectives have tags starting with `JJ` in spaCy and are denoted as `wn.ADJ` in NLTK.
- Adverbs have tags starting with `RB` in spaCy and are denoted as `wn.ADV` in NLTK.

Note that only these four parts of speech are covered by WordNet and SentiWordNet, so it would suffice to take only words of these four types into account. Listing 8.4 first implements the `convert_tags` function that translates POS tags between two toolkits and then returns a predicted label for a review based on the aggregation of positive and negative scores assigned to each synset to which the word may belong. Specifically, in this code, for each word token in the review, you check whether it is an adjective, an adverb, a noun, or a verb based on its POS tag. Then you retrieve the SentiWordNet synsets based on the lemma of the word and its POS tag. The score is aggregated as the balance between the positive and negative scores assigned to each synset for the word token. Finally, you return the list of `decisions`, where each item maps the predicted score to the actual one.

Listing 8.4 Code to aggregate sentiment scores based on SentiWordNet

```
from nltk.corpus import wordnet as wn          ◁        Import WordNet interface
                                                        from NLTK for part-of-speech
def convert_tags(pos_tag):                              tag conversion.
    if pos_tag.startswith("JJ"):
        return wn.ADJ
    elif pos_tag.startswith("NN"):
        return wn.NOUN
    elif pos_tag.startswith("RB"):
        return wn.ADV
    elif pos_tag.startswith("VB") or pos_tag.startswith("MD"):
        return wn.VERB
    return None               ◁           Function convert_tags
                                          translates between the tags
                                          used in the two toolkits.
def swn_decisions(a_dict, label):
    decisions = []
    for rev_id in a_dict.keys():
        score = 0
        neg_count = 0
        pos_count = 0
        for token in a_dict.get(rev_id):         For each word token
            wn_tag = convert_tags(token.tag_)     in the review, check
            if wn_tag in (wn.ADJ, wn.ADV,         its part-of-speech tag.
                        wn.NOUN, wn.VERB):    ◁
                synsets = list(swn.senti_synsets(     Retrieve the SentiWordNet
                    token.lemma_, pos=wn_tag))  ◁     synsets based on the
                if len(synsets)>0:                    lemma of the word and
                    temp_score = 0.0                  its part-of-speech tag.
                    for synset in synsets:
                        temp_score += synset.pos_score() - synset.neg_score()

                    score += temp_score/len(synsets)
        if score < 0:
            decisions.append((-1, label))     As before, return the list of
        else:                                 decisions, where each item
            decisions.append((1, label))      maps the predicted score to
    return decisions            ◁             the actual one.
```

Aggregate the score as the balance between the positive and negative scores of the word synsets.

Figure 8.5 visualizes the process of aggregating scores derived from SentiWordNet with a short example of a review consisting of a single phrase: "The movie was terrific!" First, POS tags for all words in the review are extracted from the linguistic containers. In this example, "The" is the determiner (tag DT), and "!" is a punctuation mark (tag "."). They are not considered further by the pipeline, and their tags are not converted to the WordNet ones, because WordNet doesn't cover these parts of speech. Other words—"movie" (tag NN), "was" (tag VBD), and "terrific" (tag JJ)—are considered further, and their tags are converted into wn.NOUN, wn.VERB, and wn.ADJ by the convert_tags function. Next, synsets are extracted from SentiWordNet applying

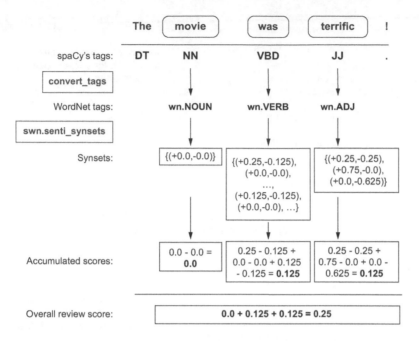

Figure 8.5   An example of how the scores are aggregated using the code from listing 8.4

swn.senti_synsets to ("movie", wn.NOUN), ("be", wn.VERB), and ("terrific", wn.ADJ). This function returns

- One synset for "movie" with scores (+0.0, -0.0); that is, it is a very unambiguous and a totally neutral word.
- As many as 13 synsets for "be," 11 of which are neural with scores (+0.0, -0.0), one mostly positive with scores (+0.25, -0.125), and one neutral on balance with scores (+0.125, -0.125).
- Three synsets for "terrific" that we've just looked into (see figure 8.4).

Without prior word sense detection, it is impossible to say in which sense each of the words is used, but you can take into account the distribution of all possible sentiments across senses and rely on the idea that, overall, the accumulated score will reflect possible deviations in sentiment. For instance, an overwhelmingly positive word that is positive in all its senses will get a higher score than a word that may be used in a negative sense once in a while. So, for example, if you sum up all sentiment scores across all synsets for "terrific," you'll get (0.25 – 0.25 + 0.75 – 0.0 + 0.0 – 0.625) = 0.125. The final score is still positive, but it is lower than the positive scores in some of its synsets (0.25 and 0.75) because it may also have a negativity component to it (-0.25 or even -0.625).

Once you've accumulated scores across all synsets of a word for each of the words in the review, the final score, as before, is an aggregation of the individual word scores. For this short review, it is 0.25, meaning that the review is quite positive. For convenience, the code in listing 8.4 converts all positive predictions into label 1 and all negative ones into -1.

Finally, let's compare the results produced by this approach to the actual sentiment labels. As before, let's calculate the accuracy of prediction by comparing the predicted scores (1 and -1) to the actual scores (1 and -1) and estimating the proportion of times your predictions are correct. Listing 8.5 implements this evaluation step in a similar manner to the evaluation in the previous chapter. In this code, you first extract and save the label predictions for the pos_docs (positive reviews with the actual label 1) and for neg_docs (negative reviews with the actual label -1) in two data structures. Next, you detect a match when the predicted score equals the actual score and calculate the accuracy as the proportion of cases where the predicted score matches the actual one. Finally, you print out the results as a table using the printing routine from before.

Listing 8.5 Code to evaluate the results for this approach

```
def get_swn_accuracy(pos_docs, neg_docs):
    decisions_pos = swn_decisions(pos_docs, 1)
    decisions_neg = swn_decisions(neg_docs, -1)          ◁   Save the label
    decisions_all = decisions_pos + decisions_neg            predictions for
    lists = [decisions_pos, decisions_neg, decisions_all]    the pos_docs
    accuracies = []                                          and neg_docs.
    for i in range(0, len(lists)):
        match = 0                        When the predicted score
        for item in lists[i]:            equals the actual score,
            if item[0]==item[1]:    ◁    consider it a match.
                match += 1
        accuracies.append(float(match)/
                          float(len(lists[i])))    ◁
    return accuracies                                   Accuracy reflects the
                                                        proportion of cases
                                                        where the predicted
                                                        score matches the
accuracies = get_swn_accuracy(pos_docs, neg_docs)       actual one.

rows = []
rows.append(["List", "Acc(positive)", "Acc(negative)", "Acc(all)"])
rows.append(["SentiWordNet", f"{accuracies[0]:.6f}",
            f"{accuracies[1]:.6f}",
            f"{accuracies[2]:.6f}"])            As before, print out the
columns = zip(*rows)                            results as a table using
column_widths = [max(len(item) for item in col) for col in columns]
for row in rows:                                            the printing routine.
    print(''.join(' {:{width}} '.format(row[i], width=column_widths[i])
                  for i in range(0, len(row))))    ◁
```

This code returns the results shown in table 8.2.

NOTE   As in other examples, you might end up with slightly different results if you are using versions of the tools different from those suggested in the installation instructions for the book. In such cases, you shouldn't worry about the slight deviations in the numbers as the general logic of the examples still holds.

Table 8.2   Results returned by the code from listing 8.5

List	Acc(positive)	Acc(negative)	Acc(all)
SentiWordNet	0.686000	0.690000	0.688000

In other words, this method achieves an overall accuracy of 68.80% and performs almost equally well on both positive and negative reviews. This is a clear improvement over the results obtained with your first, baseline classifier. To conclude this part of the chapter, let's visualize the results. Figure 8.6 presents the best accuracy of your baseline lexicon-based model (64.75%) in comparison with the current results (68.80%), with the majority class baseline for this dataset being 50%.

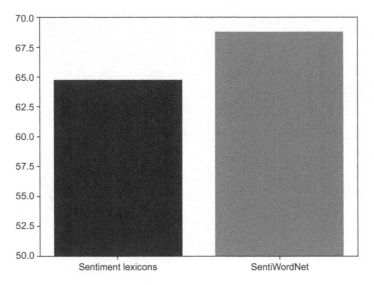

Figure 8.6   Accuracies achieved by two methods applied so far—lexicon-based and SentiWordNet-based

Exercise 8.1

The code in listings 8.4 and 8.5 takes all four parts of speech covered by WordNet into account. Before you move on to the next steps, check if the performance of the algorithm changes (e.g., improves) if you consider only some parts of speech (e.g., only adjectives) or some combinations (e.g., only nouns and adjectives).

(Note that this is an open-ended task, so feel free to experiment with your code as much as you like at this point. There are no predefined solutions for this task.)

8.2 Addressing dependence on context with machine learning

The results that you've obtained before with the simple sentiment lexicon-based approach and the advanced approach based on SentiWordNet, which allows you to adjust the sentiment score of a word based on the distribution of sentiment across its senses, still leave room for improvement. Given that a random choice of a sentiment label would be correct half of the time (since the distribution of labels is 50/50), the best accuracy you can get with a lexicon-based approach, using adjectives only, is about 0.65, and you reach around 0.69 with the SentiWordNet approach. Admittedly, the authors of the original paper cite similar accuracy figures (www.cs.cornell.edu/home/llee/papers/sentiment.pdf) for a simple lexicon-based approach that they applied. Still, their best results that they report on this task are quite a bit higher: their machine-learning models use a range of features and achieve accuracy values from around 78% up to about 83%. Even though the dataset you are working with is a slightly different version of the data (this paper used a smaller subset of 700 positive and 700 negative reviews from the same data), and it would, strictly speaking, be unfair to compare the performance on different datasets, the results in the region of 78% to 83% should provide you with a general idea of what is possible to achieve on this task. So how can you do better?

One aspect that your algorithm is currently not taking into account is the exact data you are working with. Even though you haven't yet been using a data-driven approach or machine-learning methods on this task yourself, you have already been using the product of such methods applied to this task, as both sentiment lexicons and SentiWordNet were, in fact, created using machine-learning and data-driven approaches. That means that they have potentially captured a lot of useful information about many words in language; however, there might still be a mismatch between how those words were used in their data and what you have in your reviews dataset. You are now going to look into the next challenge in sentiment analysis—*dependence of word sentiment on the surrounding context*—and you are going to learn the word sentiment dynamically based on the data at hand. It's time now to revisit approach 2 that we formulated in chapter 7:

> **Data-driven approach**
> Take a collection of positive and negative reviews. Set up a machine-learning pipeline, as you did for the applications in the previous chapters. This pipeline should rely on the dataset of reviews previously determined to be positive and negative. You should split this set into training and test data, define the set of features to learn the sentiment from, train a classifier of your choice on the training data with the selected set of features, and evaluate it on the test set.

Figure 8.7 is a reminder on the machine-learning pipeline as applied to the sentiment data.

Machine-learning pipeline

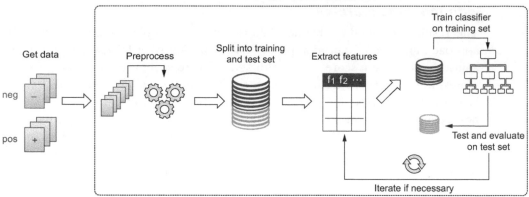

Figure 8.7   Machine-learning pipeline applied to the sentiment data

8.2.1   *Data preparation*

We are going to turn to scikit-learn now and use its functionality to prepare the data, extract features, and apply machine-learning algorithms. The first step in the process, as figure 8.7 visualizes, is preparing the texts from the dataset for classification. So far you have been working with two dictionaries: pos_docs, which store all positive reviews' IDs mapped to the content extracted from the correspondent files and processed with spaCy, and neg_docs, which store all negative reviews' IDs mapped to the linguistically processed content. The spaCy's linguistic pipeline adds all sorts of information to the original word tokens (e.g., earlier in this chapter you've used lemmas and POS tags retrieved from pos_docs and neg_docs). It's time now to decide which of these bits of information to use in your machine-learning application as features. In particular, you need to consider the following questions:

- *Question 1*—Are all words equally important for this task? For some other applications in the previous chapters, you removed certain types of words (e.g., stopwords). In addition, in chapter 7 you saw that words of certain parts of speech (e.g., adjectives or adverbs) might be more useful than others. Should you take all words into account, or should you do some prefiltering of the content?
- *Question 2*—What should be used as features for the classification? Is it word forms, so that *film* and *films* would give rise to two different features in the feature vector, or is it lemmas so that both would result in a single feature "film"? Should you consider single words like *very* and *interesting*, or should you take phrases like *very interesting* into account too?

These are reasonable questions to ask yourself whenever you are working on an NLP classification task. Regarding question 1, you might have noticed that none of the sentiment lexicons contained words like *a* or *the* (called *articles*), *of* or *in* (called *prepositions*), and other similar frequent words that are commonly called *stopwords*. In fact, the researchers who compiled these lists specified that stopwords were filtered out. SentiWordNet doesn't cover such words either. On the one hand, since stopwords mainly help link other words together (as prepositions do) or add some aspects to the meaning (as the indefinite article *a* or definite article *the* do), many of them don't express any sentiment value in addition to this main function of linking other words to each other, so you might consider filtering them out.

On the other hand, care should be taken as to what words are included in the list of stopwords: for instance, traditionally negative words like *not* and similar are also considered stopwords, but as you've seen before, they are useful for sentiment detection. You might have also noticed that lexicons and SentiWordNet do not contain any punctuation marks. Whether to include punctuation marks in the set of features is another choice you'll have to make. On the one hand, emotional statements often contain special punctuation such as exclamation marks, making them potentially useful as a feature. However, on the other hand, both positive ("This movie is a must-see!") and negative ("Don't waste your time on this movie!") reviews may contain them, making such punctuation marks less discriminative as a feature. To this end, let's implement a flexible filtering method, `text_filter`, that will allow you to customize the list of words that you'd like to ignore in processing. After filtering is done, let's consider all other words as potential features. Once you get the results with the full vocabulary, you will be able to compare the performance to the more limited sets of features (e.g., adjectives only). To see how the original content of a review may get dramatically distilled by the `text_filter` method down to content words, take a look at figure 8.8.

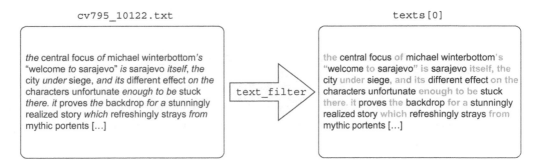

Figure 8.8 The content of the original review filtered down by a `text_filter` method

Question 2 asks you which linguistic unit should be used as the basis for the features. Recall that one of the challenges in sentiment analysis identified in the beginning of this chapter is *the size of the feature unit*. This is not a completely novel question for you. Recall that in chapters 5 and 6, you used units smaller than a word (suffixes of up to three characters in length) to classify texts as belonging to one of the authors. Although you can consider units shorter than a word as features for sentiment analysis, too, traditionally words are considered more suitable as features for this application. Use of lemmas instead of word forms will make your feature space more compact as you've seen during the data exploration phase; however, you might lose some sentiment-related information through this space-reduction step (e.g., word form *worst* might bear a stronger sentiment clue than its lemma *bad*). You might have also noticed that the sentiment lexicons used in the previous chapter contain word forms rather than lemmas. Again, let's make sure that the filtering method, `text_filter`, is flexible enough to allow you to change the level of granularity for your features if needed.

Finally, if you look into previous research on sentiment analysis—for instance, into the seminal paper "Thumbs Up? Sentiment Classification using Machine Learning Techniques" that accompanied the reviews dataset—sentiment analysis algorithms often consider units longer than single words as features. In particular, the paper mentions using *word bigrams* as well as *unigrams* as features. What does this mean?

If you continue working in NLP, you will come across such terms as *unigrams*, *bigrams*, *trigrams*, and *n-grams* in general very often. These terms define the length of a particular linguistic unit, typically in terms of characters or words. For example, *character n-grams* specify the length of a sequence of characters, with *n-* in *n-gram* standing for the length itself. Figure 8.9 illustrates how to identify *n*-grams of a specific length in terms of characters and words.

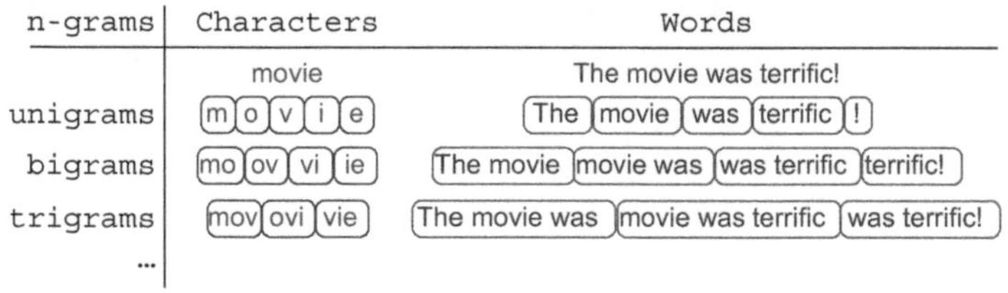

Figure 8.9   Identification of *n*-grams of various length *n* in terms of characters and words

In fact, one of the feature types used for author identification in chapters 5 and 6—suffixes—can be considered an example of character trigrams. Let's give it a proper definition.

N-grams

N-grams stand for sequences of linguistic units (e.g., characters or words) of a specific length denoted by *n-*. For instance, character *unigrams* are sequences of one character; *bigrams*, of two characters; *trigrams*, of three characters; and so on.

When thinking of using *word n-grams* as features for sentiment analysis, ask yourself whether word unigrams (e.g., *very*, *good*, and *movie* extracted from "Very good movie") are sufficiently informative, or whether addition of the word bigrams "very good" and "good movie" to the feature space will help the classifier learn the sentiment better. There is a certain tradeoff between the two options here. While bigrams might add some useful signal to the feature space, there are advantages to sticking to unigrams only. In particular:

- A word unigrams-based feature space is always *more compact*—For example, if you have 100 word unigrams, theoretically there may be up to $100*100 = 10,000$ bigrams—a very significant increase in the feature space size and a toll on the algorithm's efficiency.
- A word unigrams-based feature space is always *less sparse*—Imagine that you've seen *very* 50 times and *good* 100 times, and you are quite certain that *very* doesn't always occur in combination with *good*. How often, then, will you see "very good" in this data? You can be sure, this will be less than 50 times (i.e., the lower frequency of the words within an *n*-gram always sets up the upper bound on the frequency of the word combination as a whole), and the longer the *n*-gram becomes, the less often you will see it in the data. This might eventually mean that the *n*-gram becomes too rare to be useful in classification.

We will get to the question of using longer word *n*-grams, as well as a combination of *uni-* and longer *n*-grams a little later in this chapter once you get more familiar with the scikit-learn's functionality. Right now, let's get straight to coding and implement two functions that will allow you to apply filtering of your choice to the content of the reviews and will help you prepare the data for further feature extraction. Listing 8.6 does exactly that, filtering out punctuation marks and keeping word forms. Feel free to experiment with other types of filtering.

In this code, you start by adding some useful imports: `random` for data shuffling, `string` to access the list of punctuation marks, and finally, spaCy's stopwords list. We'll use the standard list of punctuation marks. Note that `string.punctuation` is a string of punctuation marks, so let's convert it to a list for convenience. Alternatively, you can define your own customized list instead. Next, you pass in a reviews dictionary `a_dict`, where each review's ID is mapped to its content, a label (1 for positive and -1 for negative reviews) and `exclude_lists` for the lists of words to be filtered out as arguments to the function `text_filter`. For the word forms that are not in the `exclude_lists`, you add the word forms to the output. Alternatively, you can use `token.lemma_` instead of `token.text` in this code to take lemmas instead of word forms. You return `data`—a data structure with tuples, where the first element in each tuple is a filtered down version of a review and the second is its label. After that, you apply the `text_filter` function to both types of reviews and put the tuples of filtered reviews with their labels together in one data structure. Within the `prepare_data` function, you shuffle the data entries randomly, and to ensure that this random shuffle results in the same order of reviews from one run of your system to another, you set a random seed (e.g., 42 here). Then you split the randomly shuffled tuples into two lists: `texts` for the filtered content of the reviews and `labels` for their labels. This code shows how to filter out punctuation marks using the prepare_data function. For both punctuation and stopwords filtering, you'll need to use list(stopwords_list) + punctuation_list. In the end, you apply the prepare_data function to the dataset and print out the length of the data structures (this should equal the original number—2,000 reviews here), as well as some selected text (e.g., the first one texts[0]).

Listing 8.6   Code to filter the content of the reviews and prepare it for feature extraction

```
import random          ←⎤  Add some useful imports.
import string
from spacy.lang.en.stop_words import STOP_WORDS as stopwords_list
punctuation_list = [punct for punct in string.punctuation]    ←
```
string.punctuation is a string of punctuation marks, so let's convert it to a list for convenience.

```
def text_filter(a_dict, label, exclude_lists):
    data = []
    for rev_id in a_dict.keys():
        tokens = []
        for token in a_dict.get(rev_id):
            if not token.text in exclude_lists:
                tokens.append(token.text)
        data.append((' '.join(tokens), label))
    return data
```
Pass in a_dict, a label, and exclude_lists as arguments.

For the word forms that are not in the exclude_lists, add the word forms to the output.

```
def prepare_data(pos_docs, neg_docs, exclude_lists):
    data = text_filter(pos_docs, 1, exclude_lists)
    data += text_filter(neg_docs, -1, exclude_lists)
    random.seed(42)
    random.shuffle(data)
    texts = []
    labels = []
    for item in data:
        texts.append(item[0])
        labels.append(item[1])
    return texts, labels
```
Apply the text_filter function to both types of reviews and store the results in one data structure.

Shuffle the data entries randomly.

Split the randomly shuffled tuples into two lists—texts and labels.

```
texts, labels = prepare_data(pos_docs, neg_docs, punctuation_list)    ←

print(len(texts), len(labels))
print(texts[0])    ←
```
Filter out punctuation marks.

Apply prepare_data function to the dataset and print out some results.

Return data, with the first element being a filtered down version of a review, and the second its label.

This code will print out 2,000 for the length of the texts list (i.e., the list of texts that represent filtered down content of each of the original reviews) and the length of the labels list (i.e., the list of labels, including 1 for a positive sentiment and -1 for a negative sentiment). These structures hold the processed data from the original 2,000 reviews.

To check how the data is now represented in the texts list, you use print(texts[0]) to peek into the first review in this structure. It corresponds to the positive review stored in the file `cv795_10122.txt`, the one used in the example in figure 8.8. Here is how the content looks now, with only the punctuation marks filtered out:

```
the central focus of michael winterbottom 's welcome to sarajevo is sarajevo
itself the city under siege and its different effect on the characters
unfortunate enough to be stuck there it proves the backdrop for a stunningly
realized story which refreshingly strays from mythic portents [...]
```

Now let's split this data into the usual subsets—the training set that you will use to make the classifier learn how to perform the task and the test set that you will use to evaluate the performance of the classifier (i.e., estimate how well it learned to perform the task at hand). Figure 8.10 highlights where you currently are in the machine-learning pipeline.

Machine-learning pipeline

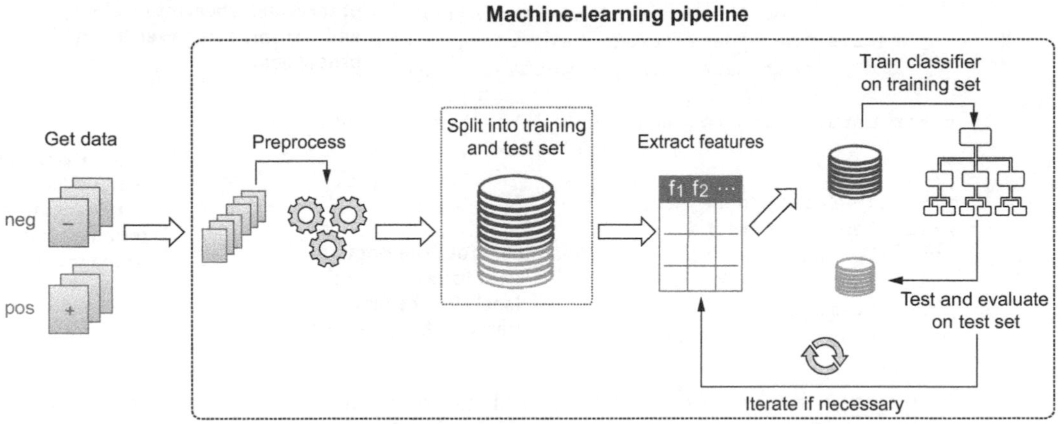

Figure 8.10   Next step in the machine-learning pipeline—split the data into the training and test sets

Let's use a simple strategy: since you've already shuffled the data, the instances with different labels should be randomly ordered in `texts` and `labels` data structures, so you can allocate the first 80% of these instances to the training set and the other 20% to the test set. We are going to improve on this splitting strategy in a bit, so let's not worry about further details of this random split for the moment. Listing 8.7 shows how to split the data into the texts for the training and test sets (called `train_data` and `test_data`) and labels for the training and test sets (`train_targets` and `test_targets`). Additionally, you can check that the data is randomly shuffled by printing out the first 10 labels from each of the subsets. Specifically, you implement the function `split`, which should split input lists of `texts` and `labels` into training and test set texts and labels using the predefined `proportion`. As the code suggests, you use `0.8` to allocate the first 80% of the input texts to the `train_data` and the first 80% of the input labels to the `train_targets`, while putting the other 20% of the input texts into the `test_data` and the other 20% of the input labels into the `test_targets`.

Finally, you print out the length of each list as well as the labels for the first 10 items in the target lists.

Listing 8.7   Code to split the data into the training and test sets

```
def split(texts, labels, proportion):
    train_data = []
    train_targets = []
    test_data = []
    test_targets = []
    for i in range(0, len(texts)):
        if i < proportion*len(texts):
            train_data.append(texts[i])
            train_targets.append(labels[i])
        else:
            test_data.append(texts[i])
            test_targets.append(labels[i])
    return train_data, train_targets, \
           test_data, test_targets

train_data, train_targets, test_data, test_targets = \
                          split(texts, labels, 0.8)

print(len(train_data))
print(len(train_targets))
print(len(test_data))
print(len(test_targets))
print(train_targets[:10])
print(test_targets[:10])
```

The split function splits input lists of texts and labels into training and test sets using predefined proportion.

Use the proportion 0.8 to allocate 80% of the data to the training set and 20% to the test set.

Print out the length of each list as well as the labels for the first 10 items in the target lists.

If you run this code as is and use 80% of the texts and labels to train the classifier, you should get 1,600 for the length of the train_data and train_targets, and 400 for the length of the test_data and test_targets. Here's the list of the first 10 labels from the training and the test data:

```
[1, -1, 1, 1, -1, -1, -1, -1, 1, -1]
[-1, 1, 1, -1, -1, 1, -1, 1, 1, 1]
```

This shows that positive reviews (label 1) are mixed with negative reviews (label -1) in a random order. Now you've done several preparation steps: you've prefiltered the content of the reviews to distill it down to what can be considered to constitute important features, you've separated texts from labels, and you've split the data into the training and the test sets. It's time now to extract features and apply the full machine-learning pipeline, as figure 8.11 shows.

8.2.2   *Extracting features from text*

One of the benefits of scikit-learn and, indeed, one of the reasons to use it in this book is that many steps in the machine-learning pipeline, such as feature extraction for NLP tasks, are made easy with this toolkit. One of the most widely used approaches

Machine-learning pipeline

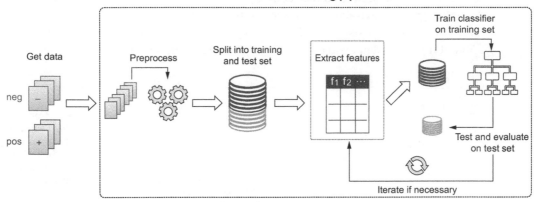

Figure 8.11 **Next step in the machine-learning pipeline—extract features**

to using words as features—in fact, the one that you've already used for some of the previous applications—is based on the idea that distribution of words contributes to the class prediction. For instance, if you see a word *good* used multiple times in a review, you would expect this review to express a positive sentiment overall. Similarly, if some negative words like *bad* or *awful* are simultaneously used in a review, it's a strong signal that the review is overall negative. Therefore, if you have a list of words to estimate the distribution of in the data, your classifier can learn how frequently they occur in the positive and in the negative reviews. In fact, scikit-learn covers these two steps—collection of the vocabulary words to estimate distribution for and calculation of frequency of words from this vocabulary in each review—with a single tool called `CountVectorizer`.

Recall why you need to split the data into the training and test sets: when the algorithm learns how to solve the task, it sees only the data and labels from the training set. Based on that, it learns how to connect the data (features) from the training set to the labels, assuming that the training set represents the task at hand perfectly; that is, whatever the distribution of the features and their correspondence to the labels in the training data is, it will be exactly the same or very closely replicated in any future data you apply the trained algorithm to. When you apply it to the test data that the algorithm has not seen during its training, you can get a rough estimate of how the algorithm will perform on new, unseen data. Therefore, it is important that whatever the algorithm learns, it does so on the basis of the training data *only*, without peeking into the test set. To this end, the `CountVectorizer` does two things. First, it builds the vocabulary of words based on the training data only (which means that if some words occur in the test set only, they will be ignored during classification), and second, it estimates the correspondence between the feature distribution and the class label based on the training data only. The particular method that allows the `CountVectorizer` to do that is called `fit_transform`. Listing 8.8 shows how `CountVectorizer` can be applied to the training data. Behind the scenes, the `fit_transform` method from scikit-learn's `CountVectorizer` extracts the shared vocabulary from all training set reviews and estimates frequency of each word from the vocabulary in each review. Once you've applied it to your data, you can print out the size of the `train_counts` data structure.

Listing 8.8   Code to apply CountVectorizer to learn the features on the training set

```
from sklearn.feature_extraction.text import CountVectorizer

count_vect = CountVectorizer()
train_counts = count_vect.fit_transform(train_data)     ⟵── The fit_transform
                                                            method extracts the
                                                            shared vocabulary
print(train_counts.shape)    ⟵──                            from the training set
                             Let's print out the size       and estimates word
                             of the train_counts            frequency.
                             data structure.
```

This code produces the following output: `(1600, 36094)`. What does this mean? The first element of the tuple tells you that the number of data entries in the training set equals 1,600. This is exactly the number of training set reviews. The second element is, in fact, the length of the collected vocabulary. This means that there are 36,094 distinct words in the vocabulary collected by the algorithm from all training set reviews. This vocabulary is then applied to each review to produce a *feature vector*, and the frequency of *each* word from this vocabulary is estimated for *each* review to fill in the values in this vector. You know from our statistical checks in the previous chapter that the average length of a review is about 800 words, and that is before punctuation marks or stopwords are filtered out. Obviously, no review will contain anything close to 36,094 distinct words in it. This means that the feature vectors will be extremely sparse (i.e., only a small portion of a vector will be filled with counts from the words that actually occur in the review, while the rest will be filled with 0s).

Let's check this out. For instance, if you want to look "under the hood" of the algorithm and see what the `CountVectorizer` collected, you can use the following command:

```
print(train_counts[:11])
```

This will print out the counts collected for the first 10 reviews in the training set. In particular, it will print out the following:

```
(0, 32056)    41
(0, 5161)     1
(0, 12240)    1
(0, 22070)    18
...
```

The first element here tells you which review you are looking at. Index `0` means the first review from the training set—the one that starts with `the central focus of . . .` as printed out above and used in figure 8.8. The second element in each tuple tells you which word is used in a review by referring to its index from the alphabetically ordered vocabulary. For instance, the index `32056` corresponds to the word *the*, `5161` to the word *central*, `12240` to the word *focus*, and `22070` to the word *of*. You can always retrieve the word from the vocabulary by its index using `count_vect.get_feature_names()[`*index*`]`. For instance, `count_vect.get_feature_names()[35056]` will return the.

> **NOTE** In newer versions of scikit-learn, the `get_feature_names()` function is replaced with `get_feature_names_out()`.

Finally, the printed-out numbers correspond to the number of occurrences of each word in the review. For example, in this review, the word *the* occurs 41 times, *of* 18 times, and the other two words discussed above occur only once.

Now, if you want to have a further look into the collected vocabulary, you can print it out using `print(count_vect.get_feature_names()[:10])`, which will print out the first 10 entries from the vocabulary:

```
['00', '000', '0009f', '007', '00s', '03', '04', '05', '05425', '10']
```

Finally, `print(count_vect.vocabulary_)` will print out the entries from the vocabulary mapped to their IDs:

```
{'the': 32056, 'central': 5161, 'focus': 12240, ...}
```

Table 8.3 provides a glimpse into the vocabulary and feature vectors. The header presents the indexes from the vocabulary mapped to the words, while the figures show the frequency of each feature in the first review from the training set. Features that don't occur in the review get a count of 0. The bottom row, therefore, shows you a small bit of the feature vector for the first review.

Table 8.3 A glimpse into the vocabulary and feature vectors

Index	0	1	...	5161	...	32056	...
Word	00	000	...	central	...	the	...
Count (first review)	0	0	...	1	...	41	...

Now, let's extract the same features from the test data and apply the classifier. In the previous chapters, you've learned that Naïve Bayes, unlike some other classifiers, can deal reasonably well with sparse features, such as distributions of words from a large vocabulary, where for each particular review only a few are present. To this end, let's apply this classifier to your task. Figure 8.12 provides a reminder of the scikit-learn's train-test routine and syntax.

Figure 8.12   A reminder of the scikit-learn's train-test routine and syntax

Before you can apply a trained model to the test set, you need to extract the features from the test set, which is achieved in a very similar manner by applying the scikit-learn's CountVectorizer. To make sure that the algorithm counts the occurrences of the words from the vocabulary that it collected from the training data only (rather than collecting a new vocabulary and counting word occurrences based on it), omit the call to the fit method of the vectorizer and use only the transform bit—that is, you are *transforming* the raw contents of the test set reviews to the feature vectors, without fitting them into a new vocabulary. Listing 8.9 walks you through these steps.

Listing 8.9   Code to apply CountVectorizer to test set and run classification

Initialize the classifier and train the model on the training data using fit method.

Extract features from the test data by applying the transform method of the CountVectorizer.

Apply the classifier to make predictions on the test set.

Print out some results, for example the predicted labels for the first 10 reviews from the test set.

```
from sklearn.naive_bayes import MultinomialNB

clf = MultinomialNB().fit(train_counts, train_targets)

test_counts = count_vect.transform(test_data)
predicted = clf.predict(test_counts)

for text, label in list(zip(test_data, predicted))[:10]:
    if label==1:
        print('%r => %s' % (text[:100], "pos"))
    else:
        print('%r => %s' % (text[:100], "neg"))
```

This code will print out the first 100 characters from the first 10 reviews mapped with their predicted sentiment. Among them, you'll see the following examples:

```
"susan granger 's review of america 's sweethearts columbia sony what a waste
    of a talented cast bill" => neg
'  the fugitive is probably one of the greatest thrillers ever made it takes
    realistic believable cha' => pos
```

This looks like a very sensible prediction; for instance, the word *waste* (as well as the whole phrase "a waste of a talented cast") strongly suggests that it is a negative review, and the classifier picked that information up. The second review contains quite positive expressions, including "one of the greatest thrillers ever made" and "realistic believable cha[racters]", thus the prediction made for this review is that it is positive.

Congratulations, you've just built a data-driven sentiment analyzer that is tuned to detecting sentiment based on your specific data! Now let's look into how these multiple steps, including feature extraction and machine-learning classification, can be put together in a single flexible pipeline, and then let's run a full-scale evaluation of the results.

8.2.3 Scikit-learn's machine-learning pipeline

You've come across processing pipelines before, such as when you used the spaCy's pipeline earlier in this chapter and in the previous chapters to apply all linguistic tools at once. Scikit-learn allows you to define your own pipeline of processing, feature extraction, and machine-learning tools as well. What's the benefit of using such a pipeline? Here are the main advantages:

- Once defined, you don't need to worry about the sequence of tool application and consistency of the tools applied to training and test data. Define your pipeline once and then simply run it on any dataset.
- Scikit-learn's pipeline is highly customizable, and it allows you to bolt together various tools and subsequently run them with a single line of code (i.e., invoking the pipeline when needed). It makes it easy to experiment with different settings of the tools and find out what works best.

So, let's find out how the pipeline works. Listing 8.10 shows how to define a pipeline. You start by importing the `Pipeline` functionality and the `Binarizer` tool, which helps record absence or presence of features. You can add any tools of your choice to the pipeline and print out the full list of tools included in it with the activated options. Once defined, the pipeline can be run using the usual `fit-predict` routine.

Listing 8.10 Code to define pipeline

Import the Pipeline functionality.

Import the Binarizer tool to record the absence or presence of features.

```
from sklearn.pipeline import Pipeline
from sklearn.preprocessing import Binarizer

text_clf = Pipeline([('vect', CountVectorizer(min_df=10, max_df=0.5)),
                     ('binarizer', Binarizer()),
                     ('clf', MultinomialNB()),
                    ])

text_clf.fit(train_data, train_targets)
print(text_clf)
predicted = text_clf.predict(test_data)
```

Add any tools of your choice to the pipeline.

You can print out the full list of tools included in the pipeline with the activated options.

Apply the usual fit-predict routine.

Note that instead of defining the tools one by one and passing the output of one tool as the input to the next tool, you simply pack them up under the `Pipeline`, and after that you don't need to worry anymore about the flow of the information between the bits of the pipeline. In other words, you can train the whole model applying `fit` method as before (which will use the whole set of tools this time) and then test it on the test set using `predict` method. Figure 8.13 is thus an update on figure 8.12.

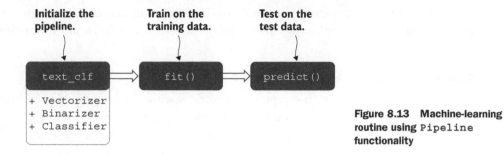

Figure 8.13   Machine-learning routine using `Pipeline` **functionality**

Now let's look more closely into the tools:

- Previous applications of the `CountVectorizer` left the brackets empty, and this time we use some options: `min_df=10` and `max_df=0.5`. What does this mean? (Check out the full list of available options at http://mng.bz/J2w0.) Recall from your earlier data explorations in this chapter that both positive and negative review collections have a large number of words in their vocabularies. The full vocabulary collected on the training set contains over 36,000 words, yet, as we've discussed, for any particular review the actual number of words occurring in it will be relatively small. The feature vectors of ~36,000 dimensionality are very expensive to create and process, especially given that they are very sparse (i.e., mostly filled with zeros for any given review). `CountVectorizer` allows you to mitigate this issue to some extent by setting cutoffs on the minimum and maximum document frequency (`min_df` and `max_df` options here). An integer value is treated as the absolute frequency, while a floating-point number denotes proportion of documents. By setting `min_df` to `10` and `max_df` to `0.5`, you are asking the algorithm to populate only the vocabulary and count the frequency for the words that occur in more than 10 reviews in the training data and in no more than 800 of them (i.e., 0.5 of the 1,600 training reviews), thus eliminating some relatively rare words that might be not frequent enough to be useful, as well as some very frequent words that might be too widely spread to carry any useful information. This makes the feature space much more compact and often not only speeds up the processing but also improves the results (as in this case).

- We are using a new tool, `Binarizer`, as part of this pipeline (check out the documentation at http://mng.bz/woZq). What does it do? Recall that with the lexicon-based approach, you tried two variations: taking absolute value of the sentiment (+1 for positive and –1 for negative words) or the relative sentiment weight. `Binarizer` allows you to do something a bit similar: it helps you to model the presence/absence of a word in a review as opposed to its frequency; in other words, it assigns a value of `1` (instead of a count) to each vocabulary word present in a review and a value of `0` to each vocabulary word absent from a review. The pipeline is very flexible in this respect. Add this tool to your pipeline and your classifier will rely on the presence/absence of features; remove it and your classifier will rely on frequencies. The authors of the "Thumbs Up?" paper report that presence/absence works better for sentiment analysis than frequency. Experiments on this version of the dataset show that the difference is very small, with presence/absence yielding slightly better results, so make sure you experiment with the different settings in the code.

Now, what are the results exactly? Let's find out! Listing 8.11 reminds you how to evaluate the performance of your classifier (here, the whole pipeline) and print out a confusion matrix where the actual labels are printed against system's predictions. Figure 8.14 shows a reminder of what information a confusion matrix contains.

Listing 8.11 Code to evaluate performance of your pipeline

```
from sklearn import metrics              ⟵┐ Import the collection
                                          │ of metrics.
print("\nConfusion matrix:")
print(metrics.confusion_matrix(test_targets, predicted))
print(metrics.classification_report(
    test_targets, predicted))    ⟵──┐ Print out the confusion matrix and
                                     │ the whole classification_report.
```

	Predicted negative	Predicted positive
Actual negative	173	29
Actual positive	41	157

Figure 8.14   A reminder of what information is contained in the confusion matrix

Here are the results:

```
Confusion matrix:
[[173  29]
 [ 41 157]]
              precision    recall  f1-score   support

          -1       0.81      0.86      0.83       202
           1       0.84      0.79      0.82       198

    accuracy                           0.82       400
   macro avg       0.83      0.82      0.82       400
weighted avg       0.83      0.82      0.82       400
```

A confusion matrix provides a concise summary of classifier performance (including both correctly classified instances and mistakes) and is particularly suitable for the analysis in binary classification cases. For instance, in this task you are classifying reviews into positive and negative ones. The example in figure 8.14 shows that in a set of 400 reviews (consisting of 202 actually negative reviews and 198 actually positive ones—you can estimate the totals following the numbers in each row), the classifier correctly identifies 173 negative and 157 positive ones. These numbers can be found on the diagonal of the confusion matrix. At the same time, the classifier incorrectly detects 29 negative reviews as positive, and 41 positive reviews as negative. The code in listing 8.11 reminds you how to print out the confusion matrix as well as the whole `classification_report`, which includes accuracy, precision, recall, and F-score for each class.

This particular pipeline run on this particular train-test split (with 202 negative and 198 positive reviews in the test set, as the support values show) achieves an accuracy of 82%, with a quite balanced performance on the two classes. In particular, it correctly classifies 173 negative reviews as negative and 157 positive reviews as positive; it incorrectly assigns a negative label to 41 actually positive reviews and a positive label to 29 actually negative ones. The last two lines of the report present macro average and weighted average for all metrics. You don't need to worry about the difference between them, as for a balanced dataset (as the one you are using in this chapter), there is no difference between the two—they simply represent averages for the values in each column. The difference will show itself when the classes have unequal distribution. Weighted average will take the proportion of instances in each class into account, while macro average will average across all classes regardless.

Now that you know how to run a whole pipeline of tools in one go, attempt exercise 8.2. Try solving these tasks before checking the solutions in the Jupyter Notebook.

Exercise 8.2

Experiment with different parameters and options for the selected tools. For example:

- Check out the documentation for available options.
- Evaluate the results with the frequency-based approach instead of the presence/absence approach.
- Compare the results to the classifier that uses lemmas instead of word forms.
- Compare the results to the classifier that filters out stopwords as well as punctuation.

8.2.4   *Full-scale evaluation with cross-validation*

Now you've obtained some results on this dataset and they seem to be quite promising. The performance is rather balanced on the two classes; the accuracy of 0.82 is similar to that reported in the "Thumbs Up?" paper (recall that we've discussed earlier in this chapter that the authors report accuracy values in the region of 78% to 83% for this task on a subset of this dataset). Well done! There is just one caveat to consider before you declare success on this task. Remember that your train-test split comes from one specific way of shuffling the dataset (using a selected random seed, 42 in listing 8.6) and training on the first 80% and testing on the other 20% of it. What happens if you shuffle the data differently, for example, using a different seed?

You might guess that the results will change. They will indeed, and if you are interested further in this question, you can try this out as an experiment. The results might change ever so slightly, but still, they would be different. What's more, you might also get "unlucky" with the new selection of the test set and get much lower results! Which results should you trust in the end? One way to make sure you get a fair range of results on different bits of the dataset, rather than on some random, perhaps some "lucky" test set (which might yield overly optimistic results), or perhaps some "unlucky" test set (that will make you believe the performance is lower than it actually is on another bit), is to run your classifier multiple times on different subsets of the data; for instance, changing the random seed and taking the mean of the results from multiple runs. How many times should you run your algorithm then?

In fact, there exists a widely used machine-learning technique called *k-fold cross-validation* that defines how such multiple runs of the algorithm over the data should be performed. *K* in the title of the technique stands for the number of splits in your data (and consequently also for the number of runs). Here is how you can apply k-fold cross-validation:

1 Split your full dataset into *k* random subsets (folds) of equal size. Traditionally, you would go for *k* = 5 or *k* = 10. Let's assume that you decided to run a ten-fold cross-validation (i.e., *k* = 10).

2 Take the subsets 1 to 9 as your training set, train your algorithm on this combined data, and use the tenth fold as your test set. Evaluate the performance on this fold.

3 Repeat this procedure nine more times, each time allocating a different fold to the test set and training your algorithm on the rest of the data; for example, in the second run, use the ninth fold as your test set and train on folds 1 to 8 plus fold 10. Evaluate the performance on each fold.

4 In the end, use the mean values for all performance metrics across all ten folds.

Note that by the end of this procedure, you would have run your classifier on every datapoint (every review) from your full dataset, because it would have ended up in some test fold in one of the runs. At the same time, you would never violate the golden rule of machine learning: since in each run the test set is separate from the training set, you never actually peek into the test set, yet you are able to fully exploit your dataset both for training and for testing purposes! Figure 8.15 visualizes the cross-validation procedure.

Like all other machine-learning techniques, cross-validation implementation is covered by scikit-learn, so you don't actually need to perform the splitting into folds yourself. Listing 8.12 shows how to invoke cross-validation for the pipeline you've built in the previous section. Specifically, in this code you rely on `cross_val_score` and `cross_val_predict` functionality. You specify the number of folds with the cv option, return the accuracy scores on each run, and calculate the average accuracy across all k-folds. In the end, you return predicted values from each fold and print out the evaluation report as you did before.

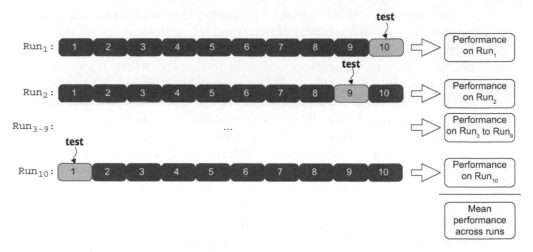

Figure 8.15   In each run in this ten-fold cross-validation scenario, the light-shaded fold is used for testing and all dark-shaded folds are used for training. In the end, the performance across all ten runs is averaged.

Listing 8.12   Code to run k-fold cross-validation

Specify the number of folds with the cv option and return the accuracy scores on each run.

Import cross_val_score and cross_val_predict functionality.

```
from sklearn.model_selection import cross_val_score, \
                              cross_val_predict

scores = cross_val_score(text_clf, texts, labels, cv=10)
print(scores)
print("Accuracy: " + str(sum(scores)/10))
predicted = cross_val_predict(text_clf, texts,
                          labels, cv=10)
print("\nConfusion matrix:")
print(metrics.confusion_matrix(labels, predicted))
print(metrics.classification_report(labels, predicted))
```

Calculate the average accuracy across k folds.

Return the predicted values from each fold.

Print out the evaluation report as you did before.

Here are the results:

```
[0.87  0.805 0.87  0.785 0.86  0.82  0.845 0.85  0.81  0.845]
Accuracy: 0.836

Confusion matrix:
[[843 157]
 [193 807]]
              precision    recall  f1-score   support

          -1       0.82      0.86      0.84      1000
           1       0.85      0.81      0.83      1000

    accuracy                           0.84      2000
   macro avg       0.84      0.84      0.84      2000
weighted avg       0.84      0.84      0.84      2000
```

The list of scores shows that, most of the time, the algorithm performs with an accuracy over 0.80, sometimes reaching an accuracy score as high as 0.87 (on fold 3). That is, if you randomly split your data into training and test sets and happened to have fold 3 for your test set, you'll be very pleased with your results. Not so much, though, if you happened to have fold 4 for your test set, as the accuracy there is 9% lower, at 0.785. In summary, the classifier performs with an average accuracy of around 0.84, which is also very close to the results you obtained before. On the full dataset of 1000 positive and 1000 negative reviews, the classifier is more precise at identifying positive reviews (precision on class="1" is 0.85) while reaching a higher recall on the negative reviews (recall on class="-1" is 0.86): this means that the classifier has a slight bias toward predicting negative reviews, so it has good coverage (recall) for them, but occasionally it makes mistakes (i.e., incorrectly predicts that a positive review is negative). Figure 8.16 visualizes the new best accuracy in comparison to previous results.

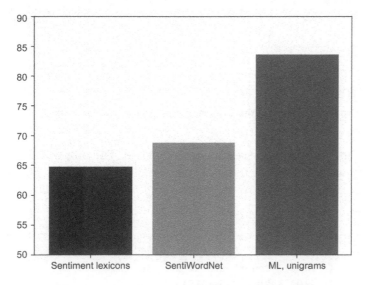

Figure 8.16   Accuracy achieved with a machine-learning (ML) approach using word unigrams

8.3   *Varying the length of the sentiment-bearing features*

The next challenge in sentiment analysis, identified in the beginning of this chapter, is the length of the sentiment-bearing unit. Are single word unigrams (like *very*, *good*, and *movie*) enough, or should you consider higher-order *n*-grams (e.g., bigrams like *very good* and *good movie*, or even trigrams like *very good movie*)? Let's find out which unit works best as the basis for features.

With scikit-learn's help, nothing can be easier! All you need to do to change the granularity of features—for example, replacing word unigrams with longer *n*-grams or combining the different types of *n*-grams—is to set the `ngram_range` option of the `CountVectorizer`. For instance, `ngram_range=(2, 2)` will allow you to use bigrams only and `ngram_range=(1, 2)` to combine unigrams and bigrams in the feature set. That is, you need to update your code from listing 8.10 and evaluate the results again using the code from listing 8.12. Figure 8.17 highlights the bit of the pipeline that is involved in this process.

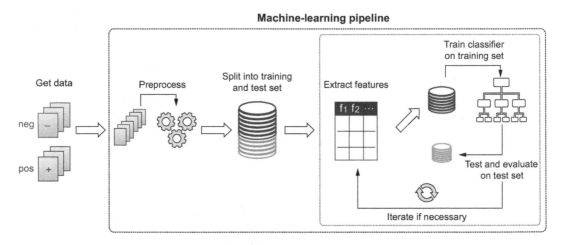

Figure 8.17   You can iterate on the final steps in the pipeline, updating your algorithm with new features.

Listing 8.13 shows how to update the scikit-learn's pipeline. The only option you need to update is the `ngram_range` of the `CountVectorizer`. Note that since most bigrams will be relatively rare in comparison to unigrams, you don't need to specify document frequency thresholds.

Listing 8.13   Code to update the Pipeline with n-gram features

```
text_clf = Pipeline([('vect', CountVectorizer(ngram_range=(1, 2))),
                     ('binarizer', Binarizer()),
                     ('clf', MultinomialNB())
                     ])

scores = cross_val_score(text_clf, texts, labels, cv=10)
print(scores)
print("Accuracy: " + str(sum(scores)/10))
predicted = cross_val_predict(text_clf, texts, labels, cv=10)
print("\nConfusion matrix:")
print(metrics.confusion_matrix(labels, predicted))
print(metrics.classification_report(labels, predicted))
```

The only option you need to update is the ngram_range of the CountVectorizer.

The rest of the code is the same as before.

This code produces the following results, showing that the performance of the sentiment analyzer improves overall and in particular on the positive class:

```
[0.865 0.845 0.875 0.795 0.89  0.82  0.865 0.88  0.795 0.875]
Accuracy: 0.8504999999999999

Confusion matrix:
[[819 181]
 [118 882]]
              precision    recall  f1-score   support

          -1       0.87      0.82      0.85      1000
           1       0.83      0.88      0.86      1000

    accuracy                           0.85      2000
   macro avg       0.85      0.85      0.85      2000
weighted avg       0.85      0.85      0.85      2000
```

Before you move on to addressing the final challenge, try to solve exercise 8.3.

> ### Exercise 8.3
> Explore how the length of the *n*-gram features impacts the results. For that, consider various settings for the `ngram_range` option; for instance, `(2, 2)` for bigrams only, `(1, 3)` for uni-, bi-, and trigrams combined, and so on. How does the performance change?

If you attempt this exercise with the combination of uni-, bi-, and trigrams as features modifying the code from listing 8.13 accordingly, you will get the following results:

```
[0.89  0.86  0.87  0.835 0.895 0.82  0.86  0.855 0.825 0.88 ]
Accuracy: 0.859

Confusion matrix:
[[810 190]
 [ 92 908]]
              precision    recall  f1-score   support

          -1       0.90      0.81      0.85      1000
           1       0.83      0.91      0.87      1000

    accuracy                           0.86      2000
   macro avg       0.86      0.86      0.86      2000
weighted avg       0.86      0.86      0.86      2000
```

To summarize, with the combination of *n*-grams of higher order, the overall accuracy of classification appears to increase, as do precision on the negative class and recall on the positive class. This means that the mistakes that the classifier makes are now mostly concerned with incorrect identification of some negative reviews as positive ones. Figure 8.18 plots the accuracies of the classifier with the new features against the previous results.

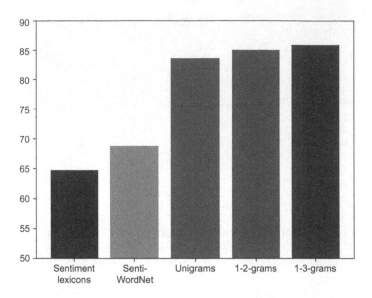

Figure 8.18   Summary of the results with various algorithms attempted so far

8.4   *Negation handling for sentiment analysis*

The final challenge for a sentiment analysis algorithm that we've identified in the beginning of this chapter is negation. Your sentiment analyzer must already be able to deal with negation to a certain extent: note that by not filtering out stopwords (that contain, among other words, *not* and similar negative markers) and taking into account longer phrases (bigrams and trigrams), you include phrases like "not good," "did not like," and similar in the feature set. The problem with this approach is twofold:

- First, since you are using both word unigrams and longer *n*-grams, even if you include phrases like "not good" or "did not like" in your feature set as bigrams and trigrams, you also include unigrams contained in them, namely *good* and *like*, which are normally associated with a positive sentiment and will confuse the classifier.
- Secondly, current approach is not able to handle any longer phrases. You are always limited by what you considered to be the optimal length of the *n*-gram. In practice, negation might apply to the whole phrase following it or to a word that doesn't follow the negative marker immediately. For example, such is the case in "This book did<u>n't</u> make for a good read and a good discussion," where "not" in "didn't" negates "good" (which wouldn't be captured even in the same trigram) if not the whole following phrase.

How should you deal with this issue, then? The authors of the "Thumbs Up?" paper suggest a solution: they mention that they use a method that adds a NEG marker to every word within the phrase that follows the negating word. Figure 8.19 illustrates what this "trick" does to the sentence that contains a negative word.

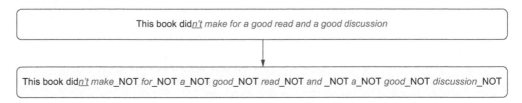

Figure 8.19   Negation can be handled by adding a prefix NEG to the words following the negation marker.

With sentiment analysis being a popular task, this "trick" has actually been already implemented in NLTK. This is yet another case where the combination of different tools proves to be useful. Listing 8.14 shows how to add this to your preprocessing. Specifically, NLTK's negation-handling functionality can be accessed via `mark_nega-tion`. In this code, you implement a `text_filter_neg` function, which is very similar to the `text_filter` function from listing 8.6, with the only difference that you apply `mark_negation` to the review content. Then you prepare the data for machine-learning classification as you did before and store the processed texts and labels in two data structures. To check how the data is represented in the end, you can print out the length of each of these data structures (this should equal to 2000 as before) and the processed content of the first review.

Listing 8.14   Code to add negation handling to your text preprocessing

```python
from nltk.sentiment.util import import mark_negation       ◁──┐ Add NLTK's negation
                                                               │ handling functionality
def text_filter_neg(a_dict, label, exclude_lists):            │ via mark_negation.
    data = []
    for rev_id in a_dict.keys():
        tokens = []
        for sent in a_dict.get(rev_id).sents:             Implement a
            neg_tokens = mark_negation(sent.text.split())  ◁── text_filter_neg
            for token in neg_tokens:                          function that
                if not token in exclude_lists:                applies mark_
                    tokens.append(token)                      negation to the
        data.append((' '.join(tokens), label))               review content.
    return data

def prepare_data_neg(pos_docs, neg_docs, exclude_lists):   ◁──┐ Prepare the data for
    data = text_filter_neg(pos_docs, 1, exclude_lists)        │ machine-learning
    data += text_filter_neg(neg_docs, -1, exclude_lists)      │ classification as
    random.seed(42)                                           │ you did before.
    random.shuffle(data)
    texts = []
    labels = []
```

```
    for item in data:
        texts.append(item[0])
        labels.append(item[1])
    return texts, labels
```

As in listing 8.6, store the processed texts and labels in two data structures.

```
texts_neg, labels_neg = prepare_data_neg(pos_docs, neg_docs, punctuation_list)
print(len(texts_neg), len(labels_neg))
print(texts_neg[0])
```

Print out the length of each of these data structures and the processed content of the first review.

Here is what you will get if you run this code: the length of both `texts_neg` (texts from the movie reviews, with punctuation marks removed and negation marked via `mark_negation`) and labels keeping the actual labels of all reviews is still 2000 as expected. The content of the first review, which as before starts with `the central focus of . . .` will be affected only where the review contains negative words. For instance:

```
he doesn't toy_NEG with_NEG our_NEG emotions_NEG
in war no one_NEG is_NEG victorious_NEG
not one_NEG moment_NEG with_NEG them_NEG involved_NEG rings_NEG false_NEG
```

Now all you need to do is run your algorithm on these newly processed texts and evaluate the results against labels using cross-validation, as the following listing (identical to listing 8.13) suggests.

Listing 8.15 **Code to update the Pipeline and run the classifier**

```
text_clf = Pipeline([('vect', CountVectorizer(ngram_range=(1, 2))),
                     ('binarizer', Binarizer()),
                     ('clf', MultinomialNB())
                    ])

scores = cross_val_score(text_clf, texts, labels, cv=10)
print(scores)
print("Accuracy: " + str(sum(scores)/10))
predicted = cross_val_predict(text_clf, texts, labels, cv=10)
print("\nConfusion matrix:")
print(metrics.confusion_matrix(labels, predicted))
print(metrics.classification_report(labels, predicted))
```

Here are the results on this pipeline:

```
[0.89  0.865 0.875 0.82  0.895 0.8   0.855 0.885 0.82  0.88 ]
Accuracy: 0.8585

Confusion matrix:
[[828 172]
 [111 889]]
```

	precision	recall	f1-score	support
-1	0.88	0.83	0.85	1000
1	0.84	0.89	0.86	1000
accuracy			0.86	2000
macro avg	0.86	0.86	0.86	2000
weighted avg	0.86	0.86	0.86	2000

In terms of the overall accuracy, these results are very close to the earlier model that uses uni-, bi-, and trigrams as features, suggesting that such a model already handles negation to a considerable extent. However, a negation "trick" also appears to help rebalance the performance between the two classes a bit, bringing the performance on the two closer together in terms of their precision and recall values. Figure 8.20 concludes this section with a summary of the accuracies you obtained with different algorithms:

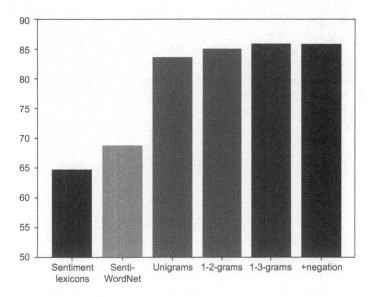

Figure 8.20 Summary of all the results

8.5　*Further practice*

Congratulations! Now you have built a fully functional sentiment analyzer, you have learned how to add as many preprocessing and feature-extraction tools as you need in a single ML pipeline, and you have learned how to evaluate the results fairly. Exercises 8.4 and 8.5 suggest more ideas for further practice with the sentiment analysis task. These tasks are open-ended; you can find some sample solutions for them in the book's Jupyter Notebook for this chapter.

Exercise 8.4: Explore contribution of adjectives and adverbs

The data-driven analyzer you've built in this chapter uses the full set of words as features. Yet, as we've discovered earlier, such words as adjectives and adverbs may bear more pronounced sentiment signal. Modify the code from this chapter to take into account *only* adjectives and adverbs. As a variation of the task, combine the data-driven approach with the sentiment lexicons; for example, only consider the words from the *adjectives lexicons*.

Hint: Instead of using the `text_filter` method to exclude words from certain lists or resources, you can implement a method that considers only words from certain lists or resources; for example, `text_filter(a_dict, label, include_lists)`.

Try solving this exercise before checking the solutions in the Jupyter Notebook.

Exercise 8.5: Classify sentiment in other data

There are several other datasets that you can experiment with and apply your sentiment analyzer to, including

- The sentence polarity dataset 1.0, available at http://mng.bz/z46g, which contains 5,331 positive and 5,331 negative sentences from movie reviews
- The Large Movie Review Dataset, available at https://ai.stanford.edu/~amaas/data/sentiment/, with as many as 25,000 highly polar movie reviews for training and another 25,000 reviews for testing
- Any other review dataset, including the ones you may have collected yourself or come across in practice

Explore these datasets, experiment with different features, and compare the results.

Summary

- This chapter looked into further, more in-depth analysis of the challenges in the sentiment classification task. Such challenges could not be handled with the baseline algorithm that you developed in the previous chapter, so this helped you define the steps to take in order to improve your classifier. In particular, (1) words are often ambiguous and may have different sentiments of different strengths associated with their multiple meanings; (2) surrounding context may change the sentiment of a word; (3) considering phrases longer than one word may be beneficial for this task, as individual words may not be able to capture intricacies of sentiment; and (4) negative words change polarity of whole phrases following them.
- The multiple senses challenge can be addressed with the use of SentiWordNet, which is a lexical database where words are assigned with three sentiment scores (positive, negative, and objective) according to their senses. SentiWordNet is closely related to WordNet, a very useful lexical resource for any application

that takes multiple senses of a word into account. Both lexical databases are available via the NLTK interface, which allows you to access synsets, groups of related words that can be used interchangeably. A sentiment analyzer based on SentiWordNet shows a 4% improvement in the results—up to 69% accuracy on the task.

- The spaCy NLP toolkit and its functionality can be combined with further linguistic resources available through NLTK, with SentiWordNet being one of such useful resources.
- The second challenge—the dynamic nature of word sentiment that may change depending on the context—can be addressed by learning the sentiment from reviews in a data-driven way through the application of machine learning.
- When building a machine learning–based sentiment analyzer, scikit-learn proves to be useful. In particular, it allows you to combine multiple tools into a single pipeline.
- A fair evaluation of your classifier's performance on the full dataset can be obtained using a k-fold cross-validation technique.
- Sequences of words are often referred to as *n*-grams in NLP applications; for instance, *bigrams* refer to sequences of words or characters of length 2, *trigrams* are sequences of length 3, and so on. This helps address the next challenge and incorporate features based on sequences longer than one word.
- Finally, the negation challenge can be addressed using NLTK functionality and marking the phrases following negative words with a special marker.
- A fully functional sentiment analyzer developed in this chapter achieves 86% accuracy on this task, which is substantially higher than the lexicon-based approach developed in the previous chapter.

Topic analysis

9

This chapter covers

- Implementing a supervised approach to topic classification with scikit-learn
- Using multiclass classification for NLP tasks
- Discovering topics in an unsupervised way
- Implementing an unsupervised approach— clustering with scikit-learn

In this chapter, you will learn how to automatically detect topics in text, either selecting from the set of known topics or discovering new, previously unseen ones. This is a challenging and practically useful task that can be approached from different perspectives using a variety of methods. This chapter will introduce new techniques, some of which are closely related to the ones that you've been using before. Let's put this task in a broader context before diving deep into the implementation issues.

Previous chapters presented a number of NLP applications that required you to build a machine-learning model that can classify text. Let's summarize them here:

- In chapter 2, you looked into how to build your own spam filter that can classify incoming email into spam or ham.

- In chapters 5 and 6, you developed an author-identification tool that can detect whether a text is written by one of the known authors (e.g., Jane Austen or William Shakespeare, or one of your contacts should you wish to apply this tool to your own data).
- In chapters 7 and 8, you learned how to build a sentiment analyzer that can classify a text (e.g., a review) as the one expressing a positive or a negative opinion.

All these applications, despite their obvious differences (e.g., detecting that an email is spam or ham is not the same as identifying who it was written by or whether it contains a positive or a negative message), bear a great deal of similarities. These similarities are related to the framework that you use to solve the task. In all these cases, you

- Rely on some data labeled with the classes of interest and build a machine-learning classifier using the classes from the annotated data. Recall that this is called *supervised machine learning*.
- Aim to distinguish between precisely two types of input (two discrete non-overlapping classes). Recall that this is called *binary classification*.

We said before that as soon as you can define separate classes in your data and have data labeled with such classes, you can apply supervised binary classification algorithms. The differences in each particular case will concern the type of features that you would select and the algorithm that you would apply. Figure 9.1 presents the now-familiar machine-learning pipeline for binary classification tasks and highlights the steps that are task-specific.

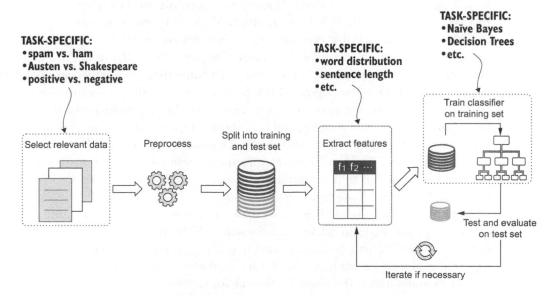

Figure 9.1 Overview of the supervised machine-learning pipeline. The selection of relevant data, feature types, and the algorithm depends on the task, as this diagram highlights.

This powerful approach is applied across the board to a wide range of *text classification* tasks, of which sentiment analysis, spam detection, and authorship identification are examples familiar to you by now. In this chapter, you will work with one more application of this powerful framework—topic classification. Let's start with a scenario. Suppose you work as a content manager for a large news platform. Your platform hosts texts from a wide variety of authors and mainly specializes in the following set of well-established topics: Politics, Finance, Science, Sports, and Arts. Your task is to decide, for every incoming article, which topic it belongs to and post it under the relevant tab on the platform. Here are some questions for you to consider:

1 Can you use your knowledge of NLP and machine-learning algorithms to help you automate this process?

2 What if you suspect that a new set of yet-uncovered topics, besides the five just mentioned, started emerging among the texts that authors send you (e.g., you get some articles on the technological advances)? How can you discover such new topics and include them in your analysis?

3 What if you think that some articles lend themselves to multiple topics, which are covered by these articles to a various extent? For instance, some articles may talk about a sports event that is of a certain political importance (e.g., Olympic Games) or about a new technological invention that results in the tech company having high valuation.

This scenario relates to the task that we can broadly define as *topic analysis*. Question 1 provides you with a hint—it suggests that you already have all the necessary skills and knowledge to use NLP and machine-learning algorithms to classify texts into topics. Indeed, this task is nothing but an extension of the old familiar scenarios where you classified texts into spam versus ham, or positive versus negative, only this time you will need to extend this framework to more than two classes. If you worked as a content manager for this platform before, one can assume that you assigned some articles to each of the categories (topics) in the past. This means that you can easily collect labeled data—just scrape some articles from each of the categories on your platform. Once your labeled data is ready, you can apply a supervised machine-learning algorithm to classify any new article into one of the familiar topics. Since by now you have vast experience working on binary classification applications to various tasks, this is just a small extension step for multiple classes. We will look into this step first, and we'll call this variety of the task *topic classification*.

Questions 2 and 3 related to this scenario are more challenging. Imagine that the content on your platform doesn't stay the same all the time. New topics may emerge in the data. Unfortunately, if you wanted to train a classification model to cover these topics in a supervised manner, you will need labeled articles for these new topics as well. Data availability is the major bottleneck for supervised machine learning. Therefore, in this and the next chapters, you will learn about alternative ways of topic discovery and will apply two unsupervised machine-learning algorithms: *clustering*, which will be covered in this chapter, and *topic modeling with latent Dirichlet allocation (LDA)*, which will be the topic of the next chapter. The diagram in figure 9.2 summarizes the set of approaches that you will apply to the task of topic analysis.

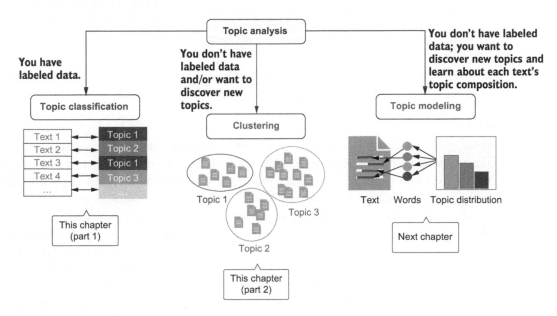

Figure 9.2   Topic analysis using three different approaches. Depending on whether you have labeled data or not, you can apply a supervised or an unsupervised approach (e.g., using clustering, as we'll cover in this chapter). If you want to discover new topics and learn about text's topic composition, apply topic modeling (next chapter).

Topic analysis and, in particular, the set of unsupervised approaches to topic discovery, provide you with powerful functionality: you can apply these algorithms to any scenario in which you would like to organize a large collection of documents without spending too much time reading them in detail, be that scientific articles, legal documents, financial documents, patent applications, or emails.

9.1   Topic classification as a supervised machine-learning task

First, let's approach topic classification using supervised machine learning (ML). By now, you have a lot of experience with supervised ML tasks, only this time you will deal with a problem that has more than two classes. This may sound challenging, but in the course of this section you will see that this is but a small extension step. As is usual with supervised ML tasks, there are several key components to think about: *data* labeled with the classes of interest, *algorithm* to apply to this multiclass classification task, and *evaluation* strategy that will help you check that your approach works well. The mental model in figure 9.3 summarizes these steps. You might recall using this mental model

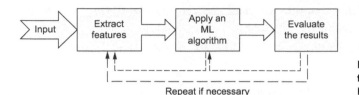

Figure 9.3   Mental model for the supervised machine-learning pipeline

in the previous chapters; this is simply what the supervised machine-learning pipeline looks like. Now let's look into each of these steps in turn.

9.1.1   Data

Chapter 5 introduced a powerful machine-learning toolkit called scikit-learn that allows you to quickly implement machine-learning applications and use a wide range of out-of-the-box techniques. In this section, you will learn about another useful functionality of this toolkit—the availability of several datasets for your use.

We've discussed before that for supervised ML scenarios, high-quality data that is labeled with the classes of interest is of utmost importance. If you are building your own application (e.g., you want to classify your own incoming emails into spam and ham, or you want to analyze your company's customers reviews), you will have to perform your own data collection and annotation. However, if your main goal is to gain more practice with the use of machine learning and NLP techniques, availability of datasets that are already collected and labeled for you is an important asset. In this chapter, we will use the famous 20 Newsgroups dataset, which is well suited for the topic classification task and is easily accessible via scikit-learn (check scikit-learn's datasets web page for more information on the various available data: http://mng.bz/yveo).

The 20 Newsgroups dataset is a collection of around 18,000 newsgroups posts on 20 topics (read about this dataset at http://qwone.com/~jason/20Newsgroups/). This dataset has been widely used in the NLP community for various tasks around text classification and, in particular, for topic classification. For the ease of comparison, the dataset is already split into training and test subsets. Table 9.1 summarizes the number of posts in each topic and each subset.

Table 9.1   Full description of the 20 Newsgroups dataset

Topic	Training size	Test size	Topic	Training size	Test size
alt.atheism	480	319	rec.sport.hockey	600	399
comp.graphics	584	389	sci.crypt	595	396
comp.os.ms-windows.misc	591	394	sci.electronics	591	393
comp.sys.ibm.pc.hardware	590	392	sci.med	594	396

Table 9.1   Full description of the 20 Newsgroups dataset

Topic	Training size	Test size	Topic	Training size	Test size
comp.sys.mac.hardware	578	385	sci.space	593	394
comp.windows.x	593	395	soc.religion.christian	599	398
misc.forsale	585	390	talk.politics.guns	546	364
rec.autos	594	396	talk.politics.mideast	564	376
rec.motorcycles	598	398	talk.politics.misc	465	310
rec.sport.baseball	597	397	talk.religion.misc	377	251

As you can see, not all newsgroups have a comparable amount of training and test data. Some, like `talk.religion.misc` and `talk.politics.misc`, are relatively small. Besides, as you will see later when it comes to visualization of results and evaluation, it might be hard to grasp the results for as many as 20 categories. To this end, let's select a subset of topics and apply classification to this subset. Luckily, scikit-learn allows you to easily change the set of categories or even include the whole lot of them, so feel free to experiment with your own selection.

Listing 9.1 shows how to initialize the training and test datasets. You start by importing libraries and functions that you will use in this module: specifically, `fetch_20newsgroups` will help you access the dataset via scikit-learn (See more information on this functionality here: http://mng.bz/M5qD). Next, you define a function `load_dataset` that will initialize a subset of the data as the `train` or `test` chunk of the 20 Newsgroups dataset and will also allow you to select particular categories listed in `cats`. You need to shuffle the dataset and remove all extraneous information such as footers, headers, and quotes. The code allows you to specify a list of categories of interest. The list of 10 topics here is used as an example. Feel free to select your own. Finally, you initialize `newsgroups_train` and `newsgroups_test` subsets. If you use `all` instead of `train` or `test`, you will get access to the full 20 Newsgroups dataset, and `None` instead of `categories` will help you access all topics.

Listing 9.1   Code to initialize the newsgroups training and test subsets

Function load_dataset will access "train" and "test" subsets for particular categories cats.

Import libraries and functions that you will use in this module.

```
from sklearn.datasets import fetch_20newsgroups
import numpy as np

def load_dataset(a_set, cats):
    dataset = fetch_20newsgroups(subset=a_set, categories=cats,
                        remove=('headers', 'footers', 'quotes'),
                        shuffle=True)
    return dataset
```

```
categories = ["comp.windows.x", "misc.forsale", "rec.autos",
    "rec.motorcycles", "rec.sport.baseball"]
categories += ["rec.sport.hockey", "sci.crypt", "sci.med", "sci.space",
    "talk.politics.mideast"]                          ◄──┐  Define a list of
                                                          categories of interest.
newsgroups_train = load_dataset('train', categories)
newsgroups_test = load_dataset('test', categories)   ◄──┐
                                                         Initialize newsgroups_train
                                                         and newsgroups_test subsets.
```

This code accesses posts from the predefined set of topics only. This can be changed to your own list of topics, or if you want to access all 20 of them, it can be changed to the full list—just use None as the second argument to the function load_dataset. The list of topics that we are going to use in this example is mainly selected based on two factors: diversity of topics and availability of a comparatively large and balanced set of posts across the training and test subsets. Table 9.2 summarizes the data you'll be working with in this chapter.

Table 9.2   Description of the data from the 20 Newsgroups dataset used in this chapter

Topic	Training size	Test size	Topic	Training size	Test size
comp.windows.x	593	395	rec.sport.hockey	600	399
misc.forsale	585	390	sci.crypt	595	396
rec.autos	594	396	sci.med	594	396
rec.motorcycles	598	398	sci.space	593	394
rec.sport.baseball	597	397	talk.politics.mideast	564	376

In total, you should get a subset of 5,913 training posts and 3,937 test posts. Listing 9.2 shows how to check what data got uploaded and how many posts are included in each subset. In this code, you first check what categories are uploaded using target_names field. This list should coincide with the one that you defined in categories earlier. Then you check the number of posts (filenames field) and the number of labels assigned to them (target field) and confirm that the two numbers are the same. The filenames field stores file locations for the posts on your computer. For example, you can access the first one via filenames[0]. The data field stores file contents for the posts in the dataset; for example, you can access the very first one via data[0]. As a final sanity check, you can also print out category labels for the first 10 posts from the dataset using target[:10].

Listing 9.2   Code to run some general checks on the uploaded data

```
def check_data(dataset):
    print(list(dataset.target_names))      ◄──┐  Check what categories
    print(dataset.filenames.shape)            are uploaded using the
                                              target_names field.
```

```
print(dataset.target.shape)
if dataset.filenames.shape[0]==dataset.target.shape[0]:
    print("Equal sizes for data and targets")
print(dataset.filenames[0])
print(dataset.data[0])
print(dataset.target[:10])

check_data(newsgroups_train)
print("\n***\n")
check_data(newsgroups_test)
```

Confirm that the two numbers above are the same.

The filenames field stores file locations for the posts on your computer.

The data field stores file contents for the posts in the dataset.

Check the number of posts (filenames) and the number of labels assigned to them (target).

Apply this function to newsgroups_train and newsgroups_test.

Print out category labels for the first 10 posts from the dataset using target[:10].

The code in the listing produces the following output:

```
['comp.windows.x', 'misc.forsale', 'rec.autos', 'rec.motorcycles',
'rec.sport.baseball', 'rec.sport.hockey', 'sci.crypt', 'sci.med',
'sci.space', 'talk.politics.mideast']
(5913,)
(5913,)
Equal sizes for data and targets
/[Your_home_directory]/scikit_learn_data/20news_home/20news-bydate-
    train/rec.sport.baseball/102665
I have posted the logos of the NL East teams to alt.binaries.pictures.misc
 [...]

[4 3 9 7 4 3 0 5 7 8]

***

['comp.windows.x', 'misc.forsale', 'rec.autos', 'rec.motorcycles',
'rec.sport.baseball', 'rec.sport.hockey', 'sci.crypt', 'sci.med',
'sci.space', 'talk.politics.mideast']
(3937,)
(3937,)
Equal sizes for data and targets
/[Your home directory]/scikit_learn_data/20news_home/20news-bydate-
    test/misc.forsale/76785
As the title says. I would like to sell my Star LV2010 9 pin printer.
[...]

[1 7 2 5 3 5 7 3 0 2]
```

The first half of this printed output is related to the training data, and the second one to the test data. To help you understand this output better, figure 9.4 first visualizes how the data is stored and how it can be accessed, and the description following it provides you with more detail.

In the first line of the output, you see that the categories have been loaded correctly. The number of posts in the training data is equal to 5913, and in the test data to 3937, as expected. Since dataset.filenames returns a list and dataset.target

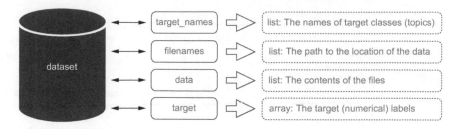

Figure 9.4   Data representation in the scikit-learn's 20 Newsgroups dataset. The dataset is stored as a `dataset` object, with various methods available to access different types of information; for example, `target_names` returns the topic labels, while `target` presents them in a numerical format; `filenames` tells you where on your computer the files are stored, while `data` shows the content of the posts. This way, you can extract any information you need from the `dataset` object.

returns an array, when you check their `shape` you see, for example, `(5913, )`. This notation means that the particular data structure has a single dimension to the length of `5913` (e.g., it is a list or an array of 5,913 elements). As a side note, if `shape` output is of the form (m, n), it means that you are working with a two-dimensional data structure—a matrix of m rows and n columns.

Note that scikit-learn allows you to not only access the dataset, but it also represents it as an object with relevant attributes that can be directly accessed via `dataset.attribute`. For example:

- `target_names` returns the list of the names for the target classes (categories).
- `filenames` is the list of paths where the files are stored on your computer.
- `target` returns an array with the target labels (note that the category names are cast to the numerical format).
- `data` returns the list of the contents of the posts (see http://mng.bz/M5qD).

The list of targets represents categories numerically. This is because machine-learning classifiers implemented in scikit-learn prefer to work with numerical format for the labels. Numbers are assigned to categories in alphabetical order: for instance, `'comp.windows.x'` corresponds to the numerical label 0, `'misc.forsale'` to 1, and so on. An output like `[4 3 9 7 4 3 0 5 7 8]` tells you that the posts on different topics are shuffled: the first one is on `rec.sport.baseball`, the second one is on `rec.motorcycles`, and so on (you can check the order of the categories in table 9.2).

9.1.2   *Topic classification with Naïve Bayes*

Now that the data is uploaded, let's turn to machine-learning techniques with scikit-learn, train a classifier on the training data, and try to predict the topic labels on the test data. As before, the next step in an ML project is to select features to be used with your classifier.

Exercise 9.1

Feature selection is an important step in a machine learning project. By selecting the features, you are pointing the algorithm at the important pieces of information that will help it learn from the data.

1 What types of features have you used before?
2 What types of features should you use in the topic classification task?

(Solution can be found at the end of this chapter.)

These considerations should help you decide upon the *type of features*—you should start by using words. The next point to consider is *word selection*—are all words equally helpful in topic classification? For instance, you've seen before that stopwords are useful in the writing style (or authorship) detection, as people use them differently and in different proportions, but given that all Newsgroups texts are posts of a relatively similar style, it is safe to assume that stopwords are not helpful and can be removed.

Finally, how should features be represented? For instance, should you assume that all words are equally important and therefore should just be simply counted? Topic classification task on the basis of word occurrences boils down to recognizing which topic a text may belong to based on which words are used in this text. Try solving the word puzzles in exercise 9.2 to see how an ML classifier may detect a topic.

Exercise 9.2

Can you guess the topic of the texts by the following lists of words occurring in them?

1 [car, engine, speed, . . .]
2 [lunar, shuttle, launch, . . .]

(Solution can be found at the end of this chapter.)

So far so good, but note that, compared to the previous applications, we've made the detection task more complex. We are considering 10 topics and a vast range of words (all but stopwords) occurring in newsgroups posts. Many of these words will occur not in a single topic but rather across lots of posts on various topics. Consider a word *post* as one example of a frequent and widely spread word: it might mean a new post that someone has got and, as such, might be more relevant to the texts in the talk.politics .mideast topic. At the same time, you will also see it frequently used in contexts like "I have posted the logos of the NL East teams to . . ." That is, despite the word *post* not being a stopword, it is quite similar to stopwords in nature. It might be used frequently across many texts on multiple topics, and thus lose its value for the task. How can you make sure that words that occur frequently in the data are given less weight than more meaningful words that occur frequently in a restricted set of texts (e.g., restricted by a topic)?

Figure 9.5 visualizes this idea, representing stopwords (e.g., "this" or "of") in regular font and highlighting the words that are specific to a particular topic (e.g., "car" for rec.autos or "launch" for sci.space) in italics and those that are distributed widely across all topics (e.g., "post" or "attend") in bold.

In this **post** I am going to tell you about my **new** *car*

US President was going to **attend** the *launch* of the *rocket*

Figure 9.5 Examples of two posts, with stopwords in regular font, words that are distributed widely across multiple topics in bold, and words that are most indicative of a specific topic in italics

In fact, you have already come across a technique that allows you to downweigh terms that occur frequently across many documents and upvalue terms that occur frequently only in some documents but not across the whole collection. This technique is called *term frequency—inverse document frequency* (TF-IDF), and it was discussed in detail in chapter 3. Here is a reminder:

- You would like to ensure that each word's contribution is not affected by the document length. For instance, a post with 100 words may use a word *car* 2 times, while another post of 200 words may use *car* 4 times. It might seem as if the post with 4 occurrences of *car* is more focused on cars, but once you take into account the overall length of text, you notice that the actual contribution of *car* in both cases is $tf(\text{"car"}) = 4/200 = 2/100 = 0.02$. This is what term frequency allows you to deduce.

- You would also like to ensure that word contribution is measured against its specificity. As the previous example shows, if you see a word *post* in virtually every text, its contribution should be lower than a contribution of some more topical words like *car*. This is what *inverse document frequency* allows you to take into account: if a word *post* is used in 80 posts out of 100, and *car* is used in 25 posts out of 100, then $idf(\text{"post"}) = 100/80 = 1.25 < idf(\text{"car"}) = 100/25 = 4$ (i.e., *car* has much more weight by way of being less widely spread across the collection of texts).

- Finally, putting the two bits together, *TF-IDF = tf*idf* gives higher weights to words that are used frequently *within* some documents but *not across* a wide variety of documents. This technique, therefore, is very useful for our task at hand.

Application of the TF-IDF technique to raw word counts is quite straightforward in scikit-learn. You've already used some vectorizers—functions that are capable of counting word occurrences in texts and then presenting each text as a vector of such word counts. For instance, CountVectorizer that you used in chapter 8 did exactly that (see more information on the CountVectorizer at http://mng.bz/aJG9). Here you are going to learn how to use another type of vectorizer, TfidfVectorizer (the documentation can be found at http://mng.bz/gwW8). As its name suggests, TfidfVectorizer performs word counting and TF-IDF weighing in one go. Listing 9.3 shows how to use it. First, you initialize the vectorizer to apply to all words but stopwords. The vectorizer estimates word counts and learns the tf-idf weights on the training data (thus method .fit_transform is applied to the train_set) and then applies the weights to the words in the test data (this is done using method .transform applied to the test_set). Using the vectorizer, you convert training and test texts into vectors and store the resulting vectors as vectors_train and vectors_test. In the end, you can run some checks on the vectors; for example, check the dimensionality of the vector structures using .shape, see how the first training text is represented, and check which word corresponds to a particular ID (33404 in this code).

Listing 9.3 Code to apply TfidfVectorizer and convert texts into vectors

```
from sklearn.feature_extraction.text \          Import
import TfidfVectorizer                           TfidfVectorizer.

                                                 Initialize the
                                                 vectorizer to apply
                                                 to all words but
vectorizer = TfidfVectorizer(stop_words = 'english')    stopwords.

def text2vec(vectorizer, train_set, test_set):   The vectorizer
    vectors_train = vectorizer.fit_transform(train_set.data)   estimates TF-IDF
    vectors_test = vectorizer.transform(test_set.data)    weights on the
    return vectors_train, vectors_test           training data and
                                                 then applies them
vectors_train, vectors_test = text2vec(          to the test data.
    vectorizer, newsgroups_train, newsgroups_test)
                                                 Convert training and
                                                 test texts into vectors
print(vectors_train.shape)                       and store the results.
print(vectors_test.shape)
print(vectors_train[0])                          Run some checks on the vectors;
print(vectorizer.get_feature_names()[33404])     use get_feature_names_out in
                                                 newer versions of scikit-learn.
```

The preceding code returns the following output ([...] shows that there are more words included in the first text, but we omit them here for space reasons):

```
(5913, 52746)
(3937, 52746)
  (0, 15218)    0.31618146678372416
  (0, 50534)    0.20153071455804605
  (0, 50435)    0.1817612919269656
  [...]
nl
```

The first two lines tell you that vectors_train is a matrix of 5,913 rows and 52,746 columns, while vectors_test is a matrix of 3,937 rows and 52,746 columns. You can imagine two large tables here, with each of the rows representing a text (remember, there are 5,913 training posts and 3,937 test posts) and each column representing a word. It is no coincidence that both matrices contain the same number of columns. The TfidfVectorizer identified 52,746 non-stopwords in the training data, and it is this set of words that is used to classify texts into topics here. The method fit_transform then calculates TF-IDF scores based on the training texts (with the `fit` part of the method) and transforms the raw counts in the training data to these scores. Finally, it applies the same transformations to the occurrences of the same 52,746 words in the test data (with the `transform` method). It is important that the TF-IDF scores are learned on the training set only. This is why we only use `transform` method on the test data and do not apply `fit_transform`, as this will rewrite our TF-IDF scores based on the test data, and we will end up with two separate sets of TF-IDF scores—one fit to the training data and another to the test data. Remember that in a real-life application, you would have access only to the training data and your test set might come, for example, from the future posts on your news platform.

A glimpse into the first text from the training set shows a list of references and scores. For example `(0, 15218)` with a rounded-up score of `0.32`. This representation means that `(0, 15218)` refers to the first text (thus, the index of `0`) and `15218` is the index of the 15,219th word in the total set of 52,746 words used for classification. Which word does it correspond to? You can always check this by applying `vectorizer`.`get_feature_names()[index]` (or `vectorizer.get_feature_names_out()[index]` in newer versions of scikit-learn) as you do in the code above for the 33,405th word (which turns out to be `nl` used in `NL East teams` that you can see in the output for listing 9.2). That is, the vectorizer collects 52,746 words, orders them alphabetically, assigns a unique identifier to each word, and finally estimates the TF-IDF score (for the 15,219th word, it is roughly 0.32). Figure 9.6 visualizes how the first training text is represented in the `vectors_train` structure.

Figure 9.6   A glimpse into the text vector for the first post in the training data. You can see what word each ID corresponds to and how highly it is weighted by TF-IDF.

Now that the data is prepared and converted to the same format with the TF-IDF weights applied to the same vocabulary of words in the training and test posts, let's train the Naïve Bayes classifier as you did in the previous applications and classify the posts from the test set into topics. Listing 9.4 shows you how to do that.

Listing 9.4   Code to perform topic classification with the Naïve Bayes classifier

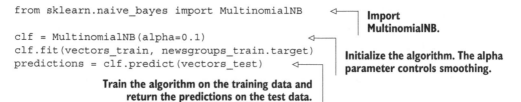

```
from sklearn.naive_bayes import MultinomialNB

clf = MultinomialNB(alpha=0.1)
clf.fit(vectors_train, newsgroups_train.target)
predictions = clf.predict(vectors_test)
```

Import MultinomialNB.

Initialize the algorithm. The alpha parameter controls smoothing.

Train the algorithm on the training data and return the predictions on the test data.

This training and testing routine should look pretty familiar to you by now. There is only one new parameter, `alpha`, that this code specifies for the Naïve Bayes algorithm, which we haven't discussed before. Let's see what this parameter does.

Imagine the following situation (we will be using a very small number of word occurrences to make the example simple, but you can scale this example up to larger numbers): the set of words that you use for classification contains `["car", "dealer", "engine", "post", "speed", . . .]`, among others. Imagine that you are working with a small training set, and the whole training set on the automotive topic contains the occurrences for the words as shown in table 9.3.

Table 9.3 An example of word counts in the automotive topic

Word	Count	Probability
car	10	10/20 = 0.50
dealer	2	2/20 = 0.10
engine	5	5/20 = 0.25
post	0	0/20 = 0.00
speed	3	3/20 = 0.15
Total	**20**	**1.00**

The probability that a particular word occurs in a text on a particular topic is estimated on the training data using the number of times a word occurs divided by the total number of all word occurrences in this topic. As table 9.3 shows, if you see *car* in the automotive texts 10 times while the sum of all word occurrences in these texts equals 20, we say that with the probability 10/20 = 0.50 (i.e., with a 50% chance), a text on the automotive topic will include the word *car*. At the same time, in your small training data, you have never seen a word *post* used in a text on the automotive topic, so its probability is 0. That may be fair enough—perhaps posts are never discussed in texts that talk mainly about cars.

However, earlier we said that actually a word like *post* may well occur across various topics. Now imagine your test set contains a text with the following sentence: "This is a post about my car". Most words here are stopwords, but two words—post and car—are part of the training set vocabulary. Let's estimate the probability that this text belongs to the automotive topic. For that, we take the probabilities that the words originate with this topic (the ones that you've estimated in table 9.3) and multiply them: `P(this text is about cars) = P(texts on cars) * P("car" occurs in a text on cars) * P("post" occurs in a text on cars)`. This formula follows the Naïve Bayes estimation that we discussed in chapter 2. Recall that the first probability is our expectation to see a text on the automotive topic in general. For example, if our training data contains 100 texts, with 10 texts on each of the 10 topics, `P(texts on cars) = 10/100 = 0.1`, or 10%. Let's multiply our probabilities now:

```
P(this text is about cars) =
P(texts on cars) * P("car" occurs in a text on cars) * P("post" occurs in a
    text on cars) =
0.1 * 0.5 * 0.0 = 0.0
```

In other words, despite the fact that this text contains a highly probable word from the automotive topic (car), it now has zero chances of being classified with the automotive topic because it also contains the word post, which has zero probability of occurring in texts on cars simply because you've never seen it occurring in automotive texts in the training data! Here is the problem with this data-driven approach to the probability estimation: if you haven't seen a word (e.g., post) in texts on a specific topic (e.g., texts on cars) in the training data, you might assume it is impossible to *ever* see this word in texts on this topic; however, it is actually much more likely that you haven't seen this word simply because you have too small or not diverse enough training data. In practice, it is very hard to make sure that you've seen all the possible texts on a specific topic (or all possible events in any supervised ML task). However large and diverse your training set is, there is always a chance that you haven't (yet) seen some examples. What can you do to fix this? Figure 9.7 proposes a solution, which is then elaborated in more detail.

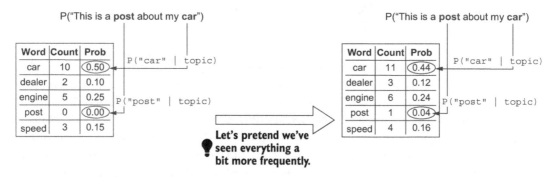

Figure 9.7   To avoid zero probabilities for some words, which is often caused by not having diverse or large enough training data, we can "pretend" that we have seen each word a bit more frequently than we did, such as by adjusting all word counts by 1.

A technique that is often used in practice is called *smoothing* and it helps ensure that you don't end up with zero probability estimates as occurred earlier because of the data effects. The most straightforward approach is called *additive* or *Laplace smoothing* (see chapter 3.5 in https://web.stanford.edu/~jurafsky/slp3/3.pdf) and here is how it works: instead of working with the actual counts, some of which might be zeros, let's pretend that we've seen every word a bit more frequently than we actually did. That is, if you've never encountered the word *post* in the texts on cars, you should pretend that you've seen it, for instance, once. Such an adjustment is called *add-one smoothing*, and it is a type of Laplace smoothing. Note in figure 9.7 that the table on the left contains actual word counts from the data and has 0 for post, while the table on the right contains adjusted word count and, thus, 1 for post. However, it would be unfair to only increment the counts for previously unseen words. The new count for post will now be 1, but what about the words that you've actually seen once in the data? To make it a fair play for all words, you need to increment the counts for *each* word in a similar way. All words that you've seen once will get a new count of 2, twice 3, and so on. Let's update the counts from table 9.3 with this add-one technique. Note that the table on the left in figure 9.7 corresponds to table 9.3, and the table on the right in figure 9.7 corresponds to table 9.4.

Table 9.4 Word counts and probabilities updated with add-one smoothing

Word	Count	Probability
car	11	11/25 = 0.44
dealer	3	3/25 = 0.12
engine	6	6/25 = 0.24
post	1	1/25 = 0.04
speed	4	4/25 = 0.16
Total	**25**	**1.00**

Two observations are due: first of all, note that all probability values from table 9.3 sum up to 1 ($0.50 + 0.10 + 0.25 + 0.00 + 0.15 = 1.00$) and so do the probability values in table 9.4 ($0.44 + 0.12 + 0.24 + 0.04 + 0.16 = 1.00$). This is important because it still allows you to say things like "If a text is on the automotive topic, the most probable word you will see is *car*," and it also allows you to reason about the word occurrence with a proper probability distribution. Note that you achieve this by adjusting the total number of all word occurrences from 20 (actual counts) to 25 (counts that take all add-ones into account). The second observation is that, even though the adjusted probabilities are different from the original ones, the total order doesn't change: $P(car) > P(engine) > P(speed) > P(dealer) > P(post)$ in both cases. It might seem like the changes to some probabilities (e.g., for the most frequent word *car*, it is –0.06 from 0.50 to 0.44, and the unseen one *post*, it is +0.04 from 0.00 to 0.04) are more radical than to others (e.g., for the words in the middle range like *speed*, +0.01 from 0.15 to 0.16). This is because the method redistributes the probabilities between all the words, "borrowing" the probability mass from the more frequent words and "donating" it to the less frequent ones, thus *smoothing* the probability across the whole range. In this toy example, we see quite radical changes of –0.06 or +0.04 because we are looking into a small word set with very few words and small counts. In real examples, the changes won't be that radical. The precise amount of probability to redistribute is controlled by the parameter alpha in the code in listing 9.4, and as the code shows, it can take values different from 1.

Finally, if you now want to estimate the probability of the text that says "This is a post about my car" belonging to the automotive topic, you will get the following:

```
P(this text is about cars) =
P(texts on cars) * P("car" occurs in a text on cars) * P("post" occurs in a
    text on cars) =
0.1 * 0.44 * 0.04 = 0.00176
```

This is what the `alpha` parameter allows you to do without explicitly adding anything to the counts yourself. Note that unlike in our toy example, in the actual task you are working with as many as 52,746 words (features), and the algorithm relies not on the raw word occurrences but on the TF-IDF scores. Unlike in our toy example, `alpha` does not have to be an integer number and does not have to be precisely 1. For instance, it is set to 0.1 in the code. You might be wondering what happens if you don't specify this parameter. In fact, scikit-learn takes care of that and assumes `alpha=1.0` by default. Finally, you might be wondering what the best setting for `alpha` is, then. In practice, you would experiment with various settings for this parameter to select the one that works best for your task, but this type of experimentation is outside the scope of this chapter.

> **NOTE**   Technically, `alpha` here is called a *hyperparameter*. It is a setting of the algorithm that is decided upon prior to training the algorithm and building the ML model. That's why if you would like to find the optimal setting for alpha depending on your task and data, you would do that in a separate set of experiments prior to training Naïve Bayes.

9.1.3   *Evaluation of the results*

Finally, it is time to evaluate the results obtained when you apply your model to the test set.

> **Exercise 9.3**
>
> What evaluation metrics do you know? How will you apply them to your task here? (Solution can be found at the end of this chapter.)

You may recall from previous chapters that accuracy is a widely used metric that helps you evaluate the performance of your algorithm at a glance; however, it doesn't tell you how well your algorithm performs on each class in particular. In contrast, precision, recall, and F-score are metrics applicable to each class and provide you with a more fine-grained insight into the performance. Let's apply these metrics to your algorithm's output, and let's also investigate which words are the most informative when detecting each topic. Listing 9.5 explains how to do that. In this code, you rely on scikit-learn's `metrics` functionality, which allows you to quickly evaluate your output. To identify the most informative features in each category, you first iterate through the categories using `enumerate(categories)`. This allows you to iterate through the tuples of (category id, category name). Within this loop, `classifier.coef_[i]` returns a list of probabilities for the features in the i-th category, and `np.argsort` sorts this list in the increasing order (from the smallest to the largest) and returns the list of identifiers for the features (see NumPy's documentation at http://mng.bz/ e79G). As a result, you can extract *n* most informative features using `[-n:]` (see additional code examples at http://mng.bz/pOnR). You can access the word features via their unique identifiers using `vectorizer.get_feature_names()` and print out the name of the category and the corresponding most informative words. In the end, you print out the full `classification_report` and the top 10 informative features per category.

Listing 9.5 Code to evaluate the results for this approach

Iterate through the categories
using enumerate(categories).

Import scikit-learn's metrics
functionality that will allow you
to quickly evaluate your output.

```
from sklearn import metrics


def show_top(classifier, categories, vectorizer, n):
    feature_names = np.asarray(vectorizer.get_feature_names())
    for i, category in enumerate(categories):
        cat_features = classifier.coef_[i]
        top = np.argsort(cat_features)[-n:]
        print(
            f'{category}: {" ".join(feature_names[top])}'
        )

full_report = metrics.classification_report(newsgroups_test.target,
                             predictions,
                             target_names=newsgroups_test.target_names)
print(full_report)
show_top(clf, categories, vectorizer, 10)
```

np.argsort sorts this list in the
increasing order and returns the
list of identifiers for the features.

Access the word features via their unique
identifiers and print out the category and
the most informative words.

Print out the full
classification_report and
the top 10 informative
features per category.

classifier.coef_[i] returns a list of probabilities
for the features in the *i*-th category.

This code returns the results as shown next. The first part of the output is presented as a table for better readability (table 9.5). Also note that some results are removed from the printout for space reasons since the performance across categories is quite similar.

Table 9.5 Classifier performance across categories

	Precision	Recall	F1-score	Support
comp.windows.x	0.92	0.90	0.91	395
misc.forsale	0.88	0.87	0.87	390

Table 9.5 Classifier performance across categories *(continued)*

	Precision	Recall	F1-score	Support
rec.autos	0.83	0.78	0.80	396
[...]				
accuracy			0.85	3937
macro avg	0.86	0.85	0.85	3937
weighted avg	0.86	0.85	0.85	3937

```
comp.windows.x: program using application windows widget use thanks motif server
     window
misc.forsale: asking email sell price condition new shipping offer 00 sale
rec.autos: know don new good dealer engine just like cars car
rec.motorcycles: don helmet riding just like motorcycle ride bikes dod bike
rec.sport.baseball: braves pitching hit think runs games game baseball team year
rec.sport.hockey: think year nhl season games players play hockey team game
sci.crypt: escrow people use nsa keys government clipper chip encryption key
sci.med: cadre dsl chastity n3jxp skepticism banks pitt geb gordon msg
sci.space: lunar just shuttle earth like moon orbit launch nasa space
talk.politics.mideast: just said arab turkish armenians people armenian jews
     israeli israel
```

The top of this printout should look familiar by now. Each row corresponds to a different category, and each column reports a different metric. Precision values range between the minimum of 0.71 for rec.sport.hockey to 0.92 for comp.windows.x, rec.sport.baseball, and sci.med. Recall values are also pretty high: from 0.78 for rec.autos to 0.94 for rec.sport.hockey. As the F1-score reports a balanced value combining both precision and recall, unless you have a reason to believe one of the two is more important as a metric for your application, it is the F1-score that you should look into. The numbers here are also quite good. The lowest F1-score of 0.80 is observed on rec.autos, and this is due to the somewhat lower recall of 0.78. Lower recall means that not all posts on rec.autos have been detected by your algorithm: 0.22 of the total amount of these posts were erroneously classified as some other topic(s).

The highest F1-score is observed on comp.windows.x, and this is because both precision (0.92) and recall (0.90) are high. This topic seems to be the most easily identifiable one. The Support column provides you with the absolute number of posts in each category. Finally, at the bottom of this bit of the printout you see the accuracy value of 0.85, and the two types of averaged values for all other metrics. Macro average calculates the values summing over the scores for all categories and dividing the sum by 10 (the number of categories), while the weighted average also takes into account the number of instances in each category, thus making sure that the contribution of each category to the average is proportionate to the category size. In this case, both sets of values are identical. This is because our categories are quite balanced in terms of their sizes, ranging from 376 posts in the `talk.politics.mideast` category to 399 in `rec.sport.hockey` (the difference is relatively small).

At the bottom of this printout, you see lists of the 10 most informative words from each category. These are the words that have the highest probabilistic weights in each category, so the classifier "trusts" them a lot when the decision about the category of a post is made. Do these word lists align with your expectations about what each topic describes? In other words, going back to exercise 9.2, if you saw a list containing words like [escrow, people, use, nsa, keys, government, clipper, chip, encryption, key], would you guess "cryptography" as the topic?

To finish with the analysis of the results, let's analyze the classifier's errors. Start with exercise 9.4.

Exercise 9.4

We noted above that `rec.autos` has a comparatively low recall of `0.78` and `rec.sport .hockey` has a comparatively low precision of `0.71`. Based on your experience with these metrics from the previous chapters, what do these figures suggest about the classifier's performance on these topics? (Solution can be found at the end of this chapter.)

The code in listing 9.6 shows how to explore the confusions that the classifier makes. In this code, you rely on scikit-learn's `plot_confusion_matrix` functionality and `matplotlib`'s plotting functionality. The `plot_confusion_matrix`'s functionality allows you to plot the predictions that the `classifier` makes on `vectors_test` against the actual labels from `newsgroups_test.target` using a heatmap. Additionally, you can set some further parameters; for instance, represent the number of correct and incorrect predictions using integer values format (i.e., `values_format="0.0f"`) and highlight the decisions on the heatmap with a particular color scheme. In this code, you use a blue color scheme, with the darker color representing higher numbers. Finally, you print out the confusion matrix and visualize correct predictions and confusions with a heatmap. For reference, you can also print out the categories' IDs that correspond to the categories' names.

Listing 9.6 Code to explore the classifier's errors and confusions

```
from sklearn.metrics import plot_confusion_matrix
import matplotlib.pyplot as plt

classifier = clf.fit(vectors_train, newsgroups_train.target)

disp = plot_confusion_matrix(classifier, vectors_test,
                    newsgroups_test.target,
                    values_format="0.0f",
                    cmap=plt.cm.Blues)
```

Import sklearn's plot_confusion_ matrix functionality and matplotlib's plotting functionality.

Plot the predictions that the classifier makes on vectors_ test against the actual labels.

Represent the number of correct and incorrect predictions using integer values format.

Highlight the decisions with a particular color scheme with darker colors for higher numbers.

```
print(disp.confusion_matrix)
```
◁——— **Print out the confusion matrix.**

```
plt.show()
for i, category in enumerate(newsgroups_train.target_names):
    print(i, category)
```
◁——— **For reference, print out the categories' IDs that correspond to the categories' names.**

Visualize correct predictions and confusions.

This code produces the output shown in figure 9.8:

a. Confusion matrix

```
[[355   8   2   2   1   8  12   2   5   0]
 [  3 339  16   9   4  11   2   1   5   0]
 [  0   9 308  25   3  27   7   3   9   5]
 [  2   8  26 320   4  15   9   4   6   4]
 [  3   7   0   2 333  33   4   5   2   8]
 [  1   0   0   2   6 374   8   2   2   4]
 [  9   7   3   3   2  18 335   2   7  10]
 [  2   4   9   5   3  17   7 324  13  12]
 [  9   3   7   2   3  18  11   6 324  11]
 [  2   0   2   7   2   9  13   2   2 337]]
```

b. Correct predictions and confusions visualized

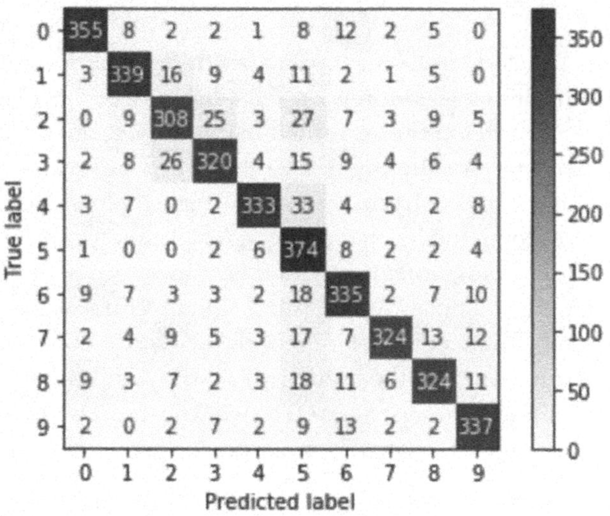

c. Categories' IDs mapped to categories' names

```
0 comp.windows.x
1 misc.forsale
2 rec.autos
3 rec.motorcycles
4 rec.sport.baseball
5 rec.sport.hockey
6 sci.crypt
7 sci.med
8 sci.space
9 talk.politics.mideast
```

Figure 9.8 The output produced by listing 9.6

As you can see from the confusion matrix, category 2 (rec.autos) indeed has the lowest number of posts (308) that are correctly assigned to this topic. In fact, some of the posts from this category end up being classified into all of the other topics: most notably, 25 posts end up in category 3 (rec.motorcycles), which may not be very surprising given the similarity of the two categories; 27 posts in category 5 (rec.sport.hockey), which is more surprising; and a smaller number of posts being erroneously assigned to other categories. It is also clear from this confusion matrix why precision on category 5 (rec.sport.hockey) is relatively low. Follow the numbers in the sixth column, and you will see that some texts from all other topics end up in this category, including 27 posts from rec.autos, 33 from rec.sport.baseball, 18 from sci.crypt, 17 from sci.med, 18 from sci.space, and so on.

Despite these classification errors, note that the overall performance of this relatively simple algorithm is quite high: 0.85 for both the accuracy and average F1-score on a 10-class prediction task. Congratulations, you have successfully built a supervised machine-learning topic classifier! This is a good starting point for an application for which you have a sufficient number of texts already labeled with their topics. What should you do if that's not the case?

9.2   Topic discovery as an unsupervised machine-learning task

It's time now to turn to the second paradigm of machine-learning approaches—*unsupervised machine learning*. This family of approaches is suitable for situations when you don't have labeled data and need to learn about the patterns from the data itself. So far, for a number of NLP applications we've looked into, we've been working under the assumption that labeled training data is easy to come by. In many real-life applications this is not the case, so let's now consider what happens if you keep receiving new texts for your news platform, but you believe that either the set of topics is not exactly the same as it used to be, or maybe new topics that you don't have the labeled data for yet keep cropping up. Why not try to learn about these topics from the texts themselves?

Figure 9.9 presents the mental model for the application of unsupervised approaches. In this section, we will look into each step of this process, starting with the selection of an appropriate algorithm.

9.2.1   Unsupervised ML approaches

Let's first discuss how unsupervised approaches work in general and then see how we can apply them to language tasks. Imagine the following scenario: suppose you are given a fruit basket and are asked to build an algorithm that can automatically sort fruits in the basket by type, so that, for example, apples will end up in one pile, oranges in another, and so on. All you know about the basket contents is that it contains fruits; you don't know which particular types of fruits are in there, and you'd like to build a general enough algorithm that can distinguish between any types of fruit based on their characteristics.

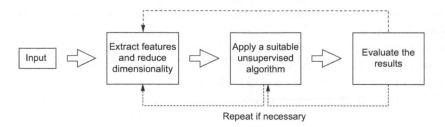

Figure 9.9   Mental model for the application of unsupervised approaches to NLP tasks. As before, you start with the selection of the input data and extract informative features. High dimensionality of the input data may be a problem for unsupervised ML algorithms, so once the dimensionality is reduced, you can apply a suitable algorithm. Finally, you should evaluate the results with an appropriate set of metrics.

This is a perfect scenario for an unsupervised ML algorithm. Note that if you want to be able to distinguish between any types of fruit, you essentially assume you are not working with any specific labeled data. How can you approach this task?

First, note that you want to be able to distinguish between fruits based on their characteristics. You might come up with the following set of characteristics: [color, size, weight, shape, taste], and perhaps some others. You can see that there comes some similarity between this approach and supervised approaches. In supervised ML, you would have used similar characteristics as features. The difference is that without labeled data, the algorithm would not be able to link these characteristics to specific named objects, but it would still be able to use them to group similar objects and distinguish between dissimilar ones. Now you decided to inspect the fruits in your basket and describe them in terms of their characteristics. You discover that all fruits can be divided into two groups. Perhaps, the first thing that you notice is that one type of fruit is green and another is red. In addition, you discover that one group can be described as [color=green, size=avg. 2.75 in, weight=avg. 0.33 pounds, shape=round, taste=sweet & sour], while the other group can be described as [color=red, size=avg. 1 in, weight=avg. 0.02 pounds, shape=round, taste=sweet]. Note that we are using average values here. In a collection of multiple fruits, individual ones may deviate from these numbers; however, you see that there is a general trend in the characteristics of the two types of fruit that helps you distinguish between them here.

In fact, the strategy that you applied earlier to divide the whole lot of fruits into two types can be adopted by your algorithm too. Each characteristic feature listed earlier needs to be considered in its own right, and this means that your algorithm will have to represent each fruit object as a collection of 5 values. Recall that machines deal best with numerical representations (i.e., you will need to represent such properties as color with some numbers), and if you want to combine multiple pieces of information, vectors and arrays are well-suited data structures. That's it: now all you need to do is transform all non-numerical values into numbers. For example, you may decide to use 1 for green and 2 for red; 1 for round; 1 for sweet, 2 for sour, 1.5 for sweet & sour; and so on. For instance, a particular fruit from your first group may now be represented as [1, 2.53, 0.35, 1, 1.5], and a fruit from the second group as [2, 0.9, 0.02, 1, 2] (for [color, size, weight, shape, taste]). Figure 9.10 visualizes your set of fruits. As we can't visualize all 5 dimensions here, let's stick to the ones illustrating weight and size.

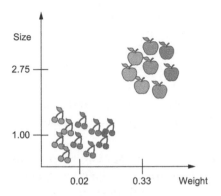

Figure 9.10   Two types of fruit to identify with an unsupervised ML algorithm. The fruits are plotted here according to their weight and size (i.e., in two dimensions). This plot visualizes two quite clearly separable groups of fruits.

NOTE   Another alternative is to use RGB codes for colors. For instance, green is commonly encoded as (0, 128, 0) and red as (255, 0, 0). See https://htmlcolorcodes.com for more examples. If you select this representation, you need to reserve three dimensions for the color feature in your vectors—one for each RGB channel.

Great, now you can clearly see that the two types of fruit are separable and quite distinct. However, your algorithm can't just "see" that; it needs to be able to learn it. How can it figure out that the two groups are distinct, and which group each particular fruit belongs to? Remember that earlier you "spotted" that the two groups of fruits are clustered around some average values for each type of fruit, for example, [color=green, size=avg. 2.75 in, weight=avg. 0.33 pounds, shape=round, taste=sweet & sour]. In fact, this is exactly what the unsupervised algorithm will try to do in this situation. It will try to identify the representative object with the averaged values for the features across the group, and cluster other objects from the same group around this central point. The representative object is technically called *centroid*, and this particular unsupervised approach is called *clustering*.

   If you know about each of the clusters in advance (e.g., it is easy to visually spot them as in figure 9.10), identifying the central point, the centroid is trivial—just take the values for all objects from the cluster and find their average. However, identification of the clusters is exactly the task your clustering algorithm is supposed to solve! In other words, you need the centroids to help you identify the clusters, but you can't identify the centroids before you know what the clusters are. This looks like a chicken-and-egg problem. Whenever you encounter a chicken-and-egg problem, the right approach is an iterative one that would allow you to make assumptions about the data and iteratively improve them based on the evidence. Here is the strategy to follow:

- *Step 1*—Choose a centroid for each cluster randomly. That's right, in this first step you don't need to worry about whether your centroid is indeed the best representative point for each cluster. Over the course of the algorithm application, you will try to improve this prediction anyway. For the task from figure 9.10, you will randomly select $centroid_1$ and $centroid_2$.

- *Step 2*—For each object in the collection, estimate how far it is located from each of the centroids. Since each of the points is represented with a set of 5 numbers, you can interpret them directly as coordinates in a multidimensional space. This is what allows you to visualize them as in figure 9.10. Having done that, you can estimate the distance between points using these coordinates and calculating Euclidean distance. Do that for each object and assign it to $cluster_1$ or $cluster_2$ based on whether the point in question is closer to $centroid_1$ or $centroid_2$.

- *Step 3*—Now that you have cluster allocations, re-estimate where centroids for each cluster lie based on the average values from the objects assigned to the relevant cluster. As a result of this step, your centroids may indeed change.

- *Step 4*—Reallocate the points to clusters measuring the distances to the new centroids (basically, repeating step 2). As a result of this step, your clusters may change too. If cluster allocation doesn't change, you can stop the algorithm at this point.

- *Steps 5 to n*—Repeat steps 3 and 4, reestimating centroids based on the new cluster allocations and then clusters based on the new centroids either for a specific number of steps *n* or until allocation of points to clusters doesn't change anymore.

Figure 9.11 visualizes these steps.

How do you actually calculate the distance between the points? We have discussed Euclidean distance in chapter 1. You first calculate the sum of squared differences between the relevant coordinates of the points, and then take the square root of this sum. Let's refresh our memory about how it works by trying to solve exercise 9.5 for two dimensions. Note that you can extend this calculation with as many dimensions as you have in your data.

Exercise 9.5

You have two centroids defined as $centroid_1 = [0.33, 2.75]$ and $centroid_2 = [0.02, 1.00]$. Allocate the following two points to two clusters based on which centroid is closest:

$point_1 = [0.25, 2.31]$ $point_2 = [0.05, 1.18]$

(Solution can be found at the end of this chapter.)

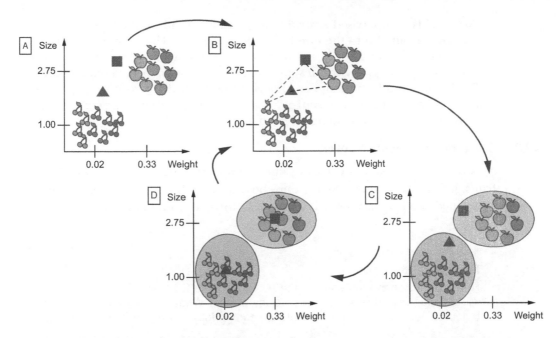

Figure 9.11 Steps of the clustering algorithm: (A) select centroids → (B) measure distances from each point to each centroid (only some points are visualized here to help readability) → (C) assign points to clusters → (D) reestimate centroids. Repeat steps B–D in sequence until the point allocation does not change anymore.

That's it! If you are lucky with your original guess of the centroids, your algorithm may find a stable solution (when no point changes its cluster allocation and eventually no centroid moves) quite quickly. This point in the algorithm, when the solution doesn't change anymore, is called *convergence*. If there are some tricky cases in your data, whose allocation is hard to establish (perhaps, they bear similarities to both groups and therefore fall somewhere between the clusters), they may flip their membership from one cluster to another over the iterations, thus stopping the algorithm from converging. For such unlucky situations, you need to specify a *stopping criterion* (e.g., requiring the algorithm to stop after several hundreds of iterations).

Finally, remember that your algorithm is meant to be quite general. You can apply this approach to *any* fruit basket, and you don't have to specify which types of fruits are contained in it. Your algorithm is agnostic to the particular clusters it is trying to identify. However, once these clusters are established by the algorithm, you can inspect the characteristics of the centroids and identify what types of fruits are captured by each cluster. For instance, even if we hadn't visualized the fruits in figures 9.10 and 9.11, you might still be able to tell that a centroid like [color=green, size=avg 2.75 in, weight=avg. 0.33 pounds, shape=round, taste=sweet & sour] is likely to describe an apple or a similar fruit with such characteristics, and [color=red, size=avg 1 in, weight=avg. 0.02 pounds, shape=round, taste=sweet] is likely to describe a cherry (or something similar).

NOTE   This unsupervised algorithm is agnostic not only to the type of clusters it discovers but also to the number of these clusters. The number of clusters that you are looking for in the data is one of the assumptions that you will need to make (e.g., based on some insights, heuristics, or data exploration). For instance, with the number of clusters set to 3, the algorithm might discover [green apples, red apples, cherries] or [apples, large cherries, small cherries], depending on the data at hand.

9.2.2 *Clustering for topic discovery*

Now that we've looked into a toy example of how clustering can be applied to a set of fruits, let's go back to our Newsgroups posts and see how the same methodology can be applied to a language task. Try answering the questions in exercise 9.6 before moving on.

> ### Exercise 9.6
> How can you apply clustering to the posts from the 20 Newsgroups dataset? What will the clusters represent? What are the points? What can you use as coordinates to locate each point in space? (Solution can be found at the end of this chapter.)

Let's apply the unsupervised approach to our data from the 20 Newsgroups dataset. In the previous section, you have already defined a set of posts on the selected 10 categories to work with. You are going to use the same set, only this time you will approach it as if you don't know what the actual topic labels are. Why is this a good idea? First of all, since you know what the labels in this data actually are, you can evaluate your algorithm at the end. Secondly, you will be able to see what the algorithm identifies in the data by itself, regardless of any assigned labels. After all, it is always possible that someone who posted to one topic actually talked more about another topic. This is exactly what you are going to find out.

First, let's prepare the data for clustering. Recall that you have already extracted the data from the 20 Newsgroups dataset. There are 5,913 posts in the newsgroups_ train and 3,937 in the newsgroups_test. Since clustering is an unsupervised technique, you don't have to separate the data into two sets, so let's combine them together in one set, all_news_data, which should then contain 5,913 + 3,937 = 9,850 posts altogether. You are going to cluster posts based on their content (which you can extract using the dataset.data field); finally, let's extract the correct labels from the data (recall from the earlier code that they are stored in the dataset.target field) and set them aside. You can use them later to check how the topics discovered in this unsupervised way correspond to the labels originally assigned to the posts. Listing 9.7 walks you through these steps. Recall that it is a good idea to shuffle the data randomly, so let's import the random functionality and set the seed to a particular value (e.g., 42) to make sure future runs of your code return the same results. Next, the code shows how you can combine the data from newsgroups_train and newsgroups_test into a single list, all_news, mapping the content of each post (accessible via .data) to its label (.target) and using the zip function. After that, you shuffle the tuples and store the contents and labels separately. You will use the contents of the posts in all_news_data for clustering and the actual labels from all_news_labels to evaluate the results. Finally, you should check how many posts you have (length of all_news_data should equal 9,850) and how many unique labels you have using np.unique (the answer should be 10), and take a look into the labels to make sure you have a random shuffle of posts on different topics.

Listing 9.7   Code to prepare the data for clustering

```
import random                    To shuffle the data randomly,
random.seed(42)          ◁————   import the random functionality
                                 and set the random seed.

all_news = list(zip(newsgroups_train.data, newsgroups_train.target))
all_news += list(zip(newsgroups_test.data,
                    newsgroups_test.target))  ◁——  Combine the data from
random.shuffle(all_news)                           newsgroups_train and
                                                   newsgroups_test into
                                                   a single list all_news.

all_news_data = [text for (text, label) in all_news]
all_news_labels = [label for (text, label) in all_news]   ◁——  Store the
                                                                contents and
print("Data:")                                                  labels separately.
print(str(len(all_news_data)) + " posts in "
    + str(np.unique(all_news_labels).shape[0])
    + " categories\n")              ◁——  Check how many
                                          posts and unique
print("Labels: ")                         labels you have.
print(all_news_labels[:10])
num_clusters = np.unique(all_news_labels).shape[0]
print("Actual number of clusters: " + str(num_clusters))  ◁——
```

Shuffle the tuples. points to `random.shuffle(all_news)`

Check the labels to make sure you have a random shuffle of posts on different topics. points to the last print line.

The preceding code produces the following output:

```
Data:
9850 posts in 10 categories

Labels:
[2, 6, 1, 9, 0, 5, 1, 2, 9, 0]
Assumed number of clusters: 10
```

You have 9,850 posts in your data, which cover 10 categories considered before. The printout on labels shows that the posts on different topics are randomly shuffled and that the assumed number of clusters is 10. This is simply what you can assume about this data based on the input (or based on some other insight into the data); however, note that from now on you will approach the task in an unsupervised manner: your algorithm will be working with the 9,850 posts in all_news_data, and it will not get access to the labels contained in all_news_labels, although you can use them at the very last, evaluation, step.

Now that the data is initialized, let's extract the features. As before, you will use words as features and represent each post as an array, or vector, where each dimension will keep the count or TF-IDF score assigned to the corresponding word—that is, for a particular post, such an array may look like [$word_0$=0, $word_1$=5, $word_2$=0, ... , $word_{52745}$=3]. To begin with, this looks exactly like the preprocessing and feature extraction steps that you did earlier for the supervised approach. However, this time there are two issues that need to be addressed:

- Remember that to assign data points to clusters, you will need to calculate distances from *each* data point to *each* cluster's centroid. This means calculating differences between the coordinates for 9,850 data points and 10 centroids in 52,746 dimensions, and then comparing the results to detect the closest centroid. Moreover, remember that clustering uses an iterative algorithm, and you will have to perform these calculations repeatedly for, say, 100 iterations. This amounts to a lot of calculations, which will likely make your algorithm very slow.

- In addition, a typical post in this data is relatively short. It might contain a couple of hundreds of words, and assuming that not all of these words are unique (some may be stopwords and some may be repeated several times), the actual word observations for each post will fill in a very small fraction of 52,746 dimensions, filling most of them with zeros. That is, it would be impossible to see any post that will contain a substantial amount of the vocabulary in it and, realistically, every post will have a very small number of dimensions filled with actual occurrence numbers, while the rest will contain zeros. What a waste—not only will you end up with a huge data structure of 9,850 posts by 52,746 word dimensions that will slow your algorithm down, but you will also be using most of this structure for storing zeros. This will make the algorithm very inefficient.

What can be done to address these problems? You've come across some solutions to these problems before, while some others will be new for you here:

1 You can ignore stopwords.
2 You can take into account only the words that are contained in a certain number of documents. It would make sense to ignore rare words that occur in less than some minimal number of documents (e.g., 2) or that occur across too many documents (e.g., above 50% of the dataset). You can perform all word-filtering steps in one go using `TfidfVectorizer`.
3 You can further compress the input data using dimensionality reduction techniques. One widely used technique is singular value decomposition (SVD), which tries to capture the information from the original data matrix with a more compact matrix. This is the technique that we will apply here.

First, let's look at the code in listing 9.8. In this code, you use `TfidfVectorizer` to convert text content to vectors, ignoring all words that occur in less that 2 documents (with `min_df=2`) or in more than 50% of the documents (with `max_df=0.5`). In addition, you remove stopwords and apply inverse document frequency weights (`use_idf=True`).

Within the `transform` function, you first transform the original data using a `vectorizer` and print out the dimensionality of this transformed data. Next, you reduce the number of original dimensions to a much smaller number using `TruncatedSVD`. `TruncatedSVD` is particularly suitable for sparse data like the one you are working with here. Then you add `TruncatedSVD` to a pipeline (`make_pipeline` from scikit-learn) together with a `Normalizer`, which helps adjust different ranges of values to the same range, thus helping clustering algorithm's efficiency. As the output of the `transform` function, you return both the data with the reduced dimensionality and the `svd` mapping between the original and the reduced data. Finally, you apply the transformations to `all_news_data` to compress the original data matrix to a smaller number of features (e.g., 300) and print out the dimensionality of the new data structure.

Note on the scikit-learn resources

To learn more about the scikit-learn classes mentioned here, see the following:

- To see documentation on `TfidfVectorizer`, visit http://mng.bz/gwW8.
- To see the documentation on `TruncatedSVD`, visit http://mng.bz/Ooqj. Visit http://mng.bz/YGyj to see more examples on how this is applied.
- You've used scikit-learn's pipelines before to stack multiple operations together. Here is a reminder on how this works: http://mng.bz/GEqA.
- Finally, for documentation on Normalizer, visit http://mng.bz/z4p6.

Listing 9.8   Code to preprocess the data with TfidfVectorizer and SVD

Use TfidfVectorizer to convert text content to vectors, ignoring words of certain frequency.

```
from sklearn.decomposition import TruncatedSVD
from sklearn.pipeline import make_pipeline
from sklearn.preprocessing import Normalizer

vectorizer = TfidfVectorizer(min_df=2, max_df=0.5,
                             stop_words='english',
                             use_idf=True)

def transform(data, vectorizer, dimensions):
    trans_data = vectorizer.fit_transform(data)
    print("Transformed data contains: " + str(trans_data.shape[0]) +
          " with " + str(trans_data.shape[1])
          + " features =>")

    svd = TruncatedSVD(dimensions)
    pipe = make_pipeline(svd, Normalizer(copy=False))
    reduced_data = pipe.fit_transform(trans_data)

    return reduced_data, svd
```

Import all functionality that you are going to use for preprocessing.

In addition, remove stopwords and apply inverse document frequency weights.

Next, reduce the number of original dimensions to a much smaller number using TruncatedSVD.

Apply a pipeline with a Normalizer.

Transform the original data using a vectorizer and print out data dimensionality.

Return both the data with the reduced dimensionality and the svd mapping.

```
reduced_data, svd = transform(all_news_data, vectorizer, 300)
print("Reduced data contains: " + str(reduced_data.shape[0]) +
    " with " + str(reduced_data.shape[1]) + " features")   ◁————┐
```

**Apply the transformations to all_news_data
to compress the original data matrix.**

Here is the output from the code listing:

```
Transformed data contains: 9850 with 33976 features =>
Reduced data contains: 9850 with 300 features
```

Let's now look more closely into this output and make sure all steps make sense. You've started out with a huge matrix of 9,850 rows (one per post) and over 50,000 columns (as you know from the supervised ML part, this is how many non-stopwords there are in the training data). This is a lot, and it will make calculations for the clustering algorithm extremely slow. Therefore, you've applied two steps in which you successfully reduced the number of columns, as figure 9.12 shows (note that to make the illustration readable, the dimensions are not visualized according to their actual proportions).

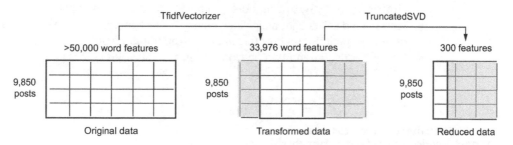

Figure 9.12   Original data dimensionality is reduced using `TfidfVectorizer` and `TruncatedSVD`. Grayed areas highlight the bits that are subsequently not considered by the algorithm. First, `Tfidf-Vectorizer` takes into account only words that occur more frequently than the minimum frequency threshold and less frequently than the maximum frequency threshold. Next, `TruncatedSVD` identifies the most informative dimensions in the data by compressing the input dimensions to a much more compact representation.

First, you remove all very rare and very frequent words, reducing the number of columns to 33,976, as figure 9.12 shows. Next, the number of considered word columns is severely reduced, from 33,976 to only 300 dimensions, essentially keeping less than 1% of the original dimensions. Let's look into what is going on under the hood and why such reduction is a justified thing to do to the data.

The goal of the SVD algorithm is to significantly reduce data dimensionality to help expensive algorithms like clustering deal with it more efficiently, while keeping as much of the valuable information in the reduced data as possible. That is, when SVD reduces the data from over 30,000 columns to 300 (thus keeping essentially about 1%), it doesn't just throw away the other 99% of the data. Instead, it tries to distill and summarize the information contained in the original huge matrix down to a much smaller number of dimensions. How does it achieve that? It relies on the matrix operations from linear algebra (you can read more on SVD, for example, in section 18.2 of https://nlp.stanford.edu/IR-book/pdf/18lsi.pdf). Don't worry, you don't need to have deep understanding of the linear algebra operations to use this method; instead let's get the general overview.

In general, SVD tries to simplify a big matrix representation by decomposing it into three smaller ones in such a way that when you multiply these three smaller matrices, you get back the original one. You can think of this as somewhat similar to decomposing a number like 24 into 4, 3, and 2, as when you multiply these numbers, you get the original number back (i.e., 4 * 3 * 2 = 24). Something similar happens to the big matrix when it gets represented as a product of three smaller ones. Figure 9.13 illustrates this idea.

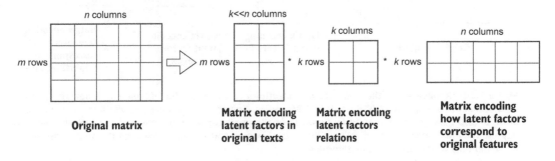

Figure 9.13   **A high-level overview of the truncated singular value decomposition. The original matrix of *m* rows (texts) and *n* columns (word features) gets decomposed into three simpler matrices. The first one encodes *m* texts in terms of a smaller number of *k* features (concepts, or latent factors); the second one describes the relations of these *k* concepts to each other; and the third one encodes the relations between the *k* concepts and the original *n* word features.**

You start with a matrix of 9,850 rows (representing posts) and 33,976 columns (representing words occurring in these posts, that you would like to use as features). That is what the original matrix on the left contains in its *m*-by-*n* dimensions (in this case, 9,850 by 33,976). Although you suppose all of these words are useful, as at this point you've already filtered out stopwords, very rare words, and very frequent words, this is still too many dimensions to consider, and you might suspect there are ways to extract more useful information from these words and their counts. For instance, consider a set of words like ["car", "cars", "automobile", "automotive"] and so on. These are different words, each with their own dimension (represented with separate columns in the original matrix) and their own counts, yet you might say they are expressing the same concept and, perhaps, there is no point in allocating each of these words separate dimensions. If you had a way to merge the dimensions for all such concept-related words, and instead of working with [$word_0$, $word_1$, $word_2$, . . . , $word_{33975}$], worked with [$concept_0$, $concept_1$, $concept_2$, . . . , $concept_{299}$], this would have simplified your task quite a lot, while keeping all the useful information. This is exactly what SVD is trying to achieve: the matrix of *m* rows by *k* columns from figure 9.13 (where the notation $k << n$ means that *k* is considerably smaller than the original *n*, as for instance $300 << 33{,}976$) represents the original *m* (9,850) posts using *k* (300) concepts, which are also often called *latent factors*—in other words, factors that are hidden from the naked eye. Let's visualize this as figure 9.14 does.

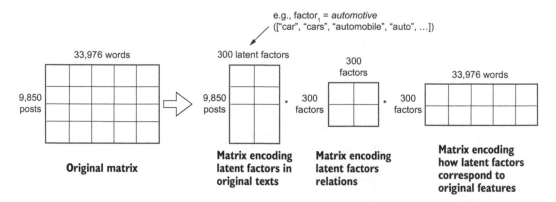

Figure 9.14   Application of the truncated SVD algorithm to our data. The original matrix describes the distribution of the original 33,976 words in 9,850 posts. Truncated SVD helps you distill these word features down to 300 most important latent factors. The smaller matrices are more efficient to work with, yet they capture the most important content from the original matrix, and you can always get the original matrix back if you multiply the three component matrices.

The second matrix, *k* by *k* (300 by 300), encodes how such latent factors correspond to each other; finally, the third one, *k* by *n* (300 by 33,976), tells you how to interpret the relations between the latent factors (or concepts) and the original *n* words. The beauty of the algorithm is that you can always get back the original *m*-by-*n* matrix by multiplying the three smaller matrices, and you don't need to estimate these constituent matrices yourself; the algorithm does it for you.

What are these *k* latent factors then and how to select them? These factors are the most prominent (i.e., salient) concepts that the algorithm finds in the data, ordered by their importance, starting with the most prominent one. That is, if you select the first $k = 100$ factors, you will end up with the most important 100 ones, while $k = 300$ will add another 200 concepts decreasingly less salient than the first 100 ones. You can continue like that as long as $k < n$. It is important that the selected number of factors is smaller than the original number of dimensions. There is no ready-made recipe, though, as to how many of such latent factors to consider. This is one of the hyperparameters of the algorithm that you can experiment with. Unfortunately, dimensionality reduction is also one of those useful algorithms that we have to treat as a "black box": while we can interpret the original 33,976 dimensions and match them to the specific words, all we can say about the reduced space is that $dimension_0$ corresponds to the most salient concept in the data, $dimension_1$ to the second most salient one, and so on, but these concepts are no longer represented with specific words. Above, we tried to impose some interpretation on the factors. For instance, we may assume that one of the factors would encode all car-related things. This is a totally reasonable interpretation, but note that the way the algorithm comes up with its "concepts" is based on the word occurrence numbers in the matrix, and what gets combined in the same "concept" is primarily based on the distribution. Despite this lack of interpretability, SVD is a very useful and powerful algorithm, which is why we are using it here.

Now that the data is ready, let's apply clustering algorithm. Listing 9.9 shows how to do that. Specifically, in this code you use the KMeans clustering algorithm from scikit-learn (see documentation at http://mng.bz/06dE). You apply the algorithm with n_clusters defining the number of clusters to form and centroids to estimate (e.g., you can use 10 here), while k-means++ defines an efficient way to initialize the centroids. The parameter max_iter defines the number of times you iterate through the dataset, and random_state set to a particular value ensures that you get the same results every time you run the algorithm. Finally, you run the algorithm on the reduced_data with the number of clusters equal to 10 (recall that this is the value stored in num_clusters, and it's based on the number of categories in the input data).

Listing 9.9   Code to run the KMeans clustering algorithm

```
from sklearn.cluster import KMeans          ←  Import KMeans clustering
                                               algorithm from sklearn.
def cluster(data, num_clusters):
    km = KMeans(n_clusters=num_clusters,       Apply the algorithm with n_clusters
                init='k-means++',          ←  defining the number of clusters to
                max_iter=100,                  form and centroids to estimate.
                random_state=0)        ←
    km.fit(data)                           max_iter defines the number
    return km                              of times you iterate through
                                           the dataset.

km = cluster(reduced_data, num_clusters)   ←  Run the algorithm on the
                                               reduced_data with the number
                                               of clusters equal to 10.
```

The code in this listing performs clustering as discussed earlier in this section. By default, the algorithm runs for up to 100 iterations (or until it converges to a stable solution) with the centroids selected randomly 10 times. Random seed makes sure such random initializations of the centroids can be replicated over multiple runs of your code. Note that here you use an insight about the number of clusters you are looking for: you try to cluster the posts into 10 clusters because you assume, based on the input data, that there are roughly 10 topics here. However, the data may tell you otherwise, and it might turn out that when people post to 10 specific topics, they actually talk about more (or less) than 10 distinct subjects. Therefore, you can change the number of clusters and experiment with other settings.

9.2.3 *Evaluation of the topic clustering algorithm*

The final step in any algorithm application is evaluation of the results. Let's see what results you get for the clustering algorithm. Listing 9.10 shows how to evaluate your clustering algorithm's performance and extract the most informative features. To identify the most informative features, you use the clustering algorithm km and the SVD mapping svd to get back the centroids using svd.inverse_transform on km.cluster_centers_. Then you sort them with argsort and return the matrix with 10 rows (one per cluster) containing the list of most informative dimensions for the cluster centroids, sorted in decreasing order using [:,::-1]. Since the resulting matrix order_centroids contains 10 rows with indices of the most significant words for cluster centroids, you can map them back to words using vectorizer.get_feature_names() and return, say, 50 per cluster. In the end, you print out the results, as well as the list of category names from the original dataset for reference.

Listing 9.10   Code to evaluate the results obtained with the clustering algorithm

```
def evaluate(km, labels, svd):
    print("Clustering report:\n")
    print(
        f"* Homogeneity: {str(metrics.homogeneity_score(labels, km.labels_))}"
        )
    print(
        f"* Completeness: {str(metrics.completeness_score(labels, km.labels_))}"
        )
    print(
        f"* V-measure: {str(metrics.v_measure_score(labels, km.labels_))}"
        )

    print("\nMost discriminative words per cluster:")
    original_space_centroids = svd.inverse_transform(
        km.cluster_centers_)
    order_centroids = \
            original_space_centroids.argsort()[:, ::-1]

    terms = vectorizer.get_feature_names()
    for i in range(num_clusters):
        print("Cluster " + str(i) + ": ")
        cl_terms = ""
        for ind in order_centroids[i, :50]:
            cl_terms += terms[ind] + " "
        print(cl_terms + "\n")

evaluate(km, all_news_labels, svd)

print("\nCategories:")
for i, category in enumerate(newsgroups_train.target_names):
    print("*", category)
```

Report the clustering evaluation metrics.

Get back the centroids using svd.inverse_transform on km.cluster_centers_.

Sort them and return the matrix containing the list of most informative dimensions for the cluster centroids.

Map them back to words using vectorizer.get_feature_names() and return 50 per cluster.

Print the list of category names from the original dataset for reference.

This code returns the following output ([...] is used to truncate the output for space reasons):

```
Clustering report:

* Homogeneity: 0.4905834160659784
* Completeness: 0.5545553250427578
* V-measure: 0.5206115419058042

Most discriminative words per cluster:
Cluster 0:
key chip encryption government keys nsa algorithm secure security encrypted [...]

Cluster 1:
doctor disease medical patients pain cause cancer treatment drug body [...]

Cluster 2:
game team hockey players season play win baseball league nhl [...]

Cluster 3:
just don like think know people does good right say [...]

Cluster 4:
window server widget display application file windows program running code [...]

Cluster 5:
sale offer shipping condition asking new drive sell interested price [...]

Cluster 6:
car bike engine cars miles ride rear speed oil road [...]

Cluster 7:
thanks mail advance know address send list email edu information [...]

Cluster 8:
space orbit launch nasa shuttle moon earth mission lunar solar [...]

Cluster 9:
israel jews israeli armenian arab people jewish armenians turkish war [...]


Categories:
* comp.windows.x
[...]
```

The metrics used here try to mirror the metrics you used for supervised ML:

- *Homogeneity*—Measures to what extent each cluster contains only members of a single class (to a certain extent, this metric is similar to *precision*). For example, does $cluster_0$ contain posts only on cryptography, and $cluster_1$ posts only on medicine, and so on?
- *Completeness*—Measures whether members of a single category end up in the same cluster. For instance, have all cryptography posts ended up in $cluster_0$ and

all medicine-related posts ended up in cluster$_1$, and so on? This is, to some extent, similar to *recall*.

- *V-measure*—Equivalent to *F-measure* in the unsupervised context, as it also represents a harmonic mean between the other two metrics.

The precise calculations for these metrics are different from those for precision, recall, and F-measure in a supervised ML setting, and the two sets of values are not directly comparable. The metrics here should be interpreted in the following way: each score lies in the range of [0, 1], with perfect assignment of posts to clusters getting scores of 1 (as in this case each topic is represented with a single cluster, and each cluster contains posts only from a single topic) and the mixed up clusters resulting in scores of 0. Thus, the closer the scores are to 1, the better the clusters identified by the algorithm. The scores that you are getting here (homogeneity of 0.49 and completeness of 0.55) show that the clusters are not perfect and there is a fair number of posts from different topics being grouped in a single cluster as well as posts from the same topic being split across several clusters.

NOTE Unsupervised measures rely on the estimation of entropy rather than simple proportions. For more details, check the original paper at www.aclweb .org/anthology/D07-1043.pdf, and for examples, take a look at scikit-learn's documentation at http://mng.bz/Kxqg.

To find out more about the precise assignment of posts to clusters, let's try to further interpret the results from listing 9.10 looking at each cluster, as exercise 9.7 suggests.

Exercise 9.7

You have originally used the data on the following categories: [comp.windows.x, misc.forsale, rec.autos, rec.motorcycles, rec.sport.baseball, rec.sport .hockey, sci.crypt, sci.med, sci.space, talk.politics.mideast]. Based on the most informative words in each cluster, can you assign each cluster with a topic from this original list?

Let's look into the solution together. Table 9.6 presents possible interpretations.

Table 9.6 Possible topic allocations for the identified clusters

Cluster ID	Topic	Cluster ID	Topic
0	sci.crypt	5	misc.forsale
1	sci.med	6	rec.autos & rec.motorcycles
2	rec.sport.baseball & rec.sport.hockey	7	misc.forsale

Table 9.6 Possible topic allocations for the identified clusters

Cluster ID	Topic	Cluster ID	Topic
3	`misc.forsale (?)` `talk.politics.mideast (?)`	8	`sci.space`
4	`comp.windows.x`	9	`talk.politics.mideast`

As you can see, the unsupervised method uncovered some new insights into the data. You've started with the assumption that the 10 topics will clearly express themselves in the word choice, thus setting the number of clusters to 10. As a result, you've identified 10 clusters, some of which (like clusters 2 and 6) may combine posts on closely related topics (e.g., baseball & hockey, or autos & motorcycles), whereas other topics may end up being spread across multiple clusters (e.g., forsale seems to be a very heterogeneous topic—put under misc, or miscellaneous—and it's probably no wonder that it gets allocated 2 or potentially 3 different clusters).

This difference in the labels from our dataset and the groups identified by the clustering algorithm on the basis of the data itself is the main reason for homogeneity and completeness scores not being equal to 1.0. Since the main goal of unsupervised approaches is to get new insights into the data, this is not necessarily a bad result. It suggests that the posts on some topics may be merged under one heading (e.g., on your news platform, you may consider putting all posts on baseball & hockey on the same page called *Sports*), while posts from some other topics that you may have assumed to be homogeneous should actually be split into several subgroups (e.g., you may consider creating multiple subtopics for selling different items).

As a final remark, we said before that the clustering algorithm is agnostic to the set of topics that it is trying to discover. It can group posts on the same topic into a single cluster and provide you with the informative words, but it won't be able to automatically assign the label for the identified topic (i.e., without further help, it won't be able to solve exercise 9.7 as you just did). Is there a way to automatically assign topic labels to the identified clusters, then? The solution is to combine supervised and unsupervised approaches. A widely used scenario for clustering is when you have a small amount of labeled data and a large amount of unlabeled data, in which case you can use clustering to identify similar posts (both among labeled and unlabeled ones) and assign the label based on the allocation of the labeled posts from the correspondent clusters. Alternatively, you can try to automatically generate topic labels based on the set of informative words returned by the clustering algorithm.

Summary

- There are two different paradigms within which you can analyze topics, *supervised* and *unsupervised.*
- If you have texts labeled with topics, you can apply a supervised machine learning algorithm. By now, you are quite familiar with this family of algorithms, but

the novelty in topic classification is that you need to extend the task to a multi-class setting.

- A machine-learning pipeline can be applied to this task, making use of the 20 Newsgroups dataset available via scikit-learn, selecting words as features, applying TF-IDF transformations to the raw word counts, and using multinomial Naïve Bayes algorithm from the scikit-learn suite.

- Additive smoothing is a technique that is widely used in classification with probabilistic algorithms, and that helps address data effects. Note that if you haven't seen a particular word in texts on a particular topic, you should assume that you don't have enough training data (which is always the most realistic assumption) rather than that this word is absolutely impossible to use with the specific topic. Smoothing helps adjust the probabilities, giving previously unseen words a small chance of occurrence in the future.

- When you don't have labeled data or you want to discover the topics from the data itself, you can use an unsupervised ML approach.

- *K*-means clustering algorithm can be applied to learn how the topics are represented in the data. This approach clusters similar texts based on word occurrences. In doing so, it identifies the representative central points for each cluster, called *centroids*. *K* in this algorithm represents the number of clusters (and centroids); for example, $k = 10$. K-means is an iterative algorithm that runs either for a predefined number of steps or until *convergence* (i.e., until a stable solution is found, and the data points don't change their cluster membership anymore).

- To estimate the centroids and find clusters, the algorithm needs to calculate distances in a multidimensional space, such as by using Euclidean distance. The number of dimensions is defined by the number of considered features. In this task, it is the words. To reduce the dimensionality of the word space, a number of familiar techniques can be used, including stopwords removal and removal of very rare and very frequent words with `TfidfVectorizer`.

- Truncated singular value decomposition is a useful technique that allows you to distill the information contained in the original vector dimensions down to a much smaller number of informative dimensions, thus making calculations much more efficient. This technique essentially allows you to convert original words into concepts (also called *latent factors*).

- Clustering algorithms can be evaluated using homogeneity (an alternative for precision in the unsupervised ML setting), completeness (alternative to recall), and V-measure (alternative to F-score). In addition, the informative words that helped the clustering algorithm identify each cluster's centroid can be extracted and analyzed. Based on these words, you can interpret the results. For instance, you can reason about the clusters identified in the data and how they correspond to the labeled topics.

- When you want to identify topics present in the data and investigate how they are distributed across the documents, which words represent each topic and to what extent, you can use another unsupervised approach—topic modeling. This will be the subject of the next chapter.

Solutions to miscellaneous exercises

Exercise 9.1

1 Previous tasks explored various types of features. Recall that in chapter 6 you did quite an extensive feature exploration for authorship identification and used features as diverse as word and sentence lengths, count and proportion of stopwords, distributions of parts of speech and word suffixes, and the presence of unique words. For sentiment analysis in chapters 7 and 8, you mostly relied on words, but recall that this also required some selection of features. For instance, you filtered out words using sentiment lexicons, considered the effect that negative words have on the rest of the text, and used *n*-grams that cover sequences of *n* words.

2 Feature selection heavily depends on the task at hand. For instance, the distribution of stopwords and word suffixes, the presence of some unique words, or sentence length may be very characteristic of a particular author's writing style. Note that the 20 Newsgroups dataset (like many other collections of texts) are written by a wide variety of authors, and even if some authors prefer to write on specific topics, identification of writing styles is peripheral to the task of topic detection. This means that such fine-grained features as unique words or distribution of suffixes and stopwords are unlikely to be helpful. It is also unlikely that different topics would vary significantly in terms of the sentence and word lengths. Although such features may help distinguish between texts of different genres (e.g., social media posts are typically shorter than scientific articles) within the Newsgroups posts, these features would probably not be very helpful. Among all the tasks addressed so far in this book, topic classification is most similar to spam detection (e.g., although it is possible that ham emails talk about "lotteries" and "medication," too, one would expect to see such words in spam emails more frequently). Words and their distributions are the most reliable feature type for topic classification too. For instance, one would expect to see a word like *car* much more frequently in `rec.autos` posts on automobiles than in `sci.med` posts on medicine, and a word like *virus* in `sci.med`, `comp.windows.x`, and, perhaps, `sci.crypt` (cryptography) posts but not so much in `misc.forsale` (sale announcements).

Exercise 9.2

A collection of words in (1) would strongly suggest a `rec.autos` topic (automobiles), while the set in (2) most likely refers to `sci.space`.

Exercise 9.3

In this book, you have come across a number of evaluation metrics in the previous tasks you worked on. Among them are

- *Accuracy*—The proportion of correctly classified examples among those that you tried to classify
- *Precision*—The proportion of texts that actually belong to the topic among those that your algorithm identifies as belonging to the topic
- *Recall*—The proportion of texts that are correctly identified as belonging to the topic among those that actually belong to this topic
- *F-score*—The harmonic mean between the precision and recall scores

Exercise 9.4

The comparatively low recall of 0.78 on rec.autos posts means that some posts from this topic are misclassified as other categories. This follows directly from the recall definition:

```
Recall = number of texts from rec.auto classified as rec.auto /
         number of texts that are actually in rec.auto
```

This means that the proportion of texts from rec.auto identified by the classifier is 0.78, suggesting that the other texts are incorrectly assigned with other categories by the classifier. The relatively low precision of 0.71 on rec.sport.hockey suggests that some of the texts that the classifier believes are related to hockey are actually from other categories. This follows from the precision definition:

```
Precision = number of texts from rec.sport.hockey classified as
    rec.sport.hockey /
          number of texts classified as rec.sport.hockey
```

This suggests that the proportion of texts that are classified as rec.sport.hockey and that are actually from this category equals 0.71, with the rest of the texts classified with this category actually belonging to some other categories. Perhaps, even to rec.auto. Listing 9.6 helps you find this out.

Exercise 9.5

Let's estimate the distances first (note, sqrt is used for square root):

```
dist(point₁, centroid₁) = sqrt ((0.25-0.33)² + (2.31-2.75)²) = sqrt (0.2000)=0.45
dist(point₁, centroid₂) = sqrt ((0.25-0.02)² + (2.31-1.00)²) = sqrt (1.7690)=1.33
dist(point₂, centroid₁) = sqrt ((0.05-0.33)² + (1.18-2.75)²) = sqrt (2.5433)=1.60
dist(point₂, centroid₂) = sqrt ((0.05-0.02)² + (1.18-1.00)²) = sqrt (0.0333)=0.18
```

These estimations show that point$_1$ is closer to centroid$_1$ (0.45 versus 1.33), so it belongs in cluster$_1$; point$_2$ is closer to centroid$_2$ (0.18 versus 1.60), so it belongs in cluster$_2$. Figure 9.15 visualizes these calculations and provides you with the general formula for Euclidean distance.

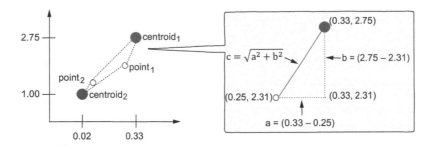

Figure 9.15　A reminder of how Euclidean distance is calculated. This graph shows two selected points and two centroids, and explains how the distance is calculated, zooming in on centroid$_1$ **and** point$_1$**, and showing the calculation steps.**

Exercise 9.6

Your "fruit basket" this time is the collection of posts from the 20 Newsgroups dataset. The goal of unsupervised approaches is to discover groups of similar objects (in this case, posts) in the data based on some characteristics that can help the algorithm tell different objects apart and combine similar objects in relatively homogeneous clusters. Here, you are trying to discover topics based on the content of the posts. Therefore, your clusters will represent topics, and each point will represent a separate post. You can use the vocabulary of the words identified by the algorithm in the training data (the set of 52,746 words as before) as coordinates in space. That is, instead of [color=green, size=avg. 2.75 in, weight=avg. 0.33 pounds, shape=round, taste= sweet & sour], you will be using something like [word$_0$=0, word$_1$=5, word$_2$=0,..., word$_{52745}$=3], where values represent either the absolute number of occurrences of a particular word in text or their TF-IDF scores. Note that this means that, unlike in our toy example, where you represented each point in a five-dimensional space, in a language task you may be dealing with thousands of dimensions.

Topic modeling

The previous chapter introduced various NLP and machine-learning techniques for topic classification and topic analysis. Here is a reminder of the scenario that you've worked on: suppose you work as a content manager for a large news platform. Your platform hosts texts from a wide variety of authors and mainly specializes in the following set of well-established topics: Politics, Finance, Science, Sports, and Arts. Your task is to decide, for every incoming article, which topic it belongs to and post it under the relevant tab on the platform. Here are some questions for you to consider:

1 Can you use your knowledge of NLP and machine-learning algorithms to help you automate this process?

2 What if you suspect that a new set of yet-uncovered topics, besides the five just mentioned, started emerging among the texts that authors send you (e.g., you get some articles on the technological advances)? How can you discover such new topics and include them in your analysis?

3 What if you think that some articles lend themselves to multiple topics, which are covered by these articles to a various extent? For instance, some articles may talk about a sports event that is of a certain political importance (e.g., Olympic Games) or about a new technological invention that results in the tech company having high valuation.

Let's summarize what you have done to address the tasks in this scenario so far:

- First of all, as question 1 suggests, you can apply your NLP and ML skills and treat this task as another *text classification* problem. You've worked on various text classification problems (spam detection, authorship profiling, sentiment analysis) before, so you have quite a lot of experience with this framework. The very first approach that you can apply to the task at hand is to use an ML classifier trained on the articles that were assigned with topics in the past, using words occurring in these articles as features. As we said in the previous chapter, this is simply an extension of the binary classification scenario to a multiclass classification one. In the previous chapter, you worked with the famous 20 Newsgroups dataset (accessed via scikit-learn at http://mng.bz/95qq) and since you focused on ten specific topics in this data, the first approach that you applied was indeed a supervised ten-class topic classification approach.

- The results looked good, but there are several drawbacks to treating this task as a supervised classification problem. First of all, it relies on the idea that high-quality data labeled with topics of interest can be easily obtained, which is not always the case in real-life scenarios. Second, this approach will not help you if the data on the news platform changes and new topics keep cropping up, as question 2 outlines. Third, it is possible that some texts on your platform belong to more than one topic, as question 3 suggests. In summary, all these drawbacks can be said to be related to availability of data and appropriate labels. What can you do if you don't have enough annotated data, or you cannot keep collecting and annotating data constantly, or you don't have access to multiple topic labels for your articles? The answer is you can use an *unsupervised machine-learning approach*. The goal of such approaches is to discover groups of similar posts in data without the use of predefined labels. If you have some labeled data, you can compare the groups discovered with an unsupervised approach to the labeled groups, but you can also use the unsupervised approach to get new insights.

- The unsupervised approach that you looked into in the previous chapter is *clustering*. With clustering, you rely on the inherent similarities between documents and let the algorithm figure out how the documents should be grouped together based on these similarities. For instance, in the previous chapter you used K-means clustering (with $k = 10$ for 10 topics in your data), and the algorithm used word occurrences in the newsgroups posts as the basis for their content similarity. Since this approach is agnostic to the particular classes that it tries to identify, it helped you to uncover some new insights into the data. For example, certain posts from originally different topics (e.g., on `baseball` & `hockey` or on `autos` & `motorcycles`) were grouped together, while certain posts originally from the same topic were split into several clusters (e.g., `forsale` turned out to be one of such heterogeneous topics with posts that can be thought of as representing different subtopics depending on what is being sold).

Unsupervised approaches such as clustering are good for data exploration and uncovering new insights. One aspect not addressed by this clustering algorithm is the possibility that some posts may naturally cover more than one topic. For example, a post where a user is selling their old car falls into two categories at once: `forsale` and `autos`. In this chapter you will learn how to build a *topic modeling* algorithm capable of detecting multiple topics in a given document using *latent Dirichlet allocation (LDA)*.

The diagram in figure 10.1 is a reminder of the full set of approaches that you can apply to analyze topics in your data. The two approaches on the left and in the center of this diagram were covered in the previous chapter, and topic modeling is the focus of this chapter.

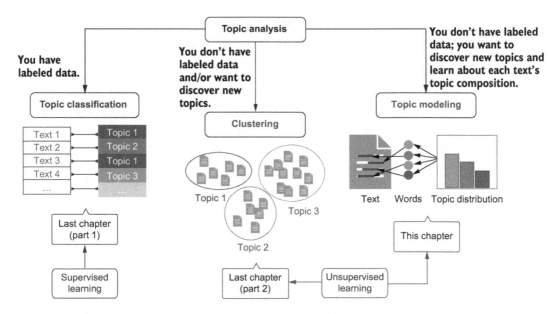

Figure 10.1 Reminder: depending on whether you have labeled data or not, you can apply a supervised (classification from the previous chapter) or an unsupervised approach (e.g., you can use clustering, as discussed in the previous chapter). If you want to discover new topics and learn about text's topic composition, apply topic modeling from this chapter.

10.1 Topic modeling with latent Dirichlet allocation

The results that you achieved using an unsupervised approach in the previous chapter revealed at least one mixed topic: misc.forsale. This shouldn't come as a surprise. Despite the fact that all posts where users were selling something ended up in one category within the newsgroups (and similarly might also be posted on the same web page on your online platform), users may be selling all sorts of things, from sports equipment to electronic devices to cars. Therefore, depending on the subject of the sale, a particular post may mix such topics as forsale & baseball, or forsale & electronics, or forsale & autos.

Let's use some concrete examples. Imagine you have the set of short posts from figure 10.2 in your collection.

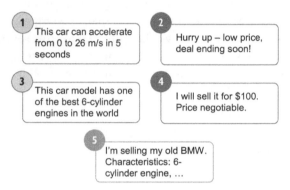

Figure 10.2   Examples of short posts on various topics

> ### Exercise 10.1
>
> Suppose you know or have reasons to believe that the set of short posts from figure 10.2 covers exactly two topics. In the previous topic analysis examples, we always assumed that each post may belong to only one specific topic. Let's lift this restriction here and allow each post to belong to either one or both topics.
>
> 1. What are your guesses on the two topics in these examples? How did you arrive at these conclusions (e.g., which words suggest these topics)?
>
> 2. Can you think of an algorithm that would detect which topics or combinations of topics each post belongs to and to what extent, as well as which words express each of these topics and to what extent?

Let's discuss the solution to this exercise together.

10.1.1 Exercise 10.1: Question 1 solution

When solving this task, you may follow a procedure like this, which wouldn't even require you to analyze the meaning of the words, only their occurrence. You start with

Post 1, which contains such words as *car, accelerate,* and *seconds,* among others. You assign Topic 1 to this post, with the set of words from Post 1 associated with this topic.

Next, you move to Post 2 . Can it also be on Topic 1? Nothing suggests that, as the set of words from this post (*hurry, low, price, deal,* etc.) don't overlap with the set that you've associated with Topic 1, so you conclude that at this point it would be safest to assign Topic 2 to this post, with the set of words from Post 2 associated with Topic 2.

You move to Post 3 and spot that there is some word overlap with Post 1 and Topic 1—specifically, both posts talk about *cars.* You decide that Post 3 also belongs to Topic 1. Similarly, Post 4 has some word overlap (specifically, the word *price*) with Post 2 and Topic 2, so you decide that Post 4 belongs to Topic 2.

Finally, you move to Post 5. Is it on Topic 1 or on Topic 2? On the one hand, it is similar to the posts on Topic 1, as it contains such words as *6-cylinder* and *engine.* On the other hand, it is also similar to the posts on Topic 2, as it contains the word *sell(ing).* However, the task description says that posts may actually belong to both topics at once. It looks like your original assignment works quite well for this set of posts, as there are no doubts about how the words are distributed among the two topics, and how topics are assigned to posts. This means that at this point you can declare that the topic distribution in these posts is as follows:

- Post 1 and Post 3 are on Topic 1 exclusively.
- Post 2 and Post 4 are on Topic 2 exclusively.
- Post 5 mixes Topic 1 and Topic 2 in some proportion.

Figure 10.3 visualizes this idea.

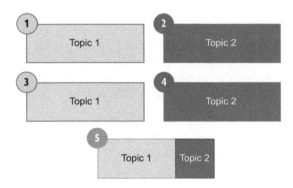

Figure 10.3   Based on the word composition of each post, Posts 1 and 3 are on Topic 1 exclusively, Posts 2 and 4 are on Topic 2 exclusively, and Post 5 combines two topics in some proportion.

Now you can also list the words that characterize each of these topics:

- Topic 1 can be characterized by *car, accelerate, 6-cylinder, engine, model,* and so on.
- Topic 2 can be characterized by *deal, sell, $, price,* and so on.

Can you tell what these topics actually *are?* Based on the sets of words, you can interpret Topic 1 as `autos`, and Topic 2 as `sales`.

10.1.2 *Exercise 10.1: Question 2 solution*

The algorithm for topic modeling that you will develop in this chapter will follow a procedure similar to the one described earlier: it will start with some topic assignment for the texts, learn about word composition of each topic, and then it will reiterate and update its topic-to-text and word-to-topic assignments to refine its predictions until it reaches the most stable allocation. We will delve into the details of this algorithm in the next section, and now let's just summarize that the goal of the approach that you will develop in this chapter—the approach that will help you to automatically solve the puzzle—would be to provide you with an answer along the lines of the following:

- Post 1 and Post 3 are 100% on Topic 1.
- Post 2 and Post 4 are 100% on Topic 2.
- Post 5 is on a mix of topics (e.g., 70% on Topic 1 and 30% on Topic 2).

When it comes to the word content, it is also desirable that such an algorithm tells you something like this:

- The composition of Topic 1 is 20% *car*, 15% *engine*, 10% *speed*, 5% *accelerate*, and so on.
- The composition of Topic 2 is 40% *sell*, 10% *deal*, 5% *price*, 5% *cheap*, and so on.

To visualize this idea, figure 10.4 illustrates some words that may contribute to each topic using word clouds, where the font size represents the relative weight (i.e., the percentage contribution) of each word within each topic.

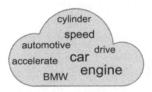 

Figure 10.4   Sample word clouds representing each of the two topics: the font size represents the relative weight or contribution of each word to each topic.

The exact contribution of the words to the topics will be detected by the algorithm based on the texts. Hopefully this small example helps you appreciate the potential of the unsupervised topic modeling algorithm that you will develop and apply in this chapter: latent Dirichlet allocation (LDA) allows you to interpret texts as combinations of topics that have produced the words that you see in your texts. Specifically, it allows you to quantitatively measure the allocation of topics and the contribution of each word to a particular topic used in your texts. Now it's time to look more closely into the inner mechanisms of this approach that allow it to come up with such estimations.

10.1.3 *Estimating parameters for the LDA*

The LDA algorithm treats each document (text, post, etc.) as a mixture of topics. For example, in exercise 10.1, such mixtures contain 100% of Topic 1 in one case, 100% of Topic 2 in another, and 70% of Topic 1 and 30% of Topic 2 in the third case. Each topic, in its turn, is composed of certain words, so once the topic or topics for the document are determined, these topics become the driving forces that are assumed to have produced the words in the document based on the word sets these topics comprise (e.g., {car, engine, speed, . . .} or {deal, sale, price, . . .}).

> **NOTE** In the context of topic modeling, the term *document* is widely used to denote any type of text (an article, a novel, an email, a post, etc.). We'll be using this term in its general meaning here too.

This is the theoretical assumption behind LDA—the words that you observe in documents are not put together in these documents in a random manner. Rather it is believed that these words are thematically related, as in exercise 10.1, where some are related to autos and others to sales. All you can observe in practice are the words themselves, but the algorithm assumes that, behind the scenes, these words are *generated* and put together in the documents by such abstract topics. Since the topics are hidden from the eye of the observer or, to use a technical term, they are *latent*, this gives the algorithm its name. The goal of the algorithm, then, is to reverse-engineer this document-generation process to detect which topics are responsible for the observed words.

The algorithm focuses on estimating two sets of parameters—*topic distribution* in the collection of documents and *word distribution* for each topic on the basis of the documents in the collection. These two sets of parameters, as you will see in the course of this chapter, are very closely related to each other. Just like in exercise 10.1, if the algorithm decides upon the topics (e.g., that Post 1 is entirely on Topic 1), then the words from the document are assigned to this topic, which means that the next time the algorithm encounters any of these words in another document, they will suggest that the other document is on the same topic. Exercise 10.1 explained this process using a small example. It worked well because the set of posts was small, with some word overlap to make things easier, with clear allocation of posts to topics, and only a single post where both topics were present. In a real document collection, there may be thousands of documents with millions of words and many more complex topic combinations. How does the algorithm deal with this level of complexity?

The answer is the algorithm starts with the best possible strategy for the cases where the correct answer is not readily available—namely, it starts by making random allocation. Specifically, it goes through each document in the collection and *randomly assigns* each word in this document to one of the topics (e.g., Topic 1 or Topic 2). Note that random allocation of words to topics within each document allows the algorithm to account for the possible presence of multiple topics in the same document. Random allocation is widely used as the first step by unsupervised algorithms. You may recall that you also had to randomly allocate documents to clusters in the first iteration of clustering in the previous chapter. Of course, it is unlikely that the algorithm would manage to guess the "right" topics randomly, but the good news is that after this first pass, you have an *initial allocation* and therefore you can already estimate both the topic distribution in the collection of posts and the word distribution in each topic based on this *random guess.* Since this guess, being random in nature, will likely not fit the real state of affairs (i.e., the actual underlying distribution), how can you do better?

You apply an iterative algorithm, adjusting the estimation in the "right" direction until your estimation is as good and as stable as possible. At this point, you may recall that the unsupervised clustering algorithm used a very similar procedure. You started with a random cluster allocation, and you kept improving the clusters iteratively until you either have run through the data a sufficient number of times (i.e., you've reached the maximum number of iterations) or your cluster allocations didn't change anymore (i.e., you've reached convergence on your solution). The algorithm that you apply here is inherently quite similar in this regard. The key difference is that, instead of one set of parameters, in this case you need to estimate two, taking into account that the topic structure (i.e., the topics themselves, their distributions in documents, and word-to-topic assignments) is a hidden structure, and this structure will need to be estimated and adjusted on the basis of the only observed parameter (i.e., words in documents). Recall that as you are using an unsupervised procedure, the algorithm doesn't have access to any predefined topic labels and doesn't know what the "correct" allocation of topics and words is. Let's summarize the steps in the algorithm. Figure 10.5 provides the mental model for the LDA.

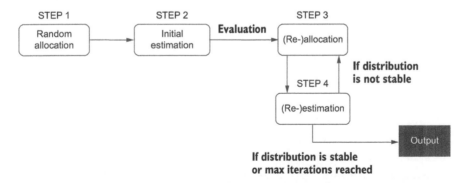

Figure 10.5   Mental model for the LDA algorithm. As in any iterative process, you start with some initial allocation and iterate on your estimates until you do not observe any significant change to the parameters anymore (i.e., until *convergence*) or until you reach the maximum number of iterations.

Here is a short description of all the steps in the algorithm:

- *Step 1: Random allocation*—Randomly assign words in documents to topics.
- *Step 2: Initial estimation*—Estimate topic and word distributions for your data based on the random allocation from step 1.
- *Step 3: Reallocation*—Evaluate your algorithm on the data, using the distributions estimated in step 2, and reallocate the words to the respective topics accordingly.
- *Step 4: Re-estimation*—Using the allocation from step 3, re-estimate distributions.
- *Iteration*—If the new estimates are not considerably different from the previous estimates, stop. Otherwise, repeat steps 3 and 4, until the difference is negligible (i.e., the algorithm converges to a stable solution).
- *Stopping criteria*—You stop either when estimates stabilize or when the maximum number of iterations has been reached.

How does this process apply to the documents, topics, and words in the topic-labeling application? Suppose on your first pass through the data you have randomly ascribed words to topics. For example, you have 100 words in the post d_1, and for each word in this post you randomly assigned it either to Topic1 (for better readability, you can think of Topic1 as some specific one, such as autos, but keep in mind that the algorithm itself doesn't "know" what the topic label is) or to Topic2 (again, think of this topic as some specific one, such as sales). Now let's pass through the data again (step 2) and estimate topic and word probability distributions. In each case, we will first look into the formal definition, then into the calculation, and finally, we'll consider a toy example.

- *Topic probability distribution*—The probability of a specific topic t for a specific post d is estimated as the number of words in the post d that have been allocated to the topic t in the previous round of the algorithm application divided by the total number of words in d. In other words, it is

```
P(topic t | post d) = number of words in post d allocated to topic t /
total number of words in post d
```

    For example, if in the first random pass you randomly assigned 52 words in post d_1 to Topic1, at this point you would estimate that $P(\text{Topic2} \mid d_1) = 0.48$ and $P(\text{Topic1} \mid d_1) = 0.52$.

- *Word probability distribution*—The probability of a particular word w, given that a specific topic t produced it, equals the number of times the word w was assigned with the topic t in the previous round in *all* posts in the collection divided by the total number of times this word has been used in the collection. In other words, it is

```
P(word w | topic t) = number of times word w is assigned to topic t in
all posts in the collection / total number of occurrences of word w
```

For example, suppose you've encountered the word `price` 50 times in your collection of posts, 35 of which you have randomly assigned to `Topic2` in the first round and 15 of which you've assigned to `Topic1`. This means that P(price | Topic2) = 0.70 and P(price | Topic1) = 0.30.

- In the next pass over the data, you start with d_1 again, and it's time to reconsider your allocation with topics in this post. Suppose in the previous round you have randomly assigned `price` to `Topic1`. Should you change your allocation in view of the new estimates? To decide, multiply the following probabilities:

P_{update}(price is from Topic2) = $P_{previous}$(Topic2 | d_1) * $P_{previous}$(price | Topic2) = 0.48 * 0.70 = 0.336, and
P_{update}(price is from Topic1) = $P_{previous}$(Topic1 | d_1) * $P_{previous}$(price | Topic1) = 0.52 * 0.30 = 0.156

Based on these estimates, since the probability of `price` being generated by `Topic2` in d_1 is higher than the probability of `price` being generated by `Topic1` (0.336 > 0.156), you should change the allocation of `price` in d_1 to `Topic2`. Note that even though post d_1 is currently more likely to be on `Topic1` overall (since P(Topic2 | d_1) = 0.48 and P(Topic1 | d_1) = 0.52), you are still able to reassign `price` to `Topic2`. This is because the distribution of the word `price` with respect to its topic allocation across all posts matters, too. Moreover, when re-estimating probability for a specific word (e.g., `price`), you keep other word probabilities as they are (i.e., probabilities for each word are re-estimated separately). This is done so that you don't need to change too many parameters at the same time, which would make estimation very complex. (A popular algorithm used to make sure the computation is done in a feasible way is based on sampling and is widely used in LDA. For more details, see Resnik and Hardisty (2009), Gibbs Sampling for the Uninitiated, http://mng.bz/j2N8).

- Now that the allocation of some words has changed, you need to pass over your data again, this time re-estimating topic probabilities.

- After multiple passes over the whole collection and re-estimation of topic assignment for all words and then distribution of topics, you will eventually reach a stable distribution where your topic assignments won't change anymore. At that point, you will be able to use these assignments to detect topic mixtures for each post in the collection by counting the proportion of words in this post belonging to each topic, just like you did earlier. Moreover, given any new post, you will be able to estimate its topic composition using the very same parameters.

Essentially, you start with a random guess and a random allocation, and you continue adjusting the estimates until the whole interaction between the components—word distribution and topic distribution—comes into a balance when nothing changes (much) anymore. Here is a real-life analogy for this process: imagine you've just started at a new company, and you've been invited to the first social event, a party at one of your new colleagues' house. You would like to know more about your colleagues' hobbies and, being a keen skier, perhaps even find fellow ski fans among your colleagues. You arrive at the party to find that people are already spread around the house in small groups chatting with each other. Can you find out what their hobbies are and, in particular, find out if there are any other ski fans among your colleagues? You can start going round the house asking everyone about their hobbies directly, or you can choose a more discreet approach.

It is reasonable to assume that people at parties talk about their hobbies rather than work matters, and you can also expect that people talking to each other in groups share interests at least to some extent. You join the first group randomly and find that people are talking about some recent political issues. You come to the conclusion that the interest of the majority of the people in this group is politics, and as this is far from your own interests, you move on to the next group(s) until you join the one discussing travel.

A couple of people from this group, Alice and Bob, mention some popular ski resorts. You assume therefore that this group represents a mixture of interests: for instance, those in this group who talk about exotic destinations may be more into traveling itself, others who mention mountains may be into hiking, but Alice and Bob may be into skiing. At this point, it is just your guess and you allocated hobbies to people somewhat randomly. To be sure that Alice and Bob indeed share your interest in skiing, you need to have more evidence. In a bit, Alice joins another group of people, where everyone is talking about active sports. Alice brings up the subject of skiing and another colleague, Cynthia, joins her in this discussion. Now you are more convinced that Alice has the same hobby as you; moreover, you conclude that Cynthia may be another fellow skier. Similarly, later you join another group of colleagues with Bob, and in this group, people are talking about the cost of equipment for their hobbies. Bob mentions that his recent pair of skis were quite expensive, at which point Denise asks him which brand he uses and tells him about her preferred brand of relatively inexpensive skis.

In this scenario, hobbies are similar to *topics*; groups of people are similar to *documents*, as they may combine mixtures of topics (or, in this analogy, people with various hobbies); and each person may be considered an analogy of a *word* representing a specific hobby (topic). As a result of your quest for colleagues with similar interests, where you've used an approach similar to the one used by LDA, you identify that Alice, Bob, Cynthia, and Denise are into skiing as much as you are, and you arrange a ski trip with your colleagues.

10.1.4 *LDA as a generative model*

We said earlier that LDA assumes that there is some abstract generation process going on behind the scenes, in which hidden (latent) topics generate words that make up the documents in the collection that you observe. The algorithm's main goal is then to reverse-engineer this generation process and to identify the components of this hidden structure—the topics, their distribution, and the distribution of words in each topic. Because of this background assumption that the data is generated by certain parameters, LDA is called a *generative model*. LDA is not the only algorithm that assumes that a generative process is behind the data observed and that tries to estimate the parameters responsible for such generation—in fact, there is a whole family of machine-learning algorithms called *generative models* (https://developers.google.com/machine-learning/gan/generative).

To give you a bit more insight into why it is reasonable to assume that such a generative process may be responsible for the observed data, let's try to replicate a generative process behind topic modeling using a small example. Suppose this process generates documents on two topics (i.e., $K = 2$). As discussed in the previous section, the algorithm doesn't know anything about topic identities and just treats them as `Topic1` and `Topic2`, but for clarity let's assume that `Topic1` = `sales` and `Topic2` = `electronics`. The generation is driven by the two sets of parameters as before—topic distribution and word distribution. In this case, they are the true, underlying parameters of the generative process that the algorithm is trying to identify as you've seen in the previous section.

To generate a document using this process, you first decide upon the length of the text to produce. For the sake of this example, let's select some small number of words (e.g., $N = 10$). The next step is to decide upon the topic mixture for your document. This decision is based on the selection of topics from the actual *topic distribution*. In this example, the process selects among two topics: $K = \{$`Topic1`, `Topic2`$\}$, with `Topic1` = `sales` and `Topic2` = `electronics`, and depending on this step, the words of the document will represent each topic in a certain proportion. You can think of this generation step as figure 10.6 illustrates. Imagine you have a wheel with sectors marked with the available topics, 1 (`sales`) and 2 (`electronics`). You spin the wheel 10 times and record the output. For instance, imagine the output returned over these 10 spins is [1, 1, 2, 2, 2, 1, 1, 2, 1, 1]. This means that out of the 10 words that you will generate for your document, 6 (or 60%) will be on `Topic 1` (`sales`) and the other 4 (40%) on `Topic 2` (`electronics`).

Topic distribution wheel

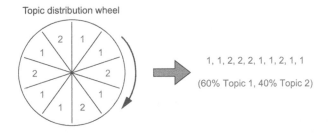

1, 1, 2, 2, 2, 1, 1, 2, 1, 1

(60% Topic 1, 40% Topic 2)

Figure 10.6   Generation of topics: you spin the wheel and output one of the available topics. In this example, 60% of the output represents `Topic 1` **and 40%** `Topic 2`.

Now comes the second part of the generation procedure. For each of the selected topics, you need to generate a word according to the actual *word distribution*. This step is very similar to the previous one, except that this time you have two wheels to spin—one for each topic—and the sectors are filled with words. You've seen an example of some possible word distributions in exercise 10.1. For instance, sales topic was represented there as [40% sell, 10% deal, 5% price, 5% cheap, etc.]. What do these percentages actually mean? When the algorithm establishes that 40% of the sales topic is represented by the word sell, this means that if you see 100 words on the sales topic in your collection of documents, 40 of them should be sell. Similarly, if the words from the sales topic are put on the wheel and the wheel has 100 sectors on it, 40 of them should be marked with the word sell. This means that when you spin the wheel, on the average 40% of the time you will get the word sell as a result, 5% of the time you will get the word price, and so on.

> **NOTE**   We say "on the average" here because if you marked 40% of the sectors on the wheel with the word sell and you actually ended up outputting every single word from this wheel over the spins, you would end up returning sell precisely 40% of the time. In reality, every round of spins is different from any other one. You may get different results from one round to another. This means that over a series of rounds, you may get sell, say, 38%, 39%, or 43% of the time in each particular series (e.g., for different documents), yet over a long range of such wheel spinning activities, the average number of sell returns will approximate its true distribution of 40%. This is what happens when you run experiments over multiple trials.

Now let's combine these two steps together: you use the topic distribution returned by the *topic distribution* wheel, and for each topic you spin the appropriate *word distribution* wheel. For the sequence of topics returned by the topic distribution wheel before (i.e., [1, 1, 2, 2, 2, 1, 1, 2, 1, 1]), you will spin the Topic1 word distribution wheel to generate the word1 and word2; then you will spin the Topic2 word distribution wheel three times to output the word3, word4, and word5; then you will spin the Topic1 word distribution wheel twice (for word6 and word7), then the Topic2 word distribution wheel once (for word8), and you will finish the sequence by spinning the Topic1 word distribution wheel to output word9 and word10. Figure 10.7 illustrates this process, although note that for simplicity only some words are visualized on the wheels.

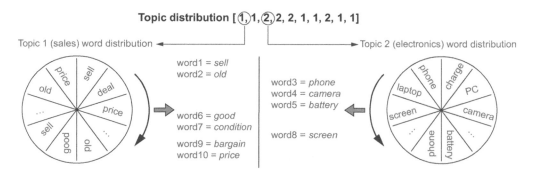

Figure 10.7   Once the topics are generated, the words in each topic are selected in a similar fashion. A special "wheel," on which the words are marked according to the word distribution within this particular topic, is spun and the output word is written down.

To summarize, the following generative process is taking place here:

- Select Topic 1 (sale) → generate sell
- Select Topic 1 (sale) → generate old
- Select Topic 2 (electronics) → generate phone
- Select Topic 2 (electronics) → generate camera
- Select Topic 2 (electronics) → generate battery
- Select Topic 1 (sale) → generate good
- Select Topic 1 (sale) → generate condition
- Select Topic 2 (electronics) → generate screen
- Select Topic 1 (sale) → generate bargain
- Select Topic 1 (sale) → generate price

This results in the following "document" consisting of 10 words on 2 topics generated by the algorithm as described earlier: "*sell old phone camera battery good condition screen bargain price*". This document doesn't exactly look like a post you may see in reality, although you probably can still get at the core meaning of the message. This generated sequence of words should rather be treated as a skeleton, which can be realized into a real-world advertisement like the following (with the generated words highlighted in italics): "Hello everyone! I'm *selling* my *old phone* X. Excellent *camera, battery* in *good condition*, small scratch on the *screen*. It's a *bargain*—I'm giving it away for just $Y (*price* negotiable)". Figure 10.8 visualizes the result, with the topics highlighted in text similar to the process visualized in figure 10.1.

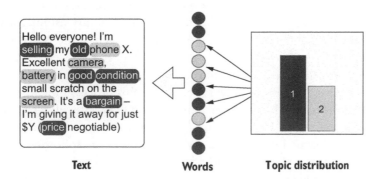

Text   Words   Topic distribution

Figure 10.8 The generative process first selects topic distribution (on the right, with `Topic1` marked in black and `Topic2` in light gray); then each topic generates some words, which are then used in the produced post (on the left).

A couple of observations are due at this point. First of all, note that the actual post may contain words other than the ones generated by the topics. After all, such words as *everyone* or *in* may occur across multiple posts and they don't bear any topic-specific meaning. Second, in our example earlier, word lemmas rather than full forms are generated first (note that sell is generated for the skeleton document, and it is then converted into selling in the actual post). In fact, the algorithm may be applied to any word representation: you may consider word stems, lemmas, or full forms. We will discuss the appropriate representation levels later in this chapter. One final observation to make is that this process uses a bag-of-words model, which means that its goal is to generate topic-relevant words, and it is agnostic to their actual order. What matters most is whether the words are generated according to the actual underlying distribution. For the sake of this toy example, generated words are put in the post in the order that makes it easier for us as readers, but in practice the wheel spinning in figure 10.7 may have output these words in a different order. Still, whichever order the words are presented in, you would be able to understand what topics are behind them.

Now, let's step back from this small-scale example and describe the overall generative procedure. The LDA algorithm represents all documents as mixtures of topics, and it assumes that the documents are originally generated based on two types of probability estimations—one describing topic distribution and another one describing word distribution within each topic. Once the number N of words to be generated for a particular document is selected, the generative process draws topics from the topic distribution, and once the topics are determined, it then produces the words drawn from these topics according to the probabilities assigned to these words within the respective topics. Hopefully the notion of probabilities and distributions does not sound unfamiliar to you anymore. You have worked with probabilities before in this book, when you used Naïve Bayes, for spam filtering, or when you looked into Decision Trees for authorship identification. Yet, it is always a good idea to solidify one's understanding; in fact, the topics and words output in our wheel-spinning activities described in figures 10.6 and 10.7 are defined by the probability estimations. The algorithm repeats the two consecutive generation steps for each of the N words in the document as figure 10.9 summarizes.

Since the LDA algorithm does not have access to the parameters that the generative process uses, it tries to "decode" or reverse-engineer this process by learning these parameters based on the data at hand. When a new document comes along, it assumes that the document is generated by the same process with the same parameters, so it applies the parameters learned on the data, trying to answer the following question: "Given what we know about the topic and word distributions, which of the topics could have generated the given document?" It then returns the topic(s) that answer this question best.

10.2 *Implementation of the topic modeling algorithm*

Now that we've discussed the inner workings of the LDA algorithm, it's time to apply it in practice. Figure 10.10 summarizes the processing pipeline for the algorithm.

In this chapter, like you did in the previous one, you are going to work with the posts from the 20 Newsgroups dataset on the selected data subset. This will allow you to compare the discoveries made by your second unsupervised algorithm, LDA, in this

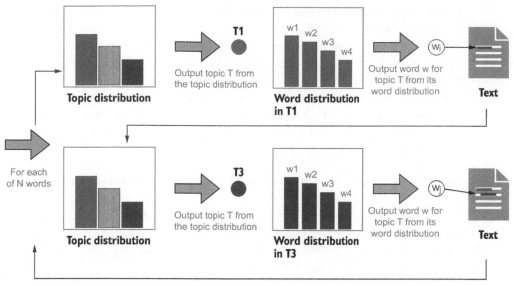

Figure 10.9 A summary of the text-generation process with LDA. For each of the *N* words, first a topic is selected according to the topic distribution, and then a word is selected according to the word distribution within this topic

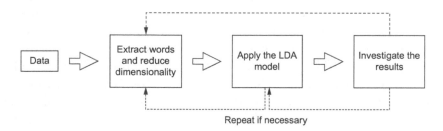

Figure 10.10 Processing pipeline for the LDA algorithm

data and see whether the assumption that the data represents the topics (i.e., labels) assigned in the original 20 Newsgroups dataset holds. Let's remind ourselves what data we are working with and load the input data as the first step in our pipeline requires.

10.2.1 Loading the data

In the previous chapter, you learned that the popular machine-learning toolkit scikit-learn provides you not only with implementation of a variety of widely used machine-learning algorithms, but also with easy access to a number of datasets to train your skills on. The specific dataset of interest here is the famous 20 Newsgroups dataset, which is well-suited for all topic analysis-related tasks and is easily accessible via scikit-learn.

(Check scikit-learn's datasets web page for more information on the various available data: http://mng.bz/WxQl.)

As a reminder, the 20 Newsgroups dataset is a collection of around 18,000 newsgroups posts on 20 "topics"; however, not all of them have a comparable amount of data. Besides, as we've discussed before, exploring the results for as many as 20 topics may be quite overwhelming. To this end, in the previous chapter we restricted ourselves to a specific set of 10 topics of interest based on their diversity and the amount of data available. Table 10.1 is a reminder on the selected newsgroups labels and the amount of data you are working with.

Table 10.1   A reminder on the data from the 20 Newsgroups dataset used for topic analysis

Topic	Training size	Test size	Topic	Training size	Test size
comp.windows.x	593	395	rec.sport.hockey	600	399
misc.forsale	585	390	sci.crypt	595	396
rec.autos	594	396	sci.med	594	396
rec.motorcycles	598	398	sci.space	593	394
rec.sport.baseball	597	397	talk.politics.mideast	564	376

Recall that scikit-learn's interface to the dataset allows you to easily choose which topic labels you want to work with and which subsets of data to consider. In particular, the dataset is already split into training and test sets. Recall that when you are working with a *supervised learning algorithm* (e.g., the one that you used for *topic classification* in the previous chapter), it is important that you train the algorithm on the training data and evaluate it on the test data. Since scikit-learn already provides you with predefined subsets, it is easy to compare your results across multiple implementations, your own as well as those from the others. At the same time, such *unsupervised approaches* as clustering applied in the previous chapter and LDA that you are going to implement in this chapter do not make any special use of the training versus test data; in fact, they are agnostic to the particular labels that may already exist in the data and aim to identify useful groups in the data by themselves. This means that you can use the whole dataset (i.e., both training and test sets combined) to build an unsupervised model.

Listing 10.1 shows you how to access the data via scikit-learn, restricting yourself to specific topic labels from the 20 Newsgroups dataset but not to specific subsets. To start with, you import sklearn's functionality that allows you to access the 20 Newsgroups dataset and define the `load_dataset` function, which takes the subset and categories list as arguments and returns the data extracted according to these restrictions. In addition, it allows you to remove extra information (e.g., headers and footers). Then you define the list of categories to extract from the data. This list contains the same categories as you've worked with before but note that you can always change the selection of labels to your own preferred list. When you run the `load_dataset`, use `all` as the first argument to access both training and test sets. Finally, you can access the uploaded posts applying the `.data` method to `newsgroups_all`, and, as a sanity check, print out the number of posts using `len`.

Listing 10.1 Code to access the Newsgroups data on specific topics

Define the load_dataset function to return the data extracted according to predefined restrictions.

Import sklearn's functionality that allows you to access the 20 Newsgroups dataset.

```
from sklearn.datasets import fetch_20newsgroups

def load_dataset(sset, cats):
    if cats==[]:
        newsgroups_dset = fetch_20newsgroups(subset=sset,
                          remove=('headers', 'footers', 'quotes'),
                          shuffle=True)
    else:
        newsgroups_dset = fetch_20newsgroups(subset=sset, categories=cats,
                          remove=('headers', 'footers', 'quotes'),
                          shuffle=True)
    return newsgroups_dset


categories = ["comp.windows.x", "misc.forsale", "rec.autos"]
categories += ["rec.motorcycles", "rec.sport.baseball", "rec.sport.hockey"]
categories += ["sci.crypt", "sci.med", "sci.space"]
categories += ["talk.politics.mideast"]

newsgroups_all = load_dataset('all', categories)
print(len(newsgroups_all.data))
```

Define the list of categories to extract from the data.

Access the uploaded posts applying the .data method to newsgroups_all; check the number of posts using len.

To access both training and test sets, use "all" as the first argument.

The code should extract all posts on the predefined list of categories (labels), both from the training and test subsets, and as a result you should get 9,850 posts in `newsgroups_all`. This is what should be printed out by the code. As a reminder, there are 5,913 posts in these categories in the training set and 3,937 in the test set. You can also check these numbers against table 10.1.

10.2.2 *Preprocessing the data*

The data loaded so far contains whole posts, and your task is to identify topics in these posts. Since LDA works with words or tokens of similar granularity, your first task is to tokenize the posts (i.e., extract word tokens from them). Once the text is split into words, you need to consider the questions from exercise 10.2.

Exercise 10.2

Like any unsupervised NLP algorithm, LDA relies on the information it can learn observing the occurrences and patterns in the use of words or tokens of similar granularity in the documents. This means that the complexity and computation time of the algorithm increase with the number of words or tokens considered. At the same time, not all tokens are equally useful and filtering them out may improve the algorithm's efficiency without doing harm to its performance.

Try answering the following questions about the selection of data and features (solution can be found at the end of this chapter):

1   Should your features include words, word lemmas, or word stems?
2   How can you reduce the dimensionality of the considered feature space further (i.e., can some words or tokens be filtered out)?

Listing 10.2 shows how to preprocess texts for your topic-modeling application. In particular, it uses a stemming algorithm called SnowballStemmer, which provides you with a good intermediate level of granularity. It helps the algorithm efficiency by reducing the word space to a higher extent than lemmatization, and at the same time it is less "aggressive" in merging words together than some other stemming algorithms (for comparison, you can look at the outputs of different stemmers; see www.nltk.org/howto/stem.html for some examples). This stemmer implementation is available via the NLTK toolkit, which you have extensively used before for other tasks. At the same time, listing 10.2 calls on a new toolkit, gensim, that you haven't used before.

So far, you have gained experience using two NLP toolkits, namely NLTK and spaCy. We've noted before that it is good to know of the wide range of opportunities in the field, and often, when you want to develop some new application of your own, you would find that the building blocks for this application (e.g., certain preprocessing tools) are readily available. You might have also noticed that, in some respects, these toolkits have comparable functionality (e.g., both can be used to do tokenization), while in other respects they may have complementary strengths (e.g., NLTK, unlike spaCy, has access to a number of various stemmers). It is time, therefore, to add another NLP toolkit—gensim—to your tool belt (for installation instructions, see https://radimrehurek.com/gensim/).

Gensim

Gensim is an NLP toolkit particularly suitable for various tasks related to topic modeling and the analysis of word meaning. In this chapter, you will learn how to use LDA functionality available via this toolkit.

Just like the other toolkits, gensim includes a number of useful preprocessing functions, some of which are used in listing 10.2. Specifically, you need to import SnowballStemmer from NLTK, and `simple_preprocess` functionality and stopwords list from gensim. `SnowballStemmer` supports several different languages, so you need to invoke the English version of the `stemmer` (other functions from NLTK and gensim are applicable to English by default). Next, you define a function `stem` that takes a word as an input and returns its stem as an output. `Simple_preprocess` functionality allows you to do several useful things at once (see detailed documentation at http://mng.bz/wo8q): it converts input text to lowercase, splits it into tokens, and returns only the tokens that are longer than `min_len` characters, which is set to 4 characters (inclusive) here. Finally, you iterate through the tokens, and if a token is not in the stopwords list, you apply the stemming algorithm to it and add the resulting stem to the output stored in `result`.

> **NOTE** The "magic" number of 4 here is based on the widely recognized observation that many frequent and not topically specific words are short (i.e., about 3 characters in length). Such are, for example, common abbreviations like *lol*, *omg*, and so on. At the same time, they are unlikely to be captured by most stopwords lists.

Listing 10.2 Code to preprocess the data using NLTK and gensim

```
import nltk
import gensim                                    Import SnowballStemmer
from nltk.stem import SnowballStemmer            from nltk.
from gensim.utils import simple_preprocess       From gensim, import the
from gensim.parsing.preprocessing \             simple_preprocess functionality
import STOPWORDS as stopwords                    and stopwords list.

stemmer = SnowballStemmer("english")            Use the English version
                                                of the stemmer.
def stem(text):
    return stemmer.stem(text)                   Define a function stem that takes
                                                a word as an input and returns
def preprocess(text):                           its stem as an output.
    result = []
    for token in gensim.utils.simple_preprocess(
        text, min_len=4):                       The simple_preprocess
        if token not in stopwords:              functionality allows you
            result.append(stem(token))          to do several useful
    return result                               things at once.

        If a token is not in the stopwords list,
     apply stemming and add the stem to result.
```

Let's see what effect this preprocessing step has on a specific document. The following listing applies the `preprocess` function to the first document from your selected newsgroups collection and prints the preprocessing result next to the original document.

Listing 10.3   Code to inspect the results of the preprocessing step

```
doc_sample = newsgroups_all.data[0]
print('Original document: ')
print(doc_sample)

print('\n\nTokenized document: ')
words = []
for token in gensim.utils.tokenize(doc_sample):
    words.append(token)
print(words)

print('\n\nPreprocessed document: ')
print(preprocess(doc_sample))
```

⊲ **Extract a specific original document from the collection (e.g., the first one at index 0).**

⊲ **Print out the original document as is.**

⊲ **Check the output of the gensim's tokenizer, which is produced by gensim.utils.tokenize.**

⊲ **Check the output of the preprocess function defined in listing 10.2.**

Here is what this code will produce for the first document from newsgroups_all:

```
Original document:
Hi Xperts!

How can I move the cursor with the keyboard (i.e. cursor keys),
if no mouse is available?

Any hints welcome.

Thanks.

Tokenized document:
['Hi', 'Xperts', 'How', 'can', 'I', 'move', 'the', 'cursor', 'with', 'the',
'keyboard', 'i', 'e', 'cursor', 'keys', 'if', 'no', 'mouse', 'is',
'available', 'Any', 'hints', 'welcome', 'Thanks']

Preprocessed document:
['xpert', 'cursor', 'keyboard', 'cursor', 'key', 'mous', 'avail', 'hint',
'welcom', 'thank']
```

You can observe the following: the original text contains over 30 word tokens, including punctuation marks. Gensim's tokenizer splits input text by whitespaces and punctuation marks, returning individual word tokens *excluding* punctuation marks as a result. (Gensim's tokenizer is part of the gensim.utils group of functions; see the description at https://radimrehurek.com/gensim/utils.html.) Finally, the preprocess function does several things at the same time: it tokenizes input text internally, converts all word tokens into lowercase, excludes not only punctuation marks but also stopwords and words shorter than 4 characters in length (thus, for example, removing "i" and "e", which come from "i.e.", often not covered by stopwords lists), and finally, outputs stems of the remaining word tokens. Figure 10.11 visualizes how this preprocessing step extracts the content from the original document, efficiently reducing the dimensionality of the original space.

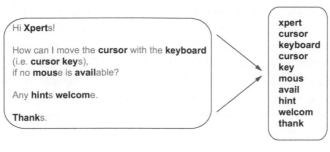

Figure 10.11 The `Preprocess` function allows you to considerably reduce the dimensionality of your original feature space. It converts all words to lowercase; removes punctuation marks, stopwords, and words shorter than 4 characters; and outputs a list of stems for the remaining words.

You can also check how a particular set of documents is represented after the preprocessing steps are applied to the original texts. The following listing shows how to extract the preprocessed output from the first 10 documents in the collection.

Listing 10.4   Code to inspect the preprocessing output for a group of documents

Iterate through the documents, such as through the list of the first 10 ones.

Print out each document's index followed by the list of up to 10 first stems from this document.

```
for i in range(0, 10):
    print(str(i) + "\t" + ", ".join(preprocess(newsgroups_all.data[i])[:10]))
```

The code from this listing outputs the following lists of stems for the first 10 documents in your collection:

```
0    xpert, cursor, keyboard, cursor, key, mous, avail, hint, welcom, thank
1    obtain, copi, open, look, widget, obtain, need, order, copi, thank
2    right, signal, strong, live, west, philadelphia, perfect, sport, fan, dream
3    canadian, thing, coach, boston, bruin, colorado, rocki, summari, post, gather
4    heck, feel, like, time, includ, cafeteria, work, half, time, headach
5    damn, right, late, climb, meet, morn, bother, right, foot, asleep
6    olympus, stylus, pocket, camera, smallest, class, includ, time, date, stamp
7    includ, follow, chmos, clock, generat, driver, processor, chmos, eras, prom
8    chang, intel, discov, xclient, xload, longer, work, bomb, messag, error
9    termin, like, power, server, run, window, manag, special, client, program
```

As you can see, each document is concisely summarized by a list of meaningful words. Can you tell which topic each document is on?

Now, since the LDA algorithm relies on word (or stem) occurrences to detect topics in documents, you need to make sure that the same word occurrences across documents can be easily and efficiently detected by the algorithm. For instance, if two documents contain the same words (e.g., *program, server,* and *processor*), there is a high chance they are on the same topic. The most suitable data structure to use in this case is a *dictionary*, where each word is mapped to a unique identifier. This way, the algorithm can detect which identifiers (words) occur in which documents and establish the similarity between documents efficiently. In fact, you have used this idea in several previous applications.

Listing 10.5 shows how to convert the full set of words occurring in the documents in your collection into a dictionary, where each word is mapped to a unique identifier, using the `gensim` functionality. You start by preprocessing all documents in your collection using the function `preprocess`, defined in listing 10.2. Then you check the length of the resulting structure. This should be equal to the number of documents you have (i.e., 9,850). After that, you extract a dictionary of terms from all processed documents, `processed_docs`, using `gensim.corpora.Dictionary` and check the size of the resulting dictionary (see the full documentation at http://mng.bz/XZX1). Finally, you check what is stored in this dictionary; for example, you can iterate through the first 10 items, printing out `key` (the unique identifier of a word stem) and `value` (the stem itself).

Listing 10.5   Code to convert word content of the documents into a dictionary

```
processed_docs = []
for i in range(0, len(newsgroups_all.data)):      ← Preprocess all documents in
    processed_docs.append(preprocess(               your collection using the function
        newsgroups_all.data[i]))                    preprocess defined in listing 10.2.

print(len(processed_docs))                        ← Check the length of the
                                                    resulting structure.

dictionary = gensim.corpora.Dictionary(processed_docs)
print(len(dictionary))                            ← Extract a dictionary of terms from
                                                    all processed documents using
index = 0                                           gensim.corpora.Dictionary.
for key, value in dictionary.iteritems():
    print(key, value)
    index += 1                    Check what is stored in
    if index > 9:                 this dictionary (e.g., iterate
        break         ←           through the first 10 items).
```

The code prints out the following output:

```
9850
39350

0 avail
1 cursor
2 hint
3 key
4 keyboard
5 mous
6 thank
7 welcom
8 xpert
9 copi
```

Exercise 10.3

How can you interpret this output? How are the word stems mapped to unique identifiers? (Solution can be found at the end of this chapter.)

Figure 10.12 visualizes how the original content of the first document is converted into a succinct summary containing only the meaningful word stems after all preprocessing steps.

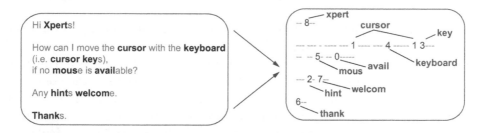

Figure 10.12   As a result of all preprocessing steps, the content of the original document is summarized by a selected set of meaningful word stems. As the visualization of the end result on the right shows, each selected word stem is represented with its unique identifier, and all the other words are filtered out.

Unfortunately, the dictionary that you end up with as a result of this step still contains a relatively high number of items—over 39,000—which would result in your algorithm being quite slow. Fortunately, there are more steps you can apply to reduce the dimensionality. For instance, as discussed in exercise 10.2, you can apply some cutoff thresholds, removing very frequent words and very rare ones, since none of these extremities are likely to help topic modeling. Listing 10.6 shows how to use the gensim functionality to first filter out the extremes (the words below and above certain frequency thresholds) and then convert each document into a convenient representation where the counts for each word from the dictionary are stored in tuples next to the word stem IDs. Specifically, in this code, you use dictionary.filter_extremes to discard word stems that occur in fewer than no_below=10 documents and in more than no_above=50% of the total number of documents in your collection (see documentation at http://mng.bz/XZX1). If the resulting number is over 10,000 word stems, you keep only the most frequent keep_n=10000 of them. Then you convert each document in the collection into a list of tuples, where the occurring word stem IDs are mapped to the number of their occurrences. In the end, you can check how a particular document is represented.

Listing 10.6   Code to perform further dimensionality reduction on the documents

```
dictionary.filter_extremes(no_below=10, no_above=0.5, keep_n=10000)
print(len(dictionary))
```
First, discard very rare and very frequent word stems; then keep only keep_n most frequent of the rest.

```
bow_corpus = [dictionary.doc2bow(doc) for doc in processed_docs]
print(bow_corpus[0])
```
Convert each document in the collection into a list of tuples and check the output.

The code produces the following output:

```
5868

[(0, 1), (1, 2), (2, 1), (3, 1), (4, 1), (5, 1), (6, 1), (7, 1), (8, 1)]
```

This means that after the "extremes"—word stems occurring in fewer than 10 and in more than 50% of the original collection of 9,850 documents—have been filtered out, you are left with 5,868 items (word stems) in the `dictionary`. This is a much more compact space than the original 39,350. If you print out the contents of the first document (the one that you've looked at in listing 10.3 and figure 10.11), you can see that the filtering step didn't remove any of the word stems from this document, as they happen to not be within any of the "extremes." In particular, the output like `[(0, 1), (1, 2), (2, 1), . . .]` tells you that the dictionary item with `id=0` occurs 1 time in this document, `id=1` occurs 2 times, `id=2` occurs 1 time, and so on. Since after filtering the "extreme" items out the dictionary IDs returned by the code from listing 10.5 might have been overwritten (i.e., if a word stem is filtered out from the dictionary because it falls within one or another extreme, its ID is reused for the next word stem that is kept in the dictionary), it is useful to check which word stems are behind particular IDs. Listing 10.7 shows how to do that. You start by extracting a particular document from `bow_corpus` (e.g., the first one here). Then you print out the IDs, the corresponding word stems (extracted from `dictionary`), and the number of occurrences of these word stems in this document extracted from `bow_corpus`.

> **Listing 10.7 Code to check word stems behind IDs from the dictionary**

```
bow_doc = bow_corpus[0]        ◁——┐ Extract a particular document
                                   │ from bow_corpus
for i in range(len(bow_doc)):
    print(f"Key {bow_doc[i][0]} =\"{dictionary[bow_doc[i][0]]}\":\
    occurrences={bow_doc[i][1]}")   ◁——┐ Print out the IDs, corresponding
                                        │ word stems, and the number of
                                        │ occurrences of these word stems.
```

This code prints out the following output, which should be familiar to you now since you've already seen in figure 10.11 what word stems the first document contains:

```
Key 0 ="avail":      occurrences=1
Key 1 ="cursor":     occurrences=2
Key 2 ="hint":       occurrences=1
Key 3 ="key":        occurrences=1
Key 4 ="keyboard":   occurrences=1
Key 5 ="mous":       occurrences=1
Key 6 ="thank":      occurrences=1
Key 7 ="welcom":     occurrences=1
Key 8 ="xpert":      occurrences=1
```

Note you can inspect any document using this code. For instance, to check the content of the 100th document in your collection, all you need to do is access `bow_doc = bow_corpus[99]` in the first line of code in listing 10.7.

10.2.3 Applying the LDA model

Now that the data is preprocessed and converted to the right format, let's run the LDA algorithm and detect topics in your collection of documents from the 20 Newsgroups dataset. With gensim, it is quite easy to do and running the algorithm is just a matter of setting a number of parameters. Listing 10.8 shows how to do that. You start by initializing `id2word` to the `dictionary` where each word stem is mapped to a unique ID. Then you initialize `corpus` to the `bow_corpus` that you created earlier. This data structure keeps the information on the stem occurrence and frequency across all documents in the collection. Next, you initialize `lda_model` to the LDA implementation from gensim (see the full documentation and description of all arguments and methods applicable to the model at https://radimrehurek.com/gensim/models/ldamodel.html). This model requires a number of arguments, which are explicitly specified in this code. Let's go through them one by one.

First, you provide the model with `corpus` and `id2word` initialized earlier in this code. Since you have a bit of an insight into the data (specifically, you have extracted the data from 10 labeled topics), it is reasonable to ask the algorithm to find `num_topics=10`. In addition, if you would like to get the same results every time you run the code, set `random_state` to some number (e.g., 100 here). You also need to specify how often the algorithm should update its topic distributions (e.g., after each document with `update_every=1`), and, for efficiency reasons, you should train it over smaller bits of data than the whole dataset (e.g., over chunks of 1,000 documents with `chunksize=1000`), passing through training `passes=10` times. Next, with `alpha='symmetric'`, you make sure that topics are initialized in a fair way, and with `iterations=100`, you put an upper bound on the total number of iterations through the data. Finally, `per_word_topics` ensures that you learn word-per-topic as well as topic-per-document distributions. In the end, you print out the results: use `-1` as an argument to `print_topics` to output all topics in the data, and for each of them, print out its index and the most informative words identified for the topic.

Listing 10.8 Code to run the LDA algorithm on your documents

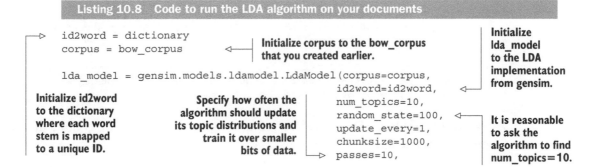

```
id2word = dictionary
corpus = bow_corpus

lda_model = gensim.models.ldamodel.LdaModel(corpus=corpus,
                                            id2word=id2word,
                                            num_topics=10,
                                            random_state=100,
                                            update_every=1,
                                            chunksize=1000,
                                            passes=10,
```

Initialize corpus to the bow_corpus that you created earlier.

Initialize lda_model to the LDA implementation from gensim.

Initialize id2word to the dictionary where each word stem is mapped to a unique ID.

Specify how often the algorithm should update its topic distributions and train it over smaller bits of data.

It is reasonable to ask the algorithm to find num_topics=10.

Output all topics and for each of them print out its index and the most informative words identified.

```
                                            alpha='symmetric',
                                            iterations=100,
                                            per_word_topics=True)       ◁

for index, topic in lda_model.print_topics(-1):       Set up the remaining
    print(f"Topic: {index} \nWords: {topic}")                parameters.
```

The code produces the following output:

```
Topic: 0
Words: 0.021*"encrypt" + 0.018*"secur" + 0.018*"chip" + 0.016*"govern" +
    0.013*"clipper" + 0.012*"public" + 0.010*"privaci" + 0.010*"key" +
    0.010*"phone" + 0.009*"algorithm"
Topic: 1
Words: 0.017*"appear" + 0.014*"copi" + 0.013*"cover" + 0.013*"star" +
    0.013*"book" + 0.011*"penalti" + 0.010*"black" + 0.009*"comic" +
    0.008*"blue" + 0.008*"green"
Topic: 2
Words: 0.031*"window" + 0.015*"server" + 0.012*"program" + 0.012*"file" +
    0.012*"applic" + 0.012*"display" + 0.011*"widget" + 0.010*"version" +
    0.010*"motif" + 0.010*"support"
Topic: 3
Words: 0.015*"space" + 0.007*"launch" + 0.007*"year" + 0.007*"medic" +
    0.006*"patient" + 0.006*"orbit" + 0.006*"research" + 0.006*"diseas" +
    0.005*"develop" + 0.005*"nasa"
Topic: 4
Words: 0.018*"armenian" + 0.011*"peopl" + 0.008*"kill" + 0.008*"said" +
    0.007*"turkish" + 0.006*"muslim" + 0.006*"jew" + 0.006*"govern" +
    0.005*"state" + 0.005*"greek"
Topic: 5
Words: 0.024*"price" + 0.021*"sale" + 0.020*"offer" + 0.017*"drive" +
    0.017*"sell" + 0.016*"includ" + 0.013*"ship" + 0.013*"interest" +
    0.011*"ask" + 0.010*"condit"
Topic: 6
Words: 0.018*"mail" + 0.016*"list" + 0.015*"file" + 0.015*"inform" +
    0.013*"send" + 0.012*"post" + 0.012*"avail" + 0.010*"request" +
    0.010*"program" + 0.009*"includ"
Topic: 7
Words: 0.019*"like" + 0.016*"know" + 0.011*"time" + 0.011*"look" +
    0.010*"think" + 0.008*"want" + 0.008*"thing" + 0.008*"good" + 0.007*"go"
    + 0.007*"bike"
Topic: 8
Words: 0.033*"game" + 0.022*"team" + 0.017*"play" + 0.015*"year" +
    0.013*"player" + 0.011*"season" + 0.008*"hockey" + 0.008*"score" +
    0.007*"leagu" + 0.007*"goal"
Topic: 9
Words: 0.013*"peopl" + 0.012*"think" + 0.011*"like" + 0.009*"time" +
    0.009*"right" + 0.009*"israel" + 0.009*"know" + 0.006*"reason" +
    0.006*"point" + 0.006*"thing"
```

Figure 10.13 visualizes this output for the first topics, listing the top 3 most highly weighted words in each for brevity.

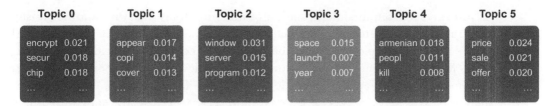

Figure 10.13   The output from listing 10.8. For brevity, only the first 6 topics with their top 3 most informative words are included.

In this output, each topic with its unique ID (since you are using an unsupervised approach, this algorithm cannot assign the labels, so it returns IDs) is mapped with a set of most informative words that help the algorithm associate documents with this specific topic. For instance, the first topic `Topic 0` is characterized by such word stems as `encrypt` (for *encryption, encrypted,* etc.), `secur` (for *secure, security,* etc.) and `chip`; the third topic `Topic 2` can be identified by the word stems like `window` (as in *Windows*), `server`, `program`, and so on. Note that the numerical values included in front of the word stems show the relative weight of each word in the topic (or its probability score), and the + sign suggests that the topic is composed of all these words in the specified proportion. Now let's attempt exercise 10.4.

> ### Exercise 10.4
> You have originally used the data on the following categories: [`comp.windows.x`, `misc.forsale`, `rec.autos`, `rec.motorcycles`, `rec.sport.baseball`, `rec.sport .hockey`, `sci.crypt`, `sci.med`, `sci.space`, `talk.politics.mideast`]. Based on the most informative words in each topic returned by the algorithm from listing 10.8, can you assign each topic ID with a topic label from this original list?

Let's discuss this exercise together. To begin with, this exercise should remind you of exercise 9.7, where you tried to interpret the clusters as topics based on the most informative words within each identified cluster. Let's use a copy of table 9.6 here (table 10.2) to interpret the topics identified by LDA and map them to the clusters from chapter 9 on the one hand and to the labels from the 20 Newsgroups dataset on the other.

Table 10.2   Possible topic labels for the identified topics

Label	Cluster	Topic	Label	Cluster	Topic
`comp.windows.x`	4	2, 6	`rec.sport.hockey`	2	8
`misc.forsale`	3(?), 5, 7	5, 7(?)	`sci.crypt`	0	0, 6(?)
`rec.autos`	6	7	`sci.med`	1	3
`rec.motorcycles`	6	7	`sci.space`	8	3
`rec.sport.baseball`	2	8	`talk.politics.mideast`	3(?), 9	4, 9

As you can see from the interpretation of the output, just like with another unsupervised approach, clustering, implemented in the last chapter, the LDA algorithm comes up with a topic allocation that does not necessarily coincide with the topic labels from the original dataset. Some original topics (e.g., `rec.sport.baseball` and `rec.sport.hockey`), appear to be merged into one topic, `Topic 8`. At the same time, such topics as `talk.politics.mideast` and `misc.forsale` are split into multiple groups. Note that you've got a similar result from the clustering algorithm, which also split these topics into two clusters each. This shows that there might truly be quite diverse subtopics discussed under both titles, and they perhaps shouldn't be thought of as single homogeneous topics. However, there is something new that is discovered by the LDA algorithm in the data, which was not observed in the clustering output. First, it seems like `sci.med` and `sci.space` correspond to a single topic, `Topic 3`. Since both topics are science-related (note that they both come from the `sci.` thread), the algorithm identifies their internal similarities. Second, the LDA algorithm identifies `Topic 1`, characterized by such word stems as `copi` (as in *copies*), `book`, and `comic`. This is a novel discovery in the data, encompassing documents that potentially cover a yet unidentified topic related to books. Figure 10.14 summarizes the topics discovered by LDA and maps them, where possible, to the labels from the 20 Newsgroups data.

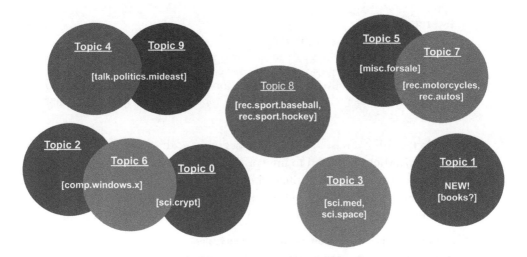

Figure 10.14   Summary of the topics discovered by the LDA algorithm with the labels from the 20 Newsgroups dataset assigned to the identified topics, where possible

10.2.4 Exploring the results

Given that you are working with an unsupervised algorithm, it may be hard to interpret the results in a precise, quantitative way. In this section, you'll be looking into several approaches to results exploration.

We've said earlier in this chapter that the LDA algorithm interprets each document as a mixture of topics. It is, in fact, possible to measure the contribution of the topics and, in particular, identify the main contributing topic for each document together with its most informative words. Listing 10.9 does exactly that. In this code, you first define the function `analyse_topics`, which takes as input the LDA model, the word-frequency-per-document structure from the `corpus`, and the original collection of `texts`. This function returns as output the main topic for each document (stored in `main_topic`), contribution of this topic to the mixture of topics in the document (stored in `percentage`), the most informative words (stored in `keywords`), and the original word stems from the document (in `text_snippets`). Then, for each document in the collection (`corpus`), you extract the most probable topic mixture identified by LDA as `topic_list[0]`, sort the topics from the most probable to the least probable using `sorted(..., reverse=True)` applied to the topic probability score stored in field `x[1]`, and extract the most probable topic from the resulting interpretation (see https://docs.python.org/3/howto/sorting.html on sorting with a lambda expression). It can be identified as the first item in the sorted list (thus, the identifier `j=0`), and it corresponds to a tuple (topic id, topic proportion). Next, you extract topic keywords using the `show_topic` functionality (check documentation at https://radimrehurek.com/gensim/models/ldamodel.html) and store the main topic ID (`topic_num`), topic contribution as percentage rounded up to 4 digits after the decimal point (`prop_topic`), the first 5 most informative topic keywords (`topic_keywords`), and a list of up to 8 word stems from the original text (the limit of 8 is chosen for readability purposes only). Finally, you apply the `analyse_topic` function to the dataset and store the results.

Listing 10.9 Code to identify the main topic for each document in the collection

Return the main topic, its contribution, the most
informative words, and the original word stems.

analyse_topics takes as input
the LDA model, corpus, and the
original collection of texts.

```
def analyse_topics(ldamodel, corpus, texts):
    main_topic = {}
    percentage = {}
    keywords = {}
    text_snippets = {}

    for i, topic_list in enumerate(ldamodel[corpus]):
        topic = topic_list[0]
        topic = sorted(topic, key=lambda x: (
                    x[1]), reverse=True)
```

For each document in the
collection, extract the most
probable topic mixture and
sort the topics.

```
                for j, (topic_num, prop_topic) in enumerate(topic):
                    if j == 0:
                        wp = ldamodel.show_topic(topic_num)
                        topic_keywords = ", ".join([word for word, prop in wp[:5]])
                        main_topic[i] = int(topic_num)
                        percentage[i] = round(prop_topic,4)
                        keywords[i] = topic_keywords
                        text_snippets[i] = texts[i][:8]
                    else:
                        break
            return main_topic, percentage, keywords, text_snippets

    main_topic, percentage, keywords, text_snippets = analyse_topics(
        lda_model, bow_corpus, processed_docs)
```

Extract the most probable topic from the resulting interpretation.

Extract topic keywords using the show_topic functionality.

Apply the analyse_topic function to the dataset and store the results.

Store the main topic ID, its contribution, the most informative topic keywords, and a list of word stems.

Next, listing 10.10 shows how to print out the results for a specified range of documents using a convenient tabulated format.

Listing 10.10   Code to print out the main topic for each document in the collection

```
indexes = []
rows = []
for i in range(0, 10):
    indexes.append(i)
rows.append(['ID', 'Main Topic', 'Contribution (%)', 'Keywords', 'Snippet'])

for idx in indexes:
    rows.append([str(idx), f"{main_topic.get(idx)}",
                f"{percentage.get(idx):.4f}",
                f"{keywords.get(idx)}\n",
                f"{text_snippets.get(idx)}"])
columns = zip(*rows)
column_widths = [max(len(item) for item in col) for col in columns]
for row in rows:
    print(''.join(' {:{width}} '.format(row[i], width=column_widths[i])
                    for i in range(0, len(row))))
```

Extract the output for the first 10 documents for simplicity.

Use the familiar printout routine to print the results in a tabulated manner.

The code returns the output shown in table 10.3 for the first 10 documents in the collection ([...] is used to truncate the output for space reasons, and a table is used to make the output more readable). Note that you can always print the output for any specified number of documents, as well as return more than 5 most informative keywords per topic and more than 8 word stems from each document—just change these settings in listing 10.9.

Table 10.3   Output printed out by the code from listing 10.10

ID	Main topic	Contribution (%)	Keywords	Snippet
0	2	0.8268	window, server, program, file, applic	['xpert', 'cursor', 'keyboard', 'cursor', 'key', 'mous', 'avail', 'hint']
1	6	0.4742	mail, list, file, inform, send	['obtain', 'copi', 'open', 'look', 'widget', 'obtain', 'need', 'order']
[...]				
3	8	0.4159	game, team, play, year, player	['canadian', 'thing', 'coach', 'boston', 'bruin', 'colorado', 'rocki', 'summari']
[...]				
9	2	0.6383	window, server, program, file, applic	['termin', 'like', 'power', 'server', 'run', 'window', 'manag', 'special']

As this output suggests, both the first and the tenth documents are on Topic 2, characterized by such keywords as server, program, and file (you can also see from the text snippets why these documents may be topically related). At the same time, document 3 is on a topic related to sports, as is exemplified by such keywords as game, team, and play.

Finally, we've started this chapter with the discussion on the LDA model saying that this is a unique model that allows you to investigate the interplay between words and topics in the documents. So far, your analysis of the results didn't allow you to appreciate the full extent of the model predictions. Luckily, there are a number of helpful visualization tools developed around this model, one of which is particularly useful for the analysis—pyLDAvis (available at https://github.com/bmabey/pyLDAvis). Install it following the instructions prior to running the code from listing 10.11. This tool provides you with an interactive interface to the LDA output, where you can explore both the topic distribution per documents in your collection and word distribution per topic, which is very useful when you try to interpret the output of the LDA model. You can run this tool and visualize the results directly in the Jupyter Notebook, or you can save the results in an external HTML file.

Listing 10.11 introduces the use of this tool in a concise piece of code. You start by importing pyLDAvis functionality (for newer versions of the tools, use import pyLDAvis.gensim_models) and making sure that the results can be visualized within the notebook. To apply the visualization tool, you'll need to pass in the LDA model, the data with the word occurrences in corpus, and the mapping between word stems and their IDs from id2word as arguments (for newer versions of the tools, use pyLDAvis.gensim_models.prepare(...)). Finally, you can run the visualization and inspect the results in the notebook.

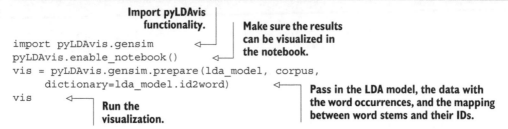

Listing 10.11   Code to visualize the output of LDA using pyLDAvis

```
import pyLDAvis.gensim              ◁─── Import pyLDAvis functionality.
pyLDAvis.enable_notebook()          ◁─── Make sure the results can be visualized in the notebook.
vis = pyLDAvis.gensim.prepare(lda_model, corpus,
    dictionary=lda_model.id2word)   ◁─── Pass in the LDA model, the data with the word occurrences, and the mapping between word stems and their IDs.
vis                                  ◁─── Run the visualization.
```

This code produces an interactive visualization of the words and topics, which you can directly explore in your notebook. The topics are represented as bubbles of the size relative to their distribution in the data (in addition, bubbles representing similar topics are located closer to each other in the space on the left), and the word stem list on the right shows contribution of each stem to each topic. You can hover your mouse over both the topics on the left, exploring word contribution to the topic, and over the words on the right, exploring word membership within various topics.

For instance, figure 10.15 visualizes word composition for a specific topic, denoted as Topic 9, which can be interpreted as a sales topic. It contains words like price, sale, offer, and so on. At the same time, the chart on the right makes it clear that sale contributes to this topic fully, while price is almost fully associated with this topic, and words like good and work contribute to this topic only partially, since they probably are widely used elsewhere.

How can you check where the rest of the word "weight" goes? If you hover over the words in the chart on the right, it will show you the topic membership for the words, highlighting the relevant topic bubbles. For instance, figure 10.16 shows that the word game (highlighted in bold) is associated with two topics—one related to sales and another to sports. Finally, if you'd like to explore other visualization techniques for topic modeling, the following post may provide you with further ideas: http://mng.bz/qYgw.

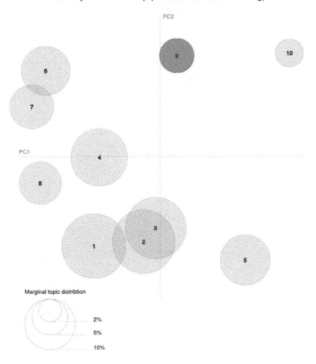

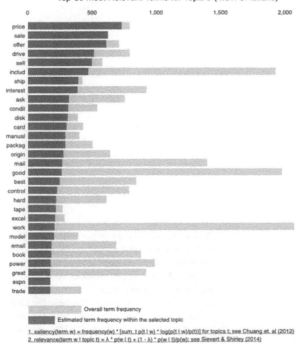

Figure 10.15 Topic 9, visualized with a bubble on the left, is composed of all the words that are highlighted in the list on the right. From these words' composition, you can tell that Topic 9 here corresponds to sales. The words are ordered by their relative contribution to the topic (e.g., price and sale are the main contributors, and most of their use corresponds to the documents on sales). At the same time, good contributes to this topic, but, as the chart shows, it is also used elsewhere.

Intertopic Distance Map (via multidimensional scaling)

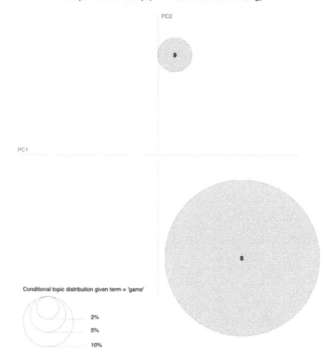

Top-30 Most Salient Terms [1]

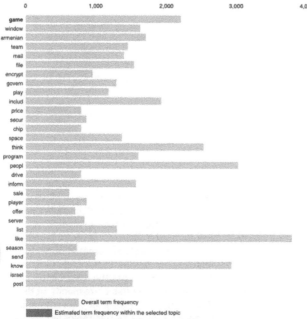

Figure 10.16 The word game is associated with two topics. When you hover over it on the right, two topic bubbles are highlighted on the left—Topic 9 associated with anything sales-related, and Topic 5 associated with sports. The relative size of the bubbles tells you that game is much more strongly associated with the sports in Topic 5.

Summary

- Topic analysis as addressed within the unsupervised paradigm allows the applied algorithm to explore the data and identify interesting correspondences without any regard to predefined labels.

- Latent Dirichlet allocation (LDA) is a widely used unsupervised approach for topic modeling. This approach treats each document as a mixture of topics and allows you to explore both document composition in terms of topics and topic composition in terms of words. If you'd like to learn more about this insightful algorithm, check David Blei's home page at http://www.cs.columbia.edu/~blei/topicmodeling.html, and take a look at his paper on Probabilistic Topic Models here: http://www.cs.columbia.edu/~blei/papers/Blei2012.pdf.

- LDA is a generative model. It assumes that each document is generated by an abstract generative process, which first selects an appropriate topic according to topic distribution and then picks words from this topic according to the word distribution per topic.

- The topic structure, including the topics themselves, their distributions in documents, and word-to-topic assignments, is a latent (i.e., hidden) structure, thus the name of the algorithm. It is estimated and adjusted on the basis of the only observed parameter—words in documents.

- Word distribution and topic distribution are the two fundamental blocks in the algorithm. The algorithm tries to estimate them directly from the data.

- Gensim is another useful NLP toolkit. It is particularly suitable for all tasks around word meaning and topic modeling.

- Using gensim, you can not only preprocess textual data but also apply an LDA model. As a result, this algorithm may help you discover new topics in the data.

- As is common with unsupervised approaches, the results may be hard to evaluate quantitatively. pyLDAvis is an interactive visualization toolkit for topic modeling interpretation, which allows you to explore topic composition in terms of words and word membership in terms of topics.

Solutions to miscellaneous exercises

Exercise 10.2

You have done feature selection and come across dimensionality reduction in a number of previous applications. Often, this process relies on your intuition or observations on the task and the data. Alternatively, you can run some preliminary experiments to figure out what the best settings for a specific algorithm would be. The following are reasonable choices for this scenario:

1 The choice you are given is between considering each word form (e.g., *car* and *cars*, *welcome* and *welcoming*) as a separate feature or converting every word form to its dictionary version (i.e., lemma), which will merge *car* and *cars* into a single

representation *car*, or extracting the core of each word form (stem), thus merging some words and lemmas even further. For instance, this will result in both *welcome* and *welcoming* to be represented as welcom. (This is a reminder of the differences between lemmas and lemmatization and between stems and stemming, discussed in chapter 3.) This means that the solution that results in the larger number of features is the one that relies on full word forms; however, there is often no topic-related difference between *car* and *cars* or *sell* and *sells*. In practice, for algorithms that quickly increase in complexity with the number of features, it is better to consider lemmatization or stemming. Stemming produces a more condensed feature space as compared to lemmatization; thus it would make the algorithm more efficient. The downside may be that, depending on the data, it might occasionally merge topically different words into a single representation.

2 You may consider any or all of the following strategies:

-   Remove stopwords since they usually do not bear any topic-related meaning (e.g., *not, of, a*).
-   Remove any other words that are likely to not bear any topic-related meaning even if they are not covered by a particular stopwords list. Often such words are short ones (e.g., various abbreviations like *lol* or *omg*).
-   Remove extremely rare words, as they might not occur in any further documents.
-   Remove very frequent words. Just like stopwords, they are unlikely to distinguish between topics (e.g., *post*, which might be used in a wide range of posts in the newsgroups data).

Exercise 10.3

The first line simply tells you that all 9,850 documents from the original collection have been successfully preprocessed and stored in the processed_docs list. The number of word stems in the dictionary is printed next; it equals 39,350. Finally, you can see a list of the first 10 word stems from the created dictionary, where each identifier is mapped uniquely to a stem. For instance, the first document that you looked into in listing 10.3 and that was analyzed in figure 10.11 consists of the stems ['xpert', 'cursor', 'keyboard', 'cursor', 'key', 'mous', 'avail', 'hint', 'welcom', 'thank']. Note that there are 10 stems altogether; however, cursor occurs in this list twice. When gensim converts the lists of words from each document into a single dictionary, it does two things: (1) each word can map to only a single identifier, so that multiple occurrences of the same word are mapped to the same identifier, and (2) the words are ordered alphabetically. If you wanted to manually convert ['xpert', 'cursor', 'keyboard', 'cursor', 'key', 'mous', 'avail', 'hint', 'welcom', 'thank'] into a dictionary of terms using this strategy, you would first sort the words alphabetically as in ['avail', 'cursor', 'cursor', 'hint', 'key', 'keyboard', 'mous', 'thank', 'welcom', 'xpert']; then you would remove duplicates; and finally, you would assign unique identifiers to each word stem as in [0='avail', 1='cursor', 2='hint', 3='key', 4='keyboard', 5='mous', 6='thank', 7='welcom', 8='xpert']. This is precisely the output that you are getting from listing 10.5. Once the algorithm is finished with document 1, it moves on to the next document, applies the same procedure, and appends the other unique words to the dictionary. For instance, you see that key 9 corresponds to the word stem copi, which comes from the second document (you can see this word stem in the output from listing 10.4).

Named-entity recognition 11

This chapter covers

- Introducing named-entity recognition (NER)
- Overviewing sequence labeling approaches in NLP
- Integrating NER into downstream tasks
- Introducing further data preprocessing tools and techniques

Previous chapters overviewed a number of NLP tasks, from binary classification tasks, such as author identification and sentiment analysis, to multiclass classification tasks, such as topic analysis. These applications deployed machine-learning models and relied on a range of linguistic features, most often related to words or word characteristics. While it is true that individual words express information useful in the context of many NLP applications, often the information-bearing unit is actually larger than a single word. In chapter 4, you looked into the task of information extraction. Remember that this task allows you to extract facts and relevant information from an otherwise unstructured data, such as raw, unprocessed text. This task is instrumental in a number of applications, from information management to database completion to question answering. For instance, suppose you have a collection of texts on various personalities, including the Wikipedia article on Albert Einstein (https://en.wikipedia.org/wiki/Albert_Einstein). Figure 11.1 shows a sentence from this article.

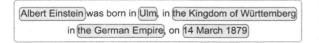

Figure 11.1 A sentence from the Wikipedia article on Albert Einstein with the critical information chunks (entities) highlighted

This single sentence provides you with answers to a whole range of questions, including

- *Who* was born in Ulm on 14 March 1879? [Albert Einstein]
- *Where* was Albert Einstein born? [in Ulm, in the Kingdom of Wurttemberg, in the German Empire]
- *Where* was Ulm located? [in the Kingdom of Wurttemberg, in the German Empire]
- *Where* was the Kingdom of Wurttemberg located? [in the German Empire]
- *When* was Albert Einstein born? [14 March 1879]

Note that the majority of these questions require groups of words rather than single words as an answer. For instance, answering *Albert* to "Who was born in Ulm on 14 March 1879?" or *14* to "When was Albert Einstein born?" would be unsatisfactory. This means that the algorithm extracting relevant information from this sentence needs to take into account the possibility that groups of words may represent a *single entity*: specifically, in this sentence such entities are "Albert Einstein," "Ulm," "the Kingdom of Wurttemberg," "the German Empire," and "14 March 1879," and each of them should be expected as a full answer to the relevant question.

In addition, you may note that the entities identified in the sentence are also of different *types*. For example, "Albert Einstein" is a *person* (so are also *Pope, Madonna, Harry Potter*, etc.), "14 March 1879" is a *date* (so are also 1879, March 1879, 14 March, etc.), and "Ulm," "the Kingdom of Wurttemberg," and "the German Empire" are *geopolitical entities*. Knowing the type of entity can also be used by the algorithm in such tasks as information extraction and question answering. For example, a question of the type *Who . . . ?* should be answered with an entity of the type person, *Where . . . ?* with a location or a geopolitical entity, and *When . . . ?* with a date, since violating these restrictions would produce nonsensical answers.

In this chapter, you will be working with the task of named-entity recognition (NER), concerned with detection and type identification of named entities (NEs). *Named entities* are real-world objects (people, locations, organizations) that can be referred to with a proper name. The most widely used entity types include *person, location* (abbreviated as LOC), *organization* (abbreviated as ORG), and *geopolitical entity* (abbreviated as GPE). You have already seen examples of some of these, and this chapter will discuss other types in the due course. In practice, the set of named entities is extended with further expressions such as dates, time references, numerical expressions (e.g., referring to money and currency indicators), and so on. Moreover, the types listed so far are quite general, but NER can also be adapted to other domains and application areas. For example, in biomedical applications, "entities" can denote different types of proteins and genes, in the financial domain they can cover specific types of products, and so on.

We will start this chapter with an overview of the named entity types and challenges involved in NER, and then we will discuss the approaches to NER adopted in practice. Specifically, such approaches rely on the use of machine-learning algorithms, but more importantly, they also take into account the sequential nature of language. Finally, you will learn how to apply NER in practice. Named entities play an important role in natural language understanding (you have already seen examples from question answering and information extraction) and can be combined with the tasks that you addressed earlier in this book. Such tasks, which rely on the output of NLP tools (e.g., NER models) are technically called *downstream tasks*, since they aim to solve a problem different from, say, NER itself, but at the same time they benefit from knowing about named entities in text. For instance, identifying entities related to people, locations, organizations, and products in reviews can help better understand users' or customers' sentiments toward particular aspects of the product or service.

To give you some examples, figure 11.2 illustrates the use of NER for two downstream tasks. In the context of *question answering*, NER helps to identify the chunks of text that can answer a specific type of a question. For example, named entities denoting locations (LOC), or geopolitical entities (GPE) are appropriate as answers for a *Where?* question. In the context of *information extraction*, NER can help identify useful

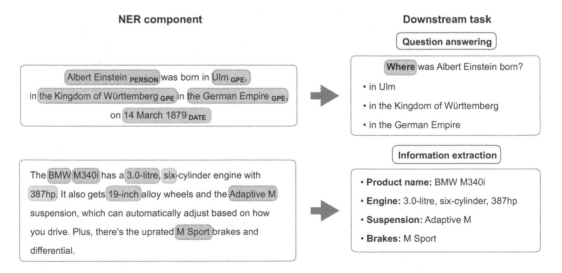

Figure 11.2   Downstream tasks relying on NER information: question answering (top) and information extraction (bottom)

characteristics of a product that may be informative on their own or as features in a sentiment analysis or another related task.

Another example of a downstream task in which NER plays a central role is stock market movement prediction. It is widely known that certain types of events influence the trends in stock price movements (for more examples and justification, see Ding et al. [2014], Using Structured Events to Predict Stock Price Movement: An Empirical Investigation, which you can access at https://aclanthology.org/D14-1148.pdf). For instance, the news about Steve Jobs's death negatively impacted Apple's stock price immediately after the event, while the news about Microsoft buying a new mobile phone business positively impacted its stock price. Suppose your goal is to build an application that can extract relevant facts from the news (e.g., "Apple's CEO died"; "Microsoft buys mobile phone business"; "Oracle sues Google") and then use these facts to predict stock prices for these companies. Figure 11.3 visualizes this idea.

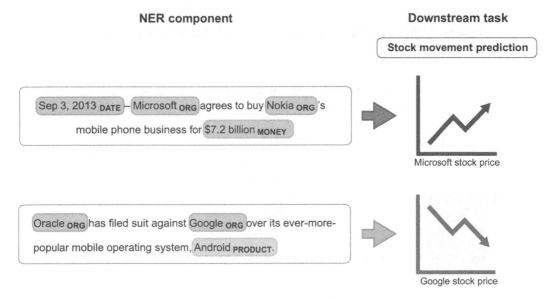

Figure 11.3 **Stock market prices movement prediction based on the events reported in the news**

Let's formulate a scenario for this downstream task. It is widely known that certain events influence the trends of stock price movements. Specifically, you can extract relevant facts from the news and then use these facts to predict company stock prices. Suppose you have access to a large collection of news; now your task is to extract the relevant events and facts that can be linked to the stock market in the downstream (stock market price prediction) application. How will you do that?

11.1   Named entity recognition: Definitions and challenges

Let's look closely into the task of named entity recognition, provide definitions for various types of entities, and discuss challenges involved in this task.

11.1.1   Named entity types

We start by defining the major named entity types and their usefulness for downstream tasks. Figure 11.4 shows entities of five different types (GPE for *geopolitical entity*, ORG for *organization*, CARDINAL for *cardinal numbers*, DATE, and PERSON) highlighted in a typical sentence that you could see on the news.

> U.S. GPE tech giant Apple Inc. ORG has acquired some 100 CARDINAL companies over the last six years DATE , the company's CEO Tim Cook PERSON said.

Figure 11.4   Named entities of five different types highlighted in a typical sentence from the news

The notation used in this sentence is standard for the task of named entity recognition: some labels like DATE and PERSON are self-explanatory; others are abbreviations or short forms of the full labels (e.g., ORG for *organization*). The set of labels comes from the widely adopted annotation scheme in OntoNotes (see full documentation at http://mng.bz/Qv5R). What is important from a practitioner's point of view is that this is the scheme that is used in NLP tools, including spaCy. Table 11.1 lists all named entity types typically used in practice and identified in text by spaCy's NER component and provides a description and some illustrative examples for each of them.

Table 11.1   A comprehensive list of named entity labels with their descriptions and some illustrative examples.

Type	Description	Example
CARDINAL	Numerals that do not fall under any other type	*I bought **two** books on Amazon for $20.*
DATE	Absolute or relative dates or periods	*I'm leaving **tomorrow**.*
EVENT	Named hurricanes, battles, wars, sports events, etc.	***The Olympic Games** are held in Tokyo.*
FAC	Facilities, such as buildings, airports, highways, bridges, etc.	*I'm flying out of the **JFK Airport**.*
GPE	Geopolitical entities, such as countries, cities, states	***New York** is about 200 miles away from **Washington, DC**.*

Table 11.1   A comprehensive list of named entity labels with their descriptions and some illustrative examples.

Type	Description	Example
LANGUAGE	Any named language	He speaks **Japanese** fluently.
LAW	Named documents made into laws	**The Constitution of the United States** was the first complete written national constitution.
LOC	Non-GPE locations, such as mountain ranges, bodies of water	They are traveling down **the Amazon River**.
MONEY	Monetary values, including unit	I bought two books on Amazon for **$20**.
NORP	Nationalities, religious or political groups	The **Canadians** won the hockey game on Sunday night.
ORDINAL	"First", "second," etc.	The Constitution of the United States was the **first** complete written national constitution.
ORG	Organizations, such as companies, agencies, institutions, sports teams, etc.	I bought two books on **Amazon** for $20.
PERCENT	Percentage (including "%")	I bought two books on Amazon with a **20%** discount.
PERSON	People, including fictional	**Harry Potter** attended Hogwarts: School of Witchcraft and Wizardry.
PRODUCT	Vehicles, weapons, foods, etc. (not services)	The new **MacBook Air** is three times faster than other laptops.
QUANTITY	Measurements, as of weight or distance	New York is **about 200 miles** away from Washington, DC.
TIME	Times smaller than a day	The Canadians won the hockey game on **Sunday night.**
WORK_OF_ART	Titles of books, songs, etc.	**The Mona Lisa** is a portrait painting by Leonardo da Vinci.

A couple of observations are due at this point. First, note that named entities of any type can consist of a single word (e.g., "two" or "tomorrow") and longer expressions (e.g., "MacBook Air" or "about 200 miles"). Second, the same word or expression may represent an entity of a different type, depending on the context. For example, "Amazon" may refer to a river (LOC) or to a company (ORG). The next section will look into details of NER, but before we do that, let's get more experience with NER in exercise 11.1.

Exercise 11.1

The NE labeling presented in table 11.1 is used in spaCy. Familiarize yourself with the types and annotation by running spaCy's NER on a selected set of examples. You can use the sentences from table 11.1 or experiment with your own set of sentences. Do you disagree with any of the results?

This is an open-ended task. Code in listing 11.1 provides you with a starting point.

Listing 11.1   Code to run spaCy's NER on a sentence

Import spacy and load a language model: en_core_web_md stands for the middle-size model.

Process a selected sentence using spacy's NLP pipeline. Experiment with other sentences.

```
import spacy
nlp = spacy.load("en_core_web_md")

doc = nlp("I bought two books on Amazon")
for ent in doc.ents:
    print(ent.text, ent.label_)
```

For each identified entity, print out the entity itself and its type.

The code from this listing prints out the following output:

```
two CARDINAL
Amazon ORG
```

NOTE   Check out the different language models available for use with spaCy: https://spacy.io/models/en. Small model (en_core_web_sm) is suitable for most purposes and is more efficient to upload and use. However, larger models like en_core_web_md (medium) and en_core_web_lg (large) are more powerful, and some NLP tasks will require the use of such larger models. The models should be installed prior to running the code examples with spaCy. You can also install the models from within the Jupyter Notebook using the command !python -m spacy download en_core_web_md.

11.1.2 Challenges in named entity recognition

NER is a task concerned with identification of a word or phrase that constitutes an entity and with detection of the type of the identified entity. As examples from the previous section suggest, each of these steps has its own challenges. Before you read about these challenges, think about the question posed in exercise 11.2.

Exercise 11.2

What challenges can you identify in NER, based on the examples from table 11.1?

Let's look into these challenges together.

- The first task that an NER algorithm solves is *full entity span identification*. As you can see in the examples from figure 11.2 and table 11.1, some entities consist of a single word, while others may span whole expressions, and it is not always trivial to identify where an expression starts and where it finishes. For instance, does the full entity consist of Amazon or Amazon River? It would seem reasonable to select the longest sequence of words that are likely to constitute a single named entity. However, compare the following two sentences:

  - Check out our [Amazon River]$_{LOC}$ maps selection.

  - On [Amazon]$_{ORG}$ [River maps]$_{PRODUCT}$ from ABC Publishers are sold for $5. (If this sentence baffles you, try adding a comma, as in "On Amazon, River maps from ABC Publishers are sold for $5.")

  The first sentence contains a named entity of the type location (*Amazon River*). Even though the second sentence contains the same sequence of words, each of these two words actually belongs to a different named entity—*Amazon* is an organization, while *River* is part of a product name *River maps*.

- The following examples illustrate one of the core reasons why natural language processing is challenging—ambiguity. You have seen some examples of sentences with ambiguous analysis before (e.g., when we discussed parsing and part-of-speech tagging in chapter 4). For NER, ambiguity poses a number of challenges: one is related to span identification, as just demonstrated. Another one is related to the fact that the same words and phrases may or may not be named entities. For some examples, consider the following pairs, where the first sentence in each pair contains a word used as a common, general noun, and the second sentence contains the same word being used as (part of) a named entity:

  - "An <u>apple</u> a day keeps a doctor away" versus "<u>Apple</u> announces a new iPad Pro."

  - "<u>Turkey</u> is the main dish served at Thanksgiving" versus "<u>Turkey</u> is a country with amazing landscapes."

  - "The <u>tiger</u> is the largest living cat species" versus "<u>Tiger</u> Woods is an American professional golfer."

  Can you spot any characteristics distinguishing the two types of word usage (as a common noun versus as a named entity) that may help the algorithm distinguish between the two? Think about this question, and we will discuss the answer to it in the next section.

- Finally, as you have seen in the examples in table 11.1, ambiguity in NER poses a challenge, and not only when the algorithm needs to define whether a word or a phrase is a named entity or not. Even if a word or a phrase is identified to be a named entity, the same entity may belong to different NE types. For example, *Amazon* may refer to a location or a company, *April* may be a name of a person or a month, *JFK* may refer to a person or a facility, and so on. The following examples are borrowed from *Speech and Language Processing* by Jurafsky and Martin and demonstrate as many as four different uses of the word *Washington* (see Section 8.3 at https://web.stanford.edu/~jurafsky/slp3/8.pdf).

– <u>Washington</u>$_{PER}$ was born into slavery on the farm of James Burroughs.
– <u>Washington</u>$_{ORG}$ went up 2 games to 1 in the four-game series.
– Blair arrived in <u>Washington</u>$_{LOC}$ for what may well be his last state visit.
– In June, <u>Washington</u>$_{GPE}$ passed a primary seatbelt law.

Note that in all these examples, Washington is a named entity, but in each case, it is a named entity of a different type, as is clear from the surrounding context.

This means that an algorithm has to identify the span of a potential named entity and make sure the identified expression or word is indeed a named entity, since the same phrase or word may or may not be an NE, depending on the context of use. But even when it is established that an expression or a word is a named entity, this named entity may still belong to different types. How does the algorithm deal with these various levels of complexity?

First of all, a typical NER algorithm combines the span identification and the named entity type identification steps into a single, joint task. Second, it approaches this task as a *sequence labeling problem*: specifically, it goes through the running text word by word and tries to decide whether a word is part of a specific type of a named entity. Figure 11.5 provides the mental model for this process.

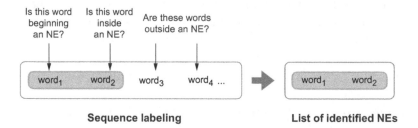

Figure 11.5   Mental model for sequence labeling used to identify NEs in text

In fact, many tasks in NLP are framed as sequence labeling tasks, since language has a clear sequential nature. We have not looked into sequential tasks and sequence labeling in this book before, so let's discuss this topic now.

11.2   *Named-entity recognition as a sequence labeling task*

Let's look closely into what it means for a task to be a sequence labeling task and how this is applied to named-entity recognition. You might have noticed from the examples overviewed in the previous section that ambiguity is present at various levels in language processing, yet whether a word or a phrase is a named entity or not and which type of a named entity it is depends on the context. Not surprisingly, named-entity recognition is addressed using machine-learning algorithms, which are capable of learning useful characteristics of the *context*. NER is typically addressed with supervised machine-learning algorithms, which means that such algorithms are trained on annotated data. To that end, let's start with the questions of how the data should be labeled for sequential tasks, such as NER, in a way that the algorithm can benefit from the most.

11.2.1 The basics: BIO scheme

Let's look again at the example of a sentence with different types of named entities, presented in figure 11.4. We said before that the way the NER algorithm identifies named entities and their types is by considering every word in sequence and deciding whether this word belongs to a named entity of a particular type. For instance, in *Apple Inc.*, the word *Apple* is at the beginning of a named entity of type ORG and *Inc.* is at its end. Explicitly annotating the beginning and the end of a named-entity expression and training the algorithm on such annotation helps it capture the information that if a word *Apple* is classified as beginning a named entity ORG, it is very likely that it will be followed by a word that finishes this named-entity expression.

The labeling scheme that is widely used for NER and similar sequence labeling tasks is called *BIO scheme*, since it comprises three types of tags: **b**eginning, **i**nside, and **o**utside. We said that the goal of an NER algorithm is to jointly assign to every word its position in a named entity and its type, so in fact this scheme is expanded to accommodate for the type tags too. For instance, there are tags B-PER and I-PER for the words beginning and inside of a named entity of the PER type; similarly, there are B-ORG, I-ORG, B-LOC, I-LOC tags, and so on. O-tag is reserved for all words that are outside of any named entity, and for that reason, it does not have a type extension. Figure 11.6 shows the application of this scheme to the short example "tech giant Apple Inc."

Figure 11.6   BIO scheme applied to "tech giant Apple Inc."

In total, there are 2n+1 tags for *n* named entity types plus a single O-tag: for the 18 NE types from the OntoNotes presented in table 11.1, this amounts to 37 tags in total. BIO scheme has two further extensions that you might encounter in practice: a less fine-grained IO scheme, which distinguishes between the **i**nside and **o**utside tags only, and a more fine-grained BIOES scheme, which also adds an **e**nd-of-entity tag for each type and a **s**ingle-word entity for each type that consists of a single word. Table 11.2 illustrates the application of these annotation schemes to the beginning of our example.

Table 11.2   NER as a sequence labeling task, showing `IO`, `BIO`, **and** `BIOES` **taggings. The notation "..." is used for space reasons for all words that are outside any named entities; they are all marked as O.**

Words	IO label	BIO label	BIOES label
U.S.	I-GPE	B-GPE	S-GPE
tech	O	O	O
giant	O	O	O
Apple	I-ORG	B-ORG	B-ORG
Inc.	I-ORG	I-ORG	E-ORG
...	O	O	O
some	I-CARDINAL	B-CARDINAL	B-CARDINAL
100	I-CARDINAL	I-CARDINAL	E-CARDINAL
...	O	O	O
the	I-DATE	B-DATE	B-DATE
last	I-DATE	I-DATE	I-DATE
six	I-DATE	I-DATE	I-DATE
years	I-DATE	I-DATE	E-DATE
,	O	O	O

This annotation is then used to train the sequential machine-learning algorithm, described in the next section. Before you look into that, try solving exercises 11.3 and 11.4.

Exercise 11.3

Table 11.2 doesn't contain the annotation for the rest of the sentence. Provide the annotation for "the company's CEO Tim Cook said" using the IO, BIO, and BIOES schemes. (Solution can be found at the end of this chapter.)

Exercise 11.4

The complexity of a supervised machine-learning task depends on the number of classes to distinguish between. The BIO scheme consists of 37 tags for 18 entity types. How many tags are there in the IO and BIOES schemes? (Solution can be found at the end of this chapter.)

11.2.2 What does it mean for a task to be sequential?

Many real-word tasks show sequential nature. As an illustrative example, let's consider how the temperature of water changes with respect to various possible actions applied to it. Suppose water can stay in one of three states—*cold, warm,* or *hot,* as figure 11.7 (left) illustrates. You can apply different actions to it. For example, heat it up or let it cool down. Let's call a change from one state to another a *state transition.* Suppose you start heating cold water up and measure water temperature at regular intervals, say, every minute. Most likely you would observe the following sequence of states: cold → . . . → cold → warm → . . . → warm → hot. In other words, to get to the "hot" state, you would first stay in the "cold" state for some time; then you would need to transition through the "warm" state, and finally you would reach the "hot" state. At the same time, it is physically impossible to transition from the "cold" to the "hot" state immediately, bypassing the "warm" state. The reverse is true as well: if you let water cool down, the most likely sequence will be hot → . . . → hot → warm → . . . → warm → cold, but not hot → cold.

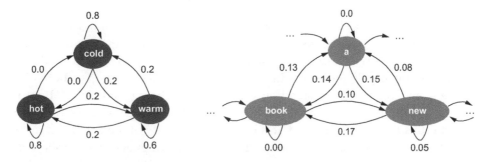

Figure 11.7   Directed graphs visualizing a chain of states (vertices in the graph), transitions (edges), and probabilities associated with these transitions marked on each edge. For example, 0.2 on the edge from "cold" to "warm" in the graph on the left means there is a 0.2 probability of temperature change from the "cold" to the "warm" state. The graph on the left illustrates the water temperature example, and the graph on the right provides an example of transitions between words.

In fact, these types of observations can be formalized and expressed as probabilities. For example, to estimate how probable it is to transition from the "cold" state to the "warm" state, you use your timed measurements and calculate the proportion of times that the temperature transitioned cold → warm among all the observations made for the "cold" state:

$$P(\text{transition cold} \rightarrow \text{warm}) = \frac{num(cold \rightarrow warm)}{num(cold \rightarrow ANY)}$$

Such probabilities estimated from the data and observations simply reflect how often certain events occur compared to other events and all possible outcomes. Figure 11.7

(left) shows the probabilities on the directed edges. The edges between hot → cold and cold → hot are marked with 0.0, reflecting that it is impossible for the temperature to change between "hot" and "cold" directly bypassing the "warm" state. At the same time, you can see that the edges from the state back to itself are assigned with quite high probabilities: P(hot → hot) = 0.8 means that 80% of the time if water temperature is hot at this particular point in time it will still be hot at the next time step (e.g., in a minute). Similarly, 60% of the time water will be warm at the next time step if it is currently warm, and in 80% of the cases water will still be cold in a minute from now if it is currently cold.

Also note that this scheme describes the set of possibilities fully: suppose water is currently hot. What temperature will it be in a minute? Follow the arrows in figure 11.7 (left) and you will see that with a probability of 0.8 (or in 80% of the cases), it will still be hot and with a probability of 0.2 (i.e., in the other 20%), it will be warm. What if it is currently warm? Then, with a probability of 0.6, it will still be warm in a minute, but there is a 20% chance that it will change to hot and a 20% chance that it will change to cold.

Where do language tasks fit into this? As a matter of fact, language is a highly structured, sequential system. For instance, you can say "Albert Einstein was born in Ulm" or "In Ulm, Albert Einstein was born," but "Was Ulm Einstein born Albert in" is definitely weird if not nonsensical and can be understood only because we know what each word means and, thus, can still try to make sense of such word salad. At the same time, if you shuffle the words in other expressions like "Ann gave Bob a book," you might end up not understanding what exactly is being said. In "A Bob book Ann gave," who did what to whom? This shows that language has a specific structure to it and if this structure is violated, it is hard to make sense of the result.

Figure 11.7 (right) shows a transition system for language, which follows a very similar strategy to the water temperature example from figure 11.7 (left). It shows that if you see a word "a," the next word may be "book" ("<u>a book</u>") with a probability of 0.14, "new" ("<u>a new</u> house") with a 15% chance, or some other word. If you see a word "new," with a probability of 0.05, it may be followed by another "new" ("a <u>new, new</u> house"), with an 8% chance it may be followed by "a" ("no matter how <u>new a</u> car is, . . ."), in 17% of the cases it will be followed by "book" ("a <u>new book</u>"), and so on. Finally, if the word that you currently see is "book," it will be followed by "a" ("<u>book a</u> flight") 13% of the time, by "new" ("<u>book new</u> flights") 10% of the time, or by some other word (note that in the language example, not all possible transitions are visualized in figure 11.7). Such predictions on the likely sequences of words are behind many NLP applications. For instance, word prediction is used in predictive keyboards, query completion, and so on.

Note that in the examples presented in figure 11.7, the sequential models take into account a single previous state to predict the current state. Technically, such models are called first-order *Markov models* or *Markov chains* (for more examples, see section 8.4.1 of Speech and Language Processing by Jurafsky and Martin at https://web.stanford.edu/~jurafsky/slp3/8.pdf). It is also possible to take into account longer history of events.

For example, second-order Markov models look into two previous states to predict the current state and so on.

NLP models that do not observe word order and shuffle words freely (as in "A Bob book Ann gave") are called *bag-of-words models*. The analogy is that when you put words in a "bag," their relative order is lost, and they get mixed among themselves like individual items in a bag. A number of NLP tasks use bag-of-words models. The tasks that you worked on before made little if any use of the sequential nature of language. Sometimes the presence of individual words is informative enough for the algorithm to identify a class (e.g., *lottery* strongly suggests spam, *amazing* is a strong signal of a positive sentiment, and *rugby* has a strong association with the sports topic). Yet, as we have noted earlier in this chapter, for NER it might not be enough to just observe a word (is "Apple" a fruit or a company?) or even a combination of words (as in "Amazon River Maps"). More information needs to be extracted from the context and the way the previous words are labeled with NER tags. In the next section, you will look closely into how NER uses sequential information and how sequential information is encoded as features for the algorithm to make its decisions.

11.2.3 *Sequential solution for NER*

Just like water temperature cannot change from "cold" immediately to "hot" or vice versa without going through the state of being "warm," and just like there are certain sequential rules to how words are put together in a sentence (with "a new book" being much more likely in English than "a book new"), there are certain sequential rules to be observed in NER. For instance, if a certain word is labeled as beginning a particular type of an entity (e.g., B-GPE for "New" in "New York"), it cannot be directly followed by an NE tag denoting inside of an entity of another type (e.g., I-EVENT cannot be assigned to "York" in "New York" when "New" is already labeled as B-GPE, as I-GPE is the correct tag). In contrast, I-EVENT is applicable to "Year" in "New Year" after "New" being tagged as B-EVENT. To make such decisions, an NER algorithm takes into account the context, the labels assigned to the previous words, and the current word and its properties. Let's consider two examples with somewhat similar contexts:

They	celebrated		New	Year
O	O		B-EVENT	I-EVENT
They	live	in	New	York
O	O	O	B-GPE	I-GPE

Your goal in the NER task is to assign the most likely sequence of tags to each sentence. Ideally, you would like to end up with the following labeling for the sentences: O – O – B-EVENT – I-EVENT for "They celebrated New Year" and O – O – O – B-GPE – I-GPE for "They live in New York." Figure 11.8 visualizes such "ideal" labeling for "They celebrated New Year" (using an abbreviation EVT for EVENT for space reasons).

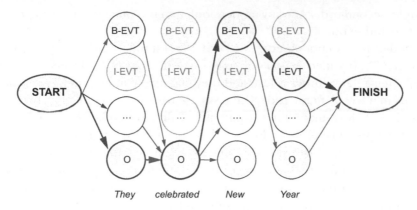

Figure 11.8   The "ideal" NE labeling for "They celebrated New Year". The circles denote states (i.e., NE labels) and the arrows denote transitions from one NE label to the next one. The implausible states for each word are grayed out (e.g., I-EVT for "New"), the implausible transitions are dropped, and the preferred states and transitions are highlighted in bold. Since there are many more labels in the NER scheme, not all of them are included: ". . ." denotes "any other label" (e.g., B-GPE, I-GPE).

As figure 11.8 shows, it is possible to start a sentence with a word labeled as a beginning of some named entity, such as B-EVENT or B-EVT (as in "Christmas$_{\text{B-EVT}}$ is celebrated on December 25"). However, it is not possible to start a sentence with I-EVT (the tag for inside the EVENT entity), which is why it is grayed out in figure 11.8 and there is no arrow connecting the beginning of the sentence (the START state) to I-EVT. Since the second word, "celebrated," is a verb, it is unlikely that it belongs to any named entity type; therefore, the most likely tag for it is O. "New" can be at the beginning of event (B-EVT as in "New Year") or another entity type (e.g., B-GPE as in "New York"), or it can be a word used outside any entity (O). Finally, the only two possible transitions after tag B-EVT are O (if an event is named with a single word, like "Christmas") or I-EVT. All possible transitions are marked with arrows in figure 11.8; all impossible states are grayed out with the impossible transitions dropped (i.e., no connecting arrows); and the states and transitions highlighted in bold are the preferred ones.

As you can see, there are multiple sources of information that are taken into account here: word position in the sentence matters (tags of the types O and B-ENTITY—outside an entity and beginning an entity, respectively—can apply to the first word in a sentence, but I-ENTITY cannot); word characteristics matter (a verb like "celebrate" is unlikely to be part of any entity); the previous word and tag matter (if the previous tag is B-EVENT, the current tag is either I-EVENT or O); the word shape matters (capital *N* in "New" makes it a better candidate for being part of an entity, while the most likely tag for "new" is O); and so on.

This is, essentially, how the algorithm tries to assign the correct tag to each word in the sequence. For instance, suppose you have assigned tags O - O - B-EVENT to the sequence "They celebrated New" and your current goal is to assign an NE tag to the word "Year". The algorithm may consider a whole set of characteristic rules—let's call them *features* by analogy with the features used by supervised machine-learning algorithms in other tasks. The features in NER can use any information related to the current NE tag and previous NE tags, current word and the preceding context, and the position of the word in the sentence. Let's define some feature templates for the features helping the algorithm predict that $word_4$ in "They celebrated New Year" (i.e., $word_4$="Year") should be assigned with the tag I-EVENT after the previous word "New" is assigned with B-EVENT. It is common to use the notation y_i for the current tag, y_{i-1} for the previous one, X for the input, and i for the position, so let's use this notation in the feature templates:

- f1(y_{i-1}, y_i, X, i)—If current word is "Year", return 1; otherwise, return 0.
- f2(y_{i-1}, y_i, X, i)—If current word is "York", return 1;otherwise, return 0.
- f3(y_{i-1}, y_i, X, i)—If previous word is "New", return 1; otherwise, return 0.
- . . .
- f12(y_{i-1}, y_i, X, i)—If current word part of speech is noun, return 1; otherwise, return 0.
- f13(y_{i-1}, y_i, X, i)—If previous word part of speech is adjective, return 1; otherwise, return 0.
- . . .
- f23(y_{i-1}, y_i, X, i)—If current word is in a gazetteer, return 1; otherwise, return 0.
- . . .
- f34(y_{i-1}, y_i, X, i)—If current word shape is Xx, return 1; otherwise, return 0.
- . . .
- f45(y_{i-1}, y_i, X, i)—If current word starts with prefix "Y", return 1; otherwise, return 0.
- f46(y_{i-1}, y_i, X, i)—If current word starts with prefix "Ye", return 1; otherwise, return 0.
- . . .

NOTE A gazetteer (e.g., www.geonames.org) is a list of place names with millions of entries for locations, including detailed geographical and political information. It is a very useful resource for identification of LOC, GPE, and some other types of named entities.

NOTE Word shape is determined as follows: capital letters are replaced with X, lowercase letters are replaced with x, numbers are replaced with d, and punctuation marks are preserved; for example, "U.S.A." can be represented as "X.X.X." and "11–12p.m." as "d–dx.x." This helps capture useful generalizable information.

Feature indexes used in this list are made up, and as you can see, the list of features grows quickly with the examples from the data. When applied to our example, the features will yield the following values:

- f1 (y_{i-1} = B-EVENT, y_i = I-EVENT, X = "They celebrated New Year", i = 4) = 1
- f2 (y_{i-1} = B-EVENT, y_i = I-EVENT, X = "They celebrated New Year", i = 4) = 0
- f3 (y_{i-1} = B-EVENT, y_i = I-EVENT, X = "They celebrated New Year", i = 4) = 1
- . . .
- f12 (y_{i-1} = B-EVENT, y_i = I-EVENT, X = "They celebrated New Year", i = 4) = 1
- f13 (y_{i-1} = B-EVENT, y_i = I-EVENT, X = "They celebrated New Year", i = 4) = 1
- . . .
- f23 (y_{i-1} = B-EVENT, y_i = I-EVENT, X = "They celebrated New Year", i = 4) = 0
- . . .
- f34 (y_{i-1} = B-EVENT, y_i = I-EVENT, X = "They celebrated New Year", i = 4) = 1
- . . .
- f45 (y_{i-1} = B-EVENT, y_i = I-EVENT, X = "They celebrated New Year", i = 4) = 1
- f46 (y_{i-1} = B-EVENT, y_i = I-EVENT, X = "They celebrated New Year", i = 4) = 1

It should be noted that no single feature is capable of correctly identifying an NE tag in all cases; moreover, some features may be more informative than others. What the algorithm does in practice is it weighs the contribution from each feature according to its informativeness and then it combines the values from all features, ranging from feature k = 1 to feature k = K (where k is just an index), by summing the individual contributions as follows:

$$\sum_{k=1}^{K} w_k f_k(y_{i-1}, y_i, X, i)$$

Sum over all features

Feature weight

Feature value (0, 1)

Equation 11.1 Sum over all features from feature with index k = 1 to k = K over the feature values f_k (equal to either 0 or 1) multiplied with respective weights w_k.

For example, if w1 for f1 is 0.4, w2 for f2 is 0.4, and w3 for f3 is 0.2, then the sum over these three features using the values for "They celebrated New Year" from above is

```
Result = w1 × f1 + w2 × f2 + w3 × f3 = 0.4 × 1 + 0.4 × 0 + 0.2 × 1 = 0.6
```

The appropriate weights in this equation are learned from labeled data as is normally done for supervised machine-learning algorithms. As was pointed out earlier, the ultimate goal of the algorithm is to assign the correct tags to all words in the sequence, so the expression is actually applied to each word in sequence, from $i = 1$ (i.e., the first word in the sentence) to $i = n$ (the last word); that is,

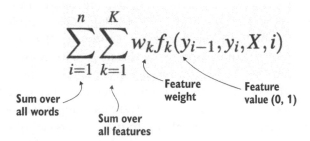

$$\sum_{i=1}^{n} \sum_{k=1}^{K} w_k f_k(y_{i-1}, y_i, X, i)$$

Sum over all words — Sum over all features — Feature weight — Feature value (0, 1)

Equation 11.2 Apply the estimation from Equation 11.1 to each word in the sequence and sum the results over all words from *i* = 1 to *i* = *n*.

Specifically, this means that the algorithm is not only concerned with the correct assignment of the tag I-EVENT to "Year" in "They celebrated New Year", but also with the correct assignment of the whole sequence of tags O - O - B-EVENT - I-EVENT to "They celebrated New Year". However, originally, the algorithm knows nothing about the correct tag for "They" and the correct tag for "celebrated" following "They", and so on. Since originally the algorithm doesn't know about the correct tags for the previous words, it actually considers *all* possible tags for the first word, then *all* possible tags for the second word, and so on. In other words, for the first word, it considers whether "They" can be tagged as B-EVENT, I-EVENT, B-GPE, I-GPE, . . . , O, as figure 11.8 demonstrated earlier; then for each tag applied to "They", the algorithm moves on and considers whether "celebrated" can be tagged as B-EVENT, I-EVENT, B-GPE, I-GPE, . . . , O; and so on. In the end, the result you are interested in is the *sequence* of *all* NE tags for *all* words that is most probable; that is,

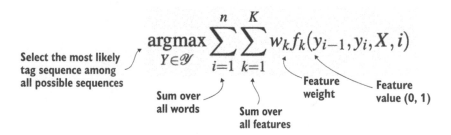

$$\arg\max_{Y \in \mathscr{Y}} \sum_{i=1}^{n} \sum_{k=1}^{K} w_k f_k(y_{i-1}, y_i, X, i)$$

Select the most likely tag sequence among all possible sequences — Sum over all words — Sum over all features — Feature weight — Feature value (0, 1)

Equation 11.3 Use the estimation from Equation 11.2 and return the sequence of tags, which results in the maximum value.

The formula in Equation 11.3 is exactly the same as the one in Equation 11.2, with just one modification: *argmax* means that you are looking for the sequence that results in the highest probability estimated by the rest of the formula; Y stands for the whole sequence of tags for all words in the input sentence; and the fancy font $\mathscr{Y}$ denotes the full set of possible combinations of tags. Recall the three BIO-style schemes introduced earlier in this chapter: the most coarse-grained IO scheme has 19 tags, which means that the total number of possible tag combinations for the sentence "They celebrated New Year", consisting of 4 words, is 19^4=130,321; the middle-range BIO scheme contains 37 distinct tags and results in 37^4=1,874,161 possible combinations; and finally, the most fine-grained BIOES scheme results in 73^4=28,398,241 possible tag combinations for a sentence consisting of 4 words. Note that a sentence consisting of 4 words is a relatively short sentence, yet the brute-force algorithm (i.e., the one that simply iterates through each possible combination at each step) rapidly becomes highly inefficient. After all, some tag combinations (like O $\rightarrow$ I-EVENT) are impossible, so there is no point in wasting effort on even considering them. In practice, instead of a brute-force algorithm, more efficient algorithms based on *dynamic programming* are used (the algorithm that is widely used for language-related sequence labeling tasks is the Viterbi algorithm; you can find more details in section 8.4.5 of Speech and Language Processing by Jurafsky and Martin at https://web.stanford.edu/~jurafsky/slp3/8.pdf).

Instead of exhaustively considering all possible combinations, at each step a dynamic programming algorithm calculates the probability of all possible solutions given only the *best, most optimal solution for the previous step*. The algorithm then calculates the best move at the current point and stores it as the current best solution. When it moves to the next step, it again considers only this best solution rather than all possible solutions, thus considerably reducing the number of overall possibilities to only the most promising ones. Figure 11.9 demonstrates the intuition behind dynamic

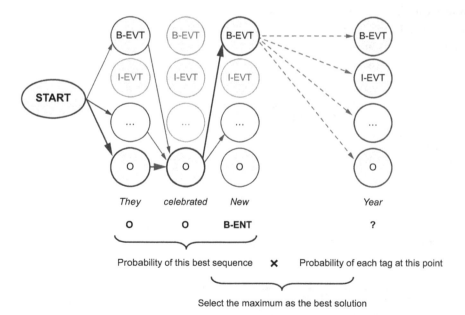

Figure 11.9   A dynamic programming algorithm solves the following task: if the best (most likely) tag sequence so far is O – O – B-ENT, what is the most likely tag for "Year" at this point?

estimation of the best NE tag that should be selected for "Year" given that the optimal solution O - O - B-EVENT is found for "They celebrated New".

This, in a nutshell, is how a sequence labeling algorithm solves the task of tag assignment. As was highlighted before, NER is not the only task that demonstrates sequential effects, and a number of other tasks in NLP are solved this way. One task that you have encountered before in this book, which is also a sequence labeling task and which, under the hood, is solved in a similar manner, is POS tagging. You looked into this task in chapter 4 and used POS tags as features in NLP applications in later chapters. The approach to sequence labeling outlined in this section is used by machine-learning algorithms, most notably, conditional random fields (for further examples, see section 8.5 of Speech and Language Processing by Jurafsky and Martin at https://web.stanford.edu/~jurafsky/slp3/8.pdf), although you don't need to implement your own NER to be able to benefit from the results of this step in the NLP pipeline. For instance, spaCy has an NER implementation that you are going to rely on to solve the task set out in the scenario for this chapter. The next section delves into implementation details.

11.3 Practical applications of NER

Let's remind ourselves of the scenario for this chapter. It is widely known that certain events influence the trends of stock price movements. Specifically, you can extract relevant facts from the news and then use these facts to predict company stock prices. Suppose you have access to a large collection of news; now your task is to extract the relevant events and facts that can be linked to the stock market in the downstream (stock market price prediction) application. How will you do that?

This means that you have access to a collection of news texts, and among other preprocessing steps, you apply NER. Then you can focus only on the texts and sentences that are relevant for your task. For instance, if you are interested in the recent events, in which a particular company (e.g., "Apple") participated, you can easily identify such texts, sentences, and contexts. Figure 11.10 shows a flow diagram for this process.

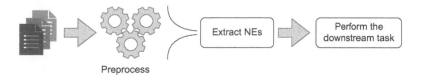

Preprocess

Figure 11.10 Practical application of NER in downstream tasks (e.g., in further information extraction)

11.3.1 Data loading and exploration

There are multiple ways in which you can get access to news articles, such as extracting the up-to-date news articles from the news portals in real time. This, of course, would be a reasonable approach if you wanted to build an application that can predict outcomes for the current events. For the sake of the exercise in this chapter, however, we are going to use the data that has already been extracted from a range of news portals. The dataset called "All the news" is hosted on the Kaggle website (www.kaggle .com/snapcrack/all-the-news). The dataset consists of 143,000 articles scraped from 15 news websites, including the *New York Times*, CNN, Business Insider, *Washington Post*, and so on. The dataset is quite big and is split into three comma-separated values (CSV) files. In the examples in this chapter, you are going to be working with the file called `articles1.csv`, but you are free to use other files in your own experiments.

Many datasets available via Kaggle and similar platforms are stored in the `.csv` format. This basically means that the data is stored as a big spreadsheet file, where information is split between different rows and columns. For instance, in `articles1.csv`, each row represents a single news article, described with a set of columns containing information on its title, author, the source website, the date of publication, its full content, and so on. The separator used to define the boundary between the information belonging to different data fields in `.csv` files is a comma. It's time now to familiarize yourselves with pandas, a useful data-preprocessing toolkit that helps you work with files in such formats as `.csv` and easily extract information from them.

> **Pandas**
>
> Pandas is a fast, powerful, flexible, and easy-to-use open source data analysis and manipulation tool, built on top of Python (see more information and installation instructions at https://pandas.pydata.org).

Let's use this toolkit to extract the information from the input file as listing 11.2 shows. In this code, you import pandas once you've installed it. Since the dataset is split into multiple files, you need to provide the path location for the files, and then you can open a particular file using pandas `read_csv` functionality. The result is stored in a `DataFrame df`.

Listing 11.2   Code to extract the data from the input file using pandas

```
import pandas as pd
path = "all-the-news/"
df = pd.read_csv(path + "articles1.csv")
```

Import pandas once you've installed it.

Provide the path location for the files.

Open the file using pandas read_csv functionality; the result is stored in a DataFrame df.

The code from listing 11.2 reads the contents of the .csv file, using a comma as a delimiter to identify which information field (column) a particular string of text in the row belongs to. The result is called a `DataFrame`, a labeled data structure with columns of potentially different types (e.g., they can contain textual as well as numerical information). Pandas provides you with extensive functionality and allows you to investigate the contents of the `DataFrame` from various perspectives. You can learn more about this tool's functionality from the documentation. The most useful functions at this point in your application are `df.shape` and `df.head()`. The function `df.shape` prints out the dimensionality of the data structure. For `articles1.csv`, it is `(50000, 10)`—that is, 50,000 rows representing individual news articles to 10 columns containing various information on these articles, from titles, to publication dates, to the full article content. The function `df.head()` prints out the first five rows from your `DataFrame`. Both these functions serve as useful sanity checks. It is always a good idea to check what the data you are working with contains. Here is what `df.head()` returns for the `DataFrame` initialized in listing 11.2:

	Unnamed: 0	id	title	publication	author	date	year	month	url	content
0	0	17283	House Republicans Fret About Winning Their Hea...	New York Times	Carl Hulse	2016-12-31	2016.0	12.0	NaN	WASHINGTON — Congressional Republicans have...
1	1	17284	Rift Between Officers and Residents as Killing...	New York Times	Benjamin Mueller and Al Baker	2017-06-19	2017.0	6.0	NaN	After the bullet shells get counted, the blood...
2	2	17285	Tyrus Wong, 'Bambi' Artist Thwarted by Racial ...	New York Times	Margalit Fox	2017-01-06	2017.0	1.0	NaN	When Walt Disney's "Bambi" opened in 1942, cri...
3	3	17286	Among Deaths in 2016, a Heavy Toll in Pop Musi...	New York Times	William McDonald	2017-04-10	2017.0	4.0	NaN	Death may be the great equalizer, but it isn't...
4	4	17287	Kim Jong-un Says North Korea Is Preparing to T...	New York Times	Choe Sang-Hun	2017-01-02	2017.0	1.0	NaN	SEOUL, South Korea — North Korea's leader, ...

You can now explore the data in your `DataFrame` in more detail. For example, since the data from 15 news sources is split between several .csv files, let's find out which news sources are covered by the current `DataFrame`. Listing 11.3 shows how to do that. Specifically, you need to extract the information from a particular column (here, `"publication"`) and apply `unique()` function to convert the result into a set.

> **Listing 11.3 Code to extract the information on the news sources only**

```
sources = df["publication"].unique()     ⟵   Extract the information from the
print(sources)                                "publication" column and convert
                                              the result into a set.
```

As you can see, pandas provides you with an easy way to extract and explore the information you need at this point. With just one line of code, you extract the contents of the column entitled `"publication"` in the `DataFrame` (this column indicates the news source for each article), and then apply the function `unique()` that converts the list into a set of unique values. Here is the output that this code produces:

```
['New York Times' 'Breitbart' 'CNN' 'Business Insider' 'Atlantic']
```

Since the `DataFrame` contains as many as 50,000 articles, for the sake of this application, let's focus on some articles only. We will extract the text (content) of the first 1,000 articles published in the *New York Times*. Listing 11.4 shows how to do that. First, you define a `condition`—the publication source should be `"New York Times"`. Then you select the content from all articles that satisfy this condition (i.e., `df.loc[condition, :]`), and from these, you extract only the first 1,000 for simplicity. In the end, you can check the dimensionality of the extracted data structure using `df.shape` as before.

> **Listing 11.4 Code to extract the content of articles from a specific source**

Define a condition for the publication source to be "New York Times".

Select the content from all articles that satisfy this condition and only extract the first 1,000 of them.

```
condition = df["publication"].isin(["New York Times"])
content_df = df.loc[condition, :]["content"][:1000]
content_df.shape
```

Check the dimensionality of the extracted data structure using df.shape as before.

The code prints out `(1000,)`, confirming that you extracted 1,000 articles from the *New York Times*. The new data structure, `content_df`, is simply an array of 1,000 news texts. You can further check the contents of these articles using the functions mentioned before; for example, `content_df.head()` will show the following content from the first five articles:

```
0    WASHINGTON  —   Congressional Republicans have...
1    After the bullet shells get counted, the blood...
2    When Walt Disney's "Bambi" opened in 1942, cri...
3    Death may be the great equalizer, but it isn't...
4    SEOUL, South Korea  —   North Korea's leader, ...
```

11.3.2 *Named entity types exploration with spaCy*

Now that the data is loaded, let's explore what entity types it contains. For that, you can rely on the NER functionality from spaCy (for more examples and more information, check spaCy's documentation at https://spacy.io/usage/linguistic-features#named-entities). Recall that you used it in an earlier exercise in listing 11.1.

Let's start by iterating through the news articles, collecting all named entities identified in texts and storing the number of occurrences in a Python dictionary, as figure 11.11 illustrates.

Listing 11.5 shows how to populate a dictionary with the named entities extracted from all news articles in `content_df`. First, you import spaCy and load a language

Figure 11.11 Extract all named entities from news articles and store them in a Python dictionary.

model (here, medium size). Next, you define the collect_entities function, which extracts named entities from all news articles and stores the statistics on them in the Python dictionary named_entities. Within this function, you process each news article with spaCy's NLP pipeline and store the result in the processed_docs list for future use. Specifically, for each entity, you extract the text with ent.text (e.g., Apple) and store it as entity_text. In addition, you identify the type of the entity with ent.label_ (e.g., ORG) and store it as entity_type. Then, for each entity type (e.g., ORG), you extract the list of entities and their counts (e.g., [Facebook: 175, Apple Inc.: 63, ...] currently stored in current_ents. After that, you update the counts in current_ents, incrementing the count for the entity stored as entity_text, and finally, you return the named_entities dictionary and the processed_docs list.

Listing 11.5 Code to populate a dictionary with NEs extracted from news articles

```
import spacy
nlp = spacy.load("en_core_web_md")          Import spaCy and load a language
                                             model (here, medium-size).

def collect_entites(data_frame):            Define the collect_entities function
    named_entities = {}                      to extract named entities and store
    processed_docs = []                      the statistics on them.

    for item in data_frame:                  Process each news article with
        doc = nlp(item)                      spaCy's NLP pipeline and store the
        processed_docs.append(doc)           result in the processed_docs list.

    for ent in doc.ents:                     For each entity, extract the text with ent.text
        entity_text = ent.text               (e.g., Apple) and store it as entity_text.
        entity_type = str(ent.label_)
        current_ents = {}                                    For each entity type,
        if entity_type in named_entities.keys():             extract the list of
            current_ents = named_entities.get(entity_type)   currently stored entities
                                                             with their counts.
```

Identify the type of the entity with ent.label_ (e.g., ORG) and store it as entity_type.

```
        current_ents[entity_text] = current_ents.get(entity_text, 0) + 1
        named_entities[entity_type] = current_ents
    return named_entities, processed_docs

named_entities, processed_docs = collect_entites(content_df)
```

Update the counts in current_ents, incrementing
the count for the entity stored as entity_text.

Return the named_entities dictionary
and the processed_docs list.

To inspect the results, let's print out the contents of the `named_entities` dictionary, as listing 11.6 suggests. In this code, you print out the type of a named entity (e.g., `ORG`) and for each type, you extract all entities assigned with this type in the dictionary (e.g., `[Facebook: 175, Apple Inc.: 63, ...]`). Then you sort the entries by their frequency in descending order. For space reasons, this code suggests that you only print out the most frequent *n* ones (e.g., 10 here) of them. Additionally, it would be most informative to only look into entities that occur more than once. In the end, you print out the named entities and frequency counts.

Listing 11.6   Code to print out the named entities dictionary

Sort the entries by their frequency in descending
order and print out the most frequent *n* ones.

Print out the type of a
named entity (e.g., ORG).

```
def print_out(named_entities):
    for key in named_entities.keys():
        print(key)
        entities = named_entities.get(key)
        sorted_keys = sorted(entities, key=entities.get, reverse=True)
        for item in sorted_keys[:10]:
            if (entities.get(item)>1):
                print("    " + item + ": " + str(entities.get(item)))

print_out(named_entities)
```

Extract all entities of
a particular type from
the dictionary.

Print out the named
entity and its frequency.

It would be most informative to only look
into entities that occur more than once.

This code prints out all 18 named entity types with up to 10 most frequent named entities for each type. The full list is, of course, much longer, with many entities occurring in the data only a few times (that is why we limit the output here to the most frequent items only). Here is the output printed out for the GPE type:

```
GPE
    the United States: 1148
    Russia: 526
    China: 515
    Washington: 498
    New York: 365
    America: 359
    Iran: 294
    Mexico: 265
    Britain: 236
    California: 203
```

NOTE These results are obtained with the versions of tools specified in the installation instructions. As before, if you are using different versions of tools or a model different from en_core_web_md, it is possible that the precise numbers that you are getting are slightly different and you shouldn't be alarmed by this difference in the results.

Perhaps not surprisingly, the most frequent geopolitical entity mentioned in the *New York Times* articles is the United States. It is mentioned 1,148 times in total; in fact, this can be combined with the counts for other expressions used for the same entity (e.g., *America* and the like). It is followed by Russia (526 times) and China (515). As you can see, there is a lot of information contained in this dictionary.

Another way in which you can explore the statistics on various NE types is to aggregate the counts on the types and print out the number of unique entries (e.g., Apple and Facebook would be counted as two separate named entities under the ORG type), as well as the total number of occurrences of each type (e.g., 175 counts for Facebook and 63 for Apple would result in the total number of 238 occurrences of the type ORG). Listing 11.7 shows how to do that. It suggests that you print out information on the entity type (e.g., ORG), the number of unique entries belonging to a particular type (e.g., Apple and Facebook would contribute as two different entries for ORG), and the total number of occurrences of the entities of that particular type. To do that, you extract and aggregate the statistics for each NE type, and in the end, you print out the results in a tabulated format, with each row storing the statistics on a separate NE type.

Listing 11.7 Code to aggregate the counts on all named entity types

Print out the results, with each row storing the statistics on a separate NE type.

Print out the entity type, the number of unique entries, and the total number of entities occurrences.

```
rows = []
rows.append(["Type:", "Entries:", "Total:"])
for ent_type in named_entities.keys():
    rows.append([ent_type, str(len(named_entities.get(ent_type))),
                str(sum(named_entities.get(
                    ent_type).values())))])

columns = zip(*rows)
column_widths = [max(len(item) for item in col) for col in columns]
for row in rows:
    print(''.join(' {:{width}} '.format(row[i], width=column_widths[i])
                for i in range(0, len(row))))
```

Extract and aggregate the statistics for each NE type.

This code prints out the results shown in table 11.3.

Table 11.3 Aggregated statistics on the named entities from the news articles dataset—the NE types, the number of unique entries, and the total number of occurrences.

Type	Entries	Total	Type	Entries	Total
GPE	1,661	14,747	EVENT	188	474
NORP	487	7,459	TIME	531	1,407

Table 11.3 Aggregated statistics on the named entities from the news articles dataset—the NE types, the number of unique entries, and the total number of occurrences. (continued)

Type	Entries	Total	Type	Entries	Total
PERSON	9,651	30,431	FAC	570	1,226
MONEY	679	1,234	ORDINAL	68	1,783
ORG	4,892	14,197	QUANTITY	337	465
CARDINAL	1,192	8,517	PERCENT	271	660
DATE	3,011	14,905	WORK_OF_ART	1,258	1,818
LAW	97	324	PRODUCT	229	527
LOC	456	1,508	LANGUAGE	12	85

As this table shows, the most frequently used named entities in the news articles are entities of the following types: PERSON, GPE, ORG, and DATE. This is, perhaps, not very surprising. After all, most often news reports on the events that are related to people (PERSON), companies (ORG), countries (GPE), and usually news articles include references to specific dates. At the same time, the least frequently used entities are the ones of the type LANGUAGE: there are only 12 unique languages mentioned in this news articles dataset, and in total they are mentioned 85 times. Among the most frequently mentioned are English (48 times), Arabic (8), and Spanish (7). You may also note that the ORDINAL type has only 68 unique entries: it is, naturally, a very compact list of items including entries like *first*, *second*, *third*, and so on.

11.3.3 *Information extraction revisited*

Now that you have explored the data, you can look more closely into the information that the articles contain on specific entities of interest. Consider the scenario again: your task is to build an information extraction application focused on companies and the news that reports on these companies. The dataset at hand, according to table 11.4, contains information on as many as 4,892 companies. Of course, not all of them will be of interest to you, so it would make sense to select a few and extract information on them.

Chapter 4 looked into the information extraction task, which was concerned with the extraction of relevant facts (e.g., actions in which certain personalities of interest are involved). Let's revisit this task here, making the necessary modifications. Specifically, the following ones:

- Let's extract actions together with their participants but focus on participants of a particular type, such as companies (ORG) or a specific company (Apple). For that, you will work with a subset of sentences that contain the entity of interest.
- Let's extract the contexts in which an entity of interest (e.g., Apple) is one of the main participants (e.g., "*Apple* sued Qualcomm" or "Russia required *Apple*

to . . ."). For that, you will use the linguistic information from spaCy's NLP pipeline, focusing on the cases where the entity is the subject (the main participant of the main action as *Apple* is in "*Apple* sued Qualcomm") or the object (the second participant of the main action as *Apple* is in "Russia required *Apple* to . . ."). This information can be extracted from the spaCy's parser output using `nsubj` and `dobj` relations, respectively.

- Oftentimes the second participant of the action is linked to the main verb via a preposition. For instance, compare "Russia <u>required</u> *Apple*" to "The New York Times <u>wrote about</u> *Apple*". In the first case, *Apple* is the direct object of the main verb *required,* and in the second case, it is an indirect object of the main verb *wrote.* Let's make sure that both cases are covered by our information extraction algorithm.

- Finally, as observed in the earlier examples, named entities may consist of a single word (*Apple*) or of several words (*Apple Inc.*). To that end, let's make sure the code applies to both cases.

Recall that spaCy's NLP pipeline processes sentences (or full documents) and returns a data structure, which contains all sorts of information on the words in the sentence (text), including the information about the word's type (part of speech, such as verb, noun, etc.), its named entity type, and its role in the sentence (e.g., main verb—`ROOT`, main action's participant—`nsubj`). Figure 11.12 provides a reminder.

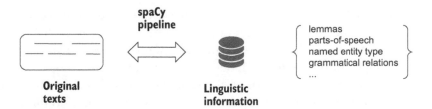

Figure 11.12 A reminder on the information provided on the word tokens by spaCy pipeline

In addition, each word has a unique index that is linked to its position in the sentence. If a named entity consists of multiple words, some of them may be marked with the `nsubj` or `dobj` relations (i.e., relevant relations in your application), but your goal is to extract not only the word marked as `nsubj` or `dobj` but also the whole named entity, which plays this role. To do that, the best way is to match the named entities to their roles in the sentence via the indexes assigned to the named entities in the sentence. Figure 11.13 illustrates this process.

Specifically, figure 11.13 looks into the following example: suppose your named entity of interest is a multiword expression "The New York Times" and the full sentence is "The New York Times wrote about Apple". Your goal is to identify whether "The New York Times" is one of the participants of the main action (*wrote*) in this sen-

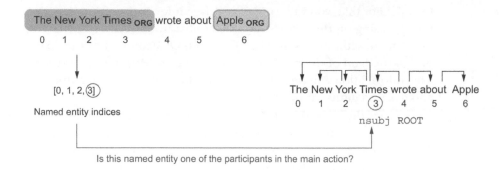

Figure 11.13   The aim of the extraction algorithm is to identify whether the named entity of interest is one of the participants in the main action; that is, a subject or an object of the main verb. In a multiword NE, only one word will be marked with the relevant role (e.g., `nsubj` here), but the code needs to return the whole NE.

tence; in other words, if it is the subject (the entity that performs the action) or an object (an entity to which the action applies). Indeed, "The New York Times" as a whole is the subject; it is the entity that performed the action of writing. However, since linguistic analysis applies to individual words rather than whole expressions, technically only the word "Times" is directly dependent on the main verb "wrote"; this is shown through the chain of relations in figure 11.13. How can you extract the whole expression "The New York Times"?

To do that, you first identify the indexes of the words covered by this expression in the sentence. For "The New York Times", these are [0, 1, 2, 3], as the left part of figure 11.13 shows. Next, you check if a word with any of these indexes plays a role of the subject or an object in the sentence. Indeed, the word that is the subject in the sentence has the index of 3 (as is shown on the right-hand side of figure 11.13). Therefore, you can return the whole named entity "The New York Times" as the subject of the main action in the sentence.

The first step concerned with the identification of the indexes of the words contained in the named entity in question is solved with the code from listing 11.8. In this code, you define `extract_span` function, which takes as input a sentence and the entity of interest. It then populates the list of `indexes` with the indexes of the words included in the NE and returns the `indexes` list as an output.

Listing 11.8   Code to extract the indexes of the words covered by the NE

```
def extract_span(sent, entity):          ◁      Define the extract_span function,
    indexes = []                                which takes as input a sentence
    for ent in sent.ents:                       and the entity of interest.
        if ent.text==entity:
            for i in range(int(ent.start), int(ent.end)):
                indexes.append(i)        ◁
    return indexes                              Populate the list of indexes with the
                                                indexes of the words included in the NE.
```

Return the indexes list as an output.

This code returns [0, 1, 2, 3] for extract_span ("The New York Times wrote about Apple", "The New York Times").

The second half of the task, the one concerned with the identification of whether a named entity in question plays the role of one of the participants in the main action, is solved with the code from listing 11.9. This code may look familiar to you. It is a modification of a solution that was applied to extract information in chapter 4. In this code, you define the extract_information function, which takes a sentence, the entity of interest, and the list of the indexes of all the words covered by this entity as an input. Then you initialize the list of actions and an action with two participants. Next, you identify the main verb expressing the main action in the sentence and initialize the indexes for the subject and the object related to this main verb. The main verb itself is stored in the action variable; you can find the subject that is related to the main verb via the nsubj relation and store it as participant1 and its index as subj_ind. If there is a preposition attached to the verb (e.g., "write about"), then you need to search for the indirect object as the second participant. If such an object is a noun or a proper noun, you store it as participant2 and its index as obj_ind. If at this point both participants of the main action have been identified and their indexes are included in the indexes of the words covered by the entity, you add the action with two participants to the list of actions. Otherwise, if there is no preposition attached to the verb, participant2 is a direct object of the main verb, which can be identified via the dobj relation (e.g., "X bought Y"). In this case, you apply the same strategy as earlier, adding the action with two participants to the list of actions. In the end, if the final list of actions is not empty, you print out the sentence and all actions together with the participants.

Listing 11.9 Code to extract information about the main participants of the action

```
def extract_information(sent, entity, indexes):          ◁─┐  Define the
    actions = []                                              extract_information
    action = ""                       Initialize the list of function.
    participant1 = ""                 actions and an action
    participant2 = ""                 with two participants.
                          ◁─                                  Identify the main verb
                                                              expressing the main
    for token in sent:                                       action in the sentence.
        if token.pos_=="VERB" and token.dep_=="ROOT":   ◁─┘
            subj_ind = -1
            obj_ind = -1         ◁─   Initialize the indexes for the subject and
            action = token.text       the object related to the main verb.
            children = [child for child in token.children]
            for child1 in children:
                if child1.dep_=="nsubj":                Find the subject via the
                    participant1 = child1.text          nsubj relation and store
                    subj_ind = int(child1.i)       ◁─   it as participant1 and its
                if child1.dep_=="prep":                 index as subj_ind.
                    participant2 = ""
                    child1_children = [child for child in child1.children]
                    for child2 in child1_children:
                        if child2.pos_ == "NOUN" or child2.pos_ == "PROPN":
```

Store the main verb itself in the action variable. ┗▷ action = token.text

Search for the indirect object
as the second participant and
store it as participant2 and
its index as obj_ind.

If both participants of
the action are identified,
add the action with two
participants to the list
of actions.

If there is no preposition
attached to the verb, find a
direct object of the main
verb via the dobj relation.

```
                        participant2 = child2.text
                        obj_ind = int(child2.i)
                if not participant2=="":
                    if subj_ind in indexes:
                        actions.append(entity + " "
                                        + action + " " + child1.text
                                        + " " + participant2)
                    elif obj_ind in indexes:
                        actions.append(participant1 + " " + action + \
                        " " + child1.text + \
                        " " + entity)
                if child1.dep_=="dobj" and (child1.pos_ == "NOUN"
                                        or child1.pos_ == "PROPN"):
                    participant2 = child1.text
                    obj_ind = int(child1.i)
                    if subj_ind in indexes:
                        actions.append(entity + " " + action + " " + participant2)
                    elif obj_ind in indexes:
                        actions.append(participant1 + " " + action + " " + entity)
```

```
        if not len(actions)==0:
            print (f"\nSentence = {sent}")
            for item in actions:
                print(item)
```

If the final list of actions is not empty,
print out the sentence and all actions
together with the participants.

Now let's apply this code to your texts extracted from the news articles. Note, however, that the code in listing 11.9 applies to the sentence level, since it relies on the information extracted from the parser (which applies to each sentence rather than the whole text). In addition, if you are only interested in a particular entity, it doesn't make sense to waste the algorithm's efforts on the texts and sentences that don't mention this entity at all. To this end, let's first extract all sentences that mention the entity in question from processed_docs and then apply the extract_information method to extract all tuples (participant1 + action + participant2) from the sentences, where either participant1 or participant2 is the entity you are interested in.

Listing 11.10 shows how to do that. In this code, you define the entity_detector function that takes processed_docs, the entity of interest, and its type as input. If a sentence contains the input entity (e.g., Apple) of the specified type (e.g., ORG) among its named entities, you add this sentence to the output_sentences. Using this function, you find all sentences for a specific entity and print out the number of such sentences found. In the end, you apply extract_span and extract_information functions from the previous code listings to extract the information on the entity of interest from the set of sentences containing this entity.

Listing 11.10   Code to extract information on the specific entity

```
def entity_detector(processed_docs, entity, ent_type):

    output_sentences = []
    for doc in processed_docs:
        for sent in doc.sents:
```

Define the entity_detector function that
takes processed_docs, the entity of
interest, and its type as input.

```
                    if entity in [ent.text for ent in sent.ents if
                            ent.label_==ent_type]:
                        output_sentences.append(sent)
        return output_sentences

entity = "Apple"
ent_sentences = entity_detector(processed_docs, entity, "ORG")
print(len(ent_sentences))

for sent in ent_sentences:
    indexes = extract_span(sent, entity)
    extract_information(sent, entity, indexes)
```

Only consider sentences that contain the input entity of the specified type among its named entities.

Find all sentences for a specific entity and print out the number of such sentences found.

Apply extract_span and extract_information functions from the previous code listings.

This code uses "Apple" as the entity of interest and specifically looks for sentences, in which the company (ORG) *Apple* is mentioned. As the printout message shows, there are 59 such sentences. Not all sentences among these 59 sentences mention *Apple* as a subject or object of the main action, but the last line of code returns a number of such sentences with the tuples summarizing the main content:

```
Sentence = Apple has previously removed other, less prominent media apps from
its China store.
Apple removed apps

Sentence = Russia required Apple and Google to remove the LinkedIn app from
their local stores.
Russia required Apple

Sentence = On Friday, Apple, its longtime partner, sued Qualcomm over what it
said was $1 billion in withheld rebates.
Apple sued Qualcomm
```

The main content of the sentences is concisely summarized by the tuples consisting of the main action and its two participants, so if you were interested in extracting only the sentences that have such informative content and that directly answer questions "What did *Apple* do to X?" or "What did Y do to *Apple*?" you could use the code from listing 11.10.

> ### Exercise 11.5
>
> The code from listing 11.10 allows you to extract information on named entities consisting of multiple words. Apply this code to the examples of such multiword entities; for example, you can search for the information on "The New York Times" or any other entity of your choice from the ones contained in the data. You can find more examples of multiword entities in the output of listing 11.6. (Solution can be found at the end of this chapter.)

11.3.4 *Named entities visualization*

One of the most useful ways to explore named entities contained in text and to extract relevant information is to visualize the results of NER. For instance, the code from listing 11.10 allows you to extract the contexts in which a named entity of interest is one of the main participants, but what about all the other contexts? Among those missed by the algorithm applied in listing 11.10 might be sentences with interesting and relevant content. To that end, let's revisit extraction of sentences containing the entity in question and explore visualization to highlight the use of the entity alongside other relevant entities.

Listing 11.11 uses spaCy's visualization tool, `displaCy`, which allows you to highlight entities of different types in the selected set of sentences using distinct colors for each type (see documentation on `displaCy` here: https://spacy.io/usage/visualizers). Specifically, after `display` is imported, you define the `visualize` function that takes `processed_docs`, an `entity` of interest, and its type as input, identifies the sentences that contain the entity in question, and visualizes the context. You can test this code by applying it to any selected example.

> **Listing 11.11   Code to visualize named entities of various types in their contexts of use**

```
from spacy import display        ◁——— Import display.

def visualize(processed_docs, entity, ent_type):        ◁
    for doc in processed_docs:
        for sent in doc.sents:
            if entity in [ent.text for ent in sent.ents
                          if ent.label_==ent_type]:
                display.render(sent, style="ent")        ◁

visualize(processed_docs, "Apple", "ORG")        ◁
```

Define visualize function that takes processed_docs, an entity of interest, and its type as input.

Identify the sentences that contain the entity in question and visualize the context.

Apply this code to a selected example.

This code displays all sentences, in which the company (`ORG`) *Apple* is mentioned. Other entities are highlighted with distinct colors. Figure 11.14 shows a small portion of the output.

Finally, you might be interested specifically in the contexts in which the company *Apple* is mentioned alongside other companies. Let's filter out all other information and highlight only named entities of the same type as the entity in question (i.e., all `ORG` NEs in this case). Listing 11.12 shows how to do that. Here, you define the `count_ents` function that counts the number of entities of a certain type in a sentence. With an updated `entity_detector_custom` function, you extract only the sentences that mention the input `entity` of a specified type as well as at least one other entity of the same type. You can print out the number of sentences identified this way as a sanity check. Then you define the `visualize_type` function that applies visualization to the entities of a predefined type only. spaCy allows you to customize the colors for visualization and to apply gradient (you can choose other colors from

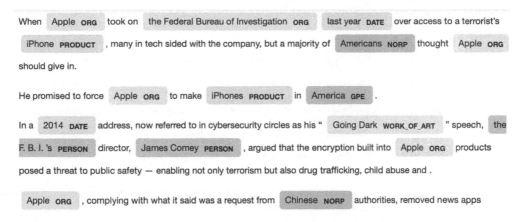

Figure 11.14   Contexts, in which the company (ORG) *Apple* is mentioned alongside other named entities. Entities of different types are highlighted using distinct colors.

https://htmlcolorcodes.com/color-chart/), and using this customized color scheme, you can finally visualize the results.

Listing 11.12   Code to visualize named entities of a specific type only

Extract sentences that mention entity of a specified type as well as at least one other entity of the same type.

Define the count_ents function that counts the number of entities of a certain type in a sentence.

```
def count_ents(sent, ent_type):
    return len([ent.text for ent in sent.ents if ent.label_==ent_type])


def entity_detector_custom(processed_docs, entity, ent_type):
    output_sentences = []
    for doc in processed_docs:
        for sent in doc.sents:
            if entity in [ent.text for ent in sent.ents
                          if ent.label_==ent_type and
                          count_ents(sent, ent_type)>1]:
                output_sentences.append(sent)
    return output_sentences


output_sentences = entity_detector_custom(processed_docs, "Apple", "ORG")
print(len(output_sentences))


def visualize_type(sents, entity, ent_type):
    colors = {"ORG":
              "linear-gradient(90deg, #64B5F6, #E0F7FA)"}
    options = {"ents": ["ORG"], "colors": colors}
    for sent in sents:
        displacy.render(sent, style="ent", options=options)


visualize_type(processed_docs, "Apple", "ORG")
```

Define the visualize_type function that applies visualization to the entities of a predefined type only.

spaCy allows you to customize the colors for visualization and to apply gradient.

Visualize the results using the customized color scheme.

Print out the number of sentences identified this way.

Figure 11.15 shows some of the output of this code.

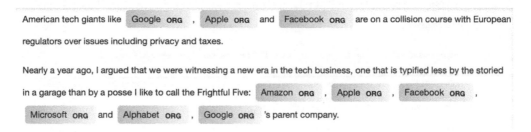

Figure 11.15   Visualization of the company names in contexts mentioning the selected company of interest (*Apple*) using customized color scheme

Congratulations! With the code from this chapter, you can now extract from a collection of news articles all relevant events and facts summarizing the actions undertaken by the participants of interest, such as specific companies. These events can be further used in downstream tasks. For example, if you also harvest data on stock price movements, you can link the events extracted from the news to the changes in the stock prices immediately following such events, which will help you to predict how the stock price may change in view of similar events in the future.

Summary

- Named-entity recognition (NER) is one of the core NLP tasks; however, when the main goal of the application you are developing is not concerned with improving the core NLP task itself but rather relies on the output from the core NLP technology, this is called a *downstream task*. The tasks that benefit from NER include information extraction, question answering, and the like.
- Named entities are real-world objects (people, locations, organizations, etc.) that can be referred to with a proper name, and named-entity recognition is concerned with identification of the full span of such entities (as entities may consist of a single word like *Apple* or of multiple words like *Albert Einstein*) and the type of the expression.
- The four most widely used types include *person, location, organization,* and *geopolitical entity,* although other types like time references and monetary units are also typically added. Moreover, it is also possible to train a customized NER algorithm for a specific domain. For instance, in biomedical texts, gene and protein names represent named entities.
- NER is a challenging task. The major challenges are concerned with the identification of the full span of the expression (e.g., *Amazon* versus *Amazon River*) and the type (e.g., *Washington* may be an entity of up to 4 different types depending on the context). The span and type identification are the tasks that in NER are typically solved jointly.

- The set of named entities often used in practice is derived from the OntoNotes, and it contains 18 distinct NE types. The annotation scheme used to label NEs in data is called a BIO scheme (with a more coarse-grained variant being the IO, and the more fine-grained one being the BIOES scheme). This scheme explicitly annotates each word as **b**eginning an NE, being **i**nside of an NE, or being **o**utside of an NE.

- The NER task is typically framed as a *sequence labeling task,* and it is commonly addressed using a feature-based approach. NER is not the only NLP task that is solved using sequence labeling, since language shows strong sequential effects. Part-of-speech tagging overviewed in chapter 4 is another example of a sequential task.

- You can apply spaCy in practice to extract named entities of interest and facts related to these entities from a collection of news articles.

- A very popular format in data science is CSV, which uses a comma as a delimiter. An easy-to-use open source data analysis and manipulation tool for Python practitioners that helps you work with such files is `pandas`.

- Finally, you can explore the results of NER visually, using the `displaCy` tool and color-coding entities of different types with its help.

Conclusion

This chapter concludes the introductory book on natural language processing. You have covered a lot of ground since you first opened this book. Let's briefly summarize what you have learned:

- The first couple of chapters provided you with a mild introduction into the field of NLP, using examples of applications in everyday life that, under the hood, rely on NLP technology. You looked into some of these applications in more detail and learned about the core tasks and techniques.

- The earlier chapters of this book focused on the introduction of the fundamental NLP concepts and methods. You learned about tokenization, stemming and lemmatization, part-of-speech tagging and dependency parsing, among other things. To put these concepts and techniques in context, each of them was introduced as part of a more focused, practical NLP task. For instance, the earlier chapters focused on the development of such applications as information search and information extraction.

- This book has taken a practical approach to learning from early on. Indeed, there is no better way to acquire new knowledge and skills than to put them in practice straightaway. Apart from the information search and the information extraction applications, you have also built your own spam filter, authorship attribution algorithm, sentiment analyzer, and topic classifier.

- Machine-learning techniques play an important role in NLP these days and are widely used across various NLP tasks. This book has introduced you to a range of ML approaches covering supervised, unsupervised, and sequence-labeling frameworks.

- Finally, this book has introduced good project development practices as each application followed the crucial steps in a data science project: from data exploration to preparation and preprocessing, to algorithm development, to evaluation.

The field of NLP is one of the most popular and quickly developing fields in artificial intelligence and data science. The primary goal of this book has been to introduce you to this exciting and highly innovative field and equip you with the core knowledge and skills that would allow you to further explore the vast number of opportunities in this area. I sincerely hope that you will continue your journey. Here are some further pointers, where you can get ideas for your future NLP projects:

- State-of-the-art NLP research is presented at the top NLP conferences of the Association of Computational Linguistics (ACL). All papers are in open access and can be found in the ACL Anthology: www.aclweb.org/anthology/.
- Google Scholar (https://scholar.google.com) and arXiv (https://arxiv.org) are other good sources of up-to-date publications.
- If you are looking for ready-to-use implementations, open access papers with code and datasets can be found on https://paperswithcode.com.
- Last but not least, if you enjoy reading textbooks, especially the ones that combine theoretical background with practical advice, you should continue with the NLP books from Manning (www.manning.com/).

Solutions to miscellaneous exercises

Exercise 11.3

Table 11.4 shows the answer to this question.

Table 11.4   BIO annotation for "the company's CEO Tim Cook said"

Words	IO label	BIO label	BIOES label
the	O	O	O
company's	O	O	O
CEO	O	O	O
Tim	I-PER	B-PER	B-PER
Cook	I-PER	I-PER	E-PER
said	O	O	O

Exercise 11.4

The IO scheme has one I-tag for each entity type plus a single O-tag for words outside any entity type. This results in $n+1$, or 19 tags for 18 entity types. The BIOES scheme has 4 tags for each entity type (B, I, E, S) plus one O-tag for words outside any entity type. This results in $4n+1$, or 73 tags.

As you can see, the more detailed schemes provide for finer granularity but also come at an expense of having more classes for the algorithm to distinguish between. While the BIO scheme allows the algorithm to train on 37 classes, the BIOES scheme has almost twice as many classes, which means the algorithm has to deal with higher complexity and may make more mistakes.

Exercise 11.5

This exercise requires you to, essentially, change one line of code in listing 11.10 (entity="The New York Times"). In addition, you can see the output of this code in the Jupyter Notebook for this chapter.

appendix
Installation instructions

To run the notebooks on your machine, check whether Python 3 is installed (all code was written and tested with Python 3.7). In addition, you will need the following libraries (notebooks were tested with the versions indicated in the brackets; if you use different versions, the code will still work but minor differences in the results are possible):

- NLTK (v3.5)—Check installation instructions for the toolkit at www.nltk .org/install.html and the accompanying data at www.nltk.org/data.html.
- SpaCy (v3.1.3)—Check installation instructions at https://spacy.io/usage. You will also need to install models (e.g., en_core_web_sm, en_core_web_md, and en_core_web_lg) using the instructions on the website.
- Gensim (v3.8.0)—Check installation instructions at https://radimrehurek .com/gensim/.
- Matplotlib (v3.1.3)—Check installation instructions at https://matplotlib.org/ users/installing.html.
- Scikit-learn (v0.22.1)—Check installation instructions at http://scikit-learn .org/stable/install.html.
- NumPy (v1.18.1)—Check installation instructions at www.scipy.org/install.html.
- Pandas (v1.0.1)—Check installation instructions at https://pandas.pydata.org/ pandas-docs/stable/getting_started/install.html.

Alternatively, a number of these libraries can be installed in one go through Anaconda distribution: www.anaconda.com/products/distribution.

For more information on Jupyter Notebooks, check https://jupyter.org.

Finally, all code examples from the book are available in the book's repository (https://github.com/ekochmar/Getting-Started-with-NLP), where all further updates to the code will be posted.

index